LESSONS 1-120

GREGG
College Keyboarding & Document Processing
for Windows™

8th Edition

Scot Ober, Ph.D.
Professor, Department of Business Education
and Office Administration
Ball State University
Muncie, Indiana

Robert N. Hanson, Ed.D.
Professor Emeritus, Department of Office Systems
and Business Education
Northern Michigan University
Marquette, Michigan

Jack E. Johnson, Ph.D.
Director of Business Education
Department of Management
and Business Systems
State University of West Georgia
Carrollton, Georgia

Arlene Rice, M.A.
Professor, Office
Administration Department
Los Angeles City College
Los Angeles, California

Robert P. Poland, Ph.D.
Professor Emeritus, Business
and Distributive Education
Michigan State University
East Lansing, Michigan

Albert D. Rossetti, Ed.D.
Professor, Information
and Decision Sciences Department
School of Business
Montclair State University
Montclair, New Jersey

GLENCOE
McGraw-Hill

New York, New York   Columbus, Ohio   Woodland Hills, California   Peoria, Illinois

REVIEWERS

Ms. Dianne S. Campbell
Athens Technical Institute
Athens, Georgia

Dr. William J. Dross
Columbus State Community College
Columbus, Ohio

Dr. Marsha Gadzera
Northshore Community College
Danvers, Massachusetts

Mrs. Marilyn Satterwhite
Danville Area Community College
Danville, Illinois

Ms. Sherry Young
Kingwood College
Kingwood, Texas

Photo Credits Cover: Aaron Haupt, Stephen Johnson, Photone library; R-2, Aaron Haupt; 1, 39, 94, Jeff Bates; 152, Tim Courlas; 217, Doug Martin; 286, Jeff Bates; SB-1, Glencoe file.

Glencoe/McGraw-Hill

A Division of The **McGraw·Hill** *Companies*

**Gregg College Document Processing for Windows, 8th Edition,
Lessons 1-120**

Send all inquires to:

Glencoe/McGraw-Hill
936 Eastwind Drive
Westerville, OH 43081

ISBN 0-02-803152-0

3 4 5 6 7 8 9 0   VH   05 04 03 02 01 00 99 98 97

Contents

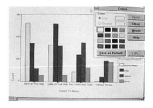

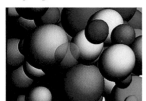

PART THREE

Correspondence, Reports, and Employment Documents

PART FOUR

Reports, Correspondence, and Tables

PART FIVE

Forms, Specialized Correspondence, Reports, and Tables

PART SIX

Designing Forms, Specialized Applications, In-Basket Exercise

SKILLBUILDING

Skillbuilding

Preface

Gregg College Keyboarding & Document Processing for Windows, 8th Edition, is a multicomponent instructional program designed to give the student and the instructor a high degree of flexibility and a high degree of success in meeting their respective goals. To facilitate the choice and use of materials, the core components of this instructional system are available in either a kit format or a book format. *Keyboarding for Windows, 4th Edition*, is also available for the development of touch-typing skills for use in shorter computer keyboarding classes.

The Kit Format

Gregg College Keyboarding & Document Processing for Windows, 8th Edition, provides a complete kit of materials for both courses in the keyboarding curriculum generally offered by colleges. Each kit, which is briefly described below, contains a softcover textbook, a student data disk for use with the correlated software instructional program, and a student word processing manual.

Kit 1: Lessons 1-60. This kit provides the text, word processing manual, and software for the first course. Since this kit is designed for the beginning student, its major objectives are to develop touch control of the keyboard and proper typing techniques, build basic speed and accuracy, and provide practice in applying those basic skills to the formatting of letters, reports, tables, memos, and other kinds of personal and business communications.

Kit 2: Lessons 61-120. This kit provides the text and software for the second course. This course continues the development of basic typing skills and emphasizes the formatting of various kinds of business correspondence, reports, tables, electronic forms, and desktop publishing projects from unarranged and rough-draft sources.

The Book Format

For the convenience of those who wish to obtain the core instructional materials in separate volumes, *Gregg College Keyboarding & Document Processing for Windows, 8th Edition*, offers a textbook for the first course (*Gregg College Keyboarding & Document Processing for Windows, 8th Edition, Lessons 1-60*), for the second course (*Gregg College Document Processing for Windows, 8th Edition, Lessons 61-120*),

for a two-semester course (*Gregg College Keyboarding & Document Processing for Windows, 8th Edition, Lessons 1-120*), as well as for a third-semester course (*Gregg College Keyboarding & Document Processing for Windows, 8th Edition, Lessons 121-180*). In each instance, the content of these textbooks is identical with that of the corresponding textbooks in the kit format.

Supporting Materials

Gregg College Keyboarding & Document Processing for Windows, 8th Edition, includes the following additional components.

Instructional Materials. The special support materials provided for the instructor can be used with either the kits or the textbooks. Special instructor's editions of the textbooks (Lessons 1-60 and Lessons 61-120) contain annotated student pages. Solution keys for all of the formatting exercises in Lessons 1-180 are contained in separate booklets for different word processing programs used with this program. Separate instructor's notes booklets for different word processing programs contain specific suggestions for teaching the features of that program and contain lesson-by-lesson tips. A separate Instructor's Manual contains teaching and grading suggestions for the entire program. Finally, test booklets are available that contain masters of the objective and alternate document processing tests for each part.

Computer Software. IBM-compatible computer software is available for the entire program. The computer software provides a complete instructional system.

Acknowledgments

We wish to express our appreciation to all the instructors and students who have used the previous editions and who have contributed much to this 8th Edition.

Scot Ober	Robert Hanson
Jack Johnson	Arlene Rice
Robert Poland	Albert Rossetti

Introduction

A. STARTING A LESSON

Each lesson begins with the goals for the lesson. Read the goals carefully so that you understand the purpose of your practice. In the example at the left, the goals for the lesson are to type 29 wam (words a minute) on a 3-minute timing with no more than 5 errors and to format simple reports.

B. BUILDING STRAIGHT-COPY SKILL

Warmups: Beginning with Lesson 11, each lesson starts with a warmup paragraph that reviews alphabet, number, and symbol keys. Type the warmup paragraph twice.
Skillbuilding: The skillbuilding portion of each lesson includes a variety of drills to build both speed and accuracy. Instructions for completing the drills are always provided beside each activity.

Additional skillbuilding drills are included in the back of the textbook. These drills are used in various lessons and are available for extra practice.

C. MEASURING STRAIGHT-COPY SKILL

Straight-copy skill is measured in wam (words a minute). All timings are the exact length needed to meet the speed goal for the lesson. If you finish a timing before time is up, you have automatically reached your speed goal for the lesson.

Timings in Lessons 1-60 and Lessons 61-120 are of equal difficulty as measured by syllabic intensity (average number of syllables per word).

D. BUILDING FORMATTING AND DOCUMENT PROCESSING SKILL

Each new document format presented is illustrated and explained. A formatting reference manual is included in the front of the textbook for quick reference. Marginal notes are sometimes used to remind you of special directions.

Symbols are used on sample documents and within document processing activities to provide visual formatting reminders. For example, ↓ 3 ds means that you should set double spacing, then press Enter 3 times.

All word processing commands needed to format documents are explained and practiced in the word processing manual. A special "GO TO" icon (shown at the left) in the textbook alerts you to the need to refer to the manual. The document processing icon is used in the manual to remind you to complete the appropriate document processing exercises in the textbook.

E. CORRECTING ERRORS

As you learn to type, you will probably make some errors. To correct an error, press BACKSPACE (shown as ← on some keyboards) to delete the incorrect character. Then type the correct character.

If you notice an error on a different line, use the up, down, left, or right arrows to move the insertion point immediately to the left or right of the error. Press BACKSPACE to delete a character to the left of the insertion point or DEL to delete a character to the right of the insertion point.

F. TYPING TECHNIQUE

Correct position at the keyboard enables you to type with greater speed and accuracy and with less fatigue. When typing for a long period, rest your eyes occasionally by looking away from the screen. Change position, walk around, or stretch when your muscles feel tired.

If possible, adjust your workstation as follows:

Chair. Adjust the height so that your upper and lower legs form a 90-degree angle and your lower back is supported by the back of the chair.

Keyboard. Center your body opposite the J key, and lean forward slightly. Keep your forearms horizontal to the keyboard.

Screen. Position the monitor so that the top of the screen is just below eye level and about 18 to 26 inches away.

Text. Position your textbook or other copy on either side of the monitor as close to it vertically and horizontally as possible to minimize head and eye movement and to avoid neck strain.

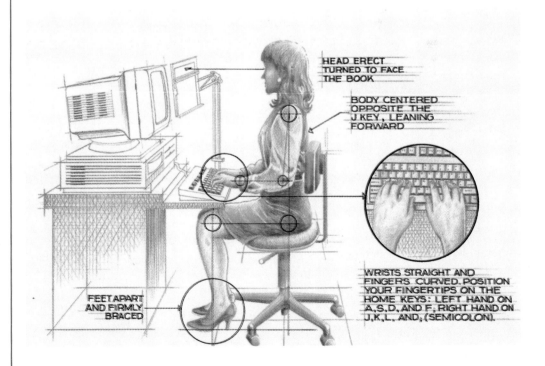

HEAD ERECT
TURNED TO FACE
THE BOOK

BODY CENTERED
OPPOSITE THE
J KEY, LEANING
FORWARD

WRISTS STRAIGHT AND
FINGERS CURVED. POSITION
YOUR FINGERTIPS ON THE
HOME KEYS: LEFT HAND ON
A,S,D, AND F; RIGHT HAND ON
J,K,L, AND, (SEMICOLON).

FEET APART
AND FIRMLY
BRACED

Reference Manual

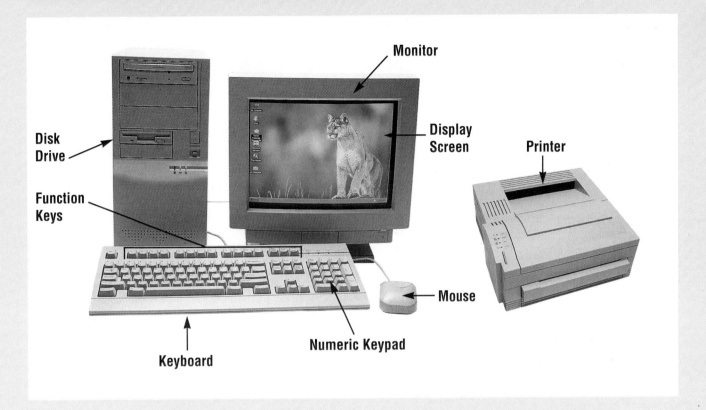

Disk Drive

Function Keys

Monitor

Display Screen

Printer

Mouse

Keyboard

Numeric Keypad

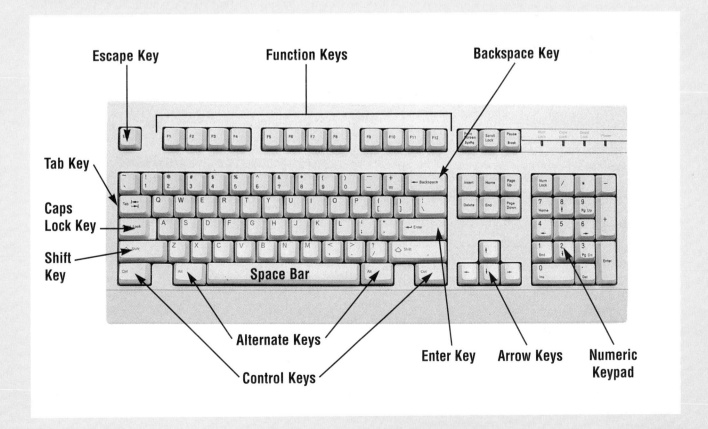

Escape Key

Function Keys

Backspace Key

Tab Key

Caps Lock Key

Shift Key

Space Bar

Alternate Keys

Control Keys

Enter Key

Arrow Keys

Numeric Keypad

Business letter in block style
(open punctuation)

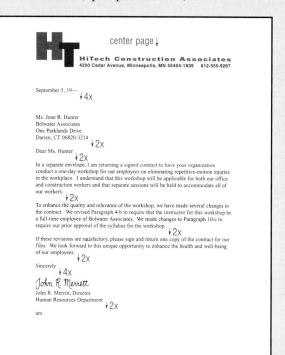

Business letter in modified-block style
(standard punctuation)

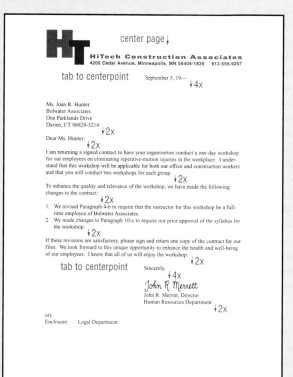

Business letter in simplified style

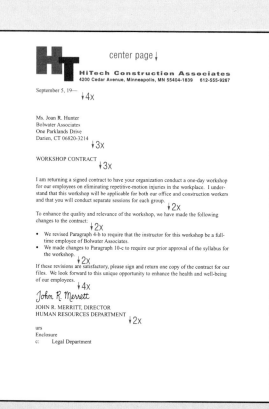

Personal-business letter
(modified-block style; indented paragraphs; standard punctuation)

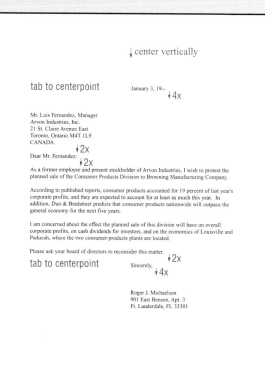

Business letter on executive stationery
(7¼″ × 10½″; 1-inch side margins)

center page ↓
WELLINGTON INDUSTRIES
550 Thornail Street, Edison, NJ 08818   201-555-8000

July 18, 19— ↓4x

Mr. Rodney Eastwood
BBL Resources
52A Northern Ridge
Mt. Stuart, Tasmania 7000
AUSTRALIA ↓2x

Dear Rodney: ↓2x

I see no reason why we should continue to consider the locality around Geraldton for our new refinery. Even though the desirability of this site from an economic point of view is undeniable, there is insufficient housing readily available for those workers whom we would have to transfer. ↓2x

In trying to control urban growth, the city has been either turning down the building permits for new housing or placing so many restrictions on foreign investment as to make it too expensive to build.

Please continue to seek out other areas of exploration where we might form a joint partnership. ↓2x

Sincerely, ↓4x

Arlyn J. Bunch

Arlyn J. Bunch
Vice President for Operations ↓2x

urs
By fax

Business letter on half-page stationery
(5½″ × 8½″; 0.75-inch side margins)

center page ↓
WELLINGTON INDUSTRIES
550 Thornail Street, Edison, NJ 08818   201-555-8000

July 18, 19— ↓4x

Mr. Rodney Eastwood
BBL Resources
52A Northern Ridge
Mt. Stuart, Tasmania 7000
AUSTRALIA ↓2x

Dear Rodney: ↓2x

I do not believe we should continue to consider Geraldton for our new refinery. There is insufficient housing for those workers whom we would have to transfer. In trying to control growth, the city has placed so many restrictions on foreign investment that it is too expensive to build.

Please continue to seek out other areas of exploration where we might form a joint partnership. ↓2x

Sincerely, ↓4x

Arlyn J. Bunch

Arlyn J. Bunch
Vice President for Operations ↓2x

urs

Business letter formatted for a window envelope

6x ↓

WELLINGTON INDUSTRIES
550 Thornail Street, Edison, NJ 08818   201-555-8000

July 18, 19— ↓3x

Mr. Rodney Eastwood
BBL Resources
52A Northern Ridge
Mt. Stuart, Tasmania 7000
AUSTRALIA ↓3x

Dear Rodney: ↓2x

I see no reason why we should continue to consider the locality around Geraldton for our new refinery. Even though the desirability of this site from an economic point of view is undeniable, there is insufficient housing readily available for those workers whom we would have to transfer.

In trying to control urban growth, the city has been either turning down building permits for new housing or placing so many restrictions on foreign investment as to make it too expensive to build.

Please continue to seek out other areas of exploration where we might form a joint partnership. ↓2x

Sincerely, ↓4x

Arlyn J. Bunch

Arlyn J. Bunch
Vice President for Operations ↓2x

urs
Enclosure ↓2x

PS: I thought you might enjoy the enclosed article from a recent *Forbes* magazine on the latest misfortunes of one of your major competitors.

Memo

↓6x

MEMO TO: Nancy Price, Executive Vice President ↓2x

FROM: Arlyn J. Bunch, Operations ↓2x

DATE: July 18, 19— ↓2x

SUBJECT: New Refinery Site ↓2x

As you can see from the attached letter, I've informed BBL Resources that I see no reason why we should continue to consider the locality around Geraldton, Australia, for our new refinery. Even though the desirability of this site from an economic standpoint is undeniable, there is insufficient housing readily available for those workers whom we would have to transfer. As of July 1, the number of appropriate single-family houses listed for sale by real estate agents within a 25-mile radius of Geraldton was as follows: ↓2x

Castleton Homes	123
Belle Real Estate	5
Red Carpet	11
Geraldton Sales	9
TOTAL	148

↓2x

In addition, in trying to control urban growth, Geraldton has been either turning down building permits for new housing or placing so many restrictions on foreign investment as to make it too expensive for us to consider building housing ourselves.

Because of this deficiency of housing for our employees, we have no choice but to look elsewhere. ↓2x

urs
Attachment

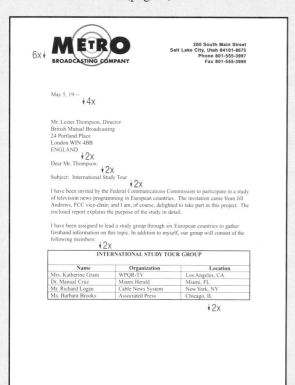

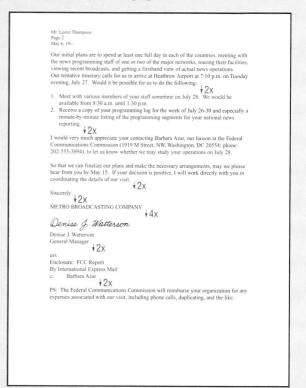

SPECIAL CORRESPONDENCE FEATURES

FOREIGN ADDRESS. Type the name of a foreign country in all capital letters on a line by itself.

SUBJECT LINE. If used, type a subject line in upper- and lowercase letters below the salutation, with 1 blank line above and below; the terms *Re:* or *In re:* may also be used.

TABLE. Leave 1 blank line above and below a table.

MULTI-PAGE LETTERS. Type the first page on letterhead stationery and the second page on matching plain stationery. On the second page, type the addressee's name, page number, and date as a header, blocked at the left margin. Leave 1 blank line after the page-2 header.

ENUMERATION. Create an enumeration by using the automatic numbering feature. Double-space a list that is part of the body of a double-spaced document. Single-space a list that is part of the body of a single-spaced document, but leave 1 blank line above and below the list.

COMPANY NAME IN CLOSING LINES. If included, type the company name in all capital letters below the complimentary closing, with 1 blank line above and 3 blank lines below it.

REFERENCE INITIALS. Type only the typist's initials (not the signer's) in lowercase letters a double space below the writer's name and/or title. (Optional: You may also include the computer filename; for example: *urs/SMITH.LET*).

ENCLOSURE NOTATION. Type an enclosure notation a single space below the reference initials if an item is enclosed with a letter. Use the term "Attachment" if an item is attached to a memo instead of enclosed in an envelope. Examples: *3 Enclosures, Enclosure: Contract, Attachment.*

DELIVERY NOTATION. Type a delivery notation a single space below the enclosure notation. Examples: *By Certified Mail, By Fax, By Federal Express.*

COPY NOTATION. Type a copy notation *(c:)* a single space below the delivery notation if someone other than the addressee is to receive a copy of the message.

POSTSCRIPT NOTATION. Type a postscript notation as the last item, preceded by 1 blank line. Indent the first line of the postscript if the paragraphs in the body are indented.

FORMATTING ENVELOPES

A standard large (No. 10) envelope is 9½ by 4⅛ inches. A standard small (No. 6¾) envelope is 6½ by 3⅝ inches. Although either address format shown below is acceptable, the format shown for the large envelope (all capital letters and no punctuation) is recommended by the U.S. Postal Service for mail that will be sorted by an electronic scanning device.

Window envelopes are often used in a word processing environment because of the difficulty of aligning envelopes correctly in some printers. A window envelope requires no formatting, since the letter is formatted and folded so that the inside address is visible through the window.

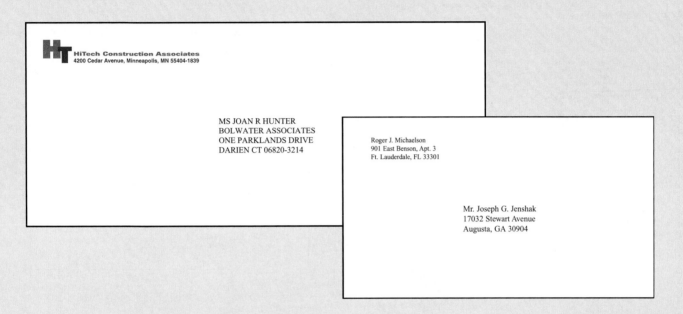

FOLDING LETTERS

To fold a letter for a large envelope:
1. Place the letter *face up* and fold up the bottom third.
2. Fold the top third down to 0.5 inch from the bottom edge.
3. Insert the last crease into the envelope first, with the flap facing up.

To fold a letter for a small envelope:
1. Place the letter *face up* and fold up the bottom half to 0.5 inch from the top.
2. Fold the right third over to the left.
3. Fold the left third over to 0.5 inch from the right edge.
4. Insert the last crease into the envelope first, with the flap facing up.

To fold a letter for a window envelope:
1. Place the letter *face down* with the letterhead at the top and fold the bottom third of the letter up.
2. Fold the top third down so that the address shows.
3. Insert the letter into the envelope so that the address shows through the window.

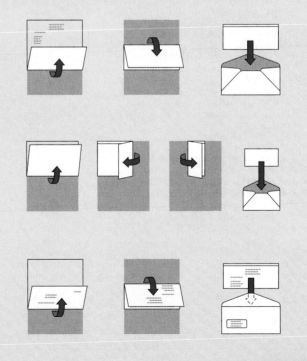

↓6x

THE FEASIBILITY OF IN-HOUSE MANUFACTURING ↓2x

OF NAIL-POLISH LACQUERS ↓2x

I.   INTRODUCTION ↓2x

    A. Statement of the Problem
    B. Scope
    C. Procedures
    D. Organization of the Report ↓2x

II.   FINDINGS

    A. Current Manufacturing Processes
       1. Contract Manufacturing
       2. In-House Manufacturing
    B. Market Differentiation
       1. Image Advertising
       2. Product Characteristics
       3. Manufacturing Control
    C. Advantages and Disadvantages

III. CONCLUSIONS

    A. Summary of Findings
    B. Conclusions and Recommendations

center page ↓

CONSOLIDATION OF THE PARTS WAREHOUSES AT ↓2x

SIOUX CITY AND CEDAR FALLS ↓2x

Maintaining Profitability in a Declining Market ↓12x

Prepared by ↓2x

Catherine Rogers-Busch
Chief Product Engineer
Helene Ponds and Associates ↓12x

December 3, 19—

↓6x

CONTENTS ↓2x

↓3 DS

PREPARING FORMAL REPORTS ↓1x

Formatting Guidelines for Writers ↓1x

By Keith Stallings ↓1x

Formatting formal reports is not a difficult task if you just take the time to study the technical aspects involved. This report discusses report headings, page numbers, reference citations, and the bibliography. ↓1x

HEADINGS ↓1x

The major heading in a report is the title. It should be centered and typed in all caps and bold approximately 2 inches from the top of the page. A subtitle or byline, if used, is typed in initial caps a double space below the title. The body of the report begins on the second line below the title or byline.

    Side Headings. A side heading (such as "PAGE NUMBERING" shown below) is typed at the left margin in all caps and bold, with a double space before and after it.

    Paragraph Headings. A paragraph heading is indented and typed in initial caps and bold a double space below the preceding paragraph. The paragraph heading is followed by a period and two spaces, with the text beginning on the same line.

PAGE NUMBERING

    Use the page numbering command of your word processing software to insert a page number at the top right of each page. Suppress the page number on the first page.

for the following reasons:

- Contrary to popular belief, modular homes are generally not less expensive than conventionally constructed homes.
- Zoning regulations and restrictive convenants often forbid the construction of modular homes especially in upscale areas.

The big advantage of modular homes is the speed with which they can be constructed.[2] Since the River Road development is not subject to time pressures, conventional construction methods were evaluated as the most appropriate for this

---

[1] Benjamin J. Ashley, "New Sales Versus Resales: Apples to Oranges?" *Real Estate Quarterly,* September 1995, p. 143.
[2] Jacqueline Miller, *Residential Real Estate: North Georgia Edition,* Georgia Real Estate Association, Atlanta, Georgia, 1995, pp. 216-224.

following reasons:

- Contrary to popular belief, modular homes are generally not less expensive than conventionally constructed homes.
- Zoning regulations and restrictive convenants often forbid the construction of modular homes especially in upscale areas.

The big advantage of modular homes is the speed with which they can be constructed.[2] Since the River Road development is not subject to time pressures, conventional construction methods were evaluated as the most appropriate for this submarket.

---

[1] Benjamin J. Ashley, "New Sales Versus Resales: Apples to Oranges?" *Real Estate Quarterly,* September 1995, p. 143.

[2] Jacqueline Miller, *Residential Real Estate: North Georgia Edition,* Georgia Real Estate Association, Atlanta, Georgia, 1995, pp. 216-224.

13

↓6x

BIBLIOGRAPHY ↓2x

Ashley, Benjamin J., "New Sales Versus Resales: Apples to Oranges?" *Real Estate Quarterly,* September 1994, pp. 143-149. ↓2x

Barrett, R. J., "Planning Your First Home," *The Long Island Herald,* September 13, 1993, pp. A3, A16.

Bullard, Mary Helen, *The Bullard Real Estate Report,* Bullard Consulting Group, Nyack, New York, 1995.

Heydenburg, Peter, and Rhonda Silver, "Restricting Covenants and the Law," *Journal of Real Estate Law,* Vol. 24, No. 3, Fall 1992, pp. 81-87.

Miller, Jacqueline, *Residential Real Estate: North Georgia Edition,* Georgia Real Estate Association, Atlanta, Georgia, 1995.

3

an option for this submarket because of the numerous developments of this type that already exist or are under construction in the area.

Modular homes, which have been partially constructed before being brought to the building site, were likewise rejected because:
↓1 DS

Contrary to popular belief, modular homes are generally not less expensive than conventionally constructed homes. Their biggest advantage, instead, is the speed with which they can be constructed. Their major disadvantage relates to the restrictions often placed on them by municipal zoning ordinances.
↓1 DS

Since the River Road development is not subject to time pressures, conventional construction methods were evaluated as the most appropriate for this submarket.

Most of the homes sold in Chestnut Log contain at least three bedrooms, but in the lowest price bracket most contain less than 1,600 square feet, as shown below.
↓1 DS

Selling Price	Number of Homes	Days Listed	Average Square Feet
Less than $90,000	55	145	1,571
$90,000-$109,000	29	81	1,917
$110,000-$129,999	7	105	2,094
$130,000-$149,999	8	85	2,291

↓1 DS

Because several planning experts have noted the importance of overall outside dimensions for first-time home buyers, the home plan selected for this submarket is only 37 feet wide, allowing it to be placed on a 67-foot-wide lot, with adequate footage on both sides.

Market research shows that smaller lots are more appealing because the landscaping needs are minimized. Reducing landscaping is a definite advantage

to whether hardware should be purchased or leased. Although many firms decide to purchase their own hardware, others have taken the route of time-sharing or remote processing whereby the costs of processing data can be shared with other users.

TRAINING OPERATORS

Many firms neglect this important phase of designing a computer system. It is not enough to offer a one-week training course in an applications package and then expect proficiency from a worker.[iii] Training must occur over time to help those who will be using computers every day on the job.

---

[i] Neal Swanson, *Information Management,* Glencoe/McGraw-Hill, Westerville, Ohio, 1992, p. 372.
[ii] Christine L. Seymour, "The Ins and Outs of Designing Your Computer System," *Information Processing Trends,* January 1991, p. 23.
[iii] Lee Bailey, *Computer Systems Management,* The University of New Mexico Press, Albuquerque, New Mexico, 1992, p. 413.

TRAINING OPERATORS

Many firms neglect this important phase of designing a computer system. It is not enough to offer a one-week training course in an applications package and then expect proficiency from a worker.[3] Training must occur over time to help those who will be using computers every day on the job.

1. Neal Swanson, *Information Management,* Glencoe/McGraw-Hill, Westerville, Ohio, 1992, p. 372.

2. Christine L. Seymour, "The Ins and Outs of Designing Your Computer System," *Information Processing Trends,* January 1991, p. 23.

3. Lee Bailey, *Computer Systems Management,* The University of New Mexico Press, Albuquerque, New Mexico, 1992, p. 413.

2

a real estate agent from North Georgia Realty, provided a copy of selected reports

that are available only to real estate agents (Miller, 1995, p. 216). Statistics for the

Chestnut Log school district for those homes selling during the past year are

shown in Table 2.

TABLE 2. CHESTNUT LOG HOME SALES
January Through December

Selling Price	Number of Homes	Days Listed	Average Square Feet
Less than $90,000	55	145	1,571
$90,000-$109,000	29	81	1,917
$110,000-$129,999	7	105	2,094
$130,000-or more	14	185	2,391

The data reflected in Table 2 are based on used homes. According to one

source, the typical residential community offers fewer new homes than resales,

new homes sell faster, and they average about 20 percent larger than resales

(Ashley, 1994, p. 143).

YOUNG FAMILY

Individuals in the young family submarket are making their first purchase of

a new home. This submarket represents households from a rental or used-home

arrangement. In the market, on the basis of current mortgage rates, these buyers

cannot afford more than $107,000 for a home. And, since family size is still small

(less than four), homes of approximately 2,000 square feet are considered to be an

adequate size.

13

References

Connor, E. (1995, June). Exploring body language cues. Management Today,
14, 250-261, 273.

LePoole, A. (1989). Your tour of duty overseas (2nd ed.). Oklahoma City:
American Press.

LePoole, A. (1991). What American business can (and must) learn from the
Japanese. New York: Management Press.

Newby, C.J. (1995). Global implications for American business: The numbers
don't Slie. Marketing Research Quarterly, 50, 190-215.

Roncaro, P. L., & Lance, G. D. (1992, June 2). Losing something in the
translation. Winston-Salem Herald, pp. 4A, 12A.

Tell it like it is: Making yourself understood in the new Russia. (1994, October
19). International Times, p. 38.

Jenson 1

↓1" top margin

Sherlon Jenson

Professor Zhao

BusCom 300

8 October 19—

Communication Skills Needed in International Business

International business plays an increasingly important role in the U.S. economy,

and U.S. companies recognize that to be competitive nationally, they must be

competitive internationally. Reflecting this trend, direct investment by U.S. private

enterprises in foreign countries increased from $409 billion in 1990 to $528 billion in

1994, an increase of 29 percent in four years (Connor 253). Today, more than 3,000

U.S. corporations have over 25,000 subsidiaries and affiliates in 125 foreign countries,

and more than 25,000 American firms are engaged in international marketing (Newby

193, 205).

International business is highly dependent on communication. According to

Arnold LePoole, chief executive officer of Armstrand Industries, an international

supplier of automotive parts:

If a company cannot communicate with its foreign subsidiaries,

customers, suppliers, and governments, it cannot achieve success.

The sad fact is that most American managers are ill-equipped to

communicate with their international counterparts. (143-144)

Because competent business communications skills are one of the most impor-

tant components for success in international business affairs, a survey instrument was

designed to explore the importance of, level of competence in, and methods of

---

Jensen 13

↓3 DS

Works Cited

Connor, Earl. "Exploring Body Language Cues." Management Today, June 1994: 250-
261, 273.

LePoole, Arnold. What American Business Can (and Must) Learn From the Japanese.
New York: Management Press, 1990.

---. Your Tour of Duty Overseas. 2nd ed. Oklahoma City: American Press, 1988.

Newby, Corrine J. "Global Implications for American Business: The Numbers Don't
Lie." Marketing Research Quarterly 50 (1994): 190-215.

Roncaro, Paul L., and Glenn D. Lance. "Losing Something in the Translation."
Winston-Salem Herald 2 June 1992: 4A+.

"Tell It Like It Is: Making Yourself Understood in the New Russia." International
Times 19 October 1993: 38.

↓6x

MILES HARDWARE EXECUTIVE COMMITTEE ↓2x

Meeting Agenda ↓2x

June 7, 19—, 3 p.m. ↓2x

1. Call to order
2. Approval of minutes of May 5 meeting
3. Progress report on building addition and parking lot restrictions (Norman Hedges and Anthony Pascarelli)
4. May 15 draft of Five-Year Plan
5. Review of National Hardware Association annual convention
6. Employee grievance filed by Ellen Burrows (John Landstrom)
7. New expense-report forms (Anne Richards)
8. Announcements
9. Adjournment

↓6x

RESOURCE COMMITTEE ↓2x

Minutes of the Meeting ↓2x

March 13, 19— ↓2x

ATTENDANCE	The Resource Committee met on March 13, 19—, at the Airport Sheraton in Portland, Oregon, in conjunction with the western regional meeting. Members present were Michael Davis, Cynthia Giovanni, Don Madsen, and Edna Pointer. Michael Davis, chairperson, called the meeting to order at 2:30 p.m. ↓2x
OLD BUSINESS	The members of the committee reviewed the sales brochure on electronic copyboards. They agreed to purchase an electronic copyboard for the conference room. Cynthia Giovanni will secure quotations from at least two vendors. ↓2x
NEW BUSINESS	The committee reviewed a request from the Purchasing Department for three new computers. After extensive discussion regarding the appropriate use of the computers in the Purchasing Department and software to be purchased, the committee approved the request. ↓2x
ADJOURNMENT	The meeting was adjourned at 4:45 p.m. The next meeting has been scheduled for May 4 in the headquarters conference room. Members are asked to bring with them copies of the latest resource planning document. ↓2x

Respectfully submitted, ↓4x

D. S. Madsen, Secretary

↓6x

PORTLAND SALES MEETING ↓2x

Itinerary for Arlene Gilsdorf ↓2x

March 12-15, 19— ↓2x

Thursday, March 12 ↓2x

Detroit/Minneapolis .... Northwest 83
Depart 5:10 p.m.; arrive 5:55 p.m.
Seat 8D; nonstop ↓2x

Minneapolis/Portland .... Northwest 2363
Depart 6:30 p.m.; arrive 8:06 p.m.
Seat 15C; nonstop; dinner ↓2x

Sunday, March 15

Portland/Minneapolis .... Northwest 360
Depart 7:30 a.m.; arrive 12:26 p.m.
Seat 15H; one stop; breakfast

Minneapolis/Detroit .... Northwest 748
Depart 1 p.m.; arrive 3:32 p.m.
Seat 10D; nonstop; snack ↓2x

NOTES ↓2x

1. Jack Weatherford, assistant western regional manager, will meet your flight on Thursday and drive you to the airport on Sunday.
2. All seat assignments are aisle seats; smoking is not allowed on any of the flights.
3. Important phone numbers:
   Jack Weatherford .... 503-555-8029, Ext. 87
   Airport Sheraton 503-555-4032

↓3 DS

POWER OF ATTORNEY

KNOW ALL MEN BY THESE PRESENTS that I, ATTORNEY LEE FERNANDEZ, of the City of Tulia, County of Swisher, State of Texas, do hereby appoint my son, Robert Fernandez, of this City, County, and State as my attorney-in-fact to act in my name, place, and stead as my agent in the management of my real estate transactions, chattel and goods transactions, banking transactions, and business operating transactions.

I give and grant unto my said attorney full power and authority to do and perform every act and thing requisite and necessary to be done in the said management as fully, to all intents and purposes, as I might or could do if personally present, with full power of revocation, hereby ratifying all that my said attorney shall lawfully do.

IN WITNESS WHEREOF, I have hereunto set my hand and seal this thirteenth day of April, 1995. ↓2 DS

centerpoint→ _____(L.S.) ↓1 DS

SIGNED and affirmed in the presence of: ↓2 DS

_____ ↓2 DS

_____

Page 1 of 1

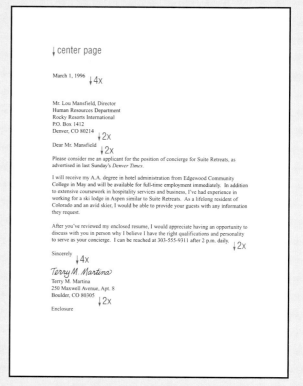

PLACING INFORMATION ON PRINTED LINES

Because of the difficulty of aligning copy on a printed line with a computer and printer, lined forms such as job-application forms are most efficiently completed on a typewriter.

When typing on a lined form, use the typewriter's variable line spacer to adjust the paper so that the line is in the position that a row of underlines would occupy. (On many machines, this is accomplished by pressing in the left platen knob.)

Do not leave any lines for requested information blank; use *N/A* ("not applicable") if necessary. Because of space limitations, it may be necessary to abbreviate some words.

Because first impressions are important, ensure that all your employment documents are in correct format, are neat in appearance, and are free from errors.

Job-application form

(first page)

(with centered column headings)

↓ center page

COMPUTER SUPPLIES UNLIMITED
Guide to Support Services*

↓1x

Support Service	Telephone	Hours
Product Literature	800-555-3867	6 a.m. to 5 p.m.
Replacement Parts	303-555-3388	24 hours a day
Technical Documentation	408-555-3309	24 hours a day
Troubleshooting	800-555-8277	6 a.m. to 5 p.m.
Printer Drivers	800-555-2377	6 a.m. to 5 p.m.
Software Notes	800-555-3496	24 hours a day
Hardware Information	303-555-4289	6 a.m. to 5 p.m.
Technical Support	800-555-1205	24 hours a day

(with blocked column headings)

↓ center page

COMPUTER SUPPLIES UNLIMITED
Guide to Support Services

↓1x

Support Service	Telephone	Hours
Product Literature	800-555-3867	6 a.m. to 5 p.m.
Replacement Parts	303-555-3388	24 hours a day
Technical Documentation	408-555-3309	24 hours a day
Troubleshooting	800-555-8277	6 a.m. to 5 p.m.
Printer Drivers	800-555-2377	6 a.m. to 5 p.m.
Software Notes	800-555-3496	24 hours a day
Hardware Information	303-555-4289	6 a.m. to 5 p.m.
Technical Support	800-555-1205	24 hours a day

(with blocked column headings)

↓ center page

COMPUTER SUPPLIES UNLIMITED
Guide to Support Services*

↓1x

Support Service	Telephone	Hours
Product Literature	800-555-3867	6 a.m. to 5 p.m.
Replacement Parts	303-555-3388	24 hours a day
Technical Documentation	408-555-3309	24 hours a day
Troubleshooting	800-555-8277	6 a.m. to 5 p.m.
Printer Drivers	800-555-2377	6 a.m. to 5 p.m.
Software Notes	800-555-3496	24 hours a day
Technical Support	800-555-1205	24 hours a day
Hardware Information	303-555-4289	6 a.m. to 5 p.m.
*All support services are available 7 days a week.		

(with centered column headings)

↓ center page

QUALITY INN SUITES		
↓1x Location	Rack Rate	Discount Rate
Los Angeles, California	$159.00	$89.50
Orlando, Florida	$125.00	$95.50
Chicago, Illinois	$149.00	$79.50
New York, New York	$239.00	$175.00
Minneapolis, Minnesota	$98.50	$59.50
Las Vegas, Nevada	$125.50	$85.00
Seattle, Washington	$79.00	$59.00
Dallas, Texas	$250.00	$185.00

↓1x

Many business forms can be created and filled in by using templates that are provided within commercial word processing software. Template forms can be used "as is" or they can be edited. Templates can also be used to create customized forms for any business.

When a template is opened, the form is displayed on screen. The user can then fill in the necessary information, including personalized company information. Data is entered into cells or fields and you can move quickly from field to field with a single keystroke—usually by pressing Tab or Enter.

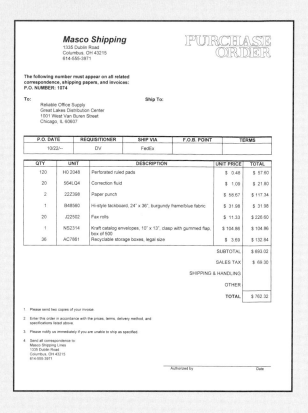

Proofreaders' Marks		Draft	Final Copy
‿	Omit space	data base	database
∨ or ∧	Insert	if he's going, not	if he's not going,
≡	Capitalize	Maple street	Maple Street
ℰ	Delete	a final draft	a draft
#	Insert space	allready to	all ready to
when ⟍	Change word	and if you	and when you
/	Use lowercase letter	our President	our president
¶	Paragraph	¶ Most of the	Most of the
•••	Don't delete	a true story	a true story
○	Spell out	the only ①	the only one
∽	Transpose	they all see	they see all

Proofreaders' Marks		Draft	Final Copy
SS	Single-space	SS [first line / second line	first line / second line
ds	Double-space	ds [first line / second line	first line / second line
⊐	Move right	Please send	Please send
⊏	Move left	May I	May I
∿	Bold	Column Heading	**Column Headin**
ital	Italic	ital Time magazine	*Time* magazine
u/l	Underline	u/l Time magazine	<u>Time</u> magazine readers
♂	Move as shown	readers will see	will see

AMPERSAND. One space before and after.
CLOSING QUOTATION MARK. *(a)* Typed *after* a period or comma and *before* a colon or semicolon. *(b)* Typed *after* a question mark or exclamation point if the quoted material is a question or an exclamation; otherwise, it is typed *before* the question mark or exclamation point.
COLON. Two spaces after.
COMMA. One space after.
EXCLAMATION POINT. Two spaces after.
PERIOD. *(a)* Two spaces after a period at the end of a sentence; *(b)* one space after the period following someone's initials or the abbreviation of a single word (for example, *Mrs. Jones*); *(c)* no space after each internal period in an abbreviation (for example, *a.m.*).
QUESTION MARK. Two spaces after.
SEMICOLON. One space after.
TABLE COLUMNS. Although six spaces are generally left between table columns, spacing varies when you use the Table feature of your word processor.
ITALICS/UNDERLINE. *(a)* Type a magazine or book title in italics or underline it, including internal spaces and punctuation. *(b)* To stress individual words, italicize or underline them separately; do not italicize or underline the punctuation or the spaces between the words.
ZIP CODE. One space before.

LANGUAGE ARTS FOR BUSINESS

PUNCTUATION

COMMAS

1. **, ind** Use a comma between independent clauses joined by a conjunction. (An independent clause is one that can stand alone as a complete sentence.)

    We requested Brown Industries to change the date, and they did so within five days.

2. **, intro** Use a comma after an introductory expression (unless it is a short prepositional phrase).

    Before we can make a decision, we must have all the facts.
    In 1992 our nation elected a president.

3. **, date** Use a comma before and after the year in a complete date.

    We will arrive at the plant on June 2, 1995, for the conference.

4. **, place** Use a comma before and after a state or country that follows a city (but not before a ZIP Code).

    Joan moved to Vancouver, British Columbia, in September.
    Send the package to Douglasville, GA 30135, by express mail.

5. **, ser** Use a comma between each item in a series of three or more.

    We need to order paper, toner, and font cartridges.

6. **, tran** Use a comma before and after a transitional expression (such as *therefore* and *however*).

    It is critical, therefore, that we finish the project on time.

7. **, quot** Use a comma before and after a direct quotation.

    When we left, James said, "Let us return to the same location next year."

8. **, non** Use a comma before and after a nonessential expression. (A nonessential expression is a word or group of words that may be omitted without changing the basic meaning of the sentence.)

    Let me say, to begin with, that the report has already been finalized.

9. **, adj** Use a comma between two adjacent adjectives that modify the same noun.

    We need an intelligent, enthusiastic individual for this job.

SEMICOLONS

1. ; noconj
Use a semicolon to join two closely related independent clauses that are not connected by a conjunction (such as *and*, *but*, or *nor*).

Management favored the vote; stockholders did not.

2. ; ser
Use a semicolon to separate three or more items in a series if any of the items already contain commas.

Region 1 sent its reports on March, April, and May; and Region 2 sent its reports on September, October, and November.

HYPHENS

1. - adj
Hyphenate compound adjectives that come before a noun (unless the first word is an adverb ending in *-ly*).

We reviewed an up-to-date report on Wednesday.
We attended a highly rated session on multimedia software.

2. - num
Hyphenate compound numbers (between twenty-one and ninety-nine) and fractions that are expressed as words.

We observed twenty-nine infractions during the investigation.
Bancroft Industries reduced their sales force by one-third.

3. - div
Turning on the hyphenation feature on your word processor takes care of most word division decisions for you. However, in some cases, you will need to make the correct choices. As a general rule, hyphenate words that are divided at the ends of lines. Do not divide one-syllable words, contractions, or abbreviations; divide other words only between syllables.

To appreciate the full significance of our actions, you must review the entire document that was sent to you.

APOSTROPHES

1. ' sing
Use *'s* to form the possessive of singular nouns.

The hurricane caused major damage to Georgia's coastline.

2. ' plur
Use only an apostrophe to form the possessive of plural nouns that end in *s*.

The investors' goals were outlined in the annual report.

3. ' pro
Use *'s* to form the possessive of indefinite pronouns (such as *someone's* or *anybody's*); do not use an apostrophe with personal pronouns (such as *hers*, *his*, *its*, *ours*, *theirs*, and *yours*).

She was instructed to select anybody's paper for a sample.
Each computer comes carefully packed in its own container.

COLONS

1. : expl
Use a colon to introduce explanatory material that follows an independent clause. (An independent clause is one that can stand alone as a complete sentence.)

The computer satisfies three criteria: speed, cost, and power.

DASHES

1. —emph   Use a dash instead of a comma, semicolon, colon, or parenthesis when you want to convey a more forceful separation of words within a sentence. (If your software has a special dash symbol, use it. Otherwise, form a dash by typing two hyphens, with no space before, between, or after.)

At this year's meeting, the speakers—and topics—were superb.

PERIODS

1. . req   Use a period to end a sentence that is a polite request. (Consider a sentence a polite request if you expect the reader to respond by doing as you ask rather than by giving a yes-or-no answer.)

Will you please call me if I can be of further assistance.

QUOTATION MARKS

1. ' title   Use quotation marks around the titles of newspaper articles, magazine articles, chapters in a book, reports, conferences, and similar items.

The best article I found in my research was entitled "Multimedia for Everyone."

2. " quote   Use quotation marks around a direct quotation.

Harrison responded by saying, "This decision will not affect our merger."

ITALICS (OR UNDERLINE)

1. _ title   Italicize (or underline) the titles of books, magazines, newspapers, and other complete published works.

I read *The Pelican Brief* last month.

GRAMMAR

AGREEMENT

1. Agr sing   Use singular verbs and pronouns with singular subjects and plural verbs and pronouns with plural subjects.

   agr plur   I was pleased with the performance of our team.
Reno and Phoenix were selected as the sites for our next two meetings.

2. Agr pro   Some pronouns (*anybody, each, either, everybody, everyone, much, neither, no one, nobody,* and *one*) are always singular and take a singular verb. Other pronouns (*all, any, more, most, none,* and *some*) may be singular or plural, depending on the noun to which they refer.

Each employee is responsible for summarizing the day's activities.
Most of the workers are going to get a substantial pay raise.

3. Agr inter   Disregard any intervening words that come between the subject and verb when establishing agreement.

The box containing the books and pencils has not been found.

4. Agr near   If two subjects are joined by *or, either/or, neither/nor,* or *not only/but also,* the verb should agree with the subject nearer to the verb.

Neither the players nor the coach is in favor of the decision.

5. Agr num   The subject *a number* takes a plural verb; *the number* takes a singular verb.

<u>A</u> number of us are taking the train to the game.
<u>The</u> number of errors has increased in the last two attempts.

6.	**Agr comp**	Subjects joined by *and* take a plural verb unless the compound subject is preceded by *each*, *every*, or *many a* (*an*).
		Every man, woman, and child is included in our survey.
7.	**Agr subj**	Verbs that refer to conditions that are impossible or improbable (that is, verbs in the *subjunctive mood*) require the plural form.
		If the total eclipse were to occur tomorrow, it would be the second one this year.

PRONOUNS

1.	**Pro nom**	Use nominative pronouns (such as *I, he, she, we*, and *they*) as subjects of a sentence or clause.
		They traveled to Minnesota last week but will not return until next month.
2.	**Pro obj**	Use objective pronouns (such as *me, him, her, us*, and *them*) as objects in a sentence or clause.
		The package has been sent to her.

ADJECTIVES AND ADVERBS

1.	**Adj/Adv**	Use comparative adjectives and adverbs (*-er*, *more*, and *less*) when referring to two nouns; use superlative adjectives and adverbs (*-est*, *most*, and *least*) when referring to more than two.
		Of the two movies you have selected, the shorter one is the more interesting.
		The highest of the three mountains is Mount Everest.

WORD USAGE

1.	**Word**	Do not confuse the following pairs of words:
		Accept means "to agree to"; *except* means "to leave out."
		We accept your offer for developing the new product.
		Everyone except Sam and Lisa attended the meeting.
		Affect is most often used as a verb meaning "to influence"; *effect* is most often used as a noun meaning "result."
		Mr. Smith's decision will not affect our programming plans.
		It will be weeks before we can assess the effect of this action.
		Farther refers to distance; *further* refers to extent or degree.
		Did we travel farther today than yesterday?
		We need to discuss our plans further.
		Personal means "private"; *personnel* means "employees."
		The letters were very personal and should not have been read.
		We hope that all personnel will comply with the new regulations.
		Principal means "primary"; *principle* means "rule."
		The principal means of research were interviewing and surveying.
		They must not violate the principles under which our company was established.

MECHANICS

CAPITALIZATION

1. ≡ sent

Capitalize the first word of a sentence.

Please prepare a summary of your activities for our next meeting.

2. ≡ prop

Capitalize proper nouns and adjectives derived from proper nouns. (A proper noun is the official name of a particular person, place, or thing.)

Judy Hendrix drove to Albuquerque in her new automobile, a Pontiac.

3. ≡ time

Capitalize the names of the days of the week, months, holidays, and religious days (but do not capitalize the names of the seasons).

On Thursday, November 25, we will celebrate Thanksgiving, the most popular fall holiday.

4. ≡ noun #

Capitalize nouns followed by a number or letter (except for the nouns *line, note, page, paragraph,* and *size*).

Please read Chapter 5, but not page 94.

5. ≡ comp

Capitalize compass points (such as *north, south,* or *northeast*) only when they designate definite regions.

The Crenshaws will vacation in the Northeast this summer.
We will have to drive north to reach the closest Canadian border.

6. ≡ org

Capitalize common organizational terms (such as *advertising department* and *finance committee*) when they are the actual names of the units in the writer's own organization and when they are preceded by the word *the*.

The quarterly report from the Advertising Department will be presented today.

7. ≡ course

Capitalize the names of specific course titles but not the names of subjects or areas of study.

I have enrolled in Accounting 201 and will also take a marketing course.

NUMBER EXPRESSION

1. # gen

In general, spell out numbers 1 through 10, and use figures for numbers above 10.

We have rented two movies for tonight.
The decision was reached after 27 precincts had sent in their results.

2. # fig

Use figures for:

Dates (use *st, d,* or *th* only if the day precedes the month).

We will drive to the camp on the 23d of May.
The tax report is due on April 15.

All numbers if two or more related numbers both above and below ten are used in the same sentence.

Mr. Carter sent in 7 receipts; Ms. Cantrell sent in 22 receipts.

Measurements (time, money, distance, weight, and percent).

At 10 a.m. we delivered the $500 coin bank in a 17-pound container.

Mixed numbers.

Our sales are up 9½ percent over last year.

3. **# word**

Spell out:

Numbers used as the first word in a sentence.

Seventy people attended the conference in San Diego last week.

The smaller of two adjacent numbers.

We have ordered two 5-pound packages for the meeting.

The words *million* and *billion* in even amounts (do not use decimals with even amounts).

The lottery is worth $28 million this month.

Fractions.

About one-half of the audience responded to the questionnaire.

ABBREVIATIONS

1. **Abb no**

In nontechnical writing, do not abbreviate common nouns (such as *dept.* or *pkg.*), compass points, units of measure, or the names of months, days of the week, cities, or states (except in addresses).

The Sales Department will meet on Tuesday, March 7, in Tempe, Arizona.

2. **Abb meas**

In technical writing, on forms, and in tables, abbreviate units of measure when they occur frequently; do not use periods (e.g., deg (degree), ft (foot/feet), hrs (hours), mi (mile), min (minute), mos (months), oz (ounce), and yrs (years).

14 oz   5 ft 10 in   50 mph   2 yrs 10 mo

3. **Abb lc**

In lowercase abbreviations made up of single initials, use a period after each initial but no internal spaces.

We will be including several states (e.g., Maine, New Hampshire, Vermont, Massachusetts, and Connecticut).

4. **Abb ≡**

In all-capital abbreviations made up of single initials, do not use periods or internal spaces. (Exception: Keep the periods in most academic degrees and in abbreviations of geographic names other than two-letter state abbreviations.)

You need to call the EEO office for clarification on that issue.

He earned a Ph.D. degree in business administration.

PART ONE — The Alphabet, Number, and Symbol Keys

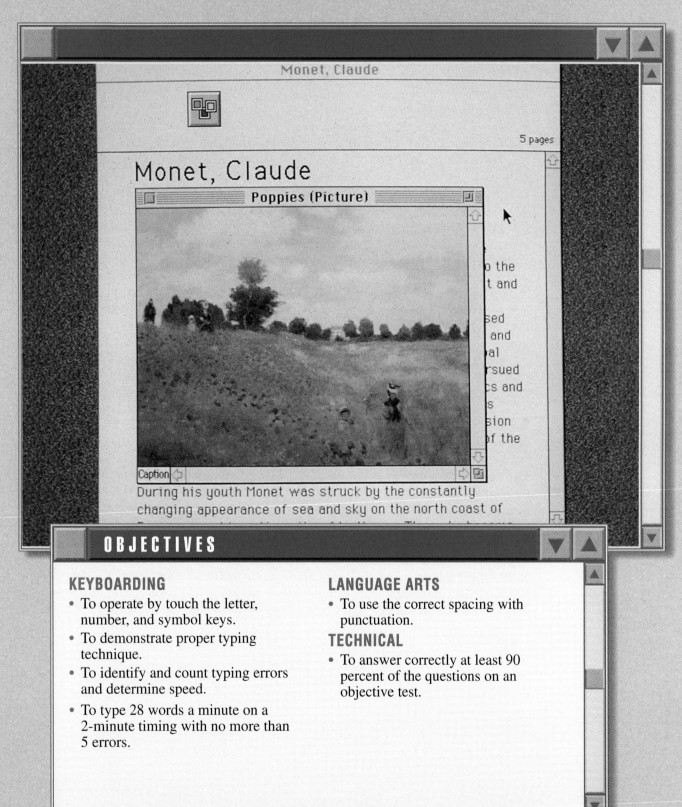

Monet, Claude

5 pages

Monet, Claude

Poppies (Picture)

o the
t and

sed
and
al
rsued
cs and
s
sion
of the

Caption

During his youth Monet was struck by the constantly
changing appearance of sea and sky on the north coast of

OBJECTIVES

KEYBOARDING

- To operate by touch the letter, number, and symbol keys.
- To demonstrate proper typing technique.
- To identify and count typing errors and determine speed.
- To type 28 words a minute on a 2-minute timing with no more than 5 errors.

LANGUAGE ARTS

- To use the correct spacing with punctuation.

TECHNICAL

- To answer correctly at least 90 percent of the questions on an objective test.

BEFORE YOU BEGIN

Using Microsoft Windows

If you are using *Gregg College Keyboarding & Document Processing, Eighth Edition for Windows*, you must know how to use a mouse and you must know some basic information about Microsoft Windows.

Before you begin Lesson 1, turn to the Introduction section in your word processing manual and read the information presented there. Then, use Windows Help to learn how to navigate within a program and to learn the skills you need to use Windows.

Moving around, or navigating, within a program with a mouse involves pointing, clicking, double-clicking, and dragging.

Through Windows Help, you will learn the names and functions of the different parts of a window. You will want to pay close attention to the menu bar and command names, as well as how to select options in a dialog box.

Starting Your Program

Once you have completed the Introduction, you are ready to begin Lesson 1. If you are using the *Gregg College Keyboarding & Document Processing for Windows* software (sometimes referred to as GDP) that is correlated with this textbook, you must first start Windows. To start the *Gregg College Keyboarding & Document Processing for Windows* software, in the Program Manager, locate the Glencoe Keyboarding group icon. Double-click the icon to open the group window. If you will be saving your data to a floppy disk, insert your data disk into the correct drive before you continue.

In the Glencoe Keyboarding group window, if there is a GDP Classes icon, double-click that icon to start the program. Choose the correct class; then choose your name from the class list. If your name does not appear on the list, click *New* to add your name to the list. Then follow the instructions to log in and begin Lesson 1.

If there is no GDP classes icon, select the icon that corresponds to your course name and the location of your data. For example, if your course is called *Lessons 1-60* and you will be saving your data to a disk in drive A, double-click the GDP Lessons 1-60 (Drive A) icon. If you will be saving your data to a disk in drive B, double-click the GDP Lessons 1-60 (Drive B) icon. If you will be saving your data to a hard drive or network drive, you may have an icon specified for your use only. (If you are unsure of which icon to use, ask your instructor.) Double-click the correct program icon, and follow the on-screen directions to log in and begin Lesson 1.

D. Type each line 2 times.

D. WORD PATTERNS

9 banister minister adapter filter master
10 disable disband discern discord discuss
11 embargo emerge embody empty employ emit
12 enforce endure energy engage engine end
13 precept precise predict preside premier
14 subtract subject subsist sublime subdue
15 teamster tearful teaches teak team tear
16 theater theirs theory thefts therm them
17 treason crimson season prison bison son
18 tribune tribute tripod trial tribe trim

E. Type each line 2 times. Keep fingers curved and wrists low but not resting on the keyboard as you practice these lines.

E. ALPHABET REVIEW

19 Alda asked Alma Adams to fly to Alaska.
20 Both Barbara and Bill liked basketball.
21 Carl can accept a classic car in Cairo.
22 David dined in a dark diner in Detroit.
23 Elmo said Eddie edited the entire text.
24 Five friars focused on the four fables.
25 Guy gave a bag of green grapes to Gina.
26 Haughty Hugh hoped Hal had helped Seth.
27 Irene liked to pickle pickles in brine.
28 Jon Jones joined a junior jogging team.
29 Kenny kept a kayak for a trek to Koyuk.
30 Lowell played a well-planned ball game.
31 Monica made more money on many markups.
32 Ned knew ten men in a main dining room.
33 Opal Orem opened four boxes of oranges.
34 Pat paid to park the plane at the pump.
35 Quincy quickly quit his quarterly quiz.
36 Robin read rare books in their library.
37 Sam signed, sealed, and sent the lease.
38 Todd caught trout in the little stream.
39 Uncle Rubin urged Julie to go to Utica.
40 Viva Vista vetoed the five voice votes.
41 Walt waited while Wilma went to Weston.
42 Xu mixed extra extract exactly as told.
43 Yes, your young sister played a cymbal.
44 Zesty zebras zigzagged in the Ohio zoo.

F. Take two 1-minute timings. Determine your speed and errors.

Goal: 19 wam/1'/3e

F. 1-MINUTE TIMING

45 Zoe expected a quiet morning to do   7
46 all of her work. Joy Day was to bring   15
47 five of the tablets.   19

| 1 | 2 | 3 | 4 | 5 | 6 | 7 | 8 |

Lesson 11 Number Keys

GOALS: To control the 5, 7, 3, and 9 keys; to type 19 wam/2′/5e.

A. Type the paragraph 2 times.

A. WARMUP

1   The law firm of Quayle, Buster, Given, and   9
2 Rizzo processed all the cases last June and July;   19
3 however, we will seek a new law firm next summer.   29

   | 1 | 2 | 3 | 4 | 5 | 6 | 7 | 8 | 9 | 10

NEW KEYS

B. Type each line 2 times.

    Use the F finger.

B. THE 5 KEY

4 fr5f fr5f f55f f55f f5f5 f5f5 5 55 555 5,555 5:55
5 55 fury 55 foes 55 fibs 55 fads 55 furs 55 favors
6 The 55 students read the 555 pages in 55 minutes.
7 He found Item 5 that weighed 55 pounds, 5 ounces.

C. Type each line 2 times.

    Use the J finger.

C. THE 7 KEY

8 ju7j ju7j j77j j77j j7j7 j7j7 7 77 777 7,777 7:77
9 77 jigs 77 jobs 77 jugs 77 jets 77 jars 77 jewels
10 The 77 men bought Items 77 and 777 for their job.
11 Joe had 57 books and 77 tablets for a 7:57 class.

D. Type each line 2 times.

    Use the D finger.

D. THE 3 KEY

12 de3d de3d d33d d33d d3d3 d3d3 3 33 333 3,333 3:33
13 33 dots 33 died 33 dine 33 days 33 dogs 33 drains
14 The 33 vans moved 73 cases in less than 33 hours.
15 Add 55 to 753; subtract 73 to get a total of 735.

E. Type each line 2 times.

    Use the L finger.

E. THE 9 KEY

16 lo9l lo9l 1991 1991 1919 1919 9 99 999 9,999 9:99
17 99 lads 99 lights 99 labs 99 legs 99 lips 99 logs
18 Their 99 cans of No. 99 were sold to 99 managers.
19 He had 39 pens, 59 pads, 97 pencils, and 9 clips.

F. NUMBER PRACTICE: 5, 7, 3, AND 9

F. Type each line 2 times.

20 The 57 tickets were for the April 3 show at 9:59.
21 Mary was to read pages 33, 57, 95, and 97 to him.
22 Kate planted 53 tulips, 39 mums, and 97 petunias.
23 Only 397 of the 573 coeds could register at 5:39.

G. TECHNIQUE PRACTICE: SHIFT KEY

G. Type each line 2 times. Keep other fingers at home as you reach to the shift keys.

24 Vera Rosa Tao Fay Jae Tab Pat Yuk Sue Ann Sal Joe
25 Andre Fidel Pedro Chong Alice Mike Juan Fern Dick
26 Carlos Caesar Karen Ojars Julie Marta Scott Maria
27 Marge Jerry Joan Mary Bill Ken Bob Ray Ted Mel Al

H. PROGRESSIVE PRACTICE: ALPHABET

Turn to the Progressive Practice: Alphabet routine beginning on page SB-7. Take a 1-minute timing on the Entry Timing paragraph. Then follow the directions at the top of page SB-7 for completing the activity.

I. 2-MINUTE TIMING

I. Take two 2-minute timings. Determine your speed and errors.

Goal: 19 wam/2'/5e

28   Jazz paid for six seats and quit because he   9
29 could not get the views he wanted near the middle   19
30 of the field. In August he is thinking of going   29
31 to the ticket office early to purchase tickets.   38
   | 1 | 2 | 3 | 4 | 5 | 6 | 7 | 8 | 9 | 10

Lesson 12   Review

GOAL: To type 20 wam/2'/5e.

A. Type the paragraph 2 times.

A. WARMUP

1   Rex played a very quiet game of bridge with   9
2 Zeke. In March they played in competition with   19
3 39 players; in January they played with 57 more.   28
   | 1 | 2 | 3 | 4 | 5 | 6 | 7 | 8 | 9 | 10

B. 12-SECOND SPEED SPRINTS

4 A good neighbor paid for these ancient ornaments.
5 Today I sit by the big lake and count huge rocks.
6 The four chapels sit by the end of the old field.
7 The signal means help is on its way to the child.

| | | |5| | | |10| | | |15| | |20| | | |25| | | |30| | | |35| | | |40| | | |45| | | |50

C. SUSTAINED PRACTICE: SYLLABIC INTENSITY

8   People continue to rent autos for personal   9
9 use and for their work, and car rental businesses   19
10 just keep growing. You may want to try one soon.   29

11   It is likely that a great deal of insurance   9
12 protection is part of the standard rental cost to   19
13 you. You may, however, make many other choices.   29

14   Perhaps this is not necessary, as you might   9
15 already have the kind of protection you want in a   19
16 policy that you currently have on the automobile.   29

17   Paying separate mileage charges could evolve   9
18 into a very large bill. This will undoubtedly be   19
19 true if your trip involves distant destinations.   29

| | 1 | 2 | 3 | 4 | 5 | 6 | 7 | 8 | 9 | 10

D. ALPHABET PRACTICE

20 Packing jam for the dozen boxes was quite lively.
21 Fay quickly jumped over the two dozen huge boxes.
22 We vexed Jack by quietly helping a dozen farmers.
23 The quick lynx from the zoo just waved a big paw.
24 Lazy brown dogs do not jump over the quick foxes.

E. NUMBER PRACTICE

25 Mary was to read pages 37, 59, 75, and 93 to Zoe.
26 He invited 53 boys and 59 girls to the 7:35 show.
27 The 9:37 bus did not come to our stop until 9:55.
28 Purchase Order 53 listed Items 35, 77, 93, and 9.
29 Flight 375 will be departing Gate 37 at 9:59 p.m.

F. TECHNIQUE PRACTICE: ENTER KEY

30 Can he go? If so, what? I am lost. Joe is ill.
31 Did he type the memo? Tina is going. Jane lost.
32 Max will drive. Xenia is in Ohio. He is taller.
33 Nate is fine; Ty is not. Who won? Where is Nan?
34 No, he cannot go. Is he here? Where is Roberta?

G. Type each line 2 times. Space without pausing.

G. TECHNIQUE PRACTICE: SPACE BAR

35 a b c d e f g h i j k l m n o p q r s t u v w x y
36 an as be by go in is it me no of or to we but for
37 Do you go to Ada or Ida for work every day or so?
38 I am sure he can go with you if he has some time.
39 He is to be at the car by the time you get there.

H. Take two 2-minute timings. Determine your speed and errors.

Goal: 20 wam/2'/5e

H. 2-MINUTE TIMING

40   Jack and Alex ordered six pizzas at a price   9
41 that was quite a bit lower than for the one they   19
42 ordered yesterday. They will order from the same   29
43 place tomorrow for the party they are planning to   39
44 have.   40

| 1 | 2 | 3 | 4 | 5 | 6 | 7 | 8 | 9 | 10

Lesson 13   Number Keys

GOALS: To control the 8, 2, and 0 keys; to type 21 wam/2'/5e.

A. Type the paragraph 2 times.

A. WARMUP

1   Mary, Jenny, and Quinn packed 79 prizes in   9
2 53 large boxes for the party. They will take all   19
3 of the boxes to 3579 North Capitol Avenue today.   28

| 1 | 2 | 3 | 4 | 5 | 6 | 7 | 8 | 9 | 10

NEW KEYS

B. Type each line 2 times.
    Use the K finger.

B. THE 8 KEY

4 ki8k ki8k k88k k88k k8k8 k8k8 8 88 888 8,888 8:88
5 88 inks 88 inns 88 keys 88 kits 88 kids 88 knives
6 Bus 38 left at 3:38 and arrived here at 8:37 p.m.
7 Kenny called Joe at 8:38 at 883-7878 or 585-3878.

C. Type each line 2 times.

Use the S finger.

C. THE 2 KEY

8 sw2s sw2s s22s s22s s2s2 s2s2 2 22 222 2,222 2:22
9 22 seas 22 sets 22 sons 22 subs 22 suns 22 sports
10 The 22 seats sold at 2:22 to 22 coeds in Room 22.
11 He added Items 22, 23, 25, 27, and 28 on Order 2.

D. Type each line 2 times.

Use the Sem finger.

D. THE 0 KEY

12 ;p0; ;p0; ;00; ;00; ;0;0 ;0;0 0 00 000 0,000 0:00
13 20 pads 30 pegs 50 pens 70 pins 80 pits 900 parks
14 You will get 230 when you add 30, 50, 70, and 80.
15 The 80 men met at 3:05 with 20 agents in Room 90.

SKILLBUILDING

E. Type each line 2 times.

E. NUMBER PRACTICE

16 Jill bought 55 tickets for the 5:50 or 7:50 show.
17 Maxine called from 777-7370 or 777-7570 for Mary.
18 Sally had 23 cats, 23 dogs, and 22 birds at home.
19 Items 35, 37, 38, and 39 were sent on October 30.
20 Did Flight 2992 leave from Gate 39 at 9:39 today?
21 Sue went from 852 28th Street to 858 28th Street.
22 He sold 20 tires, 30 air filters, and 200 wipers.

F. Indent and type each sentence on a separate line. Type 2 times.

F. TECHNIQUE PRACTICE: TAB KEY

23 Casey left. Where is John? Susan asked for Tom.
24 I drive. Where do you drive? When do you drive?
25 Pat sold cars. Don sold vans. Pete sold trucks.
26 Nick has nails. Chris has bolts. Dave has wood.

G. PACED PRACTICE

Turn to the Paced Practice routine beginning on page SB-14. Take a 1-minute timing on the Entry Timing paragraph. Then follow the directions at the top of page SB-14 for completing the activity.

H. DIAGNOSTIC PRACTICE: ALPHABET

Turn to the Diagnostic Practice: Alphabet routine beginning on page SB-2. Type one of the Pretest/Posttest paragraphs and identify any errors made. Then type the corresponding drill lines 2 times for each letter on which you made 2 or more errors and 1 time for each letter on which you made only 1 error. Finally, repeat the same Pretest paragraph and compare your performance.

I. Take two 2-minute timings. Determine your speed and errors.

Goal: 21 wam/2′/5e

I. 2-MINUTE TIMING

```
27        Jim told Bev that they must keep the liquid      9
28   oxygen frozen so that it could be used by the new    19
29   plant foreman tomorrow.  The oxygen will then be     29
30   moved quickly to its new location by transport or    39
31   rail next evening.                                   42
     |  1  |  2  |  3  |  4  |  5  |  6  |  7  |  8  |  9  |  10
```

Lesson 14 Number Keys

GOALS: To control the 4, 6, and 1 keys; to type 22 wam/2′/5e.

A. Type the paragraph 2 times.

A. WARMUP

```
1         We quickly made 30 jars of jam and won a big     9
2   prize for our efforts on March 29.  Six of the       19
3   jars were taken to 578 Culver Drive on April 28.     28
    |  1  |  2  |  3  |  4  |  5  |  6  |  7  |  8  |  9  |  10
```

 NEW KEYS

B. Type each line 2 times.

Use the F finger.

B. THE 4 KEY

```
4   fr4f fr4f f44f f44f f4f4 f4f4 4 44 444 4,444 4:44
5   44 fans 44 feet 44 figs 44 fins 44 fish 44 flakes
6   The 44 boys had 44 tickets for the games at 4:44.
7   Matthew read 4 books, 54 articles, and 434 lines.
```

C. Type each line 2 times.

Use the J finger.

C. THE 6 KEY

8 jy6j jy6j j66j j66j j6j6 j6j6 6 66 666 6,666 6:66
9 66 jabs 66 jams 66 jobs 66 join 66 jots 66 jewels
10 Tom Lux left at 6:26 on Train 66 to go 600 miles.
11 There were 56,640 people in Bath; 26,269 in Hale.

D. Type each line 2 times.

Use the A finger.

D. THE 1 KEY

12 aqla aqla alla alla alal alal 1 11 111 1,111 1:11
13 11 aces 11 adds 11 aims 11 arts 11 axes 11 arenas
14 Sam left here at 1:11; Sue at 6:11; Don at 11:11.
15 Eric moved from 1661 Main Street to 1116 in 1995.

SKILLBUILDING

E. Type each line 2 times. Focus on accuracy rather than speed as you practice the number drills.

E. NUMBER PRACTICE

16 Adding 10 and 20 and 30 and 40 and 70 totals 170.
17 On July 25, 1996, 130 girls ran in a 4-mile race.
18 Al selected Nos. 16, 17, 18, 19, and 20 to study.
19 The test took Sam 10 hours, 8 minutes, 3 seconds.
20 Alice took 14 men and 23 women to the 128 events.

21 Did the 33 men drive 567 miles on Route 23 or 27?
22 On 10/29/96, she typed lines 16-47 in 35 minutes.
23 In 1995 there were 2,934 people in the 239 camps.
24 The 18 shows were sold out by 8:37 on October 18.
25 On April 29-30 we will be open from 7:45 to 9:30.

F. PROGRESSIVE PRACTICE: NUMBERS

Turn to the Progressive Practice: Numbers routine beginning on page SB-11. Take a 1-minute timing on the Entry Timing paragraph. Then follow the directions at the top of page SB-11 for completing the activity.

G. Take two 1-minute timings. Determine your speed and errors.

G. HANDWRITTEN PARAGRAPH

26 *Good writing skills are critical for success* 9
27 *in business. Numerous studies have shown* 19
28 *that these skills are essential for job advancement.* 28

H. Take two 2-minute timings. Determine your speed and errors.

Goal: 22 wam/2′/5e

H. 2-MINUTE TIMING

29   James scheduled a science quiz next week for   9
30 George, but he did not let him know what time the   19
31 exam was to be taken. It is very important that   29
32 George scores well in this exam to be admitted to   39
33 the Mount Garland Academy.   44

| 1 | 2 | 3 | 4 | 5 | 6 | 7 | 8 | 9 | 10 |

Lesson 15   Review

GOAL: To type 23 wam/2′/5e.

A. Type the paragraph 2 times.

A. WARMUP

1   Jeffrey Mendoza quickly plowed six fields so   9
2 that he could plant 19 rows of beets, 28 rows of   19
3 corn, 37 rows of grapes, and 45 rows of olives.   28

| 1 | 2 | 3 | 4 | 5 | 6 | 7 | 8 | 9 | 10 |

SKILLBUILDING

B. Take three 12-second timings on each line. The scale below the last line shows your wam speed for a 12-second timing.

B. 12-SECOND SPEED SPRINTS

4 The lane to the lake might make the auto go away.
5 They go to the lake by bus when they work for me.
6 He just won and lost, won and lost, won and lost.
7 The man and the girl rush down the paths to town.

| | 5 | 10 | 15 | 20 | 25 | 30 | 35 | 40 | 45 | 50 |

C. Tab once between columns. Type 2 times.

C. TECHNIQUE PRACTICE: TAB KEY

8 aisle Tab→ break Tab→ crank Tab→ draft Tab→ earth
9 frame   guide   hitch   input   juice
10 knack   learn   mason   night   ocean
11 print   quest   rinse   slide   title
12 usual   vapor   where   extra   zesty

D. Type each line 2 times. Try not to slow down for the capital letters.

D. TECHNIQUE PRACTICE: SHIFT KEY

13 Sue, Pat, Ann, and Gail left for Rome on June 10.
14 The St. Louis Cardinals and New York Mets played.
15 Dave Herr took Flight 481 for Memphis and Toledo.
16 An address for Karen Cook is 5 Bar Street, Provo.
17 Harry Truman was born in Missouri on May 8, 1884.

E. Type each line 2 times.

E. PUNCTUATION PRACTICE

18 Jan Brooks-Smith was a go-between for the author.
19 The off-the-record comment led to a free-for-all.
20 Louis was a jack-of-all-trades as a clerk-typist.
21 Ask Barbara--who is in Central Data--to find out.
22 Joanne is too old-fashioned to be that outspoken.

Pretest
Take a 1-minute timing. Determine your speed and errors.

F. PRETEST: VERTICAL REACHES

23   A few of our business managers attribute the   9
24 success of the bank to a judicious and scientific   19
25 reserve program. The bank cannot drop its guard.   29
   | 1 | 2 | 3 | 4 | 5 | 6 | 7 | 8 | 9 | 10

Practice
Speed Emphasis: If you made 2 or fewer errors on the Pretest, type each *individual* line 2 times.
Accuracy Emphasis: If you made 3 or more errors, type each *group* of lines (as though it were a paragraph) 2 times.

G. PRACTICE: UP REACHES

26 at atlas plate water later batch fatal match late
27 dr draft drift drums drawn drain drama dress drab
28 ju jumpy juror junky jumbo julep judge juice just

H. PRACTICE: DOWN REACHES

29 ca cable cabin cadet camel cameo candy carve cash
30 nk trunk drink prank rinks brink drank crank sink
31 ba batch badge bagel baked banjo barge basis bank

Posttest
Repeat the Pretest timing and compare performance.

I. POSTTEST: VERTICAL REACHES

J. PROGRESSIVE PRACTICE: ALPHABET

Turn to the Progressive Practice: Alphabet routine beginning on page SB-7. Take six 30-second timings, starting at the point where you left off the last time.

K. Take two 2-minute timings. Determine your speed and errors.

Goal: 23 wam/2'/5e

K. 2-MINUTE TIMING

32   Jeff Malvey was quite busy fixing all of the   9
33 frozen pipes so that his water supply would not   19
34 be stopped. Last winter he kept the pipes from   28
35 freezing by wrapping them with an electric cord   38
36 that did not allow in any of the cold air.   46
   | 1 | 2 | 3 | 4 | 5 | 6 | 7 | 8 | 9 | 10

UNIT FOUR ▶ Keyboarding—The Symbols

Lesson 16   Symbol Keys

GOALS: To control the $, (,), and ! keys; to type 24 wam/2′/5e.

A. Type 2 times.

A. WARMUP

```
 1        Gill was quite vexed by that musician who      9
 2  played 5 jazz songs and 13 country songs at the     18
 3  fair.  He wanted 8 rock songs and 4 blues songs.     28
    | 1  | 2  | 3  | 4  | 5  | 6  | 7  | 8  | 9  | 10
```

NEW KEYS

B. **$** DOLLAR is the shift of 4. Do not space between the dollar sign and the number. Type each line 2 times.

Use the F finger.

B. THE **$** KEY

```
 4  frf fr4f f4f f4$f f$$f f$$f $44 $444 $4,444 $4.44
 5  I quoted $48, $64, and $94 for the set of chairs.
 6  Her insurance paid $150; our insurance paid $175.
 7  Season concert seats were $25, $30, $55, and $75.
```

C. **( )** PAREN-THESES are the shifts of 9 and 0. Do not space between the parentheses and the text within them. Type each line 2 times.

Use the L finger on (.

Use the Sem finger on).

C. THE **(** AND **)** KEYS

```
 8  lo9l lo9l lo(l lo(l l((l ;p0; ;p0; ;p); ;p); ;));
 9  Please ask (1) Al, (2) Pat, (3) Ted, and (4) Dee.
10  Sue has some (1) skis, (2) sleds, and (3) skates.
11  Mary is (1) prompt, (2) speedy, and (3) accurate.

12  Our workers (Lewis, Jerry, and Ty) were rewarded.
13  The owner (Ms. Parks) went on Friday (August 18).
14  The Roxie (a cafe) had fish (salmon) on the menu.
15  The clerk (Ms. Fay Green) will vote yes (not no).
```

D. **!** EXCLAMATION is the shift of 1. Space twice after an exclamation point at the end of a sentence. Type each line 2 times.

Use the A finger.

D. THE **!** KEY

```
16  aqa aq1a aq!a a!!a a!!a Where!  Why!  How!  When!
17  Put it down!  Do not move!  No!  Yes!  Stop!  Go!
18  He did say that!  Jay cannot take a vacation now!
19  You cannot leave at this time!  Jane will not go!
```

UNIT FOUR Lesson 16   **29**

E. Type the paragraph 2 times.

E. TECHNIQUE PRACTICE: SPACE BAR

```
20        We will all go to the race if I win the one
21  I am going to run today.  Do you think I will be
22  able to run at the front of the pack and win it?
```

F. Take three 12-second timings on each line. The scale below the last line shows your wam speed for a 12-second timing.

F. 12-SECOND SPEED SPRINTS

```
23  Walking can perk you up if you are feeling tired.
24  Your heart and lungs can work harder as you walk.
25  It may be that a walk is often better than a nap.
26  If you walk each day, your health will be better.
    | | | |5| | | |10| | | |15| | | |20| | | |25| | | |30| | | |35| | | |40| | | |45| | | |50
```

G. PACED PRACTICE

Turn to the Paced Practice routine beginning on page SB-14. Take three 2-minute timings, starting at the point where you left off the last time.

H. Take two 2-minute timings. Determine your speed and errors.

Goal: 24 wam/2'/5e

H. 2-MINUTE TIMING

```
27        Katie quit her zoo job seven days after she      9
28  learned that she was expected to travel to four        19
29  different zoos in the first year of employment.        28
30  After quitting that job, she found an excellent        38
31  job that required her to travel less frequently.       48
    |  1  |  2  |  3  |  4  |  5  |  6  |  7  |  8  |  9  |  10
```

Lesson 17   Review

GOAL: To type 25 wam/2'/5e.

A. Type 2 times.

A. WARMUP

```
1        Yes!  We object to the dumping of 25 toxic       9
2  barrels at 4098 Nix Street.  A larger number (36)      19
3  were dumped on the 7th, costing us over $10,000.       28
   |  1  |  2  |  3  |  4  |  5  |  6  |  7  |  8  |  9  |  10
```

UNIT FOUR Lesson 17

B. Type each line 2 times.

B. NUMBER PRACTICE

```
 4   we 23 pi 08 you 697 row 492 tire 5843 power 09234
 5   or 94 re 43 eye 363 top 590 quit 1785 witty 28556
 6   up 70 ye 63 pit 085 per 034 root 4995 wrote 24953
 7   it 85 ro 49 rip 480 two 529 tour 5974 quite 17853
 8   yi 68 to 59 toy 596 rot 495 tier 5834 queue 17373
 9   op 90 qo 19 wet 235 pet 035 rope 4903 quote 17953
```

C. Type each line 2 times.

C. WORD BEGINNINGS

```
10   tri trinkets tribune trifle trick trial trip trim
11   mil million mileage mildew mills milky miles mild
12   spo sponsor sponge sports spore spoon spool spoke
13   for forgiving forbear forward forbid forced force

14   div dividend division divine divide diving divers
15   vic vicinity vicious victory victims victor vices
16   aff affliction affiliates affirms affords affairs
17   tab tablecloth tabulates tableau tabloids tablets
```

D. Type each line 2 times.

D. WORD ENDINGS

```
18   ive repulsive explosive alive drive active strive
19   est nearest invest attest wisest nicest jest test
20   ply supply simply deeply damply apply imply reply
21   ver whenever forever whoever quiver waiver driver

22   tor inventor detector debtor orator doctor factor
23   lly industrially logically legally ideally really
24   ert convert dessert expert invert diverts asserts
25   ink shrink drink think blink clink pink sink rink
```

E. PROGRESSIVE PRACTICE: ALPHABET

Turn to the Progressive Practice: Alphabet routine beginning on page SB-7. Take six 30-second timings, starting at the point where you left off the last time.

F. Take two 1-minute timings. Determine your speed and errors.

F. HANDWRITTEN PARAGRAPH

```
26   In this book you have learned the reaches        9
27   for all alphabetic and number keys. You have    18
28   also learned a few of the symbol keys. In the   27
29   remaining lessons you will learn the remaining  36
30   symbol keys, and you will also build your       45
31   speed and accuracy when typing.                 51
```

G. DIAGNOSTIC PRACTICE: NUMBERS

Turn to the Diagnostic Practice: Numbers routine beginning on page SB-5. Type one of the Pretest/Posttest paragraphs and identify any errors made. Then type the corresponding drill lines 2 times for each number on which you made 2 or more errors and 1 time for each number on which you made only 1 error. Finally, repeat the same Pretest paragraph and compare your performance.

H. 2-MINUTE TIMING

H. Take two 2-minute timings. Determine your speed and errors.

Goal: 25 wam/2′/5e

```
32      From the tower John saw that the six big        8
33   planes would crash as they zoomed quickly over    18
34   treetops on their way to the demonstration that   27
35   was scheduled to begin early.  We hope there is   37
36   no accident and that those pilots reach their     46
37   destinations safely.                              50
```
| 1 | 2 | 3 | 4 | 5 | 6 | 7 | 8 | | 10

Lesson 18   Symbol Keys

GOALS: To control the *, #, and ' keys; to type 26 wam/2′/5e.

A. Type 2 times.

A. WARMUP

```
1      Bill Waxmann quickly moved all 35 packs of      9
2   gear for the Amazon trip (worth $987) 26 miles    18
3   into the jungle.  The move took 14 days in all.   28
```
| 1 | 2 | 3 | 4 | 5 | 6 | 7 | 8 | 9 | 10

NEW KEYS

B. [*] ASTERISK is the shift of 8. Type each line 2 times.

Use the K finger.

B. THE ⬜ KEY

```
4   kik ki8k k8*k k8*k k**k k**k This book* is great.
5   Use an * to show that a table source is included.
6   Asterisks keyed in a row (******) make a border.
7   The article quoted Hanson,* Pyle,* and Peterson.*
```

C. **#** NUMBER (if before a figure) or POUNDS (if after a figure) is the shift of 3. Type each line 2 times.

Use the D finger.

C. THE **#** KEY

8 de3d de3#d d3#d d3#d d##d d##d #3 #33 #333 #3,333
9 Al wants 33# of #200 and 38# of #400 by Saturday.
10 My favorite seats are #2, #34, #56, #65, and #66.
11 Please order 45# of #245 and 13# of #24 tomorrow.

D. **'** APOSTROPHE is to the right of the semicolon. Type each line 2 times.

Use the Sem finger.

D. THE **'** KEY

12 ;'; ';' ;'; ';' Can't we go in Sue's or Al's car?
13 It's Bob's job to cover Ted's work when he's out.
14 What's in Joann's lunch box for Sandra's dessert?
15 He's left for Ty's banquet which is held at Al's.

SKILLBUILDING

E. PACED PRACTICE

Turn to the Paced Practice routine beginning on page SB-14. Take three 2-minute timings, starting at the point where you left off the last time.

F. DIAGNOSTIC PRACTICE: ALPHABET

Turn to the Diagnostic Practice: Alphabet routine beginning on page SB-2. Type one of the Pretest/Posttest paragraphs and identify any errors made. Then type the corresponding drill lines 2 times for each letter on which you made 2 or more errors and 1 time for each letter on which you made only 1 error. Finally, repeat the same Pretest paragraph and compare your performance.

G. Take two 1-minute timings. Determine your speed and errors.

G. HANDWRITTEN PARAGRAPH

16 You have completed the first segment of   8
17 your class and have learned your alphabetic   17
18 keys, the number keys, and some of the   25
19 symbol keys. Next you will learn the   32
20 remaining symbol keys on the top row.   40

H. Take two 2-minute timings. Determine your speed and errors.

Goal: 26 wam/2'/5e

H. 2-MINUTE TIMING

21   Max had to make one quick adjustment to his   9
22 television before the football game began. The   19
23 picture during the last game was fuzzy and hard   28
24 to see. If he cannot fix the picture, he may   37
25 have to purchase a new television set; and that   47
26 may not be possible today.   52

| 1 | 2 | 3 | 4 | 5 | 6 | 7 | 8 | 9 | 10

Lesson 19   Symbol Keys

GOALS: To control the &, %, ", and @ keys; to type 27 wam/2'/5e.

A. Type 2 times.

A. WARMUP

1   The teacher (Jane Quayler) gave us some work   9
2 to do as homework for 11-28-96. Chapters 3 and   19
3 4 from our text* are to be read for a hard quiz.   28

| 1 | 2 | 3 | 4 | 5 | 6 | 7 | 8 | 9 | 10

NEW KEYS

B. **&** AMPERSAND (sign for *and*) is the shift of 7. Space before and after the ampersand. Type each line 2 times.

Use the J finger.

B. THE **&** KEY

4 juj ju7j j7j j7&j j&&j j&&j Max & Dee & Sue & Ken
5 Brown & Sons shipped goods to Crum & Lee Company.
6 Johnson & Loo brought a case against May & Green.
7 Ball & Trump vs. Vens & See is being decided now.

C. **%** PERCENT is the shift of 5. Do not space between the number and the percent sign. Type each line 2 times.

Use the F finger.

C. THE **%** KEY

8 ft5f ft5%f f5%f f5%f f%%f f%%f 5% 55% 555% 5,555%
9 Robert quoted rates of 8%, 9%, 10%, 11%, and 12%.
10 Pat scored 82%, Jan 89%, and Ken 90% on the test.
11 Only 55% of the students passed 75% of the exams.

D. THE " KEY

12 ;'; ":" ;"; ";" "That's a super job," said Mabel.
13 The theme of the meeting is "Improving Your Job."
14 John said, "Those were good." Sharon said, "No."
15 Allison said, "I'll take Janice and Ed to Flint."

E. THE @ KEY

16 sws sw2s s2@s s2@s s@@s s@@s Buy 15 @ $5 in June.
17 You can e-mail us at this address: proj@edu.com.
18 Order 12 items @ $14 and another 185 items @ $16.
19 Lee said, "I'll buy 8 shares @ $6 and 5 @ $7.55."

FORMATTING

F. PLACEMENT OF QUOTATION MARKS

Read these rules about the placement of quotation marks. Then type lines 20–23 twice.

1. The closing quotation mark is always typed *after* a period or comma but *before* a colon or semicolon.

2. The closing quotation mark is typed *after* a question mark or exclamation point if the quoted material is a question or an exclamation; otherwise, the quotation mark is typed *before* the question mark or exclamation point.

20 "Hello," I said. "My name is Al; I am new here."
21 Zack read the article "Can She Succeed Tomorrow?"
22 James said, "I'll mail the check"; but he didn't.
23 Did he say, "We lost"? She said, "I don't know."

SKILLBUILDING

G. ALPHABET AND SYMBOL PRACTICE

24 Gaze at views of my jonquil or red phlox in back.
25 Jan quickly moved the six dozen big pink flowers.
26 Joe quietly picked six razors from the woven bag.
27 Packing jam for the dozen boxes was quite lively.

28 Mail these "Rush": #38, #45, and #67 (software).
29 No! Joe's note did not carry a rate of under 9%.
30 Lee read "The Computer Today." It's here Monday.
31 This book* cost us $48.10; 12% higher than yours.

H. Take a 1-minute tim-
ing on the first paragraph
to establish your base
speed. Then take four 1-
minute timings on the
remaining paragraphs.
As soon as you equal or
exceed your base speed
on one paragraph,
advance to the next,
more difficult paragraph.

H. SUSTAINED PRACTICE: NUMBERS AND SYMBOLS

```
32      We purchased several pieces of new computer      9
33 equipment for our new store in Boston.  We were      19
34 amazed at all the extra work we could get done.      28

35      For our department, we received 5 printers,     9
36 12 computers, and 3 fax machines.  We heard that     19
37 the equipment cost us several thousand dollars.      28

38      Next week 6 computers (Model ZS86), 4 old       9
39 copiers (drums are broken), and 9 shredders will     18
40 need to be replaced.  Total cost will be high.       28

41      Last year $150,890 was spent on equipment       9
42 for Iowa's offices.  Breaman & Sims predicted a      18
43 17% to 20% increase (*over '95); that's amazing.     28
```
| 1 | 2 | 3 | 4 | 5 | 6 | 7 | 8 | 9 | 10

I. Take two 2-minute
timings. Determine your
speed and errors.

Goal: 27 wam/2'/5e

I. 2-MINUTE TIMING

```
44      Topaz and onyx were for sale at a reasonable    9
45 price last week.  When Mavis saw the rings with      19
46 these stones, she quickly bought them both for       28
47 her sons.  These jewels were difficult to find,      38
48 and Mavis was happy.  She was able to purchase       47
49 the rings before someone else did.                   54
```
| 1 | 2 | 3 | 4 | 5 | 6 | 7 | 8 | 9 | 10

Lesson 20   Review

GOAL: To type 28 wam/2'/5e.

A. Type 2 times.

A. WARMUP

```
1       Vin went to see Exhibits #794 and #860.  He     9
2 had quickly judged these zany projects that cost      19
3 $321 (parts & labor)--a 5% markup from last year.     29
```
| 1 | 2 | 3 | 4 | 5 | 6 | 7 | 8 | 9 | 10

B. PUNCTUATION PRACTICE

4 Go to Reno.   Drive to Yuma.   Call Mary.   Get Sam.
5 We saw Nice, Paris, Bern, Rome, Munich, and Bonn.
6 Type a memo; read a report.   Get pens; get paper.
7 Read the following pages: 1-8, 10-22, and 34-58.
8 No!   Stop!   Don't look!   Watch out!   Move!   Jump!

9 Can you wait?   Why not?   Can he drive?   Where to?
10 I have these reports: Sue's, Bill's, and Lisa's.
11 It's the best--and cheapest!   Don't use it--ever.
12 "I can," he said, "right now."   Val said, "Wait!"
13 Allen called Rome (GA), Rome (NY), and Rome (WI).

Pretest
Take a 1-minute timing. Determine your speed and errors.

C. PRETEST: ALTERNATE- AND ONE-HAND WORDS

14   The chairman should handle the tax problem   9
15 downtown. If they are reversed, pressure tactics   19
16 might have changed the case as it was discussed.   28

| 1 | 2 | 3 | 4 | 5 | 6 | 7 | 8 | 9 | 10

Practice
Speed Emphasis: If you made 2 or fewer errors on the Pretest, type each *individual* line 2 times.
Accuracy Emphasis: If you made 3 or more errors, type each *group* of lines (as though it were a paragraph) 2 times.

D. PRACTICE: ALTERNATE-HAND WORDS

17 the with girl right blame handle antique chairman
18 for wish town their panel formal problem downtown
19 pan busy they flair signs thrown signals problems

E. PRACTICE: ONE-HAND WORDS

20 lip fact yolk poplin yummy affect reverse pumpkin
21 you cast kill uphill jumpy grease wagered opinion
22 tea cage lump limply hilly served bravest minimum

Posttest
Repeat the Pretest timing and compare performance.

F. POSTTEST: ALTERNATE- AND ONE-HAND WORDS

G. Take three 12-second timings on each line. The scale below the last line shows your wam speed for a 12-second timing.

G. 12-SECOND SPEED SPRINTS

23 Paul likes to work for the bank while in college.
24 They will make a nice profit if the work is done.
25 The group of friends went to a movie at the mall.
26 The man sent the forms after she called for them.

| | | | 5 | | | | 10 | | | 15 | | | 20 | | | 25 | | | 30 | | | 35 | | | 40 | | | 45 | | | 50

H. HANDWRITTEN PARAGRAPH

27 In your career, you will use the 7
28 skills you are learning in this course. 15
29 However, you will soon discover that you 23
30 must also possess human relations skills. 31

I. Take two 2-minute timings. Determine your speed and errors.

Goal: 28 wam/2'/5e

I. 2-MINUTE TIMING

31   Jake or Peggy Zale must quickly fix the fax 9
32 machine so that we can have access to regional 18
33 reports that we think might be sent within the 28
34 next few days. Without the fax, we will not be 37
35 able to complete all our monthly reports by the 47
36 deadline. Please let me know of any problems. 56

| 1 | 2 | 3 | 4 | 5 | 6 | 7 | 8 | 9 | 10 |

PART TWO

Letters, Memos, Tables, and Reports

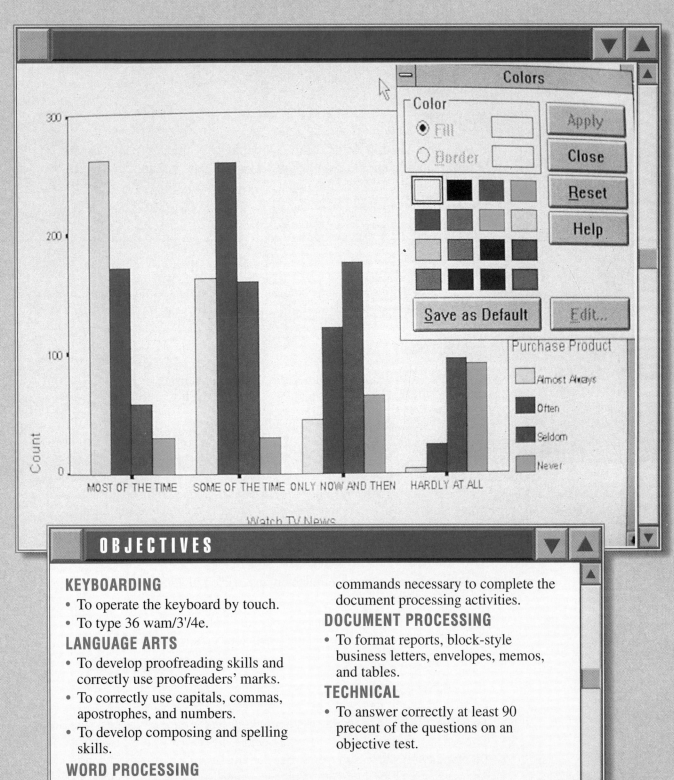

Lesson 21   Orientation to Word Processing—A

GOALS: To improve speed and accuracy; to refine language-arts skills in punctuation; to practice basic word processing commands.

A. Type 2 times.

A. WARMUP

```
1       Juan Valdez will lead 10 managers during this sales      11
2  period; his expert input has always been valuable.  Will     23
3  Quentin earn 8% commission ($534) after order #K76 arrives?   35
   | 1 | 2 | 3 | 4 | 5 | 6 | 7 | 8 | 9 | 10 | 11 | 12
```

SKILLBUILDING

B. PROGRESSIVE PRACTICE: NUMBERS

Turn to the Progressive Practice: Numbers routine beginning on page SB-11.

Take six 30-second timings, starting at the point where you left off the last time.

C. PACED PRACTICE

Turn to the Paced Practice routine beginning on page SB-14. Take three 2-minute

timings, starting at the point where you left off the last time.

LANGUAGE ARTS

D. COMMAS

D. Study the rules at the right.

Rule: Use a comma between independent clauses joined by a conjunction. (An independent clause is one that can stand alone as a complete sentence.)

,ind

Ms. Morimoto is the new president, and she will begin her term immediately.
But: Ms. Morimoto is the new president and will begin her term immediately.

Rule: Use a comma after an introductory expression (unless it is a short prepositional phrase).

,intro

When you become a network manager, you will be able to find a good job.
But: You will be able to find a good job when you become a network manager.
But: At the meeting she was very quiet.

Edit the paragraph to insert any needed punctuation.

```
4       Many companies have work-study programs in effect and
5  employ a high percentage of students after graduation.
6  Because these students have worked hard and have set goals
7  for themselves many employers will be eager to hire them.
8  On Monday interviews will be scheduled.  If students are
9  interested they should call us immediately.  A resume will
10 be required from all applicants and a letter of application
11 must be written before the interview is scheduled.
```

E. WORD PROCESSING

Study Lesson 21 in your word processing manual. Complete all of the shaded steps   while at your computer.

Lesson 22   Orientation to Word Processing—B

GOALS: To type 28 wam/3'/5e; to practice basic word processing commands.

A. Type 2 times.

A. WARMUP

```
1        Zenobia bought 987 reams of 16# bond paper from V & J    11
2   Co.  Only 2/3 of this week's order is acceptable.  About      22
3   45 percent is excellent quality; the rest cannot be used.     34
    | 1 | 2 | 3 | 4 | 5 | 6 | 7 | 8 | 9 | 10 | 11 | 12
```

SKILLBUILDING

B. PROGRESSIVE PRACTICE: ALPHABET

Turn to the Progressive Practice: Alphabet routine beginning on page SB-7. Take six 30-second timings, starting at the point where you left off the last time.

C. Take three 12-second timings on each line. The scale below the last line shows your wam speed for a 12-second timing.

C. 12-SECOND SPEED SPRINTS

```
4   Mary will be glad to see when the girls will be able to go.
5   She will not come to their office for the first time today.
6   The blue car was not very fast when he tried to speed away.
7   The work must be done when she comes to work or he will go.
    | | | | 5 | | | |10| | |15| | |20| | | |25| | |30| | |35| | | |40| | |45| | |50| | | |55| | |60
```

D. Take two 3-minute timings. Determine your speed and errors.

Goal: 28 wam/3'/5e

D. 3-MINUTE TIMING

```
8         Once you learn to use a variety of software programs,    11
9   you will feel confident and comfortable when you are using    23
10  a computer.  All you have to do is take the first step and    35
11  decide to strive for excellence.                              41
12        Initially, you might have several questions as you      52
13  gaze up at a screen filled with icons.  If you try using      63
14  just one or two commands each day, you will soon find that    75
15  learning to use software can be very exciting.                84
    | 1 | 2 | 3 | 4 | 5 | 6 | 7 | 8 | 9 | 10 | 11 | 12
```

FORMATTING

E. WORD PROCESSING

Study Lesson 22 in your word processing manual. Complete all of the shaded steps while at your computer.

Lesson 23   Orientation to Word Processing—C

GOALS: To improve speed and accuracy; to refine language-arts skills in proofreading; to practice basic word processing commands.

A. Type 2 times.

A. WARMUP

```
 1        We expect the following sizes to be mailed promptly      11
 2   on January 8:  5, 7, and 9.  Send your payment quickly so     22
 3   that the items will be sure to arrive before 2:34* (*p.m.)!   34
     | 1 | 2 | 3 | 4 | 5 | 6 | 7 | 8 | 9 | 10 | 11 | 12
```

SKILLBUILDING

B. Take a 1-minute timing on the first paragraph to establish your base speed. Then take four 1-minute timings on the remaining paragraphs. As soon as you equal or exceed your base speed on one paragraph, advance to the next, more difficult paragraph.

B. SUSTAINED PRACTICE: CAPITALS

```
 4        The insurance industry will undergo major changes due    11
 5   to the many natural disasters the United States has seen in   23
 6   the last few years in places like California and Florida.     34

 7        The recent earthquakes in San Francisco, Northridge,     11
 8   and Loma Prieta cost thousands of dollars.  Faults like       22
 9   the San Andreas are being watched carefully for activity.     33

10        Some tropical storms are spawned in the West Indies      11
11   and move from the Caribbean Sea into the Atlantic Ocean.      22
12   They could affect Georgia, Florida, Alabama, and Texas.       33

13        Some U.S. cities have VHF-FM radio weather stations.     11
14   NASA and NOAA are agencies that launch weather satellites     22
15   to predict the locations, times, and severity of storms.     34
     | 1 | 2 | 3 | 4 | 5 | 6 | 7 | 8 | 9 | 10 | 11 | 12
```

C. DIAGNOSTIC PRACTICE: ALPHABET

Turn to the Diagnostic Practice: Alphabet routine beginning on page SB-2. Type one of the Pretest/Posttest paragraphs and identify any errors made. Then type the corresponding drill lines 2 times for each letter on which you made 2 or more errors and 1 time for each letter on which you made only 1 error. Finally, repeat the same Pretest paragraph and compare your performance.

 **LANGUAGE ARTS**

D. Study the proof-reading techniques at the right.

D. PROOFREADING YOUR DOCUMENTS

Proofreading and correcting errors are an essential part of document processing. To become an expert proofreader:

1. Use the spelling feature of your word processing software to check for spelling errors; then read the copy aloud to see if it makes sense.
2. Proofread for all kinds of errors, espe-cially repeated, missing, or transposed words; grammar and punctuation; and numbers and names.
3. Use the appropriate software com-mand to see an entire page of your document to check for formatting errors such as line spacing, tabs, mar-gins, and bold.

E. Compare this para-graph with the 3-minute timing on page 41. Edit the paragraph to correct any errors.

E. PROOFREADING

8   Once you learn too use a variety of software programs
9 you will feel confidant and comfortable when you are using
10 a computr. All you have to do is take a first step and
11 decide to strive for excellence.

FORMATTING

go TO

F. WORD PROCESSING

Study Lesson 23 in your word processing manual. Complete all of the shaded steps while at your computer.

Lesson 24   Simple Reports

GOALS: To type 29 wam/3'/5e; to format simple reports.

A. Type 2 times.

A. WARMUP

1   The experts quickly realized that repairs could cost   11
2 "$985 million" and might exceed 60% of their budget. Will   23
3 Valdez & Co. begin work before 12 or just wait until 4:30?   34
    | 1 | 2 | 3 | 4 | 5 | 6 | 7 | 8 | 9 | 10 | 11 | 12

SKILLBUILDING

Pretest
Take a 1-minute timing. Determine your speed and errors.

B. PRETEST: COMMON LETTER COMBINATIONS

4   He tried to explain the delay in a logical way. The   11
5 man finally agreed to insure the package and demanded to   22
6 know why the postal worker did not record the total amount.   34
    | 1 | 2 | 3 | 4 | 5 | 6 | 7 | 8 | 9 | 10 | 11 | 12

Speed Emphasis: If you made 2 or fewer errors on the Pretest, type each *individual* line 2 times.

Accuracy Emphasis: If you made 3 or more errors, type each *group* of lines (as though it were a paragraph) 2 times.

C. PRACTICE: WORD BEGINNINGS

```
7  re reuse react relay reply return reason record results red
8  in inset inept incur index indeed intend inning insured ink
9  de dents dealt death delay detest devote derive depicts den
   | 1 | 2 | 3 | 4 | 5 | 6 | 7 | 8 | 9 | 10 | 11 | 12
```

D. PRACTICE: WORD ENDINGS

```
10  ly lowly dimly apply daily barely unruly deeply finally sly
11  ed cured tamed tried moved amused busted billed creamed fed
12  al canal total equal local postal plural rental logical pal
```

E. POSTTEST: COMMON LETTER COMBINATIONS

Posttest

Repeat the Pretest timing and compare performance.

F. 3-MINUTE TIMING

F. Take two 3-minute timings. Determine your speed and errors.

Goal: 29 wam/3′/5e

```
13      If you ever feel tired when you are typing, you should   11
14  take a rest.  Question what you are doing that is fatiguing  23
15  your muscles, and you will realize that you can change the   35
16  fundamental source of your anxiety.                          42
17      Take a deep breath, and enjoy the relaxing feeling as    53
18  you exhale slowly.  Check your posture, and be sure that     64
19  you are sitting up straight with your back against your      76
20  chair.  Stretch your neck and back for total relaxation.     87
    | 1 | 2 | 3 | 4 | 5 | 6 | 7 | 8 | 9 | 10 | 11 | 12
```

FORMATTING

G. BASIC PARTS OF A REPORT

G. Because word processing software has a variety of defaults for fonts, the number of returns will be used to express vertical spacing in all documents rather than inches.

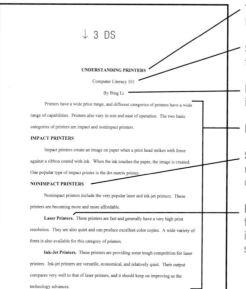

TITLE. Subject of the report; centered; typed in bold and all caps.

SUBTITLE. Secondary or explanatory title; centered; typed in initial caps.

BYLINE. Name of the writer; centered; typed in initial caps.

BODY. Text of the report; double spaced.

SIDE HEADING. Major subdivision of the report; typed at the left margin in bold and all caps.

PARAGRAPH HEADING. Minor subdivision of the report; indented 0.5 inch; typed in bold and initial caps; followed by a bold period and 2 spaces.

H. SIMPLE REPORTS

Spacing: Double-space the entire report. Change to double spacing at the beginning of the report.

Top Margin: After setting double spacing, press Enter 3 times for a top margin of approximately 2 inches.

Side Margins: Default.

Bottom Margin: Default.

Tab: Default.

I. WORD PROCESSING: LINE SPACING AND ALIGNMENT/JUSTIFICATION

Study Lesson 24 in your word processing manual. Complete all of the shaded steps while at your computer. Then format the jobs that follow.

DOCUMENT PROCESSING

Report 1

Spacing: Double

1. Set the line spacing to double, press Enter 3 times, and change to center alignment/justification.
2. Turn on bold, type the title, and immediately turn off bold.
3. Type the subtitle; then press Enter. Type the byline; then press Enter.
4. Change to left alignment/justification before pressing Tab to indent the first line of the first paragraph.
5. Let the paragraphs word wrap; that is, press Enter only at the end of each paragraph. Your lines may end differently from those shown here.
6. Spell-check, proofread, and preview your document before printing it.

↓ 3 DS

WRITING STYLE

Business Communications 101

By Amy Ho

Today's word processing software makes a variety of powerful and helpful writing tools available to you with the click of a button. You can discover interesting facts about your own style of writing by using these tools.

Many different statistics are automatically gathered as you are typing a document. For example, you can find out how many sentences are in your document and how many words or characters you have used. This information is used to determine details about your writing such as average word length, average number of words in each sentence, and maximum words per sentence.

Average word length and average sentence length determine whether it is easy or difficult for the average person to understand what you have written. Shorter words and sentences usually make writing easier to understand. Word

(continued on next page)

processing software can also analyze the formality of your writing style and suggest ways to make your writing either more formal or perhaps less formal.

If you take advantage of all the tools available in your word processing software, your writing will improve with each document you compose. Think carefully about your reader before you choose a writing style.

Report 2

Spacing: Double

Press Tab to indent paragraphs a full 0.5 inch.

OFFICE TEMP SERVICES
Business Trends Conference

Because of the rising costs of health insurance and other company-paid benefit packages, many businesses are looking to office temp services to help ease the high cost of doing business these days. A company does not have to make a long-term commitment to its temporary workers in terms of salary, benefits, or job stability.

Temp services offer many advantages to prospective employers. Sometimes temp services are available around the clock so that rush jobs can be completed on time. Often a company's reputation depends on its ability to meet deadlines and inspire confidence. Using a temp service can provide the competitive edge necessary for success.

Many temp agencies offer the services of bilingual employees. In major cities like Los Angeles, San Francisco, New York, and Miami, a bilingual employee is a necessity, not a luxury. Also, many foreign companies are based in the United States and have a growing need for bilingual employees in a variety of languages.

Sometimes a client has a need for some specialized service, software, or equipment that will be used immediately or perhaps only once. In this instance, a temporary service is certainly the answer. Because temp services are becoming indispensable for some businesses, many agencies are even sending supervisors to the job site to check on their employees. Clearly, temp services are "here to stay."

Lesson 25   Reports With Side Headings

GOALS: To improve speed and accuracy; to refine language-arts skills in composing; to format reports with side headings.

A. Type 2 times.

A. WARMUP

```
1        Exactly 610 employees have quit smoking!  About 2/3      11
2   of them just quit recently.  They realized why they can't     22
3   continue to smoke inside the buildings and decided to stop.    34
    | 1 | 2 | 3 | 4 | 5 | 6 | 7 | 8 | 9 | 10 | 11 | 12
```

SKILLBUILDING

B. Take three 12-second timings on each line. The scale below the last line shows your wam speed for a 12-second timing.

B. 12-SECOND SPEED SPRINTS

```
4   Today we want to find out if our work will be done on time.
5   Doug will be able to drive to the store if the car is here.
6   Jan will sign this paper when she has done all of the work.
7   This time she will be sure to spend two days with her sons.

| | | 5 | | | 10 | | | 15 | | | 20 | | | 25 | | | 30 | | | 35 | | | 40 | | | 45 | | | 50 | | | 55 | | | 60
```

C. Type the paragraph 2 times. Change every masculine pronoun to a feminine pronoun. Change every feminine pronoun to a masculine pronoun.

C. TECHNIQUE PRACTICE: CONCENTRATION

```
8        She will finish composing the report as soon as he has
9   given her all the research.  Her final draft will be turned
10  in to her boss; he will submit it to the company president.
```

LANGUAGE ARTS

D. COMPOSING

Composing at the keyboard can save you considerable time when you create first drafts of documents. Keep the following points in mind:

1. Type at a comfortable pace as your thoughts come to you. Do not stop to correct errors.

2. Keep your eyes on the screen as you type.

3. Do not be overly concerned with correct grammar. It is more important that you get your thoughts recorded. Any errors you make can be corrected later.

D. Answer each question with a single word.

```
11   What is your most interesting class?
12   How many miles do you travel to school?
13   Do you have a job?
14   What is your favorite color?
15   In what month were you born?
16   What type of job would you like to have?
17   Do you want to learn more about computers?
18   What day do you set aside for relaxation?
19   How many classes are you taking?
```

FORMATTING

E. REPORTS WITH SIDE HEADINGS

Spacing: Double-space the entire report, including before and after side headings.

Side Headings: Type in bold at the left margin.

Top Margin: After setting double spacing, press Enter 3 times for a top margin of approximately 2 inches.

F. WORD PROCESSING: HELP

Study Lesson 25 in your word processing manual. Complete all of the shaded steps while at your computer. Then format the jobs that follow.

DOCUMENT PROCESSING

Report 3

Spacing: Double

↓ 3 DS

SELECTING A COMPUTER

By Ina Phillips

Before selecting a computer, first consider several factors carefully. Think about what type of work you will be doing, what software is appropriate for your application, and what kinds of budget restrictions you have. Once you have made some thoughtful decisions, you will be prepared to begin shopping.

WORD PROCESSING

The most common application for the personal computer is word processing. If your computer will be used mainly for word processing, you must decide which software would be best suited to the types of documents you produce most often.

SOFTWARE SELECTION

Some word processing software is better at producing graphics that might be used in complicated desktop publishing projects. Some software can create tables with great efficiency. Study your choices, and then make your final selection.

BUDGET RESTRICTIONS

Don't make the mistake of buying the least expensive computer system available. Your primary consideration should always be to buy a system that will run your software. Remember that today's purchase could be tomorrow's mistake. Select a system that can be upgraded as technology changes.

UNDERSTANDING PRINTERS

Computer Literacy 101

By John Sanchez

Printers have a wide range of capabilities. Some print in color and others only in black and white. Some print only one or two pages a minute, while others can print several pages a minute. Their prices will vary with the number of features they offer. The two basic categories of printers are impact and nonimpact.

IMPACT PRINTERS

Impact printers create an image on paper when a print head strikes with force against a ribbon coated with ink. When the ink touches the paper, an image is created. Because the image is created by impact, these printers can be quite noisy.

Dot matrix printers are very popular impact printers for many reasons. They are fairly inexpensive and relatively durable. They can use continuous paper so that paper handling is greatly reduced. However, their output is not letter quality.

NONIMPACT PRINTERS

Nonimpact printers include the very popular laser and ink-jet printers. They are becoming more affordable and can produce a very high-quality output similar to a photocopy. These printers also produce excellent color and can use a wide variety of fonts. Ultimately, the ideal choice for a printer depends on the needs of the user.

Lesson 26 Business Letters

GOALS: To type 30 wam/3′/5e; to format a business letter in block style.

A. Type 2 times.

A. WARMUP

```
1      Mr. G. Yoneji ordered scanners* (*800 dots per inch)    11
2  in vibrant 24-bit color!  He quickly realized that exactly  23
3  31% of the work could be scanned in order to save money.    34
   | 1 | 2 | 3 | 4 | 5 | 6 | 7 | 8 | 9 | 10 | 11 | 12
```

SKILLBUILDING

B. DIAGNOSTIC PRACTICE: ALPHABET

Turn to the Diagnostic Practice: Alphabet routine beginning on page SB-2. Type one of the Pretest/Posttest paragraphs and identify any errors made. Then type the corresponding drill lines 2 times for each letter on which you made 2 or more errors and 1 time for each letter on which you made only 1 error. Finally, repeat the same Pretest paragraph and compare your performance.

C. Take three 12-second timings on each line. The scale below the last line shows your wam speed for a 12-second timing.

C. 12-SECOND SPEED SPRINTS

```
4  She went to the same store to find some good books to read.
5  Frank will coach eight games for his team when he has time.
6  Laura sent all the mail out today when she left to go home.
7  These pages can be very hard to read when the light is dim.
   | | | |5| | | |10| | |15| | |20| | |25| | |30| | |35| | |40| | |45| | |50| | |55| | |60
```

D. Take two 3-minute timings. Determine your speed and errors.

Goal: 30 wam/3′/5e

D. 3-MINUTE TIMING

```
8       Holding a good business meeting may require a great    11
9   deal of planning and preparing.  The meeting must be well   22
10  organized and an agenda must be prepared.  It may be hard    34
11  to judge how long a meeting may take or how many people      45
12  will discuss issues raised.                                  51
13       A good moderator is needed to execute the agenda.  He   62
14  or she must know when to move on to the next topic and when  74
15  a point needs more debate.  After a productive meeting,      85
16  you should feel very good.                                   90
    | 1 | 2 | 3 | 4 | 5 | 6 | 7 | 8 | 9 | 10 | 11 | 12
```

E. BASIC PARTS OF A BUSINESS LETTER

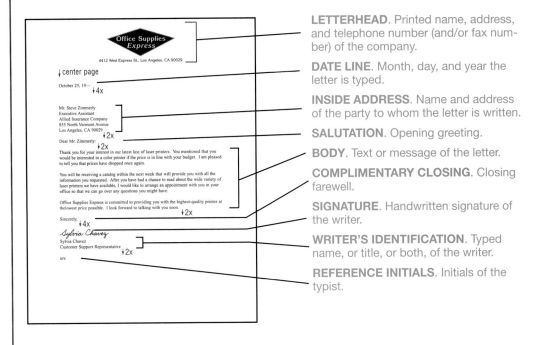

LETTERHEAD. Printed name, address, and telephone number (and/or fax number) of the company.

DATE LINE. Month, day, and year the letter is typed.

INSIDE ADDRESS. Name and address of the party to whom the letter is written.

SALUTATION. Opening greeting.

BODY. Text or message of the letter.

COMPLIMENTARY CLOSING. Closing farewell.

SIGNATURE. Handwritten signature of the writer.

WRITER'S IDENTIFICATION. Typed name, or title, or both, of the writer.

REFERENCE INITIALS. Initials of the typist.

F. BUSINESS LETTERS IN BLOCK STYLE

1. Type all lines beginning at the left margin.
2. Center the letter vertically, and then type the date.
3. After the date, press Enter 4 times and type the inside address. Leave 1 space between the state and the ZIP Code.
4. After the inside address, press Enter twice and type the salutation. Press Enter twice after the salutation.
5. Single-space the body of the letter, but press Enter twice between paragraphs.

Do not indent paragraphs.

6. Press Enter twice after the last paragraph and type the complimentary closing.
7. Press Enter 4 times after the complimentary closing and type the writer's identification.
8. Press Enter twice after the writer's identification and type your reference initials in lowercase letters with no periods or spaces.

G. WORD PROCESSING: CENTER PAGE

Study Lesson 26 in your word processing manual. Complete all of the shaded steps while at your computer. Then format the jobs that follow.

Letter 1
Block Style

1. Use standard punctuation: a colon after the salutation and a comma after the complimentary closing.
2. Use word wrap for the paragraphs. Press Enter only at the end of each paragraph. Your lines may end differently from those shown on page 52.

3. Type your initials (not *urs*) for the reference initials.
4. Always spell-check, preview, and proofread your letter when you finish for typing, spelling, and formatting errors.

(continued on next page)

↓center page
October 25, 19--
↓4X

Mr. Steve Zimmerly
Executive Assistant
Allied Insurance Company
855 North Vermont Avenue
Los Angeles, CA 90029
↓2X

Dear Mr. Zimmerly:
↓2X

Thank you for your interest in our latest line of laser printers. You mentioned that you would be interested in a color printer if the price is in line with your budget. I am pleased to tell you that prices have dropped once again.
↓2X

You will be receiving a catalog within the next week that will provide you with all the information you requested. After you have had a chance to read about the wide variety of laser printers we have available, I would like to arrange an appointment with you in your office so that we can go over any questions you might have.
↓2X

Office Supplies Express is committed to providing you with the highest-quality printer at the lowest price possible. I look forward to talking with you soon.
↓2X

Sincerely,
↓4X

Sylvia Chavez
Customer Support Representative
↓2X

urs

Letter 2
Block Style

Open the file for Letter 1 and make the following changes:

1. Change the date to October 23.

2. Change the writer's identification to:
   Agnes Gunderson Customer Service

Letter 3
Block Style

1. Be sure to center the letter vertically.
2. The slash marks in the inside address and closing lines indicate line endings. Do not type the slashes.
3. The ¶ symbol indicates the start of a new paragraph. Do *not* indent paragraphs in a block-style letter. Leave 1 blank line between paragraphs.
4. Spell-check, proofread, and preview your letter when you finish.

November 1, 19— / Ms. Sylvia Chavez / Office Supplies Express / 24133 West Del Monte / Valencia, CA 91355 / Dear Ms. Chavez:
¶Thank you for all the information you sent me on laser printers. I truly appreciate the promptness and courtesy your company has shown, and I feel confident that we will be able to order some printers very soon.

(continued on next page)

¶I am also interested in finding out if your company offers any leasing programs. Our business is interested in a state-of-the-art color copier, and we realize that the price would be prohibitive unless we lease it. Features like duplexing, collating, and size reduction and enlargement are essential.

¶Please call me in a week or so for another appointment. In the meantime, I would appreciate any information you could send regarding color copiers. Sincerely, / Steve Zimmerly / Executive Assistant / {urs}

Remember to type your initials in place of {urs}.

Lesson 27   Business Letters

GOALS: To improve speed and accuracy; to refine language-arts skills in capitalization; to format a business letter with an enclosure notation.

A. Type 2 times.

A. WARMUP

```
 1        In 7/95 the office will convert to a new phone system.      11
 2    A freeze on all toll calls is requested for July.  Account      23
 3    #GK23 has a balance of $68 and isn't expected to "pay up."      35
      |  1  |  2  |  3  |  4  |  5  |  6  |  7  |  8  |  9  |  10  |  11  |  12
```

SKILLBUILDING

Pretest
Take a 1-minute timing. Determine your speed and errors.

B. PRETEST: CLOSE REACHES

```
 4        The growth in the volume of company assets is due to       11
 5    the astute group of twenty older employees.  Their answers     23
 6    were undoubtedly the reason for the increase in net worth.     34
      |  1  |  2  |  3  |  4  |  5  |  6  |  7  |  8  |  9  |  10  |  11  |  12
```

Practice
Speed Emphasis: If you made 2 or fewer errors on the Pretest, type each *individual* line 2 times.
Accuracy Emphasis: If you made 3 or more errors, type each *group* of lines (as though it were a paragraph) 2 times.

C. PRACTICE: ADJACENT KEYS

```
 7   as ashes cases class asset astute passes chased creased ask
 8   we weave tweed towed weigh wealth twenty fewest answers wet
 9   rt worth alert party smart artist sorted charts turtles art
```

D. PRACTICE: CONSECUTIVE FINGERS

```
10   un undue bunch stung begun united punish outrun untie funny
11   gr grand agree angry grade growth egress hungry group graph
12   ol older solid tools spool volume evolve uphold olive scold
```

Posttest
Repeat the Pretest timing and compare performance.

E. POSTTEST: CLOSE REACHES

F. PACED PRACTICE

Turn to the Paced Practice routine beginning on page SB-14. Take three 2-minute timings, starting at the point where you left off the last time.

LANGUAGE ARTS

G. Study the rules at the right.

≡ sent

≡ prop

≡ time

Edit the paragraph to insert any needed capitalization.

G. CAPITALIZATION

Rule: Capitalize the first word in a sentence.

The exam is scheduled for the last week of the semester.

Rule: Capitalize proper nouns and adjectives derived from proper nouns. (A proper noun is the official name of a particular person, place, or thing.)

The American flag can be seen flying over the White House in Washington.
But: Our country's flag can be seen flying over the government buildings.

Rule: Capitalize the names of the days of the week, months, holidays, and religious days (but do not capitalize the names of the seasons).

Every summer on July 4 we celebrate Independence Day.

```
13      she will graduate in the spring from los angeles city
14   college.  the community college system in the united states
15   provides a quality education for both american and foreign
16   students.  both english and spanish are spoken in several
17   classes, like english 127 and mathematics 105.  on monday,
18   may 30, all classes will be canceled in order to observe
19   memorial day, a national holiday.  on thanksgiving and on
20   christmas, all government offices will be closed to the
21   public.  offices will reopen the following tuesday.
```

FORMATTING

H. ENCLOSURE NOTATION

1. To indicate that an item is enclosed with a letter, type the word *Enclosure* on the line below the reference initials.

Example: urs
               Enclosure
2. If more than one item is being enclosed, type the word *Enclosures.*

I. WORD PROCESSING: DATE INSERT

Study Lesson 27 in your word processing manual. Complete all of the shaded steps while at your computer. Then format the jobs that follow.

DOCUMENT PROCESSING

Letter 4

Block Style

≡ sent

Do not type the slashes and do not indent the paragraphs. Whenever you see {Current Date}, type today's date.

≡ time

≡ sent

{Current Date} / Ms. Denise Bradford / Worldwide Travel, Inc. / 1180 Alvarado, SE / Albuquerque, NM 87108 / Dear Ms. Bradford:
¶Our company has decided to hold its regional sales meeting in Scottsdale, Arizona, during the second week of January. I need information on a suitable conference site.
¶We will need a meeting room with 30 computer workstations, an overhead projector and LCD display, and a microphone and podium. We will also need a fax machine or a computer with a fax modem and on-site secretarial

(continued on next page)

54   UNIT SIX Lesson 27

services. I have enclosed a list of conference attendees and their room preferences.

¶A final decision on the conference site must be made within the next two weeks. Please send me any information you have available for a suitable location in Scottsdale immediately. Thank you for your help.

Sincerely yours, / Bill McKay / Marketing Manager / {urs} / Enclosure

Spell-check, proofread, and preview your document. Be sure you vertically centered the letter.

≡ prop

Letter 5

Block Style

Do not indent paragraphs in a block-style letter.

≡ prop

≡ time

≡ sent

{Current Date} / Mr. Bill McKay / Marketing Manager / Viatech Communications / 9835 Osuna Road, NE / Albuquerque, NM 87111 / Dear Mr. McKay:

Thank you for your inquiry regarding a conference site in Scottsdale, Arizona, for 35 people during the second week of January.

I have enclosed several brochures with detailed information on some properties in Scottsdale that provide exclusive service to businesses like yours. All these properties have meeting rooms that will accommodate your needs and also offer additional services you might be interested in using.

Please call me when you have reached a decision. I will be happy to make the final arrangements as well as issue any airline tickets you may be needing.

Yours truly, / Ms. Denise Bradford / Travel Agent / {urs} / Enclosures

Lesson 28   Envelopes

GOALS: To type 31 wam/3'/5e; to format envelopes.

A. Type 2 times.

A. WARMUP

```
1      At 8:30, Horowitz & Co. will fax Order #V546 to us for    11
2   immediate processing!  Just how many additional orders they   23
3   will request isn't known.  About 7% of the orders are here.   35
      |  1  |  2  |  3  |  4  |  5  |  6  |  7  |  8  |  9  |  10  |  11  |  12
```

B. SUSTAINED PRACTICE: PUNCTUATION

4   Anyone who is successful in business realizes that the   11
5   needs of the customer must always come first. A satisfied   23
6   consumer is one who will come back to buy again and again.   35

7   Consumers must learn to lodge a complaint in a manner   11
8   that is fair, effective, and efficient. Don't waste time   23
9   talking to the wrong person. Go to the person in charge.   34

10   State your case clearly; be prepared with facts and   11
11   figures to back up your claim--warranties, receipts, bills,   23
12   and checks are all very effective. Don't feel intimidated.   34

13   If the company agrees to work with you, you're on the   11
14   right track. Be specific: "I'll expect a check Tuesday,"   23
15   or "I'll expect a replacement in the mail by Saturday."   34

| 1 | 2 | 3 | 4 | 5 | 6 | 7 | 8 | 9 | 10 | 11 | 12

C. PROGRESSIVE PRACTICE: ALPHABET

Turn to the Progressive Practice: Alphabet routine beginning on page SB-7.

Take six 30-second timings, starting at the point where you left off the last time.

D. 3-MINUTE TIMING

16   Credit cards can make shopping very convenient, and   11
17   they frequently help you record and track your spending.   22
18   However, many card companies impose high fees for using   33
19   their credit cards.   37
20   You must realize that it may be better to pay in cash   48
21   and not use a credit card. Examine all your options. Some   60
22   card companies do not charge yearly fees. Some may offer   71
23   free extended warranties on goods you buy with their credit   83
24   cards. Judge all details; you may be surprised.   93

| 1 | 2 | 3 | 4 | 5 | 6 | 7 | 8 | 9 | 10 | 11 | 12

FORMATTING

E. ENVELOPES

A No. 10 envelope (the standard size for business letters) is 9½ by 4⅛ inches. A correctly addressed envelope should include the following:

1. **Return Address.** The sender's name and address typed or printed in the upper left corner with a minimum space of 0.25 inch from the top and side of the envelope.

2. **Mailing Address.** The receiver's name and address typed at least 2 inches from the top and 4 inches from the left edge of the envelope. The mailing address may also be typed in all caps and no punctuation for postal sorting purposes.

Trend Electronics
2206 31st Street
Minneapolis, MN 55407-1911

Mr. Charles R. Harrison
Reliable Software, Inc.
5613 Brunswick Avenue
Minneapolis, MN 55406

Standard large envelope, No. 10, is 9½ × 4⅛ inches.

F. FOLDING LETTERS

To fold a letter for a No. 10 envelope:

1. Place the letter face up, and fold the bottom third of the page up toward the top of the page.
2. Fold the top third of the page down to approximately 0.5 inch from the bottom edge of the page.
3. Insert the last crease into the envelope first with the flap facing up.

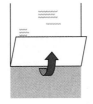 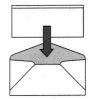

G. WORD PROCESSING: ENVELOPES

Study Lesson 28 in your word processing manual. Complete all of the shaded steps while at your computer. Then format the jobs that follow.

Envelope 1

Do not print any of these documents unless you are sure that your printer is properly set up to print envelopes.

1. Create an envelope with the following mailing address: *Mr. Charles Goldstein / Software Solutions, Inc. / 2981 Canwood Street / Roselle, IL 60172.*

2. Insert the following return address: *Shannon Stone / Data Systems, Inc. / 2201 South Street / Racine, WI 53404.*
3. Append/add the envelope to a blank document.

Envelope 2

1. Open the file for Letter 1 and create an envelope for the letter.

2. Do not insert a return address.
3. Append/add the envelope to the letter.

Envelope 3

1. Open the file for Letter 2 and create an envelope for the letter.
2. Type the following return address: *Agnes Gunderson / Office Supplies*

Express / 24133 West Del Monte / Valencia, CA 91355.

3. Append/add the envelope to the document.

Letter 6

Block Style With Envelope

1. Type the following business letter, and then create an envelope for the letter.
2. Do not insert a return address.

3. Append/add the envelope to the document.

{Current Date} / Ms. Dorothy Turner / Global Moving and Storage / 6830 Via Del Monte / San Jose, CA 95119 / Dear Ms. Turner:

Thank you for registering your PC Fax software so promptly. As a registered user, you are entitled to free technical support 24 hours a day. The enclosed brochure will explain in detail how you can reach us either by fax or by phone whenever you need help.

All our PC Fax users will receive our monthly newsletter, which is filled with tips on using your new software and other material we know you will be interested in receiving. You can now use your fax modem to access a wealth of information on a wide variety of topics.

Please call me if you have any questions or would like to receive any additional information. Your satisfaction is our number one priority.

Sincerely, / Nicholas Moore / Sales Representative / {urs} / Enclosure

---

Lesson 29   Memos

GOALS: To improve speed and accuracy; to refine language-arts skills in spelling; to format interoffice memos.

A. Type 2 times.

A. WARMUP

```
1      Will the package arrive at 11:29 or 3:45?  The exact      11
2   answer to this question could mean the difference between    22
3   losing or saving their account; Joyce also realizes this.    34
```

```
 | 1 | 2 | 3 | 4 | 5 | 6 | 7 | 8 | 9 | 10 | 11 | 12
```

B. 12-SECOND SPEED SPRINTS

4 Mary will not be able to meet them at the game later today.
5 The class is not going to be able to meet if they are gone.
6 They could not open that old door when the chair fell over.
7 This very nice piece of paper may be used to print the job.

| | | | 5 | | | |10| | | |15| | | |20| | | |25| | | |30| | | |35| | | |40| | | |45| | | |50| | | |55| | | |60

C. DIAGNOSTIC PRACTICE: NUMBERS

Turn to the Diagnostic Practice: Numbers routine beginning on page SB-5. Type one of the Pretest/Posttest paragraphs and identify any errors made. Then type the corresponding drill lines 2 times for each number on which you made 2 or more errors and 1 time for each number on which you made only 1 error. Finally, repeat the same Pretest paragraph and compare your performance.

D. PROGRESSIVE PRACTICE: ALPHABET

Turn to the Progressive Practice: Alphabet routine beginning on page SB-7. Take six 30-second timings, starting at the point where you left off the last time.

LANGUAGE ARTS

E. SPELLING

8 personnel information its procedures their committee system
9 receive employees which education services opportunity area
10 financial appropriate interest received production contract
11 important through necessary customer employee further there
12 property account approximately general control division our

13 All company personel will recieve important information.
14 Are division has some control over there financial account.
15 There comitte has received approximately three contracts.
16 The employe and the customer have an oportunity to attend.
17 There was no farther interest in the property or it's owner.
18 When it was necessary, apropriate procedurs were followed.

FORMATTING

F. INTEROFFICE MEMOS

An interoffice memo is usually sent from one person to another in the same organization. Follow these steps to format a memo on plain paper or on letterhead stationery:

1. Press Enter 6 times for a top margin of approximately 2 inches.

2. Type the headings (including the colons) in all caps and bold: ***MEMO TO:***, ***FROM:***, ***DATE:***, and ***SUBJECT:***.

3. Tab once after typing the colon to reach the point where the heading entries begin.

(continued on next page)

4. Leave 1 blank line between the heading lines and between the heading lines and the body of the memo.
5. Leave 1 blank line between paragraphs. Most memos are typed with blocked paragraphs (no indentions).
6. Leave 1 blank line between the body and the reference initials.

DOCUMENT PROCESSING

Memo 1

Spell-check, proofread, and preview your memo for errors.

Words underlined in green are spelling words from the language arts activities.

↓6X
MEMO TO: All Salaried Employees ↓2X

FROM: Linda Vigil, Human Resources ↓2X

DATE: November 2, 19-- ↓2X

SUBJECT: Health Care Benefit Plan ↓2X

Effective January 1, Allied Aerospace Industries will contract with MedNet to begin a new health benefits program for all eligible salaried personnel. A brochure outlining important program information will be mailed to you soon. ↓2X

An open enrollment period will be in effect during the entire month of January. If you and your family are interested in one of the MedNet health plan options, you may transfer yourself and your dependents into any appropriate plan. All applications must be received no later than midnight, January 31. ↓2X

If you have any questions or need any help understanding your options, please call me at Ext. 213. I will be happy to help you select the plan that is best for you. ↓2X

{urs}

Memo 2

MEMO TO: Linda Vigil, Human Resources / **FROM:** Dan Lopez / **DATE:** November 23, 19— / **SUBJECT:** MedNet Benefit Plan

¶Thank you for the brochure detailing the various options for employees under the MedNet plan. I would like clarification on some of the services included in the plan.

¶Because both my wife and I are employees of Allied Aerospace Industries, do we have the choice of enrolling separately under different options? In our present plan, I know that this is possible.

¶We have two dependents. Is it possible to enroll both dependents under different options of the plan, or do they both fall under either one option or the other? I know that in the past you have asked for evidence of dependent status and dates of birth.

¶If you need any further information, please let me know. Thank you very much for your help.

{urs}

Lesson 30 | Memos

GOALS: To type 32 wam/3′/5e; to format memos with italics, underline, and attachment notations.

A. Type 2 times.

A. WARMUP

```
1        Did Zagorski & Sons charge $876 for the renovation?      11
2   The invoice isn't quite right; the exact amount charged in    23
3   July is smeared.  Pam will try her best to get the figures.   34
    |  1  |  2  |  3  |  4  |  5  |  6  |  7  |  8  |  9  | 10 | 11 | 12
```

SKILLBUILDING

B. PROGRESSIVE PRACTICE: NUMBERS

Turn to the Progressive Practice: Numbers routine beginning on page SB-11.

Take six 30-second timings, starting at the point where you left off the last time.

C. Type the paragraph 2 times. Use the caps lock key to type a word or series of words in all caps. Reach to the caps lock with the A finger.

C. TECHNIQUE PRACTICE: SHIFT KEY AND CAPS LOCK

```
4        The new computer has CD-ROM, PCI IDE HDD controller,
5   and an SVGA card.  Mr. J. L. Jones will order one from PC
6   EXPRESS out of Orem, Utah.  IT ARRIVES NO LATER THAN JULY.
```

D. Take two 3-minute timings. Determine your speed and errors.

Goal: 32 wam/3′/5e

D. 3-MINUTE TIMING

```
7        If you want to work in information processing, you       10
8   must realize that there are steps that you must take to       22
9   plan for such an exciting career.  First, you must decide     33
10  whether or not you have the right personality traits.         44
11       Then you must be trained in the technical skills you     55
12  will need in such an important field.  The technology is      66
13  changing each day.  You must stay focused on keeping up       77
14  with these changes.  Also, you must never quit learning new   89
15  tasks each day you are on the job.                            96
    |  1  |  2  |  3  |  4  |  5  |  6  |  7  |  8  |  9  | 10 | 11 | 12
```

FORMATTING

E. ATTACHMENT NOTATION

Attachment (rather than *Enclosure*) is typed below the reference initials when material is physically attached (stapled or clipped) to a memo.

Example:

```
urs
Attachment
```

F. WORD PROCESSING: ITALICS AND UNDERLINE

Study Lesson 30 in your word processing manual. Complete all of the shaded steps while at your computer. Then format the jobs that follow.

DOCUMENT PROCESSING

Memo 3

Remember to type an attachment notation rather than an enclosure notation.

Spell-check, proofread, and preview your memo for errors.

MEMO TO: All Executive Assistants / **FROM:** Barbara Azar, Staff Development Coordinator / **DATE:** {Current Date} / **SUBJECT:** Standardizing Document Formats

¶Last month we received our final shipment of new laser printers. The installation of these printers in your offices marked the final phaseout of all dot matrix printers.

¶Because all of us can now use italicized fonts in our correspondence, please note the following change: from now on <u>all book and journal titles should be italicized rather than underlined</u> as was done in the past. This new procedure will help us to standardize our documents.

¶The latest edition of *Quick Reference for the Automated Office* has two pages of helpful information on laser printers, which I have attached. Please read them carefully, and we will discuss them at our next meeting.

{urs} / Attachment

Memo 4

MEMO TO: Barbara Azar, Staff Development Coordinator / **FROM:** Sharon Hearshen, Executive Assistant / **DATE:** {Current Date} / **SUBJECT:** Laser Printer Workshop

¶The new laser printers we received are <u>fabulous</u>! I know that you worked very hard to get these printers for us, and all of us in the Sales and Marketing Department certainly appreciate your effort.

¶Several of us would be very interested in seeing the printers demonstrated. Would it be possible to have a workshop with some hands-on training? We are particularly interested in learning about font selection, paper selection, and envelopes and labels.

¶I have attached an article on laser printers from the latest issue of *Office Technology.* It is very informative, and you might like to include it as a part of the workshop. Please let me know if I can help you in any way.

{urs} / Attachment

Letter 7

Progress Check
Block Style

1. Type the following business letter, and then create an envelope for the document.
2. Do not include a return address.
3. Do not append the envelope to the letter.

October 1, 19— / Mrs. Ruzanna Avetisyan / 844 Lincoln Boulevard / Santa Monica, CA 90403 / Dear Mrs. Avetisyan:

¶The League of Women Voters is looking for volunteers to work at the various polling places during the upcoming elections.

¶If you think you will be able to volunteer your time, please fill out and mail the enclosed card. After I receive your card, I will contact you to confirm a location, time, and date.

¶Your efforts are greatly appreciated, Mrs. Avetisyan. Concerned citizens like you make it possible for the public to have a convenient place to vote. Thank you for your interest in this very worthy cause! / Sincerely yours, / Stephanie Holt / Public Relations Volunteer / {urs} / Enclosure

Lesson 31 | Simple Tables

GOALS: To improve speed and accuracy; to refine language-arts skills in proofreading; to format simple tables.

A. Type 2 times.

A. WARMUP

```
1      You can save $1,698 when you buy the 20-part video      10
2  series!  Just ask for Series #MX5265 in the next 7 days;    22
3  ordering early qualifies you for a sizable discount of 5%.  34
   |  1  |  2  |  3  |  4  |  5  |  6  |  7  |  8  |  9  |  10  |  11  |  12
```

SKILLBUILDING

Pretest
Take a 1-minute timing. Determine your speed and errors.

B. PRETEST: DISCRIMINATION PRACTICE

```
4      Steven saw the younger, unruly boy take flight as he    11
5  threw the coin at the jury.  The brave judge stopped the    22
6  fight.  He called out to the youth, who recoiled in fear.   34
   |  1  |  2  |  3  |  4  |  5  |  6  |  7  |  8  |  9  |  10  |  11  |  12
```

Practice
 Speed Emphasis: If you made 2 or fewer errors on the Pretest, type each *individual* line 2 times.
 Accuracy Emphasis: If you made 3 or more errors, type each *group* of lines (as though it were a paragraph) 2 times.

C. PRACTICE: LEFT HAND

```
7  vbv verb bevy vibes bevel brave above verbal bovine behaves
8  wew west weep threw wedge weave fewer weight sewing dewdrop
9  fgf gulf gift fight fudge fugue flags flight golfer feigned
```

D. PRACTICE: RIGHT HAND

```
10  uyu buys your usury unity youth buoys unruly untidy younger
11  oio coin lion oiled foils foist prior recoil iodine rejoice
12  jhj jury huge enjoy three judge habit adjust slight jasmine
```

Posttest
Repeat the Pretest timing and compare performance.

E. POSTTEST: DISCRIMINATION PRACTICE

F. Take three 12-second timings on each line. The scale below the last line shows your wam speed for a 12-second timing.

F. 12-SECOND SPEED SPRINTS

```
13  The book that is on top of the big desk will be given away.
14  Bill must pay for the tape or he will have to give it back.
15  They left the meeting after all of the group had gone away.
16  The third person to finish all of the work today may leave.
    | | |5| | |10| | |15| | |20| | |25| | |30| | |35| | |40| | |45| | |50| | |55| | |60
```

G. Edit this paragraph to correct any typing or formatting errors.

G. PROOFREADING

17   It doesnt matter how fast you can type or how well
18 you now a software program if you produce documents taht
19 are filled with errors. You must learn to watch for errors
20 in spelling punctuation, and formatting. Look carefully
21 between words and sentences. Make sure that after a period
22 at the end of a sentence, you see two spaces. Sometime it
23 helps to look at the characters in the sentence justabove
24 the one you are proofreading to ensure accuracy.

FORMATTING

H. BASIC PARTS OF A TABLE

1. Tables consist of vertical columns and horizontal rows. A cell, or "box," is created where a column and a row intersect.

2. Tables formatted with horizontal and vertical lines (as shown in the illustration) are called boxed tables. Those formatted with no lines are called open tables.

3. If a table appears alone on the page, it should be centered vertically.

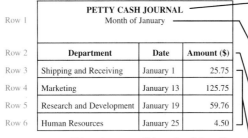

TITLE. Center and type in all caps and bold. If there is no subtitle, insert 1 blank line after the title.

SUBTITLE. Center on the line below the title, and type in initial caps. Insert 1 blank line after the subtitle.

COLUMN HEADINGS. Column headings may be centered or aligned at the left or right, depending on the table. Type column headings in initial caps and bold.

BODY. Left-justify (left-align) text columns; right-justify (right-align) number columns.

	PETTY CASH JOURNAL		
Row 1	Month of January		
Row 2	**Department**	**Date**	**Amount ($)**
Row 3	Shipping and Receiving	January 1	25.75
Row 4	Marketing	January 13	125.75
Row 5	Research and Development	January 19	59.76
Row 6	Human Resources	January 25	4.50
	Column A	Column B	Column C

I. WORD PROCESSING: TABLE—CREATE AND LINES

Study Lesson 31 in your word processing manual. Complete all of the shaded steps while at your computer. Then format the jobs that follow.

DOCUMENT PROCESSING

Table 1
2-Column Boxed Table

Simple tables such as this often do not have titles, subtitles, or column heads.

Follow these steps to format Table 1:

1. Center the table vertically on the page.
2. Create a 2-column, 4-row table.
3. Format this table as a boxed table (with lines).

Jose Robledo, President	Administration, Room 210
Carol Seinfeld, Vice President	Administration, Room 304
Martin Hashibe, Dean	Admissions and Records, Room 203
Karine Erkatyan, Associate Dean	Student Services, Room 101

Table 2
3-Column Open Table

The vertical space between table rows differs depending on the word processing software being used to create the table.

Follow these steps to format Table 2:

1. Center the table vertically.
2. Create a 3-column, 3-row table.
3. Format this table as an open table (without lines).

Linda Scher	Office Administration	Da Vinci Hall
Gary Finkle	Dental Technology	Franklin Hall
Gloria Hernandez	Political Science	Holmes Hall

Table 3
3-Column Boxed Table

Follow these steps to format Table 3:

1. Open the file for Table 2.
2. Reformat the table as a boxed table.

Table 4
3-Column Boxed Table

Follow these steps to format Table 4:

1. Center the table vertically.
2. Create a 3-column, 3-row table.
3. Format this table as a boxed table (with lines).

Thomas Freidman	Executive Editor	Los Angeles, California
Dawn Seidman	Associate Editor	St. Louis, Missouri
Martin Gonzalez	Art Director	Seattle, Washington

Lesson 32   Tables With Column Headings

GOALS: To type 33 wam/3'/5e; to format tables with column headings.

A. Type 2 times.

A. WARMUP

```
1      Sales by two travel agencies (Quill, Virgil, & Johnson     11
2  and Keef & Zane) exceeded all prior amounts.  Total sales       23
3  for that year were as follows:  $1,540,830 and $976,223.        34
   |  1  |  2  |  3  |  4  |  5  |  6  |  7  |  8  |  9  |  10  |  11  |  12
```

SKILLBUILDING

B. PROGRESSIVE PRACTICE: ALPHABET

Turn to the Progressive Practice: Alphabet routine beginning on page SB-7.

Take six 30-second timings, starting at the point where you left off the last time.

C. Take two 3-minute timings. Determine your speed and errors.

Goal: 33 wam/3'/5e

C. 3-MINUTE TIMING

4   To create documents that are easy to read, you may   10

5 want to include tables. Joining complex data in a table   22

6 makes the facts clear and quick to understand. Tables   33

7 include rows, columns, and cells.   40

8   Another way to make your reports easy to read is to   50

9 use color. Note how the quality of a document improves   61

10 when you add a zippy color to such features as headings.   73

11 As you try several new formats, you will find that your   84

12 writing comes alive. People who read your reports will   95

13 like your efforts.   99

| 1 | 2 | 3 | 4 | 5 | 6 | 7 | 8 | 9 | 10 | 11 | 12

FORMATTING

D. FORMATTING COLUMN HEADINGS

Column headings are used to describe the information contained in the columns. To format column headings:

1. Type the column headings in initial caps and bold.
2. Align column headings at the left over text columns, at the right over number columns, or centered over all columns.
3. When a column contains dollar amounts or percents, you may include the dollar sign or the percent sign as part of the column heading or add them to each of the column entries.

E. WORD PROCESSING: TABLE—JOIN CELLS

Study Lesson 32 in your word processing manual. Complete all of the shaded steps while at your computer. Then format the jobs that follow.

DOCUMENT PROCESSING

Table 5
2-Column Boxed Table With Centered Column Headings

Format Table 5 as follows:

1. Center the table vertically.
2. Create a table structure with 2 columns and 5 rows.
3. Center the column headings, and type them in bold with initial caps.
4. Type the column text aligned at the left.
5. Join the cells in Row 1; then center and type the title in bold and all caps.
6. Press Enter once to insert 1 blank line after the title.

WORLDWIDE LIFE INSURANCE COMPANY	
Investment Portfolio	**Degree of Risk**
Aggressive Stock Portfolio	Very high risk
Global Portfolio	Moderate to high risk
Common Stock Portfolio	Moderate risk

Table 6
3-Column Open Table With Left-Aligned Column Headings

Format Table 6 as follows:

1. Center the table vertically.
2. Create a table structure with 3 columns and 5 rows.
3. Type the column headings aligned at the left in bold with initial caps.
4. Type the column text aligned at the left.
5. Join the cells in Row 1; then center and type the title in bold and all caps.
6. Press Enter once to insert 1 blank line after the title.

SCHOLARSHIP RECIPIENTS

Student Name	College Department	Community College
Steven Fernandez	Office Administration	Los Angeles City College
Chin Lee	Information Management	College of the Canyons
Anthony West	Computer Science	Saddleback College

Table 7
3-Column Boxed Table With Left-Aligned Column Headings

HOMEOWNERS' INSURANCE RATINGS		
Company	**Overall Satisfaction**	**Speed of Payment**
Allied Insurance	Completely satisfied	Very fast
Coast Casualty	Somewhat satisfied	Moderate to fast
Citywide Insurance	Completely dissatisfied	Slow to moderate

Lesson 33   Tables With Number Columns

GOALS: To improve speed and accuracy; to refine language-arts skills in composing; to format tables with number columns.

A. Type 2 times.

A. WARMUP

```
1      Does Quentin know if 1/2 of the January order will be     11
2  ready?  At 5:30 about 46% of the orders still hadn't been     23
3  mailed!  Mr. Gray expects a very sizable loss this month.     34
      | 1  | 2  | 3  | 4  | 5  | 6  | 7  | 8  | 9  | 10 | 11 | 12
```

SKILLBUILDING

B. Take a 1-minute timing on the first paragraph to establish your base speed. Then take four 1-minute timings on the remaining paragraphs. As soon as you equal or exceed your base speed on one paragraph, advance to the next, more difficult paragraph.

B. SUSTAINED PRACTICE: ALTERNATE-HAND WORDS

4   When eight of them began a formal discussion on some   11
5   of the major issues, the need for a chair was very evident.   23
6   A chair would be sure to handle the usual work with ease.   34

7   The eight people in that group decided that the work   11
8   would get done only if they selected one person to be chair   23
9   of their group. They began to debate all the major issues.   35

10   One issue that needed to be settled right up front was   11
11   the question of how to handle proxy votes. It seemed for a   23
12   short time that a fight over this very issue would result.   35

13   The group worked diligently in attempting to solve the   11
14   issues that were being discussed. All of the concerns that   23
15   were brought to the group were reviewed in depth by them.   35

| 1 | 2 | 3 | 4 | 5 | 6 | 7 | 8 | 9 | 10 | 11 | 12

C. Type each sentence on a separate line. Type 2 times.

C. TECHNIQUE PRACTICE: ENTER KEY

16   Debit the account. Balance the checkbook. Add the assets.
17   Take the discount. Send the statement. Compute the ratio.
18   Review the account. Credit the amount. Figure the total.
19   Prepare the statement. Send the catalog. Call the client.

LANGUAGE ARTS

D. Answer each question with a single word.

D. COMPOSING

20   Have you ever learned a word processing program before?
21   Have you ever been on an interview?
22   Do you own a computer?
23   Do you have a CD-Rom drive?
24   How many blank lines do you leave after the title of a table?
25   Do you enjoy typing tables?
26   Do you know how to center a table vertically?
27   Have you ever had a job before?

FORMATTING

E. FORMATTING TABLES WITH NUMBER COLUMNS

1. Columns of numbers should be aligned or justified at the right.

2. The column heading over a column of numbers should be aligned or justified at the right also, except when all of the column headings are centered.

3. Because number columns are often much narrower than text columns, you may need to adjust the width of the number columns so that the table appears balanced.

4. Always adjust column widths *before* joining any cells to ensure that the column widths are adjusted correctly.

5. Adjusting the column widths will reposition the table horizontally on the page. You must issue a command to horizontally center the table.

F. WORD PROCESSING: TABLE—FORMAT AND RESIZE CELLS

Study Lesson 33 in your word processing manual. Complete all of the shaded steps while at your computer. Then format the jobs that follow.

Table 8
3-Column Boxed
Table With Number
Columns

1. Center the table vertically.
2. Create a table structure with 3 columns and 6 rows.
3. Center and type the column headings in initial caps and bold.
4. Type the column text left-aligned and right-align the number columns.
5. Automatically adjust the column widths for all columns.
6. Join the cells in Row 1.
7. Center and type the title in all caps and bold. Center and type the subtitle in initial caps.
8. Press Enter once to insert 1 blank line after the subtitle.
9. Center the table horizontally.

COLOR PRINTERS Inventory		
Type	**Total**	**Sold**
Laser	194	94
Ink-jet	117	37
Bubble-jet	9	2
Dot matrix	29	110

Table 9
3-Column Boxed
Table With Number
Columns

1. Center the table vertically.
2. Create a table structure with 3 columns and 6 rows.
3. Center and type the column headings in initial caps and bold.
4. Type the column text left-aligned and right-align the number columns.
5. Automatically adjust the column widths for all columns.
6. Join the cells in Row 1.
7. Center and type the title in all caps and bold. Center and type the subtitle in initial caps.
8. Press Enter once to insert 1 blank line after the subtitle.
9. Center the table horizontally.

PAYROLL SUMMARY Week Ending December 31, 19--		
Name	**Gross Pay ($)**	**Tax ($)**
Ferguson, Ruth	932	204
Chen, Robert	354	84
Prior, David	93	9
James, Michael	356	37

Table 10
3-Column Boxed
Table With Number
Columns

1. Open the file for Table 9.
2. Change the title to **EMPLOYEE EARNINGS**.

3. Delete the words *Week Ending* from the subtitle and change the first column heading to *Employee*.

Lesson 34 Tables With Totals

GOALS: To type 34 wam/3'/4e; to format tables with totals.

A. Type 2 times.

A. WARMUP

```
1       This series* (*6 films, 28 minutes) by J. Zeller goes      11
2  beyond the "basics" of computers.  Viewers keep requesting      23
3  an extension on the dates; this includes 3/2, 5/5, and 8/9.     35
   |  1  |  2  |  3  |  4  |  5  |  6  |  7  |  8  |  9  |  10  |  11  |  12
```

SKILLBUILDING

B. DIAGNOSTIC PRACTICE: ALPHABET

Turn to the Diagnostic Practice: Alphabet routine beginning on page SB-2. Type one of the Pretest/Posttest paragraphs and identify any errors made. Then type the corresponding drill lines 2 times for each letter on which you made 2 or more errors and 1 time for each letter on which you made only 1 error. Finally, repeat the same Pretest paragraph and compare your performance.

C. Take two 3-minute timings. Determine your speed and errors.

Goal: 34 wam/3'/4e

Note: The error limit has been lowered from 5 errors to 4 errors.

C. 3-MINUTE TIMING

```
4        Job security is an important factor for most students      11
5   who expect to have a bright future in the world of work.        23
6   Those who have computer training will have a much easier        34
7   time.  Jobs that require computer skills will pay more than     46
8   those that do not need these very critical skills.              56
9        If you can learn one or more word processing programs,     67
10  you are almost guaranteed a good job.  If you have a good       79
11  job right now, acquiring more computer skills could lead        90
12  to a big promotion or perhaps a sizable raise in your pay.     102
    |  1  |  2  |  3  |  4  |  5  |  6  |  7  |  8  |  9  |  10  |  11  |  12
```

FORMATTING

D. WORD PROCESSING: TABLE—NUMBER FORMAT AND FORMULAS

Study Lesson 34 in your word processing manual. Complete all of the shaded steps while at your computer. Then format the jobs that follow.

DOCUMENT PROCESSING

Table 11
2-Column Open Table With Number Column and Total

1. Center the table vertically.
2. Create a table structure with 2 columns and 5 rows.
3. Type the text in the columns including the word *TOTAL* in the last row, but leave the total amount blank.
4. Format the number column with dollar signs and two places after the decimal point.
5. With the insertion point in the total amount cell, insert the SUM command to get a total amount. (Do not type the question mark.)
6. Automatically adjust the column widths.
7. Join the cells in Row 1 and type the title in all caps and bold. Type the subtitle in initial caps.
8. Center the table horizontally.

UNITED CASUALTY
Liabilities

Net policy reserves	$44,726,719.00
Policy claims	$111,909.00
Other liabilities	$30,551.00
TOTAL	?

Table 12
2-Column Boxed Table With Number Column and Total

1. Center the table vertically.
2. Create a table structure with 2 columns and 7 rows.
3. Type the column headings in bold, then type the information in the columns.
4. Right justify/align the number column, including the column heading.
5. Format the number column with dollar signs and two places after the decimal point.
6. Use the SUM command to total the column.
7. Automatically adjust the column widths.
8. Join the cells in Row 1, type the title in all caps and bold, then center the table horizontally.

OPERATING EXPENSES	
Utilities	**Amount**
Electricity	$19,000.00
Gas	$18,500.00
Telephone	$1,475.00
Water	$7,500.00
TOTAL UTILITIES	?

Table 13
2-Column Open Table
With Number Column
and Total

1. Open the file for Table 12.
2. Change the table from a boxed table to an open table.

3. Add the subtitle *Homeowners' Association.*

Lesson 35   Formatting Review

GOALS: To improve speed and accuracy; to refine language-arts skills in spelling; to practice basic word processing commands.

A. Type 2 times.

A. WARMUP

```
1        Item #876 won't be ordered until 9/10.  Did you gather    11
2  all requests and input them exactly as they appeared?  Jack    23
3  will never be satisfied until a profit has been realized.    35
   |  1  |  2  |  3  |  4  |  5  |  6  |  7  |  8  |  9  |  10  |  11  |  12
```

SKILLBUILDING

B. PACED PRACTICE

Turn to the Paced Practice routine beginning on page SB-14. Take three 2-minute timings, starting at the point where you left off the last time.

C. DIAGNOSTIC PRACTICE: NUMBERS

Turn to the Diagnostic Practice: Numbers routine beginning on page SB-5. Type one of the Pretest/Posttest paragraphs and identify any errors made. Then type the corresponding drill lines 2 times for each number on which you made 2 or more errors and 1 time for each number on which you made only 1 error. Finally, repeat the same Pretest paragraph and compare your performance.

LANGUAGE ARTS

D. SPELLING

D. Type this list of frequently misspelled words, paying special attention to any spelling problems in each word.

```
4  prior activities additional than faculty whether first with
5  subject material equipment receiving completed during basis
6  available please required decision established policy audit
7  section schedule installation insurance possible appreciate
8  benefits requirements business scheduled office immediately
```

Edit the sentences to correct any misspellings.

```
9   We requierd the office to schedule all prior activities.
10  The business scheduled the instalation of the equipment.
11  The decision established the basis of the insurance policy.
12  Please audit any additionl material available to faculty.
13  If possible, we would appreciate recieving it immediately.
14  The section requirements to receive benefits were completed.
```

DOCUMENT PROCESSING

Report 5

BENEFITS PROGRAM OPTIONS
Insurance Alliance of America
By Martin VanWagner

Beginning January 1, our company has contracted with Insurance Alliance of America for a new benefits program for all employees. Please review the information below carefully before you reach any decision.

ENROLLMENT INFORMATION

The open enrollment period for the new benefits program will begin on January 1 and end on January 31. During this time, you are required to submit a completed application for enrollment in either the contributory or noncontributory policy plan. Any dependents must be enrolled in the same plan.

If you do not enroll in a medical insurance plan on or before January 31, you will automatically be enrolled in the noncontributory plan. Your new plan will become effective on the first of the month following your enrollment.

CHANGING BENEFIT PLANS

During the open enrollment period, it is possible to transfer to any available medical plan for which you are eligible. After the open enrollment period ends, you may not change plans again until the next scheduled open enrollment period.

Letter 8
Block Style

December 1, 19--

Mrs. Yvonne Spillotro
105 Northfield Avenue
Edison, NJ 08837

Dear Mrs. Spillotro:

Open enrollment for your medical insurance plan is scheduled to begin the first day of January. I hope it was possible for you to review the material you received last week.

Selecting the right benefit plan for you and your family can be an overwhelming

(continued on next page)

task. To make this decision a little easier, I have enclosed a brochure with this letter summarizing the key features of each policy. Please call me if I can help in any way.

Thank you for choosing Insurance Alliance of America.

Sincerely yours,

Keith Richards
Customer Support

{urs}

Enclosure

Envelope 4

1. Open the file for Letter 8 and create an envelope for the document.

2. Do not insert a return address.

3. Append the envelope to the letter.

Table 14
Progress Check

2-Column Boxed Table With Centered Column Headings, a Number Column, and a Total

1. Center the column headings.

2. Follow standard table format for the rest of this table.

OPERATING INCOME	
West Valley Homeowners' Association	
Category	**Amount**
Homeowner Dues	$207,090.00
Interest Income	$2,750.00
Late-Charges Income	$1,500.00
Prior-Year Excess Funds	$9,986.00
TOTAL INCOME	?

UNIT EIGHT ▶ Reports

Lesson 36 Multipage Rough-Draft Reports

GOALS: To type 35 wam/3′/4e; to learn basic proofreaders' marks; to format multipage rough-draft reports.

A. Type 2 times.

A. WARMUP

```
1      A plain paper reader/printer must be ordered; it must    11
2  accept jackets and have a footprint of 15 × 27* (*inches).    23
3  Please ask Gary to request Model Z-340 whenever he arrives.   35
   | 1 | 2 | 3 | 4 | 5 | 6 | 7 | 8 | 9 | 10 | 11 | 12
```

SKILLBUILDING

B. Take three 12-second timings on each line. The scale below the last line shows your wam speed for a 12-second timing.

B. 12-SECOND SPEED SPRINTS

```
4  Blake was paid to fix the handle on the bowls that he made.
5  Alan led the panel of four men until the work was all done.
6  Jan will sign this paper when she has done all of the work.
7  They will focus on their main theme for the last six weeks.
   | | | |5| | | |10| | | |15| | |20| | |25| | |30| | |35| | |40| | |45| | |50| | |55| | |60
```

C. Type the paragraph 2 times. Every time a number appears in the paragraph, replace it with a number that is two higher. For example, replace *two* with *four* and *five* with *seven*.

C. TECHNIQUE PRACTICE: CONCENTRATION

```
8      The two clerks placed an order for two computers, two
9  printers, three monitors, and four scanners.  The last
10 time he called, two people told him three different things.
```

D. Take two 3-minute timings. Determine your speed and errors.

Goal: 35 wam/3′/4e

D. 3-MINUTE TIMING

```
11     The use of videotapes for training company employees    11
12 is an exciting trend in the business world.  The range of    22
13 topics is wide and varied.  These tapes are designed to      34
14 instruct and entertain.  You can learn anything from office  46
15 etiquette to how and when to hire an office temp.            56
16     Most tapes are sold for a fair price when you stop to    67
17 realize just how many ways you could use these tapes.  One   78
18 use might be to launch a lively debate on some key topics    90
19 during a meeting.  Your prospects are limited only by your   102
20 own imagination.                                             105
   | 1 | 2 | 3 | 4 | 5 | 6 | 7 | 8 | 9 | 10 | 11 | 12
```

FORMATTING

E. BASIC PROOFREADERS' MARKS

1. Proofreaders' marks are used to indicate changes or corrections to be made in a document (called a rough draft) that is being revised for final copy.

2. Study the chart to learn what each proofreaders' mark means.

Proofreaders' Marks	Draft	Final Copy
⌒ Omit space	data base	database
∨ or ∧ Insert	if he's going (not)	if he's not going,
≡ Capitalize	Maple street	Maple Street
✀ Delete	a final draft	a draft
# Insert space	allready to	all ready to
when / if Change word	and if you (when)	and when you
/ Use lowercase letter	our President	our president
¶ Paragraph	¶ Most of the	Most of the

F. MULTIPAGE REPORTS

To format a multipage report:

1. Use the same side margins for all pages of the report.
2. Leave an approximate 2-inch top margin on page 1.
3. Leave an approximate 1-inch bottom margin on all pages. When you reach the end of a page, a soft page break will automatically be inserted by your software.
4. Leave a 1-inch top margin on continuing pages.
5. Do not number the first page. However, number all continuing pages at the top right.

G. WORD PROCESSING: PAGE NUMBERING AND PAGE BREAK

Study Lesson 36 in your word processing manual. Complete all of the shaded steps while at your computer. Then format the jobs that follow.

DOCUMENT PROCESSING

Report 6
Multipage, Rough-Draft Report

1. Insert the page numbers at the top right, and suppress the page number on the first page.
2. Change line spacing to double; then press Enter 3 times.
3. Center and type the title in all caps and bold.
4. Center and type the subtitle and byline in initial caps.

(continued on next page)

LEASING OFFICE EQUIPMENT

Hi-tech Research, Inc.

by Deborah Springer

Many companies are facing a dilemma these days. In order to remain competitive, businesses must use equipment that is state-of-the-art, technologically speaking. They must decide whether to invest their dollars in buying or in leasing their equipment.

Advantages of Leasing

For businesses that are simply not large enough to afford a major capital outlay, leasing can offer many advantages. **Avoid Technological Obsolescence.** Technology is making very dramatic and sweeping changes almost daily. As new products come on the market, they are very expensive initially. Over time, prices tend to drop dramatically and features continue to improve. It just doesn't make sense to make a huge major investement in an item that will likely become obsolete in a short period of time.

using state-of-the-art equipment

Upgrade Easily. If it is critical to a Company's success, leasing would allow the company to upgrade faster and with reduced cost. The short-term cost of a lease leasing must be compared with the long-term cost of investing in equipment that will not be used any longer when it becomes out dated. A company will not be locked into using hardware that is second-rate because too much money was invested when it was bought purchased. Innovation will be encouraged rather than inhibited.

Option to Buy. if a company leases with an option to buy, the money used to lease could end up being used to help purchase the equipment. If the item being leased ends up being undesirable, the company is not locked into buying it. This option could surely result in some significant savings.

DISADVANTAGES OF LEASING

If the equipment being leased is likely to be used over a long period of time, leasing it could end up costing much more than buying it over the long run. Also, if leasing rates are very high, the cost could be prohibitive or unreasonable when compared with the cost of buying. Sometimes leasing does not include a contract to service the equipment. If a service contract is considered an

(continued on next page)

additional expense, the cost of leasing might be too high. Leasing is an important alternative in today's business world. The pros and cons must be weighed ˄carefully before ~~making~~ any final decisions are made.

Report 7
Multipage Report

Open the file for Report 6 and make the following changes:

1. Change the title to **OFFICE EQUIP-MENT: LEASING VS. BUYING.**
2. Use your name in the byline.
3. Change the sideheadings to:
   LEASING ADVANTAGES
   LEASING DISADVANTAGES
4. Delete the last sentence in the paragraph headed **Option to Buy.**

Lesson 37   Bulleted and Numbered Lists

GOALS: To improve speed and accuracy; to refine language-arts skills in punctuation; to format bulleted and numbered lists.

A. Type 2 times.

A. WARMUP

```
1      The check for $432.65 wasn't mailed on time!  Late        10
2  charges of up to 10% can be expected.  To avoid a sizable      22
3  penalty, just mail the check quickly before it is too late.    34
   | 1 | 2 | 3 | 4 | 5 | 6 | 7 | 8 | 9 | 10 | 11 | 12
```

SKILLBUILDING

B. DIAGNOSTIC PRACTICE: ALPHABET

Turn to the Diagnostic Practice: Alphabet routine beginning on page SB-2. Type one of the Pretest/Posttest paragraphs and identify any errors made. Then type the corresponding drill lines 2 times for each letter on which you made 2 or more errors and 1 time for each letter on which you made only 1 error. Finally, repeat the same Pretest paragraph and compare your performance.

C. PACED PRACTICE

Turn to the Paced Practice routine beginning on page SB-14. Take three 2-minute timings, starting at the point where you left off the last time.

LANGUAGE ARTS

D. Study the rules at the right.

'sing

'plur

'pro

Edit the sentences to insert any needed punctuation.

D. APOSTROPHES

Rule: Use 's to form the possessive of singular nouns.

My secretary's office is being painted.

Rule: Use only an apostrophe to form the possessive of plural nouns that end in *s.*

The students' grades were posted in the hall.

Rule: Use 's to form the possessive of indefinite pronouns (such as *someone's* or *anybody's*); do not use an apostrophe with personal pronouns (such as *hers, his, its, ours, theirs,* and *yours*).

It is anybody's guess whether or not the car is hers.

4 The womans purse was stolen as she held her childs hand.
5 If the book is yours, please return it to the library now.
6 The girls decided to give the parents donations to charity.
7 The childs toy was forgotten by his mothers good friend.
8 The universities presidents submitted the joint statement.
9 The four secretaries salaries were raised just like yours.
10 One boys presents were forgotten when he left the party.
11 If these blue notebooks are not ours, they must be theirs.
12 The plant was designed to recycle its own waste products.

FORMATTING

E. BULLETED AND NUMBERED LISTS

1. Use bullets or numbers to call attention to items in a list. If the sequence of the items is important, use numbers rather than bullets.

2. Bullets and numbers appear at the left margin and are followed by an indent.

3. Carryover lines indent to align with the text in the previous line, not the bullet or number.

F. WORD PROCESSING: BULLETS AND NUMBERING

Study Lesson 37 in your word processing manual. Complete all of the shaded steps while at your computer. Then format the jobs that follow.

DOCUMENT PROCESSING

Report 8
Bulleted List

1. Read the information in Report 8 carefully before you type the report.

2. Type the report using the standard report format.

3. Use the bullet command to add bullets to the list as you type.

(continued on next page)

BULLETED LISTS

'plur

- To make items in a list easier to read, use either bullets or numbers.

- When the items' order is not important, use bullets instead of numbers.

'sing

- The software command for automatically inserting bullets positions the bullet at the left margin and sets the indent for the list's first line as well as any turnover (second and succeeding) lines.

- The circle you see at the left of this sentence is just one example of a bullet. Large circles, diamonds, squares, or triangles may also be used as bullets.

- A list that is part of the body of a double-spaced document (such as a report) should be double spaced.

- A list that is part of a single-spaced document (such as a letter) should be single spaced with a blank line before and after it.

- If additional text follows the bulleted list, press Enter after typing the bulleted item, then issue the command to end automatic bulleting. If a bulleted item is the last line of a report, do not press Enter.

Report 9
Numbered List

1. Carefully read the information in Report 9 before you type the report.
2. Type the report using the standard report format.
3. Use the numbering command to add numbers to the list as you type.

NUMBERED LIST

'sing

1. A numbered list's format is similar to a bulleted list's format. When the sequence of items in a list is important, use numbers instead of bullets.

2. The numbering command automatically inserts the number at the left margin and sets the indent for the first line of the list as well as any turnover lines.

3. A numbered list that is part of a double-spaced document should be double spaced.

4. A numbered list that is part of a single-spaced document should be single spaced with a blank line before and after it.

5. The numbering feature enables you to rearrange the items in your list without having to retype the numbers. As you move items, they will be

(continued on next page)

automatically renumbered in the correct sequence.

6. *If additional text follows the numbered list, press Enter after typing the last numbered item; then issue the command to end automatic numbering. If a numbered item is the last line of a report, do not press Enter.*

Report 10
Bulleted List

1. Open the file for Report 8.
2. Make the changes to the report as indicated by the proofreaders' marks.
3. Add this additional item to the end of the list: *When additional items are added to a list, position the insertion point at the end of the last item, press Enter, and type the new item.*

BULLETED LISTS

- To make ~~in a list~~ items easier to read, use either bullets or numbers. [a list's]

- When the ~~items~~ order is not important, use bullets instead of numbers. [of the items]

- The software command for automatically inserting bullets positions the bullet at the left margin and sets the indent for the ~~list's~~ first line as well as any turnover (second and succeeding) lines. [s] [of the item]

- The circle you see at the left of this sentence is ~~just one~~ example of a bullet. Large circles, diamonds, squares, or triangles may also be used as bullets. [an]

- A list ~~that is part of the body of~~ a double-spaced document (such as a report) should be double spaced. [within]

- A list ~~that is part of~~ a single-spaced document (such as a letter) should be single spaced with a blank line before and after it. [within]

- If additional text follows the bulleted list, press Enter after typing the bulleted item, then ~~issue the command to~~ end automatic bulleting. If a bulleted item is the last line of a report, do not press Enter.

Lesson 38 — Rough-Draft Reports With Numbered Lists

GOALS: To type 35 wam/3'/4e; to learn more proofreaders' marks; to format rough-draft reports with numbered lists.

A. Type 2 times.

A. WARMUP

```
1        Jerry wrote a great article entitled "Interviewing        10
2   Techniques" on pp. 78 and 123!  A & B Bookstore expected a     22
3   sizable number of requests; thus far, 65% have been sold.      34
    |  1  |  2  |  3  |  4  |  5  |  6  |  7  |  8  |  9  | 10  | 11  | 12
```

SKILLBUILDING

B. Take three 12-second timings on each line. The scale below the last line shows your wam speed for a 12-second timing.

B. 12-SECOND SPEED SPRINTS

```
4   They used about two cubic feet of dirt to fill the planter.
5   The rocks she dug up made the work much harder than before.
6   Nancy will spend as much time as she must to fix the signs.
7   The men kept the keys to the town hall inside the blue box.
    | | | |5| | | |10| | |15| | | |20| | |25| | |30| | |35| | |40| | |45| | |50| | |55| | |60
```

C. DIAGNOSTIC PRACTICE: NUMBERS

Turn to the Diagnostic Practice: Numbers routine beginning on page SB-5. Type one of the Pretest/Posttest paragraphs and identify any errors made. Then type the corresponding drill lines 2 times for each number on which you made 2 or more errors and 1 time for each number on which you made only 1 error. Finally, repeat the same Pretest paragraph and compare your performance.

D. Take two 3-minute timings. Determine your speed and errors.

Goal: 35 wam/3'/4e

D. 3-MINUTE TIMING

```
8         Telecommuting is a word you may have heard before but     11
9    don't quite understand.  Very simply, it means working at      23
10   home instead of driving in to work.  Many people like the      34
11   convenience of working at home.  They realize they can save     46
12   money on expenses like gas, clothes, and child care.           57
13        Most home office workers use a computer in their job.      68
14   When their work is completed, they can just fax it to the       80
15   office.  If they need to communicate with other employees,      91
16   they can route calls to a fax or phone and never have to       103
17   leave home.                                                    105
     |  1  |  2  |  3  |  4  |  5  |  6  |  7  |  8  |  9  | 10  | 11  | 12
```

E. MORE PROOFREADERS' MARKS

1. Review the most frequently used proofreaders' marks introduced in Lesson 36.
2. Study the additional proofreaders' marks presented here.
3. Learn what each proofreaders' mark means before typing Report 11.

Proofreaders' Marks		Draft	Final Copy
SS	Single-space	SS ⌈ first line ⌊ second line	first line second line
ds	Double-space	ds ⌈ first line second line	first line second line
...	Don't delete	a ~~true~~ story	a true story
◯	Spell out	the only ①	the only one
⌐	Move right	Please send	Please send
⌐	Move left	May I	May I
∿	Bold	Column Heading	**Column Heading**
ital	Italic	*ital* Time magazine	*Time* magazine
u/l	Underline	u/l Time magazine	Time magazine readers
⚥	Move as shown	(readers) will see	will see
∽	Transpose	they all see	they see all

F. WORD PROCESSING: CUT, COPY, AND PASTE

Study Lesson 38 in your word processing manual. Complete all of the shaded steps while at your computer. Then format the jobs that follow.

Report 11
Report With List

1. Type this report following the standard report format. If necessary, refer to the illustration on page 44 in Lesson 24.
2. Use the numbering command to type the numbered list.
3. After typing the last item in the list, remember to end the automatic numbering.

(continued on next page)

ds CONTROLLING COPIER COSTS
By Yong Lee

Controlling how and when the copier is used is one of the most difficult

challenges facing an office manager. The office copier is an essential tool that

u/l must be convenient and accessible. However, it is also one of the most

misused pieces of office equipment. Here are ⑥ guidelines for controlling

copier costs:

1. Monitor copier use by installing a system # of accountability such as a

    keypad unit. This unit identifies both the user and the ∧ number of copies

    made.

ital
2. If a keypad unit is not convenient ∧ use a card with a magnetic stripe that

    performs the same accountability functions as a keypad.

3. Use a debit # card system to limit the number of copies if excessive

    copying is the main concern.
    Begin
4. Implement a Records Management program to educate employees about

    the basic principles of controlling records in an office. Records ital

ital Management Quarterly should be required reading.

5. Implement a paper recycling plan to raise awareness of wasted paper
    caused by
    through excessive ∧ unnecessary copying.

6. Encourage employees to store and exchange data electronically using

    their computer s systems.

    If these methods are implemented and enforced, copier costs will drop
                                                        should
significantly. Ultimately, the goal is to provide employees with convenient and
                                while
reasonable access to a copier and keeping costs as low as possible.

Report 12
Report With List

Open the file for Report 11 and make the following changes:

1. Change the title to **COPIER COST MANAGEMENT**.

2. Delete the last sentence in Item 1.

3. Add the words *for all employees* to the last sentence in Item 4.

4. Transpose the two sentences in the last paragraph.

GOALS: To improve speed and accuracy; to refine language-arts skills in number expression; to format bound reports with bulleted lists.

A. Type 2 times.

A. WARMUP

1   Does Xavier know that at 8:04 a.m. his July sales   10
2 quota was realized? Invoice #671 indicates a 9% increase!   22
3 Several of the employees weren't able to regain their lead.   34

| 1 | 2 | 3 | 4 | 5 | 6 | 7 | 8 | 9 | 10 | 11 | 12

SKILLBUILDING

B. Take a 1-minute timing on the first paragraph to establish your base speed. Then take four 1-minute timings on the remaining paragraphs. As soon as you equal or exceed your base speed on one paragraph, advance to the next, more difficult paragraph.

B. SUSTAINED PRACTICE: SYLLABIC INTENSITY

4   Taking care of aging parents is not a new trend. This   11
5 issue has arisen more and more, since we are all now living   23
6 longer. Companies are now trying to help out in many ways.   35

7   Help may come in many ways, ranging from financial aid   11
8 to sponsoring hospice or in-home respite care. Employees may   23
9 find it difficult to work and care for aging parents.   34

10   Why are employers so interested in elder care? Rising   11
11 interest is the result of a combination of several things.   23
12 The most notable is a marked increase in life expectancy.   34

13   Another trend is the increased participation of women,   11
14 the primary caregivers, in the workforce. Businesses are   23
15 recognizing that work and family life are intertwined.   34

| 1 | 2 | 3 | 4 | 5 | 6 | 7 | 8 | 9 | 10 | 11 | 12

C. PROGRESSIVE PRACTICE: ALPHABET

Turn to the Progressive Practice: Alphabet routine beginning on page SB-7. Take six 30-second timings, starting at the point where you left off the last time.

LANGUAGE ARTS

D. Study the rules at the right.   # gen

D. NUMBER EXPRESSION

Rule: In general, spell out numbers 1 through 10, and use figures for numbers above 10.

Only nine copies of the report were mailed, even though 17 people requested a copy.

Rule: Use figures for dates (use *st, d,* or *th* only if the day precedes the month); all numbers if two or more related numbers both above and below ten are used in the same sentence; measurements (time, money, distance, weight, and percent); mixed numbers.

(continued on next page)

On July 1 at 10 a.m., she ordered 2 printers, 3 keyboards, and 12 printer cartridges. The monthly budget allows 12 percent for office supplies.

On the 4th of July, we spent $65 to buy 20 pounds of meat for the picnic, which was held 4 3/5 miles away.

Rule: Spell out numbers used as the first word in a sentence; the smaller of two adjacent numbers; the words *million* and *billion* in even amounts (do not use decimals with even amounts); fractions.

Two million votes were counted, thereby assuring the two-thirds majority needed.

On Wednesday three 5-page reports were presented to the assembly.

Edit the sentences to correct any errors in number expression.

16 On the third of June, when she turns 60, 2 of her annuities
17 will have earned an average of 10 3/4 percent.
18 Seven investors were interested in buying 2 15-unit condos
19 if they were located within fifteen miles of each other.
20 The purchase price will be over $3,000,000.00 at 11 percent
21 interest; escrow will close on June 3d before five p.m.
22 The agent sent 7 ten-page letters to all the investors.
23 The parcel weighed two pounds. She also mailed three post-
24 cards, twelve packages, and twenty-one letters on June 4.

 **FORMATTING**

E. BOUND REPORTS

1. A left-bound report requires a wider left margin to allow for binding so that text is not hidden.

2. To format a bound report, add additional space to the left margin by increasing the margin by 0.5 inch.

F. WORD PROCESSING: MARGINS

Study Lesson 39 in your word processing manual. Complete all of the shaded steps while at your computer. Then format the jobs that follow.

 **DOCUMENT PROCESSING**

Report 13
Multipage Bound Report With Bulleted List

1. Position the page number at the top right, and suppress the page number on the first page.

2. Change the left margin to add an extra

0.5 inch.

3. Set double spacing, and follow the standard report format to complete the report.

EMPLOYEE HEALTH CARE

By Peggy Stevens

Health care reform has been hotly debated in Congress for at least 18 months in an effort to curb the rising cost of health care. Businesses are spending more than $800 billion a year on health care. Although it is unlikely that Congress will ever reach a unanimous decision regarding health care

(continued on next page)

reform, it is clear that companies are going to have to take an active role in controlling their health care costs if they are to survive financially.

WELLNESS PROGRAMS

fig

gen

Every year on January 1 at exactly 12 a.m., a new year begins. For most people, this means at least one or two resolutions for making the coming year a healthful one. Businesses are realizing that if they implement innovative employee wellness programs, such resolutions can translate into substantial

word

savings in health care costs. Three examples of innovative approaches are as follows:

fig

- Some businesses offer employees as much as a 40 percent reduction in their health care premium as an incentive to participate in a wellness program.

fig

- Some businesses are giving employees cash rebates of $100 or more if they show improvement in things like blood pressure and cholesterol.
- Educating employees about topics such as how to manage stress and quit smoking has been an effective approach.

Health care costs should be reduced because a healthier employee will need fewer visits to the doctor and fewer medications and treatments. Also, if employees are healthier, it makes sense that they will have fewer sick days. A healthier body should also lead to more productivity and energy on the job.

PROGRAM IMPLEMENTATION

Clearly, there is a great incentive for both employers and employees to be interested in implementing some type of wellness program. With proper planning, such innovative programs could be a positive and productive answer to reducing health care costs for everyone involved.

Report 14
Multipage Bound Report With Bulleted List

Open the file for Report 13 and make the following changes:

1. Change the title to **_HEALTH CARE REFORM_**.
2. Add the subtitle _Business Alliance Symposium._
3. Change the byline to _Elaine Shibata._
4. Move the last sentence of the first paragraph (_Although it is unlikely . . ._) to the end of the report directly after the last sentence.
5. Add this sentence to the end of the first paragraph: _Some companies cannot afford to wait for Congress to act and have devised their own solutions to health care._
6. Delete both side headings.

Lesson 40 · Reports With Displays

GOALS: To type 36 wam/3'/4e; to format reports with displays.

A. Type 2 times.

A. WARMUP

1   On July 15, a check for exactly $329.86 was mailed to   11
2 Zak & Quinn, Inc.; they never received Check #104. Does   22
3 Gary know if the check cleared the company's bank account?   34

| 1 | 2 | 3 | 4 | 5 | 6 | 7 | 8 | 9 | 10 | 11 | 12

SKILLBUILDING

Pretest
Take a 1-minute timing. Determine your speed and errors.

Practice
  Speed Emphasis: If you made 2 or fewer errors on the Pretest, type each *individual* line 2 times.
  Accuracy Emphasis: If you made 3 or more errors, type each *group* of lines (as though it were a paragraph) 2 times.

Posttest
Repeat the Pretest timing and compare performance.

F. Take two 3-minute timings. Determine your speed and errors.

Goal: 36 wam/3'/4e

B. PRETEST: HORIZONTAL REACHES

4   The chief thinks the alarm was a decoy for the armed   11
5 agent who coyly dashed away. She was dazed as she dodged   22
6 a blue sedan. He lured her to the edge of the high bluff.   34

| 1 | 2 | 3 | 4 | 5 | 6 | 7 | 8 | 9 | 10 | 11 | 12

C. PRACTICE: IN REACHES

7 oy foyer loyal buoys enjoy decoy coyly royal cloy ploy toys
8 ar argue armed cared alarm cedar sugar radar area earn hear
9 lu lucid lunch lured bluff value blunt fluid luck lush blue

D. PRACTICE: OUT REACHES

10 ge geese genes germs agent edges dodge hinge gear ages page
11 da daily dazed dance adapt sedan adage panda dash date soda
12 hi hints hiked hired chief think ethic aphid high ship chip

E. POSTTEST: HORIZONTAL REACHES

F. 3-MINUTE TIMING

13   Employee complaints are often viewed as a negative   10
14 power in a workforce. In fact, these complaints should   22
15 be viewed as a chance to communicate with an employee and   34
16 improve morale. Ignoring complaints does not make them   46
17 go away. Listening to complaints objectively can help to   57
18 solve a small problem before it turns into a big one.   68
19   Often workers expect a chance to be heard by a person   79
20 who is willing to listen quite openly. You must learn to   91
21 recognize when a person wants to remain unknown so that   102
22 he or she will be free to talk.   108

| 1 | 2 | 3 | 4 | 5 | 6 | 7 | 8 | 9 | 10 | 11 | 12

G. REPORTS WITH INDENTED DISPLAYS

1. A paragraph that is quoted or needs special emphasis in a report may be made to stand out from the rest of the report by displaying it single-spaced and indented 0.5 inch from both the left and the right margins (instead of enclosing it in quotation marks).
2. Use the indent commands in your word processing software to display a paragraph.

H. WORD PROCESSING: INDENT AND WIDOWS AND ORPHANS

Study Lesson 40 in your word processing manual. Complete all of the shaded steps while at your computer. Then format the jobs that follow.

DOCUMENT PROCESSING

Report 15
Multipage Report With Displayed Paragraph

1. Position the page number at the top right, and suppress the page number on the first page.
2. Follow the standard report format.
3. Change to single spacing at the start of the displayed paragraph, and indent the displayed paragraph 0.5 inch from both margins.
4. After typing the displayed paragraph, press Enter twice; then change to double spacing.

TRAVEL POLICY

Effective July 1, 19—

Rockmart International

As of July 1, 19— the travel *policy* guidelines will be changed to adhere to Rockmart Internationals limited expenditures position that was mandated at the board meeting on June 1, 19—. This travel policy will apply to all employees of Rockmart International and will cover both in-state and out-of-state travel.

The new travel policy, as stipulated by the board on June 1 and to become effective on July 1, is as follows:

ss + indent displayed paragraph

All Rockmart International employee travel will be restricted to an amount not greater than $500 per month for in-state travel and $1,000 per month for out-of-state travel. This dollar amount will apply to meals, transportation, lodging, and miscellaneous expenses.

(continued on next page)

Travel budgets for each division vary during the months of the year. Because of this variation, division managers may request that their travel moneys be "banked" so that the months of extensive ~~excessive~~ travel can be accommodated by this policy. Any banked travel moneys remaining at the end of the fiscal year will be reallocated.

Divisions are requested to submit quarterly travel reports to the Albuquerque office no later than <u>14 days</u> prior to the quarter during which travel is anticipated. Travel form A94-022 is to be used for all requests submitted after July. The form should be sent via E-mail to the office ~~in~~ Albuquerque.

Form A94-022 requires that all transportation costs, lodging expenses, and meals be filed with the division--and subsequently with ~~regional~~ headquarters--no later than 7 days after completion of the travel. These expenses will be individually itemized for each trip. Related expenses (duplicating, telephone, and similar expenses) are to be included on Page 2 of the travel form. This policy supersedes Policy A90-324, dated March 1994, and will be in effect until further notice.

ds

Report 16

Progress Check
Multipage Bound
Report With List

1. Format this report as a multipage bound report with a numbered list.

2. Make all changes as indicated by the proofreaders' marks.

ERGONOMICS ~~IN THE~~ OFFICE

By Joyce Moore

How many times have you sat down in front of the computer only to find that after a few minutes of work, your neck ~~hurts~~ aches and your wrists are stiff? Unfortunately, this condition is more often the norm rather than the exception as repetitive stress injuries ~~are increasing~~ continue to increase at an alarming rate. So far, the government is doing very little to provide any guidelines for work place standards. Clearly, office ergonomics will ~~continue to~~ become increasingly important to corporations as they struggle with ~~lowered~~ decreased productivity and increased health care costs. Ergonomics is a broad term that includes adjusting the work environment to suit the comfort and needs of the employee rather than having the employee adjust to the work environment.

(continued on next page)

Most people associate ergonomics primarily with office furniture--for example, adjustable chairs and desks. however, it also includes things like lighting, air quality, and noise control. Providing a workstation that is sound ergonomically is the responsibility of the employer. 5 guidelines can help an employer design such a workstation:

1. Choose lighting that is adjustable such as swivel-based, swing-arm lamps that can be relocated.

2. Choose office furniture that is adjustable. Chair and desk heights should be adjustable for both height and angle.

3. Provide wrist rests on keyboards to avoid carpal tunnel syndrome injuries.

4. use air filtration systems that screen out allergens and pollutants.

5. Provide noise shields on all printers and carpeting in all work areas to reduce noise pollution.

Clearly, each employee has individual needs that must be considered in the planning of an ergonomically sound work station. Corporate leaders must continue to focus on providing a work station that is comfortable and safe for everyone. In doing so, they will fulfill their responsibility to all employees and in turn find a workforce that is more productive, happier, and healthier.

ds

Test 2-A
3-Minute Timing

1	You need to give yourself a huge pat on the back right 11
2	now. You have just finished learning about letters, memos, 23
3	reports, and tables. You have also increased your speed 35
4	and accuracy well beyond the first day of class. All of 46
5	this hard work is quite an amazing accomplishment. 56
6	You have seen that you can learn a wide range of word 67
7	processing commands and master them. You can expect even 79
8	more progress if you will just continue to learn as much 90
9	as you can each day. Ask questions and keep moving toward 102
10	a new goal each and every day. 108

| 1 | 2 | 3 | 4 | 5 | 6 | 7 | 8 | 9 | 10 | 11 | 12

Test 2-B

Letter 9

Block Style

February 14, 19— / Ms. Rose Garcia / Dean, Patten, & Epstein / 2700 Mission Boulevard / Santa Clara, CA 95052 / Dear Ms. Garcia:

Each year the Office Administration Department honors students who will graduate at the end of the semester. These students have worked long and hard to reach their goals, and the Certificates and Awards Program is very important to them.

Your presentation at our last Advisory Committee Meeting was very impressive! I have enclosed a copy of the minutes for you. Because of your outstanding reputation in the legal field, I would like to invite you to be the keynote speaker for our annual Certificates and Awards Program to be held on April 12.

I know that you began your higher education here at our community college. Having you return as a successful attorney with a promising future would be an inspiration to the students. I will be calling you in the next few days so that we can discuss the program in more detail.

Sincerely, / Janet McKay / Chairperson / {urs} / Enclosure

1. Center the table vertically.
2. Center column headings and adjust the column widths.

3. Center the table horizontally.

ADVISORY COMMITTEE MEMBERS		
Name	**Title**	**Company**
Stacey Erranova	Vice President	Office Temps, Inc.
William Zimmerman	Attorney at Law	Baird & Findling
Brenda Chandler	Account Manager	Worldwide Surety

PARKING POLICY

Fall semester

Please read these following guidelines regarding the rules and regulations governing the parking of vehicles on school property:

FACULTY AND STAFF PARKING

Certain lots have been reserved and designated specifically for use by the Faculty and Staff. These lots require a key card to gain entry. A valid and current parking permit must be prominently displayed on the dashboard of all vehicles. If such permits are missing, the vehicle will be cited and could be towed.

Student parking

Several parking lots and parking structures have been assigned designated for Student parking. A valid, current student parking permit must be affixed to the rear bumper of all vehicles. If such permits are missing, the vehicles may be cited. The following lots have been designated for student use:

• Lot 1 on the corner of Melrose Blvd. and Vermont Ave.
• Lot 3 on the corner of Heliotrope and Santa Monica Blvd. This lot will also accommodate 9 disabled parking spaces.

The city of Los Angeles maintains the streets on a regular basis. Please check all signs before parking in any location.

PART THREE

Correspondence, Reports, and Employment Documents

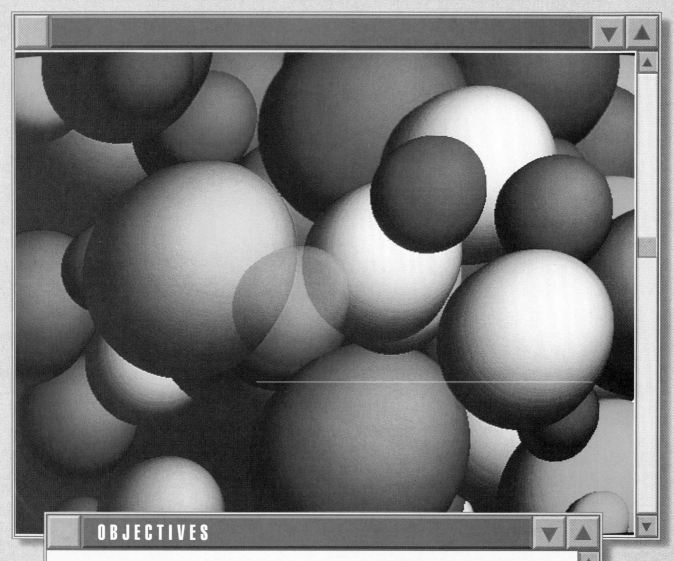

UNIT NINE ▶ Correspondence

<table>
<tr><td>Lesson 41</td><td>Business Letters</td></tr>
</table>

GOALS: To improve speed and accuracy; to refine language-arts skills in the use of commas; to format business letters.

A. Type 2 times.

A. WARMUP

```
1      Quite a night!  All sixty senior citizens (including    11
2 the handicapped) really enjoyed that play.  Over 3/4 of      22
3 the tickets were sold; most had been sold by Jeff's group.   34
  | 1 | 2 | 3 | 4 | 5 | 6 | 7 | 8 | 9 | 10 | 11 | 12
```

SKILLBUILDING

B. Take three 12-second timings on each line. The scale below the last line shows your wam speed for a 12-second timing.

B. 12-SECOND SPEED SPRINTS

```
4 Many of the men were at the auction when the vase was sold.
5 Some of the women were also there to buy some old antiques.
6 Jan was hoping to buy two chairs and a lamp at the auction.
7 Len was one of the six people who found an old wooden desk.
  | | | 5 | | | 10 | | | 15 | | | 20 | | | 25 | | | 30 | | | 35 | | | 40 | | | 45 | | | 50 | | | 55 | | | 60
```

C. PROGRESSIVE PRACTICE: ALPHABET

Turn to the Progressive Practice: Alphabet routine beginning on page SB-7. Take six 30-second timings, starting at the point where you left off the last time.

LANGUAGE ARTS

D. Study the rules at the right.

,date

D. COMMAS

Rule: Use a comma before and after the year in a complete date.

On December 7, 1996, the *Tribune* reviewed the Pearl Harbor events.
But: The *News Monthly* dated December 1996 reviewed the same events.

Rule: Use a comma before and after a state or country that follows a city (but not before a ZIP Code).

,place

Sioux City, Iowa, is a lovely place in which to live.
But: Sioux City, Iowa 51102, is where she was born.

Edit the sentences to correct any errors in the use of commas.

```
8 The warehouse building will be ready in September, 1998.
9 The attorney told a clerk to use June 30, 1994 as the date.
10 The report was sent to Nagoya, Japan on March 14, 1996.
11 The move to Toledo, Ohio, was scheduled for November, 1996.
```

E. TITLES IN CORRESPONDENCE

1. Always use a courtesy title before a person's name in the inside address of a letter; for example, *Mr., Mrs.,* or *Dr.*
2. In the closing lines, do not use a courtesy title before a man's name. A courtesy title may be included in a woman's typed name or her signature.
3. Type a person's title on the same line with the name (separated by a comma) if the title is short, or on the line below.
4. When possible, use a person's name in the salutation. The correct form for the salutation is the courtesy title and the last name. If you do not know the name of the person, use a job title or *Ladies and Gentlemen.*

INSIDE ADDRESSES	CLOSING LINES
Mrs. Rose E. Nebel, Owner Nebel Financial Services	Sincerely yours,
Dr. Prayad Chayapruks Executive Director Foy Memorial Hospital	*Mildred D. King* Miss Mildred D. King Adjunct Instructor
Mr. Craig R. Weiger Manager, Dahlke Oil Co.	Cordially,
Waynesville Printing Company	*(Ms.) Evelyn Marketto* Evelyn Marketto Senior Programmer Analyst
SALUTATIONS	Respectfully yours,
Dear Ms. Nebel:	
Dear Dr. Chayapruks:	*Jose R. Minuego* Jose R. Minuego Service Representative
Dear Mr. Weiger:	
Dear Sales Manager:	
Ladies and Gentlemen:	

F. COMPLIMENTARY CLOSINGS

Every letter should end with a complimentary closing. Some frequently used complimentary closings are *Sincerely, Sincerely yours, Yours truly, Cordially,* and *Respectfully yours.*

DOCUMENT PROCESSING

Letter 10
Business Letter in Block Style

,place
,date

{Current Date} / Mrs. Phyllis Fenske / 4304 Keller Lane / Mount Vernon, WA 98273-4156 / Dear Mrs. Fenske:

¶We at Garner Homes feel that your selection of a Suncourt town house is just the right choice for you.

¶All units at the Timber Creek site in Mount Vernon, Washington, have been built since March 1993. The Suncourt was awarded three national awards.

¶Thank you, Mrs. Fenske. If you have questions, please let us know. Sincerely, / Alfred A. Long / Sales Director / {urs}

Letter 11
Business Letter in Block Style

,place

,date

{Current Date} / Mr. Lawrence S. Alwich / 1800 East Hollywood Avenue / Salt Lake City, UT 84108 / Dear Mr. Alwich:

¶Our radio station would like you to reply to our editorial about the proposed airport site that aired from Provo, Utah, on May 15.

¶Of the more than 100 request letters for equal time, we selected yours because you touched on most of the relevant points of this topic.

¶We will contact you further about taping your rebuttal on June 4. Sincerely, / Karin L. Londgren / General Manager / {urs}

Letter 12
Business Letter in Block Style

Open the file for Letter 10 and revise it to be sent to Mr. and Mrs. Tony L. Carravetti, who live at 2906 28th Avenue South in Lilliwaup, WA 98555. They recently purchased a Delcourt town house, which has received two national awards.

Lesson 42   Personal-Business Letters

GOALS: To type 37 wam/3'/3e; to format personal-business letters.

A. Type 2 times.

A. WARMUP

1   B & Z requested 4 boxes at $37/box. The items they   11
2   wanted were #6 and #7. A discount of 20% would bring the   22
3   total to approximately $950. Will you verify the order?   33

| 1 | 2 | 3 | 4 | 5 | 6 | 7 | 8 | 9 | 10 | 11 | 12

SKILLBUILDING

Pretest
Take a 1-minute timing. Determine your speed and errors.

B. PRETEST: VERTICAL REACHES

4   Kim knew that her skills at the keyboard made her a   11
5   top rival for the job. About six persons had seen her race   23
6   home to see if the mail showed the company was aware of it.   34

| 1 | 2 | 3 | 4 | 5 | 6 | 7 | 8 | 9 | 10 | 11 | 12

Practice
Speed Emphasis: If you made 2 or fewer errors on the Pretest, type each *individual* line 2 times.
Accuracy Emphasis: If you made 3 or more errors, type each *group* of lines (as though it were a paragraph) 2 times.

C. PRACTICE: UP REACHES

7   se seven reset seams sedan loses eases serve used seed dose
8   ki skids kings kinks skill kitty kites kilts kite kids kick
9   rd board horde wards sword award beard third cord hard lard

D. PRACTICE: DOWN REACHES

10 ac races pacer backs ached acute laced facts each acre lace
11 kn knave knack knife knows knoll knots knelt knew knee knit
12 ab about abide label above abode sable abbey drab able cabs

Posttest
Repeat the Pretest timing and compare performance.

E. POSTTEST: VERTICAL REACHES

F. Take two 3-minute timings. Determine your speed and errors.

Goal: 37 wam/3'/3e

F. 3-MINUTE TIMING

13   The size of their first paychecks after they finish   11
14 college seems quite high to some young men and women. They   23
15 then rent a place to live that is just too expensive, or   35
16 they may buy a new car with a huge monthly payment. For   47
17 some it takes a while to learn that there are other items   58
18 in the monthly budget.   63
19   Some of these items are food, student loans, renters'   74
20 insurance, credit cards, car insurance, health insurance,   86
21 utilities, and miscellaneous expenses. One further goal   97
22 should be to start a savings plan by putting a small amount   109
23 aside from each paycheck.   114

| 1 | 2 | 3 | 4 | 5 | 6 | 7 | 8 | 9 | 10 | 11 | 12

G. PERSONAL-BUSINESS LETTERS

Personal-business letters are prepared by individuals to conduct their personal business affairs. To format a personal-business letter:

1. Type the letter on plain paper or personal stationery, not letterhead.
2. Include the writer's address in the let-

ter directly below the writer's name in the closing lines. (Another acceptable format is to type the return address before the date at the top of the letter.)

3. Since the writer of the letter usually types the letter, reference initials are not used.

DOCUMENT PROCESSING

Letter 13
Personal-Business
Letter in Block Style

↓center vertically
{Current Date}
↓4X

Mr. Phillip M. Fesmire, Director
City Parks and Recreation Department
4507 Renwick Avenue
Syracuse, NY 13210-0475

Dear Mr. Fesmire:

Thank you for the excellent manner in which your department accommodated our family last summer. About 120 Fensteins attended the reunion at Rosedale Park on July 28.

I should like to again request that Shelter 5 be reserved for our next year's family reunion on July 27, 19--. A confirmation of the date from your office will be appreciated.

The facilities at Rosedale are in very good condition. The new kitchen area is excellent. Please express our appreciation to those who help make it an exemplary facility.

Sincerely,
↓4X

Miss Vivian L. Fenstein
2410 Farnham Road
Syracuse, NY 13219

Personal-business letter in block style with (*a*) all lines beginning at the left margin and (*b*) standard punctuation.

Letter 14
Personal-Business
Letter in Block Style

This personal-business letter is from Walter G. Halverson, who lives at 482 22d Street East in Lawrence, KS 66049. Use today's date, and supply the appropriate salutation. The letter is to be sent to Mr. Robert A. Sotherden, Administrator / Glencrest Nursing Home / 2807 Crossgate Circle / Lawrence, KS 66047.

(continued on next page)

¶Thanks to you and dozens of other people, the fall crafts sale at Glencrest was highly successful. I am very appreciative of the ways in which you helped.

¶I particularly wish to thank you for transporting the display tables and chairs to Glencrest and back to the community center. Many people from the community center attended the sale and commented about how nice it was of you and your staff to support such an activity.

¶Having a parent who is a resident of the home, I am grateful that so many people from the Lawrence area volunteer their services to help make life more pleasant for the residents. Please accept my special thanks to you and your staff for supporting the many activities that benefit all Glencrest residents.

Letter 15
Personal-Business
Letter in Block Style

Open the file for Letter 14 and revise it as follows: Send the letter to Mrs. Diana Hagedon / Hagedon Associates / 2014 30th Street West / Lawrence, KS 66047. Replace the second paragraph with the following: *I particularly wish to thank* *you and your team for handling the* *financial transactions for residents in* *need of help. Their day was brighter* *because of you and the others who* *helped. Thank you for your kindness.*

Lesson 43   Memos

GOALS: To improve speed and accuracy;
to refine language-arts skills in proofreading;
to format memos.

A. Type 2 times.

A. WARMUP

```
1       "Rex analyzed the supply," Marge said.  Based on the      11
2    results, a purchase request for 7# at $140 (2% of what we    22
3    needed) was issued.  Was Jack surprised by this?  Vi was!    34
     |  1  |  2  |  3  |  4  |  5  |  6  |  7  |  8  |  9  |  10  |  11  |  12
```

SKILLBUILDING

B. Take three 12-second timings on each line. The scale below the last line shows your wam speed for a 12-second timing.

B. 12-SECOND SPEED SPRINTS

```
4   Nine of those new women were on time for the first session.
5   She could see that many of those old memos should be filed.
6   Forty of the men were at the game when that siren went off.
7   The line at the main hall was so long that I did not go in.
    | | | |5| | | |10| | | |15| | |20| | | |25| | | |30| | | |35| | | |40| | | |45| | | |50| | | |55| | | |60
```

C. PROGRESSIVE PRACTICE: NUMBERS

Turn to the Progressive Practice: Numbers routine beginning on page SB-11. Take six 30-second timings, starting at the point where you left off the last time.

D. Type the columns 2 times. Press Tab to move from column to column.

D. TECHNIQUE PRACTICE: TAB

8	J. Barnes	P. Varanth	S. Childers	M. Christenson
9	F. Gilsrud	J. Benson	D. Bates	M. Jordan
10	B. Harringer	J. Suksi	J. Lee	P. North
11	V. Hill	A. Budinger	T. Gonyer	S. Kravolec

LANGUAGE ARTS

E. Compare this paragraph with the 3-minute timing on page 102. Edit the paragraph to correct any errors.

E. PROOFREADING

12   Some type of insurance of this kind are straight life
13 for single and children, student health, dread disease,
14 and hospitable indemnity. Others are home morgage, credit
15 card, rental-car, job-loss, and contact-lens loss. A study
16 of policies may save you money every year.

DOCUMENT PROCESSING

Memo 5

Most memos are typed with blocked paragraphs (no indentations) and 1 blank line between paragraphs.

The use of *MEMO TO:* eliminates the need to type the word *MEMO-RANDUM* at the top of the document.

After typing the colon at the end of each bold heading, tab once to reach the point where the heading entries begin.

Type your own reference initials.

MEMO TO: Charles Cornelius, President

FROM: Alfred A. Long, Sales Director

DATE: October 20, 19—

SUBJECT: Marketing of Deer Run site

¶The Deer Run project continues to be a high priority venture. Curtis Marlowe and his staff assure me that the the models have been designed to attract first-time homes buyers. I am asking Melissa Sampson to assume total marketing responsibility for the project. A tentative plan for media exposure will be due with in ten days of her appointment. She will likely have some quite imaginative strategies in her plan. I am confident that the fine reputation of Cornelius Homes, Inc., will be further enchanced by the Deer Run project. A schedule of progress reports for the next year is attached.

{urs}

Attachment

Memo 6

MEMO TO: Melissa Sampson, Sales Associate / **FROM:** Alfred A. Long, Sales Director / **DATE:** October 20, 19— / **SUBJECT:** Deer Run Model Homes

¶The first model homes at the Deer Run site will be ready for showing by January 1. On the basis of your sales performance during the past year, I would like to have you assume total marketing responsibility for the project.

¶This may well come as a complete surprise to you. For that reason, please delay your decision until November 1. You likely will want to think through the nature of this assignment and discuss implications with your family.

¶I know that you can do a fine job with this project; I hope your answer will be "Yes!" / {urs}

Memo 7

The use of nicknames and the omission of middle initials and courtesy titles reflect the informal nature of memos as compared with letters.

The word *RE* is sometimes used in place of the word *SUBJECT* in a memo or letter.

Remember, do not indent the paragraphs in a memo.

Remember to type your own reference initials.

MEMO TO: Pat Fillmore
FROM: Hank Swanson, Personnel Director
DATE: October 20, 19--
RE: Promotion to Department Head

You will be pleased to learn that on November 1 you will be promoted to the position of head of the Housewares Department. This is a reflection of the confidence we have in you based on your performance at Layton's Department Store over the past 18 months.

The Housewares Department plays a big role in achieving the objectives of our anchor store in downtown Lowell. There is a need for someone with broad experience in the retail field who can provide leadership in this department.

Pat, I am confident that as head of the Housewares Department you will fit in well as a member of the Layton management team. Congratulations!

Lesson 44 Business Letters

GOALS: To type 37 wam/3′/3e; to format business letters.

A. Type 2 times.

A. WARMUP

1   Three travel agencies (Jepster & Vilani, Quin & Bott,   11
2 and Zeplin & Wexter) sold the most travel tickets for the   23
3 past 6 months. They sold 785, 834, and 960 total tickets.   34

| 1 | 2 | 3 | 4 | 5 | 6 | 7 | 8 | 9 | 10 | 11 | 12

SKILLBUILDING

B. DIAGNOSTIC PRACTICE: ALPHABET

Turn to the Diagnostic Practice: Alphabet routine beginning on page SB-2. Type one of the Pretest/Posttest paragraphs and identify any errors made. Then type the corresponding drill lines 2 times for each letter on which you made 2 or more errors and 1 time for each letter on which you made only 1 error. Finally, repeat the same Pretest paragraph and compare your performance.

C. SUSTAINED PRACTICE: NUMBERS AND SYMBOLS

4   The proposed road improvement program was approved   10
5 by the county commissioners at their last meeting. There   22
6 were about ten citizens who spoke on behalf of the project.   34

7   The plan calls for blacktopping a 14-mile stretch on   11
8 County Road #235. This is the road that is commonly called   23
9 the "roller coaster" because of all the curves and hills.   34

10   There will be 116 miles blacktopped by J & J, Inc.   10
11 (commonly referred to as the Jones Brothers*). J & J's   22
12 office is at 1798 30th Avenue past the 22d Street bridge.   33

13   Minor road repair costs range from $10,784 to a high   11
14 of $63,450 (39% of the total program costs). The "county   22
15 inspector" is to hold the project costs to 105% of budget!   34

| 1 | 2 | 3 | 4 | 5 | 6 | 7 | 8 | 9 | 10 | 11 | 12

D. Take two 3-minute timings. Determine your speed and errors.

Goal: 37 wam/3'/3e

D. 3-MINUTE TIMING

16   Many people would be quite amazed to find out that   10
17 they are buying insurance which has the same coverage they   22
18 already have or which is too expensive for what one may get   34
19 back after a loss. We should all take time to check our   46
20 policies to ensure that we do not make this mistake.   56
21   Some types of insurance of this kind are straight life   67
22 for singles and children, student health, dread-disease,   79
23 and hospital indemnity. Others are home mortgage, credit   90
24 card, rental-car, job-loss, and contact-lens loss. A study   102
25 of policies might save you money each year.   111

| 1 | 2 | 3 | 4 | 5 | 6 | 7 | 8 | 9 | 10 | 11 | 12

FORMATTING

E. COPY NOTATIONS

Making file copies of all documents you prepare is a good business practice. At times you may also need copies to send to people other than the addressee of the original document.

A copy notation is typed on a document to indicate that someone else besides the addressee is receiving a copy. (See the illustration on page 103.)

1. Type the copy notation on the line below the reference initials or below the attachment or enclosure notation.
2. At the left margin type a lowercase *c* followed by a colon.
3. Press Tab and type the name of the person receiving the copy.
4. If more than one person is receiving a copy, list the names, single spaced, one beneath the other and aligned at the tab.

(continued on next page)

Sincerely,

Lester A. Fagerlie

Lester A. Fagerlie
Superintendent

urs
Enclosure
c: Mrs. Coretta D. Rice
        Dr. Thomas Moore

Letter 16
Business Letter in Block Style

{Current Date} / Mr. and Mrs. Richard Belson / 783 Wellcourt Lane / Mount Vernon, WA 98273-4156 / Dear Mr. and Mrs. Belson:

¶Marian Dickenson has informed me of the visits that she has had with you, and we are pleased that you have made a decision to purchase a home from Garner Homes. We can understand your indecision about purchasing a town house or a one-family house.

¶Your decision likely will be based on these basic differences. With a one-family house you will have the responsibility for the maintenance of both the interior and the exterior. With a town house, of course, you will have responsibility for only the interior. However, you will share the building with one, two, or three other families. Also, you must pay monthly fees to the homeowners' association and abide by their policies.

¶Either Marian or I will be happy to discuss your concerns with you at a time that is convenient. We shall look forward to your call.

Sincerely, / Alfred A. Long / Sales Director / {urs} / c: Marian Dickenson

Letter 17
Business Letter in Block Style

Prepare another letter from Mr. Long (Letter 16). Use the current date and send the letter to Miss Allison E. Grinager / 2408 12th Street / Ellenburg, WA 98926. Use the appropriate salutation and add a copy notation to Marian Dickenson.

¶Thank you for making the decision to purchase a Garner home. Marian Dickenson and I both think that the Delcourt model was the right choice for you. You will enjoy your beautiful new town house for many years.

¶As we agreed, the closing date has been set for November 27 at our office. The interior is completely finished, and the remaining landscaping work will be completed early in the spring of next year.

¶Again, thank you for selecting the Delcourt from Garner Homes. We will have pleasant memories of our several planning sessions.

Letter 18
Business Letter in Block Style

Open the file for Letter 17 and revise it as follows:
1. Send the letter to Ms. Lois Peterson, who lives at 1900 Madison Street in Mount Vernon, WA 98273-0456.
2. Change the closing date to December 1.
3. Delete the last sentence of the letter.

Lesson 45   Letters in Modified-Block Style

GOALS: To improve speed and accuracy; to refine language-arts skills in composing; to format modified-block-style letters.

A. Type 2 times.

A. WARMUP

```
1        Lex was quite pleased with his travel plans; the trip      11
2    to Bozeman was on Flight #578 on July 30, and the return is      23
3    on August 12 on Flight #64.  The ticket will cost $1,090.      34
     |  1  |  2  |  3  |  4  |  5  |  6  |  7  |  8  |  9  |  10  |  11  |  12
```

SKILLBUILDING

B. PACED PRACTICE

Turn to the Paced Practice routine beginning on page SB-14. Take three 2-minute timings, starting at the point where you left off the last time.

LANGUAGE ARTS

C. COMPOSING

C. Answer each question with a complete sentence.

4   What are your best traits that you will bring to your job when you graduate?
5   What are the best traits that you will want to see in your new boss?
6   Would you like to work for a small company or a large company?
7   How much money will you expect to earn each month in your first job?
8   Would you like that first job to be in a small town or a large city?
9   As you begin your first job, what career goal will you have in mind?

FORMATTING

D. MODIFIED-BLOCK-STYLE LETTERS

The modified-block style is one of the most commonly used formats for business letters.

1. Center the letter vertically.
2. Type the date beginning at the centerpoint of the page.
3. Press Enter 4 times and type the inside address at the left margin.
4. Insert 1 blank line before and after the salutation.
5. Type the paragraphs blocked at the left margin (the preferred style) or indented 0.5 inch. Leave 1 blank line between paragraphs.
6. Press Enter twice after the body of the letter and type the complimentary closing at the centerpoint.

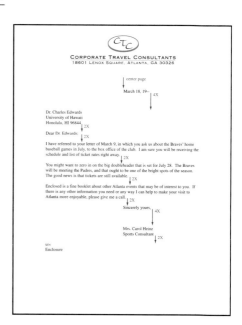

(continued on next page)

7. Press Enter 4 times and type the writer's identification beginning at the centerpoint.

8. Double-space and type your reference initials.

E. WORD PROCESSING: TAB SET AND RULER

Study Lesson 45 in your word processing manual. Complete all of the shaded steps while at your computer. Then format the jobs that follow.

Letter 19
Business Letter in Modified-Block Style

Do not indent the paragraphs.

↓ center vertically

November 29, 19— ↓4X

Mr. and Mrs. Arvey Gates-Henderson

2308 Hannegan Road

Bellingham, Wa 98225 ⁶ ↓2X

Dear Mr. and Mrs. Gates-Henderson: ↓2X

Delores Matlon, who hosted our Ridgeway open house last Saturday, has referred your unanswered questions to me. We are pleased that you are interested in a Garner home. ↓2X

The usual down payment is 20 per cent of the total selling price, but some lending agencies require a smaller amount in certain situations. Garner Homes is not itself involved in home financing, but we work with the financial institutions shown on the enclosed list. ↓2X

Yes, the lot you prefer can accommodate a walk out basement. Delores will be in touch with you soon. We can have your new ridgeway ready for occupancy within 90 days. ↓2X

Sincerely, ↓4X

ss ⌈ Alfred A. Long

Sales Director ↓2X

urs

Enclosure

UNIT NINE Lesson 45 105

Letter 20
Personal-Business Letter in Modified-Block Style

Use November 30, 19—, as the date as you format this personal-business letter to be sent to the Sales Manager at Bachmann's Nursery and Landscaping / 3410 Oneta Avenue / Youngstown, OH 44500-2175. The letter is from Marvin L. Norgaard / 4782 Saranac Avenue / Youngstown, OH 44505-6207. Use the automatic numbering feature for the numbered paragraphs.

If necessary, reset a tab for the numbered list.

Dear Sales Manager:

As you requested on the telephone, I am providing the following list of events relating to my tree problem.

1. On April 15 my wife and I purchased four silver maples at your branch in Warren.

2. We purchased four Japanese red maples at your branch in Niles later that afternoon.

3. After about three months one silver maple and one red maple had died. I phoned both the Warren and Niles branches several times, but no one returned my messages.

As these trees were expensive, I fully expect that you will replace them next spring. I shall look forward to hearing from you.

Sincerely yours,

Letter 21

Progress Check
Business Letter in Modified-Block Style

Set tabs where necessary.

{Current Date} / Mr. Marvin L. Norgaard / 4782 Saranac Avenue / Youngstown, OH 44505-6207 / Dear Mr. Norgaard:

¶This is in response to your recent letter:

¶1. Your two trees will be replaced without cost next spring. The new trees will match the others in both size and color. A copy of our warranty is enclosed.

¶2. The survival rate for trees cannot be perfect; however, we are indeed sorry that you have had to have this temporary setback.

¶3. The communication breakdown with our two branch offices should not have occurred. We will take steps to ensure that this will not happen in the future.

¶You can be confident that the appearance of your yard will be restored as soon as conditions are right next spring.

Yours truly, / Mrs. Alice G. Schmidt, Co-owner / {urs} / Enclosure / c: Mr. George Lambrecht, Co-owner

Reset a 0.5 inch tab for the copy notation.

Lesson 46 — Reports With Author/Year Citations

GOALS: To type 38 wam/3′/3e; to format reports with author/year citations.

A. Type 2 times.

A. WARMUP

```
1      The giant-size trucks, all carrying over 600 bushels,     11
2  were operating "around the clock"; quite a few of them had    23
3  dumped their boxes in Jenks during the last 18 to 20 hours.   35
   | 1 | 2 | 3 | 4 | 5 | 6 | 7 | 8 | 9 | 10 | 11 | 12
```

SKILLBUILDING

B. DIAGNOSTIC PRACTICE: ALPHABET

Turn to the Diagnostic Practice: Alphabet routine beginning on page SB-2. Type one of the Pretest/Posttest paragraphs and identify any errors made. Then type the corresponding drill lines 2 times for each letter on which you made 2 or more errors and 1 time for each letter on which you made only 1 error. Finally, repeat the same Pretest paragraph and compare your performance.

C. Type the paragraph 2 times, using your right thumb to press the space bar in the center.

C. TECHNIQUE PRACTICE: SPACE BAR

```
4      Dee is it.  Abe is here.  Cal is home.  Bev was lost.
5  Edna can see.  Faye can knit.  Gail can fly.  Hal can type.
6  Fly the kite.  Swim a mile.  Hit that ball.  Shut the door.
```

D. Take two 3-minute timings. Determine your speed and errors.

Goal: 38 wam/3′/3e

D. 3-MINUTE TIMING

```
7       The most common type of mortgage for most people over    11
8  the past years has been the fixed-rate mortgage.  With this   23
9  type of loan, the amount of the payment is the same each      34
10 month through the length of the loan period.  This is true    46
11 even if the period of the loan, for example, is as long as    58
12 thirty years.                                                 61
13      Some lenders will quickly point out that for a lot of     72
14 people there may be a better mortgage.  Depending on the       83
15 economy, the size of the monthly payment varies up or down     95
16 each year for an adjustable-rate mortgage.  A cap is set on   107
17 any increases to protect the buyer.                           114
   | 1 | 2 | 3 | 4 | 5 | 6 | 7 | 8 | 9 | 10 | 11 | 12
```

FORMATTING

E. AUTHOR/YEAR CITATIONS

Any information taken from other sources and used in a report must be documented or cited. The author/year method of citation includes the source information in parentheses at the appropriate point within the text.

1. If a source has one author, give the author's last name followed by a comma, the year of publication followed by a comma, and the page number. Example: (Smith, 1995, p. 52).

2. If the author's name appears within the text, give only the year and the page number in parentheses.

3. If a source has two authors, give both last names joined by *&*.

4. If a source has three or more authors, give the last name of the first author followed by *et al.*

DOCUMENT PROCESSING

Report 18
Two-Page Unbound Report

JUDGING A COMPUTER SYSTEM

By Marilyn Clark

Judging the effectiveness of a computer system has taken on a new dimension in the past few years, if for no ~~particular~~ reason other than the wide range of computer systems from which the user can select. It is important ,therefore, that we investigate the criteria that *should* be considered in making this *important* decision.

CRITERION 1: SPEED

This is probably the most ~~critical~~ *obvious* criterion considered when one purchases a computer system. The value of a computer is *directly* related to its speed, and a computer's speed is typically measured in megahertz (MHz). A MHz is one million cycles per second, and many of today's microcomputers run *in the range of* 90 to 100 MHz (Crenshaw, 1996, p. 173).

CRITERION 2: FLEXIBILITY This second criterion is ~~now~~ especially important because of the rapid turnover of hardware and software in the computer ~~industry.~~ The flexibility of a computer system is important for two general reasons:

To accommodate a variety of programs. Hundreds and possibly thousands of software packages are available today to meet the needs of computer users. The computer you purchase must be able to accommodate this variety of software and be flexible enough to change with the increasing sophistication of software packages.

ds To Permit Expandability. Because of the substantial investment you make in a computer, you do not want to commit your resources to a computer that cannot be expanded to handle (1) newer, more powerful operating systems; (2) "memory-hungry" software packages; (3) network interfaces; and (4) additional users (Hartung and Kallock, 1996, p.239)

(continued on next page)

CRITERION 3: CONVENIENCE

A third consideration is convenience. It is easy to learn ~~how to~~ operate your computer? Does the manufacturer stand by it's waranty, and is it difficult to obtain repairs? How convenient is it to buy parts for your computer (such as memory boards and drives) if you want to expand your system? these questions need to be answered, and the answers should be weighed carefully before you purchase a new computer system.

Report 19

Open the file for Report 18 and make the following changes:

1. Change the title to **_JUDGING COMPUTER EFFECTIVENESS._**
2. Use your name in the byline.
3. Change the side headings to the following:
   COMPUTER OPERATING SPEED
   SYSTEM FLEXIBILITY
   OVERALL CONVENIENCE

4. Transpose the two paragraphs that begin with paragraph headings (Paragraphs 4 and 5).
5. Replace the final question in the **Convenience** section with the following: _How far would you have to travel to secure replacement parts (if needed), or how many days would you have to wait if you ordered them from the dealer?_

Reports With Footnotes

GOALS: To improve speed and accuracy; to refine language-arts skills in the use of quotation marks and italics (or the underline); to format reports with footnotes.

A. Type 2 times.

A. WARMUP

```
1      Tag #357X was attached to a black jug that was 1/3      10
2   full of a creamy liquid.  Tags #491Z and #478V were both   22
3   attached to beautiful large lamps (crystal and porcelain).  34
    |  1  |  2  |  3  |  4  |  5  |  6  |  7  |  8  |  9  |  10  |  11  |  12
```

SKILLBUILDING

B. PACED PRACTICE

Turn to the Paced Practice routine beginning on page SB-14. Take three 2-minute timings, starting at the point where you left off the last time.

C. DIAGNOSTIC PRACTICE: NUMBERS

Turn to the Diagnostic Practice: Numbers routine beginning on page SB-5. Type one of the Pretest/Posttest paragraphs and indentify any errors made. Then type the corresponding drill lines 2 times for each number on which you made 2 or more errors and 1 time for each number on which you made only 1 error. Finally, repeat the same Pretest paragraph and compare your performance.

LANGUAGE ARTS

D. Study the rules at the right.

D. QUOTATION MARKS AND ITALICS (OR UNDERLINE)

Rule: Use quotation marks around the titles of newspaper articles, magazine articles, chapters in a book, reports, conferences, and similar items.

"title

The next assignment is to read the chapter entitled "The Kennedy Years."
Kurt read and reread the article, "An Interview With Joe Montana."

Rule: Use quotation marks around a direct quotation.

"quot

The officer replied, "The fingerprints are in the lab for analysis."
"All books are to be returned within one week," the statement reads.

Rule: Italicize (or underline) the titles of books, magazines, newspapers, and other complete published works.

——title

The Fifties by David Halberstam has an excellent coverage of the decade.
The article in Sports Illustrated covered the new basketball rules changes.

Edit the sentences to correct any errors in the use of quotation marks and the underline (or italics).

4 The interest rates were discussed in the November 24 "Tribune."
5 *Types of Life Insurance* is an excellent chapter.
6 His reply was very short and to the point: Definitely!
7 Her proposed title for the report was "Reactions to GATT."
8 The December 2 issue of "Newsweek" had an excellent coverage.
9 The Realtor replied, "The first thing to consider is location."

FORMATTING

E. REPORTS WITH FOOTNOTES

Footnote references indicate the sources of facts or ideas used in a report. Although the footnotes may be formatted in a variety of ways, they have many things in common:

1. Footnotes are indicated in the text by superior figures.
2. Footnotes are numbered consecutively throughout the report.
3. Footnotes appear at the bottom of the page on which the references appear.
4. A footnote should include the name of the author, the title of the book or article, the publisher, the place of publication, the year of publication, and the page number(s).

(continued on next page)

and those workers who initially resisted the technology declare it is easy to learn and has enabled them to compete with any business that has previously published such documents as reports, newsletters, and company brochures.[1] The cost of laying out a page has now been cut considerably with this revolutionary technology.[2] It is no wonder, then, that companies worldwide are enthusiastic about hiring trained personnel with these skills.[3]

---
[1] Louise Plachta and Leonard E. Flannery, *The Desktop Publishing Revolution*, 2d ed., Computer Publications, Inc., Los Angeles, 1991, pp. 558-559.
[2] Terry Denton, "Newspaper Cuts Costs, Increases Quality," *The Monthly Press*, October 1992, p. 160.
[3] Mary Ann Kennedy, "Office Skill Trends," *Personnel Digest*, August 1992, p. 43.

newsletters, and company brochures.[1] The cost of laying out a page has now been cut considerably with this revolutionary technology.[2] It is no wonder, then, that companies worldwide are enthusiastic about hiring trained personnel with these skills.[3]

---
[1] Louise Plachta and Leonard E. Flannery, *The Desktop Publishing Revolution*, 2d ed., Computer Publications, Inc., Los Angeles, 1991, pp. 558-559.

[2] Terry Denton, "Newspaper Cuts Costs, Increases Quality," *The Monthly Press*, October 1992, p. 160.

[3] Mary Ann Kennedy, "Office Skill Trends," *Personnel Digest*, August 1992, p. 43.

F. LONG QUOTATIONS

A paragraph that is quoted or considered essential to a report may be "highlighted" or displayed by using single spacing and indenting the paragraph 0.5 inch from both the left and right margins to make it stand out from the rest of the report.

G. WORD PROCESSING: FOOTNOTES

Study Lesson 47 in your word processing manual. Complete all of the shaded steps while at your computer. Then format the jobs that follow.

Report 20
One-Page Unbound Report With Footnotes

"quot

SHOPPING FOR A HOME

(Part I)

Buying a home is a process that many of us will go through in our lifetime. If we are like many other prospective buyers, we will experience this decision three or four major times in our working years. A home is typically the largest purchase we will make, and it deserves therefore our careful attention.

"Most people think that the most important criteria in shopping for a home is its site."[1]

The site should be on land that is well drained and free from flooding. Check the local city zoning plan to determine if you have chosen a site that is free from flooding and highwater levels. You should also check to see if the ground is stable. Ground that shifts considerably can cause cracks in foundations and walls.

Moreau suggests that a house survey be undertaken in the early stages:

Key problems are encroachments—trees, buildings, or additions to the house that overlap the property line or may violate zoning regulations. The solution can be as simple as moving or removing trees or bushes.[2]

The buying of a house is a major undertaking with a long list of items that must be investigated. To ensure that the building is structurally sound, many prospective buyers use the services of a building inspector.

(continued on next page)

[1]"Building a Home for Tomorrow," *homes & gardens,* (Apr.) 27, 1992, pp. 17-24.
[2]Dan Moreau, "Home Buyers: 7 Traps at Settlement," *Kiplinger's Personal Finance Magazine,* July 1994, p. 68.

Report 21
Two-Page Unbound
Report With
Footnotes

Remember to add a
page number.

Open the file for Report 20 and make the following changes.
1. Change the page reference in footnote 1 to p. 19.

2. Add the following paragraphs and references to the end of the report.

¶The walls, ceiling, and floors (if you have a basement) need to be checked for proper insulation. "Both the depth and 'R' factor need to be checked for proper levels."[3] In addition, cross braces should have been used between the beams supporting a floor.

¶Finally, a thorough check should be made of the heating, cooling, and electrical systems in the home. "These features are often overlooked by prospective homeowners; nevertheless, they are as critical as any others to be examined."[4]

---

[3]"Home Construction in the '90s," *Family Living,* October 9, 1992, p. 75.
[4]Randall Evans and Marie Alexander, *Home Facilities Planning,* Bradshaw Publishing, Salt Lake City, Utah, 1992, p. 164.

Lesson 48   Reports With Endnotes

GOALS: To type 38 wam/3'/3e; to format reports with endnotes.

A. Type 2 times.

A. WARMUP

```
1      "Baxter & Heimark, Inc., sold 63 new vehicles (47 cars    11
2  and 16 trucks) during June," the sales manager reported.      23
3  This is 41.2% of quarterly sales, an amazing achievement!     34
    | 1 | 2 | 3 | 4 | 5 | 6 | 7 | 8 | 9 | 10 | 11 | 12
```

SKILLBUILDING

Pretest
Take a 1-minute timing.
Determine your speed
and errors.

B. PRETEST: ALTERNATE- AND ONE-HAND WORDS

```
4      The chair of the trade committee served notice that    11
5  the endowment grant exceeded the budget.  A million dollars  23
6  was the exact amount.  The greater part will be deferred.    34
    | 1 | 2 | 3 | 4 | 5 | 6 | 7 | 8 | 9 | 10 | 11 | 12
```

Speed Emphasis: If you made 2 or fewer errors on the Pretest, type each *individual* line 2 times.

Accuracy Emphasis: If you made 3 or more errors, type each *group* of lines (as though it were a paragraph) 2 times.

Posttest
Repeat the Pretest timing above and compare performance.

F. Take two 3-minute timings. Determine your speed and errors.

Goal: 38 wam/3'/3e

C. PRACTICE: ALTERNATE-HAND WORDS

7 visible signs amendment visual height turndown suspend maps
8 figment usual authentic emblem island clemency dormant snap
9 problem chair shamrocks profit thrown blandish penalty form

D. PRACTICE: ONE-HAND WORDS

10 trade poplin greater pumpkin eastward plumply barrage holly
11 exact kimono created minikin cassette opinion seaweed union
12 defer unhook reserve minimum attracts million scatter plump

E. POSTTEST: ALTERNATE- AND ONE-HAND WORDS

F. 3-MINUTE TIMING

13   Many people are quite amazed to learn that through   10
14 the years there have been large differences in the average   22
15 annual incomes of those who live in rich states and those   34
16 who live in poorer regions of the country. However, during   46
17 the past decade the states with low per capita incomes have   58
18 pulled closer to the national norm. At the same time some   70
19 of the high-income states have fallen back.   78
20   A reason is that there is now a better-paying mix of   89
21 jobs in the rural states. Many industrial firms have moved   101
22 to these states in an effort to keep down their operating   113
23 costs.   114

| 1 | 2 | 3 | 4 | 5 | 6 | 7 | 8 | 9 | 10 | 11 | 12

FORMATTING

G. REPORTS WITH ENDNOTES

Like footnotes, endnotes indicate sources of facts or ideas used in a report. However, endnotes appear at the end of a report on the last page. Although endnotes may be formatted in a variety of ways, they also have many things in common:

1. Endnotes are indicated in the text by superior figures.

2. Endnotes are numbered consecutively throughout the report.

3. Endnotes appear at the end of the report, either on the last page or on a separate page.

4. Endnotes should include the name of the author, the title of the book or article, the publisher, the place of publication, the year of publication, and the page number(s).

(continued on next page)

H. WORD PROCESSING: ENDNOTES

Study Lesson 48 in your word processing manual. Complete all of the shaded steps while at your computer. Then format the jobs that follow.

Report 22
Two-Page Unbound Report With Endnotes

DESIGNING A COMPUTER SYSTEM

Designing a computer system involves a variety of different operations such as word processing, data processing, communications, printing, and other office-related functions. These areas can be integrated into a very powerful computer system.

DESIGNING THE SYSTEM

One of the first steps is to determine what information is going to be computerized and what personnel will need these resources.[i] This decision should involve all departments in the planning stage of system design. If necessary, you may have to invite input from those departments which are going to be closely involved in computer use after the system has been designed.

There may also be a need to acquire the systems design experience of outside experts—people whose careers consist primarily of planning and developing computer systems for management.[ii]

SELECTING HARDWARE AND SOFTWARE

Bailey believes that "the selection of software precedes any hardware choices. Too many people, however, select the hardware first and then try to match their software with the computer."[iii] After the software has been selected, a decision must be made as to whether hardware should be purchased or leased. Although many firms decide to purchase their own hardware, others have taken the route of time-sharing or remote processing whereby the costs of processing data can be shared with other users.

TRAINING OPERATORS

Many firms neglect this important phase of designing a computer system. It is not enough to offer a one-week training course in an applications package and then expect proficiency from a worker. Training must occur over time to help those who will be using computers every day on the job.

(continued on next page)

Your endnotes may not look like those shown here.

[i]Neal Swanson, *Information Management,* Glencoe/McGraw-Hill, Westerville, Ohio, 1992, p. 372.
[ii]Christine L. Seymour, "The Ins and Outs of Designing Computer Systems," *Information Processing Trends,* January 1991, p. 23.
[iii]Lee Bailey, *Computer Systems Management,* The University of New Mexico Press, Albuquerque, New Mexico, 1992, p. 413.

Report 23
Two-Page Unbound Report With Endnotes

Open the file for Report 22, and add the following paragraph, as well as the accompanying endnote, as the final paragraph and the final endnote in the report.

Finally, it should be recognized that training is an ongoing responsibility. As technology, software, hardware, and procedures change, training must occur regularly and on a continuing basis.[4]

4. Paula Blair, *Administrative Management,* Southern Publishing Company, Atlanta, Georgia, 1992, p. 420.

Lesson 49   Bibliography and Reference Lists

GOALS: To improve speed and accuracy; to refine language-arts skills in spelling; to format a bibliography and a reference list.

A. Type 2 times.

A. WARMUP

```
1       The prize troop received the following extra gifts:        11
2   $20 from Larson's Bakery; $19 from Calsun, Ltd.;* $50 from      22
3   some judges; and quite a number of $5 gift certificates.        34
    |  1  |  2  |  3  |  4  |  5  |  6  |  7  |  8  |  9  | 10  | 11  | 12
```

B. Take three 12-second timings on each line. The scale below the last line shows your wam speed for a 12-second timing.

B. 12-SECOND SPEED SPRINTS

```
4   Joe must try to type as fast as he can on these four lines.
5   The screens were very clear, and the print was easy to see.
6   We will not be able to print the copy until later on today.
7   The disk will not store any of the data if it is not clean.
    | | |5| | |10| | |15| | |20| | |25| | |30| | |35| | |40| | |45| | |50| | |55| | |60
```

C. SUSTAINED PRACTICE: ROUGH DRAFT

```
 8        Various human responses are asymmetrical.  This means     11
 9   that we ask more from one side of the body than the other      23
10   each time we wave, wink, clap our hands, or cross our legs.     34

11        Each one of these actions demands a clear decision,        11
                                                          c
12   usually unconscious and instantaneous, to start the process    23
                                                   begin
13   of moving parts of the body in very different directions.       34
              two

14   All children go though remarkably involved stages as they      12
         infants        r
15   develop their preferried.  As children grows she or he may     24
                        ence        a child
16   favor the right hand, the left, or both the same at times.     35

17   By the time most kids are eibgt or seven stability ocurrs,      12
                                                             c
18   and one hand is permenantly dominent over the other.  For      24
                      a e        a
19   some unknown reason, choose the right hand.                     36
         nine out of ten
   | 1 | 2 | 3 | 4 | 5 | 6 | 7 | 8 | 9 | 10 | 11 | 12
```

LANGUAGE ARTS

D. Type this list of frequently misspelled words, paying special attention to any spelling problems in each word.

Edit the sentences to correct any misspellings.

D. SPELLING

```
20   per provided international receipt commission present other
21   questions maintenance industrial service following position
22   management absence proposal corporate mortgage support well
23   approval recommendations facilities balance experience upon
24   premium currently because procedure addition paid directors

25   The international comission provided a list of proceedures.
26   That industrial maintainance proposal is curently in place.
27   The directers and management supported the recomendations.
28   Those present raised a question about a corperate morgage.
29   Six of the folowing persons have now given their aproval.
30   In adition, Kris has premium experience at the facilitys.
```

E. BIBLIOGRAPHIES

A bibliography is an alphabetic listing of sources typed on a separate page at the end of a report. To format a bibliography:

1. Use the same side margins as the report pages.

2. Center and type the title in all caps and bold approximately 2 inches from the top of the page followed by a double space (press Enter twice).

(continued on next page)

3. Type the first line at the left margin and indent carry over lines 0.5 inch (a hanging indent).

4. Arrange book entries in this order: author (last name first), title (in italics), publisher, place of publication, and year.

5. Arrange journal articles in this order: authors (last name first), article title (in quotation marks), journal title (in italics), series number, volume num-

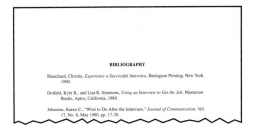

BIBLIOGRAPHY

Blanchard, Christie, *Experience a Successful Interview,* Beringson Printing, New York, 1990.

Dolfeld, Kyle B., and Lisa R. Simmons, *Using an Interview to Get the Job,* Masterson Books, Aptos, California, 1989.

Johnston, Karen C., "What to Do After the Interview," *Journal of Communication,* Vol. 17, No. 6, May 1980, pp. 17-20.

ber, issue number, date, and page number(s).

F. REFERENCE LISTS IN APA FORMAT

Reference lists also indicate sources of ideas or facts used in a report. To format an APA (the American Psychological Association) reference list:

1. Use the same side margins as the report and double spacing.

2. Center and type the title with initial caps approximately 1 inch from the top of the page followed by a double space.

3. Indent the first line of each entry.

4. Arrange book entries in this order: author (last name first), publication date in parentheses, chapter title with only the first word capitalized (no quotation marks or underline), book title (underlined), publisher's city and 2-letter state abbreviation, publisher's name.

5. Arrange periodical entries in this order: author (last name first), publication date in parentheses, article title with only the first word capitalized (no quotation marks or underline), periodical title and volume number underlined, page numbers.

DOCUMENT PROCESSING

Report 24
Bibliography

BIBLIOGRAPHY

Bilanski, Charles R., "Corporate Structures in the Year 2000," *Modern Management,* Vol. 34, July 1994, pp. 21-24.

Calhoun, Josten C., "Warehouse Facilities Needs," *Realty Services Reports,* November 1995, pp. 82-86.

Dahlman, Leland, and Joyce C. Fahler, "Trends for Boards of Directors," *International Press,* Vol. 19, November 1993, pp. 38-47.

Hammersmith Institute, *Bold Positions of the New Administration,* Hammersmith Institute Press, Baltimore, Maryland, 1992.

Jefferson, R. C., *Challenges for Industrial Commissions,* Sampson Books, Des Moines, Iowa, 1994.

Lowell, James T., et al., "Mortgage Experiences of Three Entrepreneurs," *Journal of Free Enterprise,* No. 28, June 1992, pp. 53-56.

Report 25
Reference List in APA
Format

Be sure to underline
titles. Do not type them
in italics.

References

Bilanski, Charles R. (1994, July). Corporate structures in the year 2000. Modern Management, 34, 21-24.

Calhoun, Josten C. (1995, November). Warehouse facilities needs. Realty Services Reports, 82-86.

Dahlman, Leland, & Fahler, Joyce C. Trends for boards of directors. International Press, 19, 38-47.

Hammersmith Institute. (1992). Bold positions of the new administration. Baltimore, MD: Hammersmith Institute Press.

Jefferson, R. C. (1994). Challenges for industrial commissions. Des Moines, Iowa: Sampson Books.

Report 26
Bibliography

BIBLIOGRAPHY *ital*

Byers, Ed, "Newsletter Design," Personal Publisher, Apr. 1994, pp. 14-15.

Collins, Wanda, "Taking a Journey with DTP, TDP Computeing, May 1993, p. 28.

Hirsh, Mitch, DTP Manual for Executives, Computer Press, Denver, 1995.

Salde, Beth, Desk Top Publishing Comes Of Age, Midwestern book company, Kansas City, Missouri, p. 48. 1994

Lesson 50   Preliminary Report Pages

GOALS: To type 39 wam/3'/3e; to format preliminary report pages.

A. Type 2 times.

A. WARMUP

```
1       Did Jack and Hazel see the first Sox ball game?  I've     11
2  heard there were 57,268 people there (a new record).  Your     23
3  home crowd was quiet when the game ended with a 4-9 loss.      34
   |  1  |  2  |  3  |  4  |  5  |  6  |  7  |  8  |  9  |  10  |  11  |  12
```

B. PROGRESSIVE PRACTICE: ALPHABET

Turn to the Progressive Practice: Alphabet routine beginning on page SB-7. Take six 30-second timings, starting at the point where you left off the last time.

C. 12-SECOND SPEED SPRINTS

4 Some of the new pups will be sold to the men who work here.
5 Most of the boys and girls got to go to the fair last week.
6 She has to take six of the top teams to the games that day.
7 Dick said that the right way to do it is also the easy way.

| | | |5| | | |10| | | |15| | | |20| | | |25| | | |30| | | |35| | | |40| | | |45| | | |50| | | |55| | | |60

D. Take two 3-minute timings. Determine your speed and errors.

Goal: 39 wam/3'/3e

D. 3-MINUTE TIMING

8   Just imagine that you are buying your first house and   11
9 have given notice to your landlord that you will move out   23
10 at the end of the month. Then you are amazed to find out   34
11 that a local plumber has a lien on the property. Both the   46
12 seller and the buyer are involved in the legal closing, but   58
13 the buyer is more likely to run into trouble by being lax.   70
14   Whether you are using an attorney or a real estate   80
15 person to help you, problems can be avoided by acquainting   92
16 yourself well in advance with papers to be signed. The   103
17 title search should be conducted well in advance of the   114
18 final closing.   117

| 1 | 2 | 3 | 4 | 5 | 6 | 7 | 8 | 9 | 10 | 11 | 12

FORMATTING

E. TITLE PAGES

Reports should have a title page, which at the very least shows the report title, the writer's name and identification, and the date. The title (and subtitle, if any) are typed on the top part of the page; the writer's name and identification are typed in the center of the page; and the date is typed on the lower part of the page.

To format a title page, follow these steps:

1. Center the page vertically.
2. Center the title in all caps and bold. Double-space, and center the subtitle with initial caps in regular type.
3. Press Enter 12 times, and center the words *Prepared by* followed by a blank line.
4. Center the writer's name and identification on separate lines, single-spaced.
5. Press Enter 12 times, and center the date.

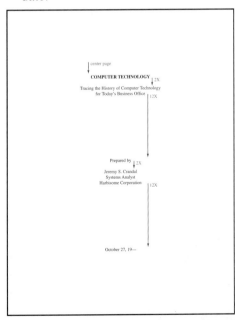

F. TABLE OF CONTENTS

A table of contents (see Report 28) is usually supplied with long reports. The table of contents identifies the major sections of a report and the page numbers where they can be found.

1. Use the same margins that were used for the report.

2. Center and type the word **CONTENTS** approximately 2 inches from the top of the page in all caps and bold, followed by a double space.

3. Type the major headings in all caps; double-space before and after them.

4. Indent subheadings (using default tabs) and type them with initial caps and single spacing.

5. Align page numbers flush right, and type them with dot leaders—a series of periods that helps guide the reader's eye across the page to the page number on the same line.

G. WORD PROCESSING: TAB SET—DOT LEADERS

Study Lesson 50 in your word processing manual. Complete all of the shaded steps while at your computer. Then format the jobs that follow.

DOCUMENT PROCESSING

Report 27
Title Page

THE SECRETARY IN TODAY'S AUTOMATED OFFICE

Maintaining Traditional Skills While Developing High-Tech Competence

*Prepared by
Phyllis G. Browe
Systems Analyst
The Western Office Group*

December 9, 19--

Report 28
Table of Contents

↓2 inches **CONTENTS**

(continued on next page)

Report 29

Progress Check
Two-Page Unbound
Report With Endnotes

MANAGING YOUR TIME

The Key to Success in an Office

Using your time efficiently in an office will help you get more work done in less time. Wasted time can never be recovered; therefore, the ideas in this report will help you better manage your time.

PLAN YOUR WORK EACH DAY

Take a few minutes at the beginning of each workday to plan your day's activities.[1] Decide which tasks should be first and which tasks can be completed later.

Obtaining Necessary Materials. Gather all necessary supplies and materials that you will need to accomplish the tasks that must be completed.[2] Have all your paper, pens and pencils, and other materials at your desk and within easy reach whenever you need to use them.

Completing Individual Tasks. Regardless of the work in which you are involved, it is usually better to finish one task before beginning another. However, if your supervisor assigns you a task that must be accomplished immediately, the original task may have to be completed later. If this happens, identify the point of your progress on your original task so that you can resume your work with little hesitation.

Before you begin any task, be sure you have a thorough understanding of what must be done. If you need to ask a question, be sure you have reviewed all of your materials for a possible answer before interrupting someone. If

(continued on next page)

there are several questions, write them down so that you ask them in the proper sequence.

SPEND YOUR TIME WISELY

Although you may want to work from beginning to end on a task, it may be better to take a short break or two when the task is of considerable length. By taking a few minutes to relax both mentally and physically, you likely will finish your task in less time.

1. Dorothy R. Crattburg, *Managing Time Wisely,* Trafton Valley Press, Monterey, California, 1995, p. 7.

2. Donald E. Wilkins and Lila G. Wahlstrom, "Time Is Money," *The New Office,* March 1995, pp. 35-37.

Lesson 51 Resumes

GOALS: To improve speed and accuracy; to refine language-arts skills in the use of commas; to format resumes.

A. Type 2 times.

A. WARMUP

```
1      "Look at them!  Have you ever seen such huge birds?"    11
2    When questioned later on an exam, about 80% to 90% of the   23
3    junior girls were amazed to learn that they were ospreys.   34
   |  1  |  2  |  3  |  4  |  5  |  6  |  7  |  8  |  9  |  10  |  11  |  12
```

SKILLBUILDING

B. DIAGNOSTIC PRACTICE: ALPHABET

Turn to the Diagnostic Practice: Alphabet routine beginning on page SB-2. Type one of the Pretest/Posttest paragraphs and identify any errors made. Then type the corresponding drill lines 2 times for each letter on which you made 2 or more errors and 1 time for each letter on which you made only 1 error. Finally, repeat the same Pretest paragraph and compare your performance.

C. PACED PRACTICE

Turn to the Paced Practice routine beginning on page SB-14. Take three 2-minute timings, starting at the point where you left off the last time.

LANGUAGE ARTS

D. Study the rules at the right.

D. COMMAS

Rule: Use a comma between each item in a series of three or more.

,ser

,ser

The invoice, contract, and cashier's check were enclosed.
Ms. Dolezal, Mr. Kneisl, and Mrs. Sperry signed the document.

Rule: Use a comma before and after a transitional expression (such as *therefore* or *however*).

,tran

,tran

They learned, however, that Mrs. Kneisl also had to sign.
Therefore, the closing will be delayed until November 26.

Rule: Use a comma before and after a direct quotation.

,quot

,quot

Ms. Dolezal inquired, "What materials shall we bring along?"
"We will meet at 3 p.m. at the bank," Ms. Trask informed us.

(continued on next page)

4 Liz sent items to the lawyer, the bank and the courthouse.
5 The abstract, deed, and sales contract were all in order.
6 However Mrs. Sperry's flight was two hours late.
7 Therefore, the closing was also delayed for two hours.
8 "The occupancy date is November 28" replied Ms. Trask.
9 Mrs. Kneisl said, "We want to thank you for your kindness."

FORMATTING

E. RESUMES

When you apply for a job, you may be asked to submit a resume. The purpose of a resume is to convey your qualifications for the position you are seeking. A resume should include the following:

1. Personal information (name, address, telephone number).
2. A summary of your educational background and special training.
3. Previous work experience.
4. Any activities or accomplishments that relate to the position for which you are applying.
5. (Optional) Your career goal.
6. (Optional) References. References

should consist of at least three people who can tell a prospective employer what kind of worker you are.

Often, your resume creates the first impression you make on a prospective employer; be sure it is free of errors.

A variety of styles is acceptable for formatting a resume (see Illustrations 1 and 2 that follow). Choose a style (or design one) that is attractive and which enables you to get all the needed information on one or two pages. A one-page resume should be vertically centered; the first page of a two-page resume should start approximately 2 inches from the top of the page.

Illustration 1   Illustration 2

F. WORD PROCESSING: FONT/FONT SIZE AND LINES

Study Lesson 51 in your word processing manual. Complete all of the shaded steps while at your computer. Then format the jobs that follow.

Type the following resume in the same format as Illustration 1 on page 124. Follow these steps:

1. Center the page vertically.
2. Center and type the name in 18-point font size, all caps, and bold.
3. Turn off bold, return to 12-point font size, press Enter twice, and insert a horizontal line.
4. Insert a blank line after the line, then center and type the address and telephone number.
5. At the left margin, type the side heading *EDUCATION* in all caps and bold.
6. Align the remaining text for the section approximately 1.5 inches from the left margin. Type the name of the school and any degrees earned.
7. Press Enter twice and type the course information aligned with the previous text. Press Enter twice and complete the remaining information.
8. Press Enter twice before beginning each new section.

SHANNON T. ANDREWS

349 Sycamore Terrace, Sioux City, IA 51104
712-555-7256
↓2X

EDUCATION   West Iowa Business College, Sioux City, Iowa
Degree: A.A. in Office Systems, May 1995
↓2X

Courses in accounting, business communication, computer application software (Lotus, dBase, WordPerfect, and Microsoft Word), office systems management, and telecommunications.
↓2X

Wayne High School, Wayne, Nebraska
Graduated: May 1993
↓2X

EXPERIENCE   Computer Systems Technician, June 1993-Present
Kramer & Kramer, Sioux City, Iowa
Duties include reviewing, installing, and updating software programs used for processing legal documents and monitoring computer network system for branch offices of Kramer & Kramer.
↓2X

Salesclerk, May 1991 to May 1993 (part-time)
Blanchard's Department Store, Wayne, Nebraska
Duties included selling sporting goods and operating Panasonic cash register. Assisted sales manager in completing monthly sales reports generated by WordPerfect and Lotus software programs.
↓2X

(continued on next page)

ACTIVITIES   President, FBLA Chapter, 1992

Spanish Honor Society, 1993

Academic Scholarships, 1994-1995

Member, Intramural Soccer Team, 1994-1995

Captain, American Legion Softball Team, 1994

↓2X

REFERENCES   References available on request.

Report 31
Resume

Open the file for Report 30 and make the following changes:

1. Change the name to 20-point font size, and change the address to: *927 Dace Avenue, Sioux City, IA 51101.*

2. Change the side headings to 14-point font size, and center them. Press Enter 2 times before and after the headings. Begin all of the section text at the left margin.

3. Add desktop publishing and program-ming (Pascal) to the Education section before telecommunications.

4. Replace the first work experience with *Programmer, June 1993-Present / Teledyne Inc. / Sioux City, Iowa / Duties include writing Pascal programs to monitor quality control within Research and Development.*

5. Delete the Spanish Honor Society and the Softball Team entries in the Activities section.

Lesson 52   Letters of Application

GOALS: To type 39 wam/5′/5e; to format letters of application.

A. Type 2 times.

A. WARMUP

```
1      Mark these quilts down by 25%:  #489, #378, and #460.   11
2  Leave the prices as they are for the remainder of the sizes  23
3  in that section.  Three adjoining sections will be next.   34
   |  1  |  2  |  3  |  4  |  5  |  6  |  7  |  8  |  9  |  10  |  11  |  12
```

SKILLBUILDING

B. Take three 12-second timings on each line. The scale below the last line shows your wam speed for a 12-second timing.

B. 12-SECOND SPEED SPRINTS

```
4  Most of those boys and girls said they would go to college.
5  Some said that they would need to gain some new job skills.
6  Many of them plan to go on to school for two or four years.
7  Most of them do have a good idea what their majors will be.
   | | | |5| | | |10| | | |15| | | |20| | | |25| | | |30| | | |35| | | |40| | | |45| | | |50| | | |55| | | |60
```

C. PROGRESSIVE PRACTICE: NUMBERS

Turn to the Progressive Practice: Numbers routine beginning on page SB-11. Take six 30-second timings, starting at the point where you left off the last time.

D. Take two 5-minute timings. Determine your speed and errors.

Goal: 39 wam/5'/5e

D. 5-MINUTE TIMING

8   We hear and read a lot about the importance of being   11

9 conscientious about our jobs. While this cannot be denied,   23

10 it is also important for individuals to learn how to relax   35

11 and enjoy their hobbies, their friends, and their family   46

12 when they are away from their place of work.   55

13   There are dozens of different types of vacations that   66

14 are unique in different parts of the country. But many   77

15 people all over the country elect to take their vacations   89

16 in the fall during the color season. They head north to   101

17 the mountains so that they can experience the breathtaking   112

18 beauty of the tree leaves as they change color. Leaves may   124

19 turn to gold or to orange before they fall from the trees;   136

20 some turn to red or to burgundy.   142

21   These scenes have been described by some as wildfires   153

22 of beauty. In addition to the many mountain ranges across   165

23 the country where fall colors abound, the northern states   177

24 from the west coast to the east coast are favorite sites   188

25 during the prime foliage season.   195

| 1 | 2 | 3 | 4 | 5 | 6 | 7 | 8 | 9 | 10 | 11 | 12

FORMATTING

E. LETTERS OF APPLICATION

A letter of application is sent along with a resume to a prospective employer. Together, the letter and the resume serve to introduce a person to the organization.

The letter of application should be no longer than one page and should include (1) the job you are applying for and how you learned of the job, (2) the highlights of your enclosed resume, and (3) a request for an interview.

DOCUMENT PROCESSING

Letter 22
Modified-Block Style

March 15, 19— / Ms. Kay Brewer, Personnel Director / Blanchard Computer Systems / 2189 Dace Avenue / Sioux City, IA 51107 / Dear Ms. Brewer:
¶Please consider me as an applicant for the position of data records operator advertised in the March 13 edition of the *Sioux City Press*.
¶In May I will graduate with an A.A. degree in Office Systems from West Iowa Business College. My enclosed resume shows that I have completed courses

(continued on next page)

in Lotus, dBase, WordPerfect, Microsoft Word, and office systems. These software packages are used in your Blanchard offices in Sioux City.

¶The position with your company is very appealing to me. If you wish to interview me for this position, please call me at 712-555-7256.

Sincerely, / Shannon T. Andrews / 349 Sycamore Terrace / Sioux City, IA 51104 / Enclosure

Letter 23
Block Style

August 10, 19— / Personnel Director / Arlington Communications / 2403 Sunset Lane / Arlington, TX 76015-3148 / Dear Personnel Director:

Please consider me as an applicant for a position with~~you~~. *Arlington Communications*

The two part~~-~~time jobs I held during the summer months at your company convinced me that <u>arlington</u> <u>comunications</u> is the place_I want to work. My strengths have always been in the_arts, as you can see on the_resume, which ~~reveals~~ a number of courses in English_~~and~~ speech. *communication* *where* *enclosed* *lists* *, and communication technology*

If you would like to interview me_this summer or fall,_call me at 214-255-2340. I look forward to hearing from you. *for any possible openings* *please* *5,*

Sincerely yours, / Kenneth R. Talbot / 6892 Center_Road / Garland, TX 75041-9285 / Enclosure *ville*

Letter 24
Block Style

Open the file for Letter 23, and revise it to be sent to Ms. Lila Mae Colbert, of Texas Media, Inc., at 3809 Fourth Street West in Arlington, TX 76013. Delete the second sentence in the second paragraph.

Lesson 53   Employment Test

GOALS: To improve speed and accuracy; to refine language-arts skills in proofreading; to format documents used in employment tests.

A. Type 2 times.

A. WARMUP

```
 1      Janice had sales of over $23,000; Kathy's sales were      11
 2   only $17,368 for the same quiet period.  They agreed that    22
 3   some inventory sizes were wrong and should be exchanged.      34
       | 1  | 2  | 3  | 4  | 5  | 6  | 7  | 8  | 9  | 10 | 11 | 12
```

Pretest
Take a 1-minute timing. Determine your speed and errors.

B. PRETEST: COMMON LETTER COMBINATIONS

4   They formed an action committee to force a motion for   11
5   a ruling on the contract case. This enabled them to comply   23
6   within the lawful time period and convey a common message.   35

| 1 | 2 | 3 | 4 | 5 | 6 | 7 | 8 | 9 | 10 | 11 | 12

Practice
Speed Emphasis: If you made 2 or fewer errors on the Pretest, type each *individual* line 2 times.
Accuracy Emphasis: If you made 3 or more errors, type each *group* of lines (as though it were a paragraph) 2 times.

C. PRACTICE: WORD BEGINNINGS

7   for forget formal format forces forums forked forest formed
8   per perils period perish permit person peruse perked pertly
9   com combat comedy coming commit common compel comply comets

D. PRACTICE: WORD ENDINGS

10   ing acting aiding boring buying ruling saving hiding dating
11   ble bubble dabble double enable feeble fumble tumble usable
12   ion action vision lesion nation bunion lotion motion legion

Posttest
Repeat the Pretest timing and compare performance.

E. POSTTEST: COMMON LETTER COMBINATIONS

F. Type the paragraph 2 times, keeping your eyes on the copy so that you do not lose your place as you type these long, difficult words.

F. TECHNIQUE PRACTICE: CONCENTRATION

13   The syncopated rhythm titillated the audience as the
14   musicians performed. The music of Mauritania, Zimbabwe,
15   Guinea, Zaire, Mozambique, Namibia, and Zambia was played.

LANGUAGE ARTS

G. Edit this paragraph to correct any typing or formatting errors.

G. PROOFREADING

16   The Smith were please to learn from their insurance
17   agent that the covrage ona $50,000 life insurance policy
18   policy would be increased by $ 20,000 at no extra cost.
19   The continued to pay the same premum, not knowing that the
20   cash value of thier original policy was being taped each
21   month to pay an addditional premium for hte new coverage.

DOCUMENT PROCESSING

Employment Test A

Letter 25   ,quot
Block Style

November 1/4, 19— / Mr. Margin T. Hegman / 182 Bonanza Avenue /

Anchorage, AK 99502 / Dear Mr. Hegman:

¶I recently told Sid Loft about your (Feb.) 15th visit. He replied, "That's terrific!"

Your discussion on the future of multi/media presentations with CD-ROM

(continued on next page)

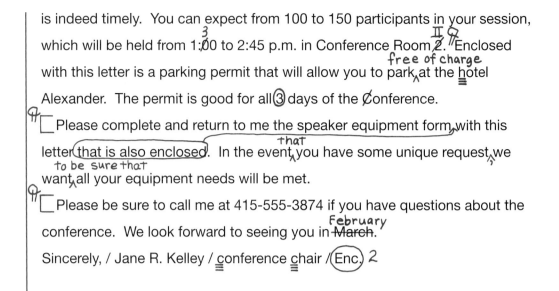

is indeed timely. You can expect from 100 to 150 participants in your session, which will be held from 1:00 to 2:45 p.m. in Conference Room 2. "Enclosed with this letter is a parking permit that will allow you to park free of charge at the hotel Alexander. The permit is good for all 3 days of the conference.

Please complete and return to me the speaker equipment form with this letter that is also enclosed. In the event that you have some unique request, we want to be sure that all your equipment needs will be met.

Please be sure to call me at 415-555-3874 if you have questions about the conference. We look forward to seeing you in February March.

Sincerely, / Jane R. Kelley / conference chair / Enc. 2

Employment Test B
Report 32

This is *Page 3* of a company report which contains several errors in punctuation, spelling, and grammar that must be identified and corrected.

Double-space the report, and use standard margins for an unbound report.

¶**Income Stock Fund.** The Income Stock Funds' objective is current income, and the potential for capital appreciation.

¶The first six month's of the fiscal year produced a total return of 25.4%, including a dividend income distribution. Electric utilities petroleum and drugs is the largest holdings in the portfolio. Net assets has grown to $225.7 million from $104.5 million on September 1.

¶**Income fund.** The Income Fund's investment objective are maximum current income without undue risk to principle. Consistant with this objective, the fund held 48.3% in mortgage securities, 12.8% in corporate bonds, and 19.9% in electric utility common stocks,

,ser

,tran

¶In addition, the fund also has a portion invested in high-yeild common stocks, which have yeilds almost as high as bonds.

¶**Money Market Fund.** The money Market Fund's investment objective is maximum current yield without undue risk to principle. There are no deviation from this policy in order to achieve additional yield. During the past six months the yield advantage increased from 25 basis points to 29 basis points. Net assits of the fund have grown to $1,375.5 milion from $927.5 milion on September 30.

Employment Test C

Table 16
Boxed Table

Prepare a copy of this table, supplying missing information where necessary.

Size the table so that Column 1 entries fit on a single line.

STATEMENT OF EXPENSES June 30, 19--			
Expense	Income Stock ($)	Income Fund ($)	Money Market ($)
Management Fees	923,928	232,687	2,418,661
Registration Fees	35,427	11,855	66,121
TOTAL	?	?	?

Lesson 54   Follow-Up Letters

GOALS: To type 39 wam/5'/5e; to format follow-up letters.

A. Type 2 times.

A. WARMUP

```
1        The new firm, Kulver & Zweidel, will be equipped to      11
2   handle from 1/6 to 1/4 of Martin's tax needs after they       22
3   move to the new location at 1970 Gansby, just east of Main.   34
```
| 1 | 2 | 3 | 4 | 5 | 6 | 7 | 8 | 9 | 10 | 11 | 12

SKILLBUILDING

B. Take three 12-second timings on each line. The scale below the last line shows your wam speed for a 12-second timing.

B. 12-SECOND SPEED SPRINTS

```
4   Pat went back to the store where he had seen the red shirt.
5   The salesclerk acted as though she had not seen him before.
6   There was a huge change when he walked into a second store.
7   Pat was met at the front door with a smile and a handshake.
```
| | | |5| | |10| | |15| | |20| | |25| | |30| | |35| | |40| | |45| | |50| | |55| | |60

C. PROGRESSIVE PRACTICE: ALPHABET

Turn to the Progressive Practice: Alphabet routine beginning on page SB-7. Take six 30-second timings, starting at the point where you left off the last time.

D. 5-MINUTE TIMING

D. Take two 5-minute timings. Determine your speed and errors.

Goal: 39 wam/5'/5e

8	While most home-repair contractors are trustworthy,	10
9	honest, hardworking people, most of us have heard stories	22
10	about individuals who have been cheated by unscrupulous con	34
11	artists. If you are urged to sign a contract quickly for	46
12	home repairs, that should be a signal that it is time to	57
13	slow down and take a better look at your position.	67
14	It does not make sense to go forward without getting	78
15	an estimate from at least one other contractor or business.	90
16	Most people have been surprised to see the wide range of	102
17	estimates they have received.	108
18	You should not even think of signing a contract with a	119
19	business or any contractor before you check its record of	131
20	performance in the city or town in which you live. You may	143
21	be well rewarded for the extra time that it takes. Ask for	155
22	names of past customers so you can ask about the quality of	167
23	the work and whether or not it was completed on schedule.	178
24	You may even be able to view some jobs that were recently	190
25	finished and then decide.	195

| 1 | 2 | 3 | 4 | 5 | 6 | 7 | 8 | 9 | 10 | 11 | 12 |

FORMATTING

E. FOLLOW-UP LETTERS

As soon as possible after your interview (preferably the next day), you should send a follow-up letter to the person who conducted your interview.

In the letter, thank the person who conducted the interview, highlight your particular strengths, and restate your interest in working for that organization. A positive tone is very important.

DOCUMENT PROCESSING

Letter 26
Modified-Block Style With Blocked Paragraphs

September 12, 19-- / Ms. Carole Rothchild / Personnel
Director / Arlington Communications / 2403 Sunset
Lane / Arlington, TX 76015-3148 / Dear Ms. Rothchild:
It was a real pleasure meeting with you
yesterday and learning of the wonderful career

(continued on next page)

opportunities at Arlington Communications. I enjoyed meeting all the people, especially those working in the Publications Division. Thank you for taking the time to tell me about the interesting start-up history of the company and its location in Arlington.

I believe my experience and job skills match nicely with those you are seeking for a desktop publishing individual, and this position is exactly what I have been looking for. You may recall that I have had experience with all of the equipment and software that are used in your office.

Please let me hear from you when you have made your decision on this position. I am very much interested in joining the professional staff at Arlington Communications.

Sincerely yours, / Kenneth R. Talbot / 6829 Centerville Road / Garland, TX 75041-9285

Letter 27
Block Style

April 7, 19— / Ms. Kay Brewer, Personnel Director / Blanchard Computer Systems / 2189 Dace Avenue / Sioux City, IA 51107 / Dear Ms. Brewer:

Thanks for the opportunity of interviewing you with Blanchard computer Systems yesterday. Please express my appreciation to all of those who were involved.

The interview gave me a very good feeling about the company. The positive description that you shared me with convinced me that blanchard is in deed a company at which I would like to work. I was greatly impressed with the summary of social service programs for citizens throughout the community that are sponsored by Blanchard.

You may recall that I have had experience with all of the equipment that is used. It appears to me that my strengths in software application computer soft ware and office systems would blend in well with your company profile.

I look forward to hearing you from soon regarding your decision on the position of data records operator.

(continued on next page)

Sincerely, / Shannon T. Andrews / 349 Sycamore Terrace / Sioux City, IA 51104

Letter 28
Block Style

Open the file for Letter 27, and revise it to be sent to Mr. William E. Boyd / Personnel Director / Hawkeye Computers, Inc. / 5604 Melrose Avenue / Sioux City, IA 51105. It will be necessary to replace *Blanchard Computer Systems* with *Hawkeye Computers, Inc.* in both the first and the second paragraphs.

Lesson 55 — Integrated Employment Project

GOALS: To improve speed and accuracy; to refine language-arts skills in composing; to format employment documents.

A. Type 2 times.

A. WARMUP

```
1       Prices were quickly lowered (some by as much as 50%)        11
2  at Rich's garage sale.  He could see that extra sales would     23
3  not be over the 25%* he had projected to finance the prize.     35
   | 1 | 2 | 3 | 4 | 5 | 6 | 7 | 8 | 9 | 10 | 11 | 12
```

SKILLBUILDING

B. Take a 1-minute timing on the first paragraph to establish your base speed. Then take four 1-minute timings on the remaining paragraphs. As soon as you equal or exceed your base speed on one paragraph, advance to the next, more difficult paragraph.

B. SUSTAINED PRACTICE: CAPITALIZATION

```
4        There are several different approaches that one can       11
5  take when considering a major purchase.  Some people make       22
6  the mistake of simply going to a store and making a choice.     34

7        When one couple decided to buy a chest-type freezer,      11
8  they looked at a consumer magazine in the library.  The         22
9  Sears, Amana, and General Electric were shown as best buys.     34

10       That same issue of their magazine compared electric       11
11 ranges.  Jonathan and Mary Ann found that the Maytag, Magic     23
12 Chef, Amana, and Gibson were determined to be best buys.        34

13       Best buys for full-size microwave ovens were the Sharp    11
14 Carousel, Panasonic, and GoldStar Multiwave.  The midsize       23
15 models were the Frigidaire, Panasonic, and Sears Kenmore.       34
   | 1 | 2 | 3 | 4 | 5 | 6 | 7 | 8 | 9 | 10 | 11 | 12
```

LANGUAGE ARTS

D. Answer each question with a complete sentence.

D. COMPOSING

16 Why do you need to prepare in advance for an interview?
17 What do good grades have to do with getting the right job?
18 How can good communication skills help in the world of work?
19 How might knowledge of a foreign language help on the job?
20 Why are ethics important in business?
21 How can you improve your confidence in speaking before a group?

DOCUMENT PROCESSING

Report 33
Resume

Letter 29
Application Letter

Letter 30
Follow-up Letter

In this unit you have learned how to prepare a resume, an application letter, and a follow-up letter—all of which are frequently used by job applicants.

You will now use these skills in preparing the documents necessary to apply for the job described in the newspaper ad that follows.

Prepare a resume for yourself as though you are applying for the job described in the ad in the next column. Use actual data in the resume. Assume that you have just graduated from a postsecondary program. Include school-related activities, courses you have completed, and any part-time or full-time work experience you may have acquired. Make the resume as realistic as possible, and provide as much information as you can about your background.

Prepare an application letter to apply for the position described in the ad. Date your letter March 10. Emphasize the skills you have acquired during your years in school and while working in any part-time or full-time positions. Use Letters 22 and 23 (pages 127 and 128) as guides for your letter.

Assume that your interview was held on March 25 and that you would very much like to work for Tri-State Publishing. It is now the day after your interview. Prepare a follow-up letter expressing your positive thoughts about working for Tri-State. Use Letters 26 and 27 (pages 132 and 133) as guides for your letter.

COMPUTER APPLICATIONS SPECIALIST

Tri-State Publishing, a New York City-based publisher specializing in trade and industrial titles, has an immediate opening for a Computer Applications Specialist whose primary responsibilities include word processing and desktop publishing.

This is an entry-level position within the Public Relations Department in our Philadelphia office. Applicant must have had training in WordPerfect and desktop publishing (preferably PageMaker or Ventura). Knowledge of computer operating systems is also helpful.

Excellent company benefits available that include a comprehensive medical and dental program, disability insurance, and a company credit union.

If interested, send a letter of application and resume to:

Mr. David E. Frantelli
Personnel Department
Tri-State Publishing
9350 Andover Road
Philadelphia, PA 19114

Tri-State is an Equal Opportunity Employer

Lesson 56   Allwood Publications

GOALS: To type 40 wam/5'/5e; to format various business documents.

A. Type 2 times.

A. WARMUP

```
1      Kyu Choi jumped at the opportunity to assume 40% of      11
2  the ownership of the restaurant.  Alverox & Choi Chinese     22
3  Cuisine will be opening quite soon at 1528 Wayzata Street.    34
   |  1  |  2  |  3  |  4  |  5  |  6  |  7  |  8  |  9  |  10  |  11  |  12
```

SKILLBUILDING

B. PROGRESSIVE PRACTICE: ALPHABET

Turn to the Progressive Practice: Alphabet routine beginning on page SB-7. Take six 30-second timings, starting at the point where you left off the last time.

C. Type the paragraph 2 times, using the caps lock key and the shift key correctly.

C. TECHNIQUE PRACTICE: SHIFT/CAPS LOCK

```
4      RHONDA KORDICH was promoted on APRIL 1 to SENIOR
5  SECRETARY.  The SOLD sign replaced the FOR SALE sign at
6  1904 ELM DRIVE.  The trip to DULUTH was on INTERSTATE 35.
```

D. Take two 5-minute timings. Determine your speed and errors.

Goal: 40 wam/5'/5e

D. 5-MINUTE TIMING

```
7       All of us have seen too many newspaper articles that     11
8   describe tragic auto accidents on our nation's highways.    22
9   This is true in spite of the efforts of both the government  34
10  and the auto industry to reduce the number of accidents.     46
11  The development of air bags and antilock brakes in recent    58
12  years has been very good.  And there will be many more       69
13  momentous safety breakthroughs in the future.               78
14       There will be cruise control that automatically slows   89
15  a car to prevent it from getting too close to the vehicle   100
16  in front.  The system will use radar to check the space     112
17  between the cars and will quickly apply the brakes.         122
18       Infrared sensors will be introduced that will extend a  133
19  driver's night vision, enabling the driver to see people or 145
20  objects in the dark.  Video cameras will be controlled by   157
21  computers to read lane markings and alert all drivers to    168
22  take corrective action when needed.  We will also see autos 180
23  that can sense a skid and apply one brake to keep the car   192
24  straight.  All these changes are amazing.                   200
    |  1  |  2  |  3  |  4  |  5  |  6  |  7  |  8  |  9  |  10  |  11  |  12
```

DOCUMENT PROCESSING

Situation: Today is November 25, 19—. You are working as an administrative assistant to Ms. Maridel B. Ash, editorial director of Allwood Publications. The following jobs are to be completed in the order shown.

Letter 31
Block Style

Ms. Victoria F. Eng
85 Holly Drive
Chadron, NE 69337

Dear Ms. Eng:

Thank you very much for your inquiry about Allwood Publications. It is a pleasure to respond.

We publish four magazines. Their names, the names of their editors, and their cost per year are listed on the enclosed table. All are subscription magazines. None are sold at newsstands.

If you would like any other details, please let me know.

Sincerely yours,

M. Ash

Remember to add the enclosure notation.

Table 17
Open Table

ALLWOOD PUBLICATIONS

Title	Editor	Cost Per Year
Parenting Today	Roberta Holt	$19.97
Just for Fun	Greg Harrison	$12.95
Puzzle Quest	Tina Ho	$12.95
Only for Children	Maria Montoya	$17.20
TOTAL		$63.07

Memo 8
Rough Draft

MEMO

TO: All Editors

FROM: Maridel B. Ash, Editorial Director

DATE: November 52, 19—

SUBJECT: Meeting on December 8

A meeting for all editors has been scheduled for 1 p.m. on December 8. We will be discussing these the following topics:

1. The use of eye-catching icons to highlight the that will regular features in our monthly magazines.

2. The introduction of a new feature entitled "Small talk" for in Only for Children *ital* as proposed by Maria Montoya.

3. The integration of some of the features that are now used in Parenting *ital* exclusively *ital* Today into our other publications.

Lesson 57   International Marketing

GOALS: To improve speed and accuracy; to refine language-arts skills in the use of hyphens, grammar, and abbreviations; to format various business documents.

A. Type 2 times.

A. WARMUP

```
1       Lex issued an ultimatum:  Quit driving on the lawn or    11
2  I will call the police.  A fine of $50 (or even more) may    22
3  be levied against Kyle who lives at 12549 Zaine in Joplin.   34
   |  1  |  2  |  3  |  4  |  5  |  6  |  7  |  8  |  9  |  10  |  11  |  12
```

B. DIAGNOSTIC PRACTICE: ALPHABET

Turn to the Diagnostic Practice: Alphabet routine beginning on page SB-2. Type one of the Pretest/Posttest paragraphs and identify any errors made. Then type the corresponding drill lines 2 times for each letter on which you made 2 or more errors and 1 time for each letter on which you made only 1 error. Finally, repeat the same Pretest paragraph and compare your performance.

C. PACED PRACTICE

Turn to the Paced Practice routine beginning on page SB-14. Take three 2-minute timings, starting at the point where you left off the last time.

LANGUAGE ARTS

D. HYPHENS, AGREEMENT, AND ABBREVIATION

D. Study the rules at the right.

Rule: Hyphenate compound adjectives that come before a noun (unless the first word is an adverb ending in *ly*).

-adj
-adj

The determination of production goals is a high-level decision.
The reduction in hard-copy files saved the company thousands of dollars.

Rule: Use singular verbs and pronouns with singular subjects and plural verbs and pronouns with plural subjects.

Agr sing
Agr plur

Neither Karla nor Marie must change her computer.
Both Richard and Erik sold their used books at a good price.

Rule: In nontechnical writing, do not abbreviate common nouns (such as *dept.* or *pkg.*), compass points, units of measure, or the names of months, days of the week, cities, or states (except in addresses).

Abb no
Abb no

Regular department meetings are on the first and third Mondays each month.
The proposed office site is 2 miles north of the old one in Los Angeles.

Edit the sentences to correct any errors in the use of the hyphen, verb-pronoun agreement, or abbreviations.

4 The purchasing director was good at locating low-cost software.
5 All newly-hired employees attended three orientation workshops.
6 Either Glenda or Phyllis are handling the payroll this month.
7 The auditor and the treasurer are meeting with the president.
8 The new fleet cars are averaging about 21 miles per gal.
9 The remaining men will be transferred in Jan. to Athens, Ga.

DOCUMENT PROCESSING

Situation: Today is July 16, 19—, and you are the secretary to Mr. Carter B. Phillips, vice president for marketing of Rockford International in Jacksonville, Florida. The company markets electronic products all over the world. Mr. Phillips wants the letter typed first; he prefers the modified-block-style letter with standard punctuation.

Memo 9

MEMO TO: Jim Watters
(Legal Department)

From: Carter B. Phillips

~~DATE:~~
Subject: Contract for Rockford;China

—

(continued on next page)

several

There are still ˄unresolved issues relating to our establishment of a wholly

foreign‑owned enterprise in the People's Republic of China (PRC).

-adj

1. ~~Our first concern is that~~ Rockford-China must be able to accept orders from
   s
   ~~any~~ customer ˄ within the PRC in either local or foreign currency without

   Government interference.

2. ~~Also,~~ Rockford-China must be able to pay duties in local chinese currency

   for imported components, sub‑assemblies, and complete products in order to

   utilize locally generated revenues.

3. Rockford-China must have the freedom to set sales prices in any currency

   and to pay dividends without Government interference.

   Please incorporate these provisions in the draft agreement, which, it is hoped,

   will be ready for signing by (Thurs.) of next week.

Abb no

Table 18
Boxed Table

QUOTATION FOR PROPOSED INITIAL ORDER

Kangas‑Rockford

Effective ~~on~~ August 1, 19—

Item	~~Item~~ Price
Temperature Text Station	$184,000.00
(Test Strength) Fixture	$12,047.00
Oscilloscope	$7,855.00
XBL Transformer	$19.60
4B Resister network	$3.12
2CD Diode	$.89
4DC Capacitor Ceramic	~~$.65~~ 56
6D Resister	$.12
mpn Transistor	$.07
TOTAL	

Letter 32
Modified-Block Style

Mr. G. Leland Paulin

Krevitz and Paulin, Attorneys-at-Law

12406 Old Olden Avenue

Trenton, NJ 08610

Dear Mr. Paulin:

(continued on next page)

Agr plur

I have been informed that Talmo & Associates and your firm are now representing Lanmoore Engineering Designs, Inc., with respect to our joint arbitration hearing. The case will be heard before the London Court of International Arbitration on November 15.

Agr sing

Neither Rockford International nor Lanmoore has questioned our actions in the years since we began our business relationship. This is the first time that our marketing efforts have resulted in arbitration.

I look forward to receiving a summary from Jim Watters of our Legal Department after your meeting with him in early August.

Sincerely yours,

Carter B. Phillips
Vice President for Marketing

Lesson 58   Surgical Associates

GOALS: To type 40 wam/5'/5e; to format various business documents.

A. Type 2 times.

A. WARMUP

```
1        Do you think 1/3 of the contents of the five quart-    10
2  sized boxes would be about right?  I do!  If not, we can     22
3  adjust the portions by adding 6 or 7 gallons of warm water.   34
   | 1 | 2 | 3 | 4 | 5 | 6 | 7 | 8 | 9 | 10 | 11 | 12
```

Pretest
Take a 1-minute timing. Determine your speed and errors.

Practice
Speed Emphasis: If you made 2 or fewer errors on the Pretest, type each *individua*l line 2 times.
Accuracy Emphasis: If you made 3 or more errors, type each *group* of lines (as though it were a paragraph) 2 times.

Posttest
Repeat the Pretest timing and compare performance.

F. Take two 5-minute timings. Determine your speed and errors.

Goal: 40 wam/5'/5e

B. PRETEST: CLOSE REACHES

```
4        Sally took the coins from the pocket of her blouse      10
5   and traded them for fifty different coins.  Anyone could     22
6   see that Myrtle looked funny when extra coins were traded.   34
    |  1  |  2  |  3  |  4  |  5  |  6  |  7  |  8  |  9  |  10  |  11  |  12
```

C. PRACTICE: ADJACENT KEYS

```
7   as asked asset based basis class least visas ease fast mass
8   we weary wedge weigh towel jewel fewer dwell wear weed week
9   rt birth dirty earth heart north alert worth dart port tort
```

D. PRACTICE: CONSECUTIVE FINGERS

```
10  sw swamp swift swoop sweet swear swank swirl swap sway swim
11  gr grade grace angry agree group gross gripe grow gram grab
12  ol older olive solid extol spool fools stole bolt cold cool
```

E. POSTTEST: CLOSE REACHES

F. 5-MINUTE TIMING

```
13        An acquaintance of mine always seems to get her house    11
14  chores completed on time and never seems to be rushed.  So    23
15  I asked her what her special secret was.  She replied that    35
16  the only explanation she could offer was what she refers to   47
17  as her "bonus time."                                          51
18        While waiting in her auto for her son to finish his     61
19  piano lesson or while waiting to visit her dentist, she       73
20  takes a notepad and finalizes her grocery list.  Or she may   85
21  write out some monthly checks and reconcile her checkbook.    97
22  Other things she mentioned were planning the guest list and  109
23  menu for a dinner party and sorting through money-saving     120
24  coupons that she had previously clipped.                     128
25        Picking up on her ideas, I discovered over several     139
26  months that I was adding to her bonus-time list.  My purse   150
27  was cleaned out, and old photographs had been sorted and     162
28  mailed to relatives and friends.  Thank-you notes were in    173
29  the mail early, and my fingernails appeared better than      185
30  they had in years.  And I had listened to a lot of favorite  197
31  cassette tapes.                                              200
    |  1  |  2  |  3  |  4  |  5  |  6  |  7  |  8  |  9  |  10  |  11  |  12
```

DOCUMENT PROCESSING

Report 34
Surgery Report

Situation: Today is August 4, 19—, and you are a medical office assistant for Ann M. Michaels, M.D., at Surgical Assoc-iates in Bloomington, Illinois. Complete the following jobs.

Please prepare a surgery report for Dr. Michaels. Center **BLOOMINGTON GENERAL HOSPITAL / 2013 MAIN STREET / BLOOMINGTON, IL 61704** in all caps, bold, and single spaced at the top of the page. Press Enter 2 times, and then add the following headings in bold at the left just as you would position them for a memo: **PATIENT:**, **SURGEON:**, **DATE:**. The patient is Edna F. Applewick; the surgery was performed on August 4, 19—. Complete the report as follows:

> **BLOOMINGTON GENERAL HOSPITAL**
> **2013 MAIN STREET**
> **BLOOMINGTON, IL 61704**
>
> **PATIENT:** Edna F. Applewick
>
> **SURGEON:** Ann M. Michaels, M. D.
>
> **DATE:**   August 4, 19—
>
> The right hip was prepped and draped in the usual sterile fashion. A standard lateral incision was made through skin and subcutaneous tissue down to the tensor fascia, which

¶The right hip was prepped and draped in the usual sterile fashion. A standard lateral incision was made through skin and subcutaneous tissue down to the tensor fascia, which was incised along its length. The vastus lateralis was then reflected away from the lateral femoral cortex.

¶Under image intensification, a guidewire was placed at an angle through the lateral cortex into the femoral head. A 125-mm Ambi nail with four-hole sideplate was then placed over the guidewire and attached to the femur with four bone screws, each appropriately drilled, measured, and placed.

¶The wound was irrigated with lactated Ringer's. The vastus lateralis was closed using interrupted 0 Dexon; the tensor fascia was closed using interrupted 0 Dexon over a medium Hemovac drain. The subcutaneous tissue was closed with 3-0 Dexon, and the skin was closed with staples. A light compression dressing was applied. The patient tolerated the procedure well and left the operating room in satisfactory condition. Estimated blood loss was 250 cc.

Memo 10

MEMO TO: Kate Peterson

FROM: Ann M. Michaels, M.D.

DATE: August 4, 19--

SUBJECT: Supplemental Dental and Optical Insurance Coverage

Welcome to Surgical Associates. I am confident that you are the type of person who will provide the kind of care that our patients need.

(continued on next page)

You indicated on your employment form that you would like to have both supplemental dental and optical coverage under your health insurance coverage. Please provide the necessary information on the attached form.

I want everyone at Surgical Associates to have a positive feeling about our work environment. If at any time you have a concern, please let me know so that remedial action can be taken.

Attachment

August 4, 19—

Mrs.
~~Ms.~~ Rebecca F. Pedrin

1244 Mt. Vernon Drive

Normal, IL 61706

Dear Mrs. ~~Ms.~~ Pedrin:

The post-operative report from the audiologist indicates that there is still a 50 per cent loss in hearing in your right ear. You may wish to consider the use of a hearing aid. A copy of an article entitled "Hearing aid update" is enclosed for your review.

¶ I do recall that you were not pleased with the hearing aid you had about 4 or 5 years ago. However, the new technology has ~~dramatically~~ significantly improved the quality of these instruments. I would like both you and Mr. Pedrin to read the article and ~~dissues~~ discuss the contents.

Sincerely Yours,

Ann M. Michaels, M. D.

Lesson 59 Valley State Bank

GOALS: To improve speed and accuracy; to refine language-arts skills in spelling; to format various business documents.

A. Type 2 times.

A. WARMUP

```
1       Crowne and Metzner, Inc., employees* joined with 68    10
2   youngsters to repair the brick homes of 13 elderly persons;   22
3   several became very well acquainted with six of the owners.    34
     |  1  |  2  |  3  |  4  |  5  |  6  |  7  |  8  |  9  |  10  |  11  |  12
```

SKILLBUILDING

B. DIAGNOSTIC PRACTICE: NUMBERS

Turn to the Diagnostic Practice: Numbers routine beginning on page SB-5. Type one of the Pretest/Posttest paragraphs and identify any errors made. Then type the corresponding drill lines 2 times for each number on which you made 2 or more errors and 1 time for each number on which you made only 1 error. Finally, repeat the same Pretest paragraph and compare your performance.

C. Take three 12-second timings on each line. The scale below the last line shows your wam speed for a 12-second timing.

C. 12-SECOND SPEED SPRINTS

```
4   Kay Sue is on her way to that new show to take some photos.
5   Most of the ones who go may not be able to make it on time.
6   When they got to their seats, they were glad they had come.
7   Both men and women might take some of their pets with them.
     | | | |5| | | |10| | |15| | |20| | |25| | |30| | |35| | |40| | |45| | |50| | |55| | |60
```

 **LANGUAGE ARTS**

D. Type this list of frequently misspelled words, paying special attention to any spelling problems in each word.

Edit the sentences to correct any misspellings.

D. SPELLING

```
8   complete recent members enclosed determine development site
9   medical facility permanent library however purpose personal
10  electrical implementation representative discussed eligible
11  organization discuss expense minimum performance next areas
12  separate professional changes arrangements reason pay field

13  Members of the medicle and profesional group discussed it.
14  The development of the seperate cite will be completed.
15  A recent representive said the libary facility may be next.
16  A perpose of the electricle organization is to get changes.
17  However, the implimentation of changes will be permenant.
18  Arrangments for the enclosed eligable expenses are listed.
```

DOCUMENT PROCESSING

Situation: Today is Wednesday, October 1. You are the secretary to Mr. G. A. Lohrsbach, a senior vice president at Valley State Bank in Casper, Wyoming. Mr. Lohrsbach prefers the modified-block-style letter.

Letter 34
Modified-Block Style

Please prepare a letter to be sent to Ms. Lisa B. Dahl-Borg, President / Dahl & Associates / 8420 El Rio Road / Casper, WY 82604 / Dear Ms. Dahl-Borg:

¶Congratulations on making the decision to move your firm to the Mountain View Mall. You and your employees will enjoy the pleasant and modern surroundings as well as the availability of excellent restaurants and shops.

¶Valley State Bank, with a branch located right in the mall, would like to serve your various banking needs. We have been providing banking services for merchants and employees in the mall for over six years.

¶I look forward to visiting with you after your move on December 1 in order to identify the different ways in which we can help you. I am optimistic that we will have a long and mutually beneficial business relationship.

Sincerely,

Table 19
Open Table

Reformat this as an open table.

Press Enter once before typing the column headings in Row 2, Cells A and D to align them correctly.

IMPORTANCE OF BANKING SERVICES Mountain View Mall Employees			
Service	Very Important	Moderately Important	Unimportant
Free checking	96%	4%	0%
Teller machines	74%	18%	8%
Drive-in service	76%	16%	8%
Installment loans	83%	15%	2%
Personal banker	65%	9%	26%
Bank credit card	93%	5%	2%
Trust department	38%	17%	45%
Financial planning	33%	42%	25%
Safe-deposit boxes	74%	20%	6%

Memo 11

MEMO TO: Avis Culpepper, President

DATE: October 1, 19--

FROM: G. A. Lohrsbach, Senior Vice President

SUBJECT: Mountain View Mall survey

The survey of Mountain View Mall Employes was completed on schedule. A table that summarizes hte results is attached for your information. A meeting to discuss follow-up strategies will be held inthe conference room at 9:00 a.m. on Oct. 8. Your presense at the meeting will be helpful.

Lesson 60 Metro Security Systems

GOALS: To type 40 wam/5'/5e; to format various business documents.

A. Type 2 times.

A. WARMUP

1   "The #6 report shows increases from 2,649 to 3,779   10
2 units," the proud CEO announced. Ms. Bailey's reaction was   22
3 quite amazing as 80 jobs were validated with checked boxes.   34

| 1 | 2 | 3 | 4 | 5 | 6 | 7 | 8 | 9 | 10 | 11 | 12

SKILLBUILDING

B. Take a 1-minute timing on the first paragraph to establish your base speed. Then take four 1-minute timings on the remaining paragraphs. As soon as you equal or exceed your base speed on one paragraph, advance to the next, more difficult paragraph.

B. SUSTAINED PRACTICE: PUNCTUATION

4   The men in the warehouse were having a very difficult   11
5 time keeping track of the inventory. Things began to go   22
6 much more smoothly for them when they got the new computer.   34

7   Whenever something was shipped out, a computer entry   11
8 was made to show the change. They always knew exactly what   23
9 merchandise was in stock; they also knew what to order.   34

10   Management was pleased with the improvement. "We   10
11 should have made the change years ago," said the supervisor   22
12 to the plant manager, who was in full agreement with him.   34

13   This is just one example (among many) of how the work   11
14 area can be improved. Workers' suggestions are listened   22
15 to by alert, expert managers. Their jobs go better, too.   34

| 1 | 2 | 3 | 4 | 5 | 6 | 7 | 8 | 9 | 10 | 11 | 12

C. Take two 5-minute timings. Determine your speed and errors.

Goal: 40 wam/5'/5e

C. 5-MINUTE TIMING

16   Compost piles have become more and more common all   10

17 over the country in recent years. Backyard and food wastes   22

18 are turned into humus, which can be applied to vegetable   34

19 gardens, flower gardens, and lawns. When mixed with soil,   46

20 the humus will help break up clay, help hold moisture, and   57

21 encourage the growth of friendly bacteria.   66

22   There are two desirable reasons why people who live in   77

23 houses should have a compost pile in their backyards. The   89

24 first reason is that compostable materials, such as leaves,   101

25 grass, and food waste, are about one-fourth of the rubbish   113

26 in landfills. As most good sites for landfills are quickly   125

27 being used up, the use of a compost pile is an important   136

28 contribution to the environment.   143

29   A second reason is suggested in the first paragraph.   154

30 The use of a free soil conditioner makes a lot of sense.   165

31 However, sizable amounts of food scraps must be joined with   177

32 grass and leaves so there is nitrogen to put composting   189

33 bacteria to work. Also, compost piles must be kept moist.   200

| 1 | 2 | 3 | 4 | 5 | 6 | 7 | 8 | 9 | 10 | 11 | 12

DOCUMENT PROCESSING

Report 35
Unbound Report

Situation: Today is Monday, March 4. You are the administrative assistant to Mrs. Louise Short, the marketing manager for Metro Security Systems, located in St. Louis, Missouri. Mrs. Short wants *Mrs.* used in closing lines of letter.

METRO SECURITY SYSTEMS

Metro Security Systems is pleased to announce the introduction of its newest home security system-- THE OBSERVER, Model 1023!

THE OBSERVER includes such standard features as:

- State-of-the-art infrared motion detectors.
- Built-in microprocessor to eliminate false alarms.
- Eight door and window sensors for maximum security.
- Battery power to keep the system active during power failures!
- Easy-to-use control panel.

Metro Security is pleased to offer a two-year

(continued on next page)

warranty with this new system. The cost of the system to dealers is $850, and the suggested retail price is $1,280. Discounts are available for large orders.

Over 7,000 homes in the St. Louis metropolitan area are now protected with Metro's security systems. Names of satisfied users will be provided on request.

For any technical questions about this new product, call our engineers at 1-800-555-3473. For sales information, call our marketing personnel at 1-800-555-3797.

Letter 35
Block Style

Mr. Alvin R. Schilling / 2437 Barken Avenue, Suite 1506 /

St. Louis, MO 63121 / Dear Mr. Schilling:

Thank you for your letter recently about our Security Systems. We have

carried a full line of residential and industrial security systems for the past

twelve years. As you open your new law office, it is understandable that you

are concerned about the security of your office files. Our sales representative

in your area of St. Louis, Carlos Jiminez, will be contacting you soon to

dicsuss your needs. Metro security will have a booth at the trade show at the

St. Louis Convention Ctr. on March 14. If you plan to attend, please stop by

and introduce yourself.

Sincerely Yours,
C: Carlos Jiminez

Table 20
Boxed Table

METRO SECURITY SYSTEMS New Industrial Clients in Past Quarter			
Company	**City, State**	**Phone**	**Contact**
ABD Controls	Leadwood, MO	314-555-9042	Donald Guidi
Chester Products	St. Louis, MO	314-555-1565	Thomas Perez
Crane Electronics	Farmington, MO	314-555-1420	Rita Clarke
Datatronics, Inc.	St. Louis, MO	314-555-3148	Vera Crispen
DK Plumbing	Danville, MO	314-555-2731	Richard Cruse

Ask your instructor for the General Information Test on Part 3.

Test 3-A
5-Minute Timing

```
 1      Many people are aware that their eating habits are          10
 2   surely not what they should be.  All of the various media      22
 3   put out so much information that most of us know what we        33
 4   need to do to change.  There is agreement that the goal         47
 5   should be to develop a lifetime eating pattern which is         56
 6   low in fat and high in fruits and vegetables.                   65
 7       If one is really sincere about making a commitment to       76
 8   healthy eating routines, the first thing to do is to take       88
 9   stock of existing habits.  Jot down all of the foods that       99
10   you eat for one week and how much of them you eat.  After      111
11   identifying the high-fat foods, look for lower-fat versions    123
12   that you can learn to accept as substitutes.  For example,     135
13   pretzels are a preferred choice to chips, and ice milk or      146
14   frozen nonfat yogurt can be substituted for ice cream.         157
15       Good eaters acquaint themselves with food labels and       168
16   watch out for fat content.  They also eat on a set schedule    180
17   and limit their snacking.  They also change their favorite     192
18   recipes to reduce the fat content in them.                     200
```
| 1 | 2 | 3 | 4 | 5 | 6 | 7 | 8 | 9 | 10 | 11 | 12

Test 3-B

Letter 36
Modified-Block Style

Use the current date and type a letter addressed to Mr. Robert D. Beilow, Director of Athletics / Mountainview Community College / 157 Valley Road / Winslow, AZ 86047.

As you are aware, the eight conferences of the quad states have now agreed to sponsor a basketball tournament to determine a champion from the quad states of Arizona, Colorado, New Mexico, and Utah.

¶1. The tournament will be held on the campus of Farmington Community College in Farmington, New Mexico, on March 19-21.

¶2. Each school must make its own travel arrangements. Lodging and meals will be available at Farmington. (Details are enclosed.)

¶3. On the basis of advertising and ticket revenues, each school participating in the tournament will receive some compensation.

¶Please call me if you have any questions about this invitation.

Sincerely, / Carline J. Wuoka / Administrator / {urs} / Enclosure

BASKETBALL TOURNAMENT

By Charlotte Luna

On March 19, 19—, an exciting new basketball competition will be be inaugurated. The eight conference winners in the basket ball programs in the community colleges of the quad states of AZ, CO, NM and UT will meet in farmington, NM.

New Agreement

The community college Athletic Directors in the quad states have agreed that each league will send its conference champion to a tournament during the third week end of March to determine a quad states champion.[1]

Financial Benefits

The raised revenues after expenses, will be returned to the colleges. Each college's share will be based on it's performance in the tournament.[2] Thus the tournament champion will collect the biggest share of revenues.

_____

[1] Pat Muranka Thomas Foley, "Basketball Tournament Becomes a Reality," *Quad States Community College Newsletter*, July 1994, p. 12.

[2] Ibid.

Use the current date and type this memo to Marvin Palomaki, Athletic Director from Debra Marchant, Tournament Manager. The memo concerns the Quad States Tournament.

¶The participating colleges in the quad states tournament have been sent the packet of information and forms. As this is my first experience in coordinating the activities for an event like this, I am very appreciative of everything that you have done to help me.

¶Housing arrangements have been made at the Manson Inn, and all meals will be provided at the Farmington Community College dining hall. The contracts for the officials (including referees) have all been received. All media personnel are being kept informed of the developments.

¶Please look over the attached list. Have I overlooked anything?

{urs} / Attachment

PART FOUR | Reports, Correspondence, and Tables

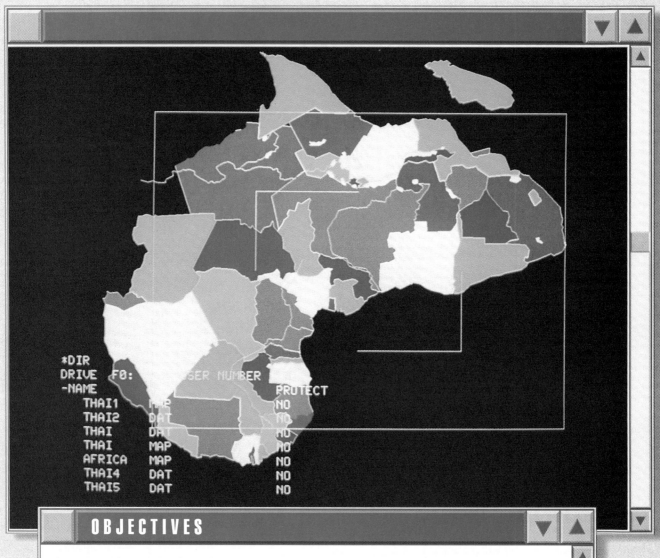

```
*DIR
DRIVE F0:        USER NUMBER
-NAME                PROTECT
    THAI1    MAP        NO
    THAI2    DAT        NO
    THAI     DAT        NO
    THAI     MAP        NO
    AFRICA   MAP        NO
    THAI4    DAT        NO
    THAI5    DAT        NO
```

OBJECTIVES

KEYBOARDING
- To type 43 wam/5'/5e.

LANGUAGE ARTS
- To refine proofreading skills and correctly use proofreaders' marks.
- To correctly abbreviate, capitalize, punctuate, and spell.
- To recognize subject/verb agreement and refine composing skills.

WORD PROCESSING
- To use the word processing commands necessary to complete the document processing activities.

DOCUMENT PROCESSING
- To review report, letter, memo, and table formats; to format business reports, special letter parts, and tables with special features.

TECHNICAL
- To answer correctly at least 90 percent of the questions on an objective test.

Lesson 61 — Skillbuilding and Report Review

GOALS: To improve speed and accuracy; to refine language-arts skills in the use of commas; to format reports.

A. Type 2 times.

A. WARMUP

```
1        A queen quickly adjusted 12 blinds as the bright sun    11
2   blazed down from the sky; she then paced through the 19      22
3   rooms (all very large) next to the castle for 38 minutes.    33
    |  1  |  2  |  3  |  4  |  5  |  6  |  7  |  8  |  9  |  10  |  11  |  12
```

SKILLBUILDING

B. Take three 12-second timings on each line. The scale below the last line shows your wam speed for a 12-second timing.

B. 12-SECOND SPEED SPRINTS

```
4  Most of those autos on the road had only one or two people.
5  Those boys and girls did the right thing by doing the work.
6  Some of the men ran to the gym to work out with their kids.
7  All of the new male workers were given a tour of the plant.
   | | | |5| | | |10| | |15| | |20| | |25| | |30| | |35| | |40| | |45| | |50| | |55| | |60
```

C. PROGRESSIVE PRACTICE: ALPHABET

Turn to the Progressive Practice: Alphabet routine beginning on page SB-7. Take six 30-second timings, starting at the point where you left off the last time.

LANGUAGE ARTS

D. Study the rules at the right.

D. COMMAS

Rule: Use a comma before and after a nonessential expression. (A nonessential expression is a word or group of words that may be omitted without changing the basic meaning of the sentence.)

,non   A typewriter, which is rarely used, is still available for addressing envelopes and filling in forms.

,non   The basic intent, agreed to by both parties, was to set a deadline that could be met.

Rule: Use a comma between two adjacent adjectives that modify the same noun.

,adj   Most of the applicants' resumes indicated fast, accurate typing skills.

,adj   Both of the top two candidates were described as being assertive, poised people.

(continued on next page)

Edit the sentences to correct any errors in the use of the comma.

8 John Ault, one of her students, purchased a laser printer.
9 One must be a patient, understanding person to be a counselor.
10 Jenny emphasized that it is a speedy user-friendly computer.
11 The young guests at the office were eager attentive listeners.
12 The new man in the warehouse is an honest, dependable worker.
13 The cook who recently underwent surgery is back on the job.

DOCUMENT PROCESSING

Report 37
One-Page Bound Report

Review the format for a report on page R-8 in the reference manual.

EMPLOYEE TRAINING PROGRAMS

Your Name

Various training techniques are used in business and industry to ~~update~~ *help* employees' ~~skills and to assist them in~~ acquiring new skills. ~~It is no surprise that conscientious employees are eager to participate in training programs.~~ Some of the various *effective training* ~~techniques~~ ~~used in training~~ are described *discussed in this report* ~~below~~.

ON-THE-JOB TRAINING AND LECTURES

Two of the most frequently used and *highly effective* training methods are on-the-job training and lectures.

On-the-Job Training. On-the-job training saves time and money by ~~permitting~~ *enabling* individuals to train at the workplace. ~~This method lets~~ the trainer uses the workstation in place of a classroom. ~~While there are many benefits from this type of experience,~~ on-the-job training requires careful coordination to ensure that learning objectives are achieved.

Lectures. Lectures are used often because they are a low-cost method of ~~training~~ *instruction*. Lectures, which require little action on the part of the trainer, may not be effective when introducing employees to new techniques and work programs.

(continued on next page)

CONFERENCES

In ~~the~~ conference ~~method of instruction~~ small groups of employees are taught by a ~~conference~~ director. ~~This method of instruction results in~~ considerable give-and-take ~~between the director and the employees~~ For learning to occur, the director must be in the use of interactive techiques.

a *Conferences provide* *skilled* *n*

Report 38
Two-Page Unbound Report With Footnotes

Review the format for a report with footnotes on page R-8 in the reference manual.

,adj

,non

,adj

LEADERSHIP SKILLS NEEDED IN BUSINESS

By Sally Rodriguez

Leadership skills are needed now more than ever in business and industry if our nation is to maintain a leading role in the business world of tomorrow. With the advent of a common European community without boundaries, the Japanese influence throughout the world, and the development of a common North American business community, we must have leaders with vision and the appropriate skills for meeting the challenges of the new, very technical century.

Each of the new skills that a successful leader needs is discussed in the following pages.

LEADERSHIP

Leadership has been defined in a variety of ways. One definition is "the behavior of an individual when he (or she) is directing the activities of a group toward a shared goal."[1]

A successful leader is one who is committed to ideas—ideas for future products and services, for improving the firm's market position, and for the well-being of his or her employees. A leader possesses a value system that is ethically and morally sound. Leaders, who make decisions affecting the firm, employees, and society, have a set of beliefs that influence decision making.

SKILLS THAT A LEADER NEEDS

A good, effective leader must have the prerequisite skills if he or she is to be effective in business. Many textbooks and business journal writers have used various terms to describe these skills. Quible[2] lists such skills as characteristics. They are "getting others to cooperate, delegating responsibilities, understanding subordinates, and using fairness." However, Quible discusses human relations, teaching, coaching, and communications as special skills that a leader should possess. These skills are often acquired on the job with the assistance of other leaders within the firm.

(continued on next page)

[1] Judith R. Gordon, *A Diagnostic Approach to Organizational Behavior,* 2d ed., Allyn and Bacon, Inc., Boston, 1997, p. 393.

[2] Zane K. Quible, *Administrative Office Management: An Introduction,* 4th ed., Prentice-Hall, Englewood Cliffs, New Jersey, 1996, pp. 212–216.

Report 39
Two-Page Unbound Report With Footnotes

Open the file for Report 38 and make the following changes:

1. Assume that you wrote the report, and change the byline accordingly.
2. Delete the third paragraph. Note that this results in the elimination of the first footnote.
3. Delete the last sentence of the report.
4. Add a third side heading, *THE LEADER AS TEACHER.* Then add the

following information: *Those in leadership positions too often assume that workers learn how to perform a job simply by doing it without guidance. The real leader plans well-structured orientation sessions for new workers and does the same for all workers whenever there is new technology to be learned or if there is a change in policies or procedures.*

Lesson 62   Skillbuilding and Letter Review

GOALS: To type 40 wam/5′/5e; to format business letters and personal-business letters.

A. Type 2 times.

A. WARMUP

```
1      Quist & Zenk's sales were exactly $247,650; but the      11
2   cost of goods sold was $174,280 (70.37%).  The profit made   22
3   was small after other, extensive expenses were subtracted.   34
       | 1  | 2  | 3  | 4  | 5  | 6  | 7  | 8  | 9  | 10  | 11  | 12
```

SKILLBUILDING

Pretest
Take a 1-minute timing.
Determine your speed and errors.

B. PRETEST: DISCRIMINATION PRACTICE

```
4      The entire trip on a large train was better than we      11
5   had hoped.  Polite police looked out for both the young and   23
6   old.  One unit was outnumbered by herds of frolicking deer.   34
       | 1  | 2  | 3  | 4  | 5  | 6  | 7  | 8  | 9  | 10  | 11  | 12
```

Practice
Speed Emphasis: If you made no more than 1 error on the Pretest, type each *individual* line 2 times.
Accuracy Emphasis: If you made 2 or more errors, type each *group* of lines (as though it were a paragraph) 2 times.

Posttest
Repeat the Pretest timing and compare performance.

F. Take two 5-minute timings. Determine your speed and errors.

Goal: 40 wam/5′/5e

C. PRACTICE: LEFT HAND

```
 7  rtr trip trot sport train alert courts assert tragic truest
 8  asa mass salt usage cased cease astute dashed masked castle
 9  rer rear rest overt rerun older before entire surest better
```

D. PRACTICE: RIGHT HAND

```
10  mnm menu numb hymns unmet manly mental namely manner number
11  pop post coop opera pools opens polite proper police oppose
12  iui unit quit fruit suits built medium guided helium podium
```

E. POSTTEST: DISCRIMINATION PRACTICE

F. 5-MINUTE TIMING

```
13      Parents agree that there is no firm age at which a       10
14  child should be allowed to stay home alone.  Experts in the  22
15  field of child growth and development support this belief.   34
16  There are some children who are responsible enough to stay   46
17  alone at the age of ten.  Amazingly, though, there are some  58
18  teenagers who have to be judged quite differently.           68
19      No matter what their age, those who stay alone must      79
20  have guidelines that are established by the parents.  The    91
21  child should telephone a responsible adult each day after   102
22  arriving home safely.  There should be agreement on which   114
23  snacks are acceptable and which appliances are not to be    125
24  used.  There should be no quibbling later about household   137
25  chores, homework, piano practice, or any other tasks.       148
26      Rules must be established for outside play, visits to   159
27  friends' homes, and times friends may come in the house.   170
28  The two biggest concerns are strangers and emergencies.  As 182
29  communities and neighborhoods are not alike, each family    194
30  should have its own set of rules.                           200
```
```
|  1  |  2  |  3  |  4  |  5  |  6  |  7  |  8  |  9  |  10  |  11  |  12
```

DOCUMENT PROCESSING

Letter 37
Personal-Business Letter in Block Style

Review the format for a business letter on pages R-3–R-4 in the reference manual.

October 1, 19— / Dr. James L. Rowe / 2345 South Main Street / Bowling Green, OH 43402 / Dear Jim:

¶Thank you for your letter of September 25 in which you inquired about my trip to New York City. Your letter brought back a lot of memories of those days when I was one of your students.

¶I plan to leave on October 15 for a two-week business and vacation trip to the city. While at Columbia University, I will be conducting a workshop

(continued on next page)

on the utilization of voice-activated equipment.

¶My work at Columbia will be completed on October 22, after which I plan to attend a number of plays, visit the Metropolitan Museum of Art, and take one of the sightseeing tours of the city.

¶If you and your wife would care to join me on October 22, please let me know. I would be most happy to make reservations at the hotel for you and to purchase theater tickets. Why don't you consider joining me in the "Big Apple."

Sincerely, / Bryan Goldberg / 320 South Summit Street / Toledo, OH 43604

Letter 38
Business Letter in Modified-Block Style

June 3, 19-- 4X ↓

Director of Product Development

Hampton Associates, Inc.

830 Market (St.)

San Francisco, Ca 9410̶3̶-1925 (2)

italic

Dear Director of Product Development:

I recently read an article in <u>Business Week</u> concerning how computer buyers can make standards happen. It was a very interesting article. It indicate**s** **d** that if customers demand (products/standard) when they purchase computers, participate in standard-setting groups, and band together with other customers, they will do better in the long run. Have you had customer groups

assist
~~help~~ you or provide you with information on the adoption of more ∧ *computer* standards**?** ~~:~~

These standards include
~~such as in the areas of~~ industry ∧ wide interfaces, a mix and match of

computer **#** gear and programs, and building the best system for each

application utilized**.**

I would appreciate any data that you might furnish for me with ~~relationship~~ *regard* to customers and your firm working together to set past or future standards.

Sincerely yours, ↓ 4X

Alice Karns
Vice President

Type your reference initials in place of *urs.*

{urs}

Letter 39
Business Letter in Block Style

Revise Letter 38, making the following changes:

1. Change the letter to block style.
2. Change the date to June 5, 19--.
3. Send the letter to Ms. Heidi M. Fischer at Gramstad Brothers, Inc., located at 5417 Harbord Drive in Oakland, CA 94618.
4. Combine the second and third paragraphs into one paragraph.
5. Add the following text as a new third paragraph: *Some of my colleagues and I would like to get involved with others in an effort to make desired changes. I am confident that there are others around the Bay area who feel the same way.*
6. Create an envelope for the letter, but do not append it.

Lesson 63 — Skillbuilding and Memo Review

GOALS: To improve speed and accuracy; to refine language-arts skills in proofreading; to format memos.

A. Type 2 times.

A. WARMUP

```
1        "When is the quarterly jury report due?" asked Glenn.     11
2   He had faxed forms* to 64 of the 135 prospective jurors.       23
3   Only about one dozen of 596 citizens could not be located.     34
    |  1  |  2  |  3  |  4  |  5  |  6  |  7  |  8  |  9  |  10  |  11  |  12
```

SKILLBUILDING

B. Take three 12-second timings on each line. The scale below the last line shows your wam speed for a 12-second timing.

B. 12-SECOND SPEED SPRINTS

```
4   Kate knew when only ten that she would someday own a store.
5   She had worked at six hat shops by the time she was twenty.
6   Two years later she had a chance to buy one of those shops.
7   She now owns a chain of eighty stores and is a rich person.
    | | | | 5 | | | |10| | |15| | |20| | |25| | |30| | |35| | |40| | |45| | |50| | |55| | |60
```

C. PROGRESSIVE PRACTICE: ALPHABET

Turn to the Progressive Practice: Alphabet routine beginning on page SB-

7. Take six 30-second timings, starting at the point where you left off the last time.

D. Type the paragraph 2 times, but press Enter after each sentence.

D. TECHNIQUE PRACTICE: ENTER

```
8         Start a business.  See the banker.  Rent a building.
9    Check state codes.  Check city codes.  Get needed licenses.
10   Contact suppliers.  Call utility companies.  Buy furniture.
11   Hire the employees.  Open the doors.  Hope for customers.
```

E. PROOFREADING

E. Compare this paragraph with the fourth paragraph of Report 38 on page 155. Edit the paragraph to correct any errors.

```
12      A successful leader is one who is commited to ideas-
13   ideas for future product and services for improving the
14   firms market position, and for the wellbeing of his or her
15   employes.  A leeder possesses a value system that is
16   ethicly and morally sound.  leaders who make decisions
17   effecting the firm, employees, and society, have set of
18   beleifs that influence decision-making.
```

DOCUMENT PROCESSING

Memo 13

Review the format for a memo on page R-4 of the reference manual.

MEMO TO: Frank Janowicz, Ticket Manager / **FROM:** Sam Steele, Executive Director / **DATE:** March 1, 19— / **SUBJECT:** Ticket Sales Campaign

¶We tentatively have scheduled 114 concerts for Orchestra Hall for the calendar year beginning September 1, 19—. The attached list shows the new season ticket prices for the main floor, mezzanine, balcony, and gallery.

¶These prices are grouped in 11 different concert categories, which reflect the varied classical tastes of our patrons. These groupings also consider preferences for day of the week, time of day, and season of the year.

¶Please see me at 3 p.m. on March 10 so that we can review our ticket sales campaign. Last year's season ticket holders have had ample time to renew their subscriptions; we must now concentrate on attracting new season subscribers. I shall look forward to reviewing your plans on the tenth.

{urs} / Attachment

Memo 14

MEMO TO: Edo Dorati, Cabaret pops Conductor

FROM: Sam Steele, Executive Director

DATE: March 2, 19--

Subject: Irving Berlin Concert

Our Patron Advisory Program Committee recomments in its their attached letter that the Irving Berlin concert begin with some pre-World War I hits, followed by music *songs* from the '20s and '30s. Favorites from this era are hit songs from *Music Box Review, Puttin' on The Ritz,* and *Follow the the Fleet.* After the intermission, the committee suggests songs from the '40s and '50s, hits from *Annie get Your Gun, Call Me Madam, and Easter parade.* A

(continued on next page)

planning meeting has been scheduled for you, Dolly Carpenter (the Rehearsals Coordinator), and me on Mar. 9 at 10 A.M. at Orchestra Hall. I shall look forward to seeing you then.

{urs}

Attachment

c: Dolly Carpenter

Memo 15

Do not indent paragraphs in a memo.

MEMO TO: Dolly Carpenter, Rehearsals Coordinator

FROM: Sam Steele, Executive Director

DATE: March 3, 19--

SUBJECT: Summer Cabaret Pops Concerts

We are pleased that you will be our rehearsals coordinator for this summer's Cabaret Pops concerts. The five biweekly concerts will run from June 13 through August 8.

As the concert schedule is much lighter during the summer months, I am quite confident that you will be able to use the Orchestra Hall stage for all rehearsals. This is the preference of Edo Dorati, who will be the conductor for this year's Cabaret Pops concerts.

I look forward to seeing you on June 1.

Remember to type your reference initials.

Lesson 64 — Skillbuilding and Table Review

GOALS: To type 40 wam/5'/5e; to format tables.

A. Type 2 times.

A. WARMUP

```
1      There were two big questions:  (1) Would both have to      11
2  be present to pick up the license? and (2) Is a blood test      23
3  required?  Jeff and Faye were quite dizzy with excitement!      34
   |  1  |  2  |  3  |  4  |  5  |  6  |  7  |  8  |  9  |  10  |  11  |  12
```

B. SUSTAINED PRACTICE: ALTERNATE-HAND WORDS

B. Take a 1-minute timing on the first paragraph to establish your base speed. Then take four 1-minute timings on the remaining paragraphs. As soon as you equal or exceed your base speed on one paragraph, advance to the next, more difficult paragraph.

4   The town council decided to shape its destiny when a   11
5 rich landowner lent a hand by proposing to chair the audit   23
6 committee. He will be a good chairman, and eight civic   34
7 club members will work to amend some troublesome policies.   45

8   One problem relates to the change in profit for many   11
9 of the firms in the city. As giant property taxes do not   22
10 relate to income, they wish to make those taxes go down.   34
11 The result means increases in their sales or income taxes.   46

12   All eight members of the town council now agree that   11
13 it is time to join with other cities throughout the state   22
14 in lobbying with the state legislature to bring about the   34
15 needed change. The right balance in taxes is the goal.   45

16   The mayor pointed out that it is not only business   10
17 property owners who would be affected. Homeowners should   22
18 see a decrease in property taxes, and renters might see   33
19 lower rents, as landlords' property taxes would be lowered.   45

| 1 | 2 | 3 | 4 | 5 | 6 | 7 | 8 | 9 | 10 | 11 | 12

C. 5-MINUTE TIMING

C. Take two 5-minute timings. Determine your speed and errors.

Goal: 40 wam/5′/5e

20   I soon learned at a recent dinner party that I was the   11
21 only person there who had ever taken a vacation trip on a   23
22 train. In fact, just about all of the people present had   34
23 never even been a passenger on a train. Many of them were   46
24 surprised when I informed them that there are more than a   58
25 dozen specialized rail adventures available throughout the   70
26 country. These adventures are in addition to established   81
27 railroads that now carry passengers across the country or   93
28 provide leisurely scenic trips.   99
29   There are different names for the various kinds of   110
30 excursions, such as quiet scenic trains, theme railroads,   121
31 dinner trains, novelty trains, and tourist railroads. Most   133
32 specialty train rides are about two or three hours, but   144
33 some rides may be for an entire day.   152
34   Passenger cars used on the various railroads can be   162
35 quite different. Some cars may be furnished with plush   174
36 carpeting, paneling, crystal, china, and silver. A mining   185
37 train or a logging train may have tin plates and wooden   197
38 benches for seats.   200

| 1 | 2 | 3 | 4 | 5 | 6 | 7 | 8 | 9 | 10 | 11 | 12

DOCUMENT PROCESSING

Table 21
Open Table With Left-Aligned Column Headings

Review table formats on page R-12 in the reference manual.

Table 22
Boxed Table With Centered Column Headings

Left-align Column 1; right-align Columns 2 and 3.

---

1. Center the table vertically.
2. Create a table with 3 columns and 9 rows.
3. Type the column headings left-aligned in initial caps and bold.
4. Automatically adjust the column widths for all columns.
5. Join the cells in Row 1.
6. Center and type the title in all caps and bold. Center and type the subtitle in initial caps. Press Enter once after typing the subtitle.
7. Center the table horizontally.

SALES CONFERENCES
All Sessions at Regional Offices

Date	City	Leader
October 7	Boston	D. G. Gorham
October 17	Baltimore	James B. Brunner
October 24	Miami	Becky Taylor
November 3	Dallas	Rodney R. Nordstein
November 10	Minneapolis	Joanne Miles-Tyrell
November 17	Denver	Becky Taylor
November 26	Los Angeles	Rodney R. Nordstein

$700 COMPOUNDED ANNUALLY FOR 7 YEARS AT 7 PERCENT		
Beginning of Year	**Interest**	**Value**
First	$00.00	$700.00
Second	$49.00	$749.00
Third	$52.43	$801.43
Fourth	$56.10	$857.53
Fifth	$60.03	$917.56
Sixth	$64.23	$981.79
Seventh	$68.72	$1,050.51
Eighth	$78.68	$1,129.19

Table 23
Boxed Table With Left-and Right-Aligned Column Headings

Left-align Column 1; right-align Columns 2 and 3.

SECOND HALF-YEAR SALES Ending December 31, 19—		
Month	**Sales Quotas ($)**	**Actual Sales ($)**
July	335,400	350,620
August	370,750	296,230
September	374,510	425,110
October	390,270	390,110
November	375,890	368,290
December	360,470	378,690
TOTAL	2,207,290	2,209,050

Lesson 65

Skillbuilding and Employment Documents Review

GOALS: To improve speed and accuracy; to refine language-arts skills in composing; to format employment documents.

A. Type 2 times.

A. WARMUP

1 Only 6 of the 18 competitors weighed more than 149#. 11
2 All Big Five matches were scheduled in Gym #3. Amazingly, 23
3 about 1/3 of the #1 Jaguars were picked to acquire titles. 34

| 1 | 2 | 3 | 4 | 5 | 6 | 7 | 8 | 9 | 10 | 11 | 12

SKILLBUILDING

B. DIAGNOSTIC PRACTICE: ALPHABET

Turn to the Diagnostic Practice: Alphabet routine beginning on page SB-2. Type one of the Pretest/Posttest paragraphs and identify any errors made. Then type the corresponding drill lines 2 times for each letter on which you made 2 or more errors and 1 time for each letter on which you made only 1 error. Finally, repeat the same Pretest paragraph and compare your performance.

C. PACED PRACTICE

Turn to the Paced Practice routine, beginning on page SB-14. Take three 2-minute timings, starting at the point where you left off the last time.

LANGUAGE ARTS

D. COMPOSING

Read through the paragraphs in the 5-minute timing in Lesson 62 on page 157. Then compose a paragraph in which you state at what age you were left alone and the type of "check-in" system that was used. Also tell about the rules you had for back-and-forth visiting at your friends' homes and your home.

DOCUMENT PROCESSING

Report 40
Resume

Follow these steps to format this resume correctly:

1. Center the page vertically.
2. Center and type the name in 18-point font size.
3. Press Enter twice; then center and type the address and telephone number in 16-point font size.
4. Press Enter twice. Type the major section headings in 12-point font size and bold at the left margin.
5. Type the section information in 12-point regular type approximately 1.5 inches from the left margin.
6. Insert a blank line between each section as shown below.

TIMOTHY J. ROBINSON

5816 Foxfire Road, Lawton, OK 73501
405-555-3039

EDUCATION

Lawton Community College, Lawton, Oklahoma
Associate in Business degree, Office Systems, June 1996

Specialization in computer application software (WordPerfect, Microsoft Word, Lotus, dBase), business communication, and office systems management.

Frederick High School, Frederick, Oklahoma
Graduated: May 1994

Selected courses recommended by Lawton Community College for entry into their business program.

EXPERIENCE

Computer Systems Technician, September 1994-Present
Selkirk & Associates, Lawton, Oklahoma
Duties include installing and updating computer software programs throughout the firm.

Secretary II, July 1992 to August 1994 (part-time)
Kittredge Insurance Agency, Frederick, Oklahoma
Duties included typing and word processing while reporting to the administrative assistant to the owner.

ACTIVITIES

College Choir, 1994-1996
Business Students Club, 1994-1996 (Secretary, 1995-1996)
Varsity basketball, 1994-1996
Intramural soccer, 1994-1996

REFERENCES

References available upon request.

Letter 40
Application Letter in Block Style

{Current Date} / Mrs. Denise F. Klenzman / Director of Human Resources / Cole Enterprises / 3714 Crestmont Avenue / Norman, OK 73069 / Dear Mrs. Klenzman:

Please consider me an applicant for the position of Computer Systems Coordinator with your firm. I became aware of the ~~new~~ position through a friend who is an employee at Cole Enterprises. ¶ I have been employed at Selkirk & Associates since graduating from high school in 1994. During this time I have also earned an (Assoc.) in Business degree at Lawton Community College. ¶ The resume enclosed shows that I have had extensive courses in computer application soft ware and office systems. I am confident that my educational ~~experience~~ background and my computer systems experience make me highly qualified for the position with your firm. ¶ You may call me for an interview at 405-555-~~4572~~ 3039.

Sincerely yours, / Timothy J. Robinson / 5816 Foxfire Road / Lawton, OK 73501 / Enclosure

Letter 41

Progress Check
Follow-Up Letter in Block Style

Do not indent paragraphs in a block-style letter.

{Current Date} / Mrs. Denise F. Klenzman / Director of Human Resources / Cole Enterprises / 3714 Crestmont Avenue / Norman, OK 73069

Dear Mrs. Klenzman:
Thank you for the opportunity to meet with you yesterday and to learn of the exciting career opportunities at Cole Enterprises. It was inspiring for me to learn about future plans for your forward-looking company.
I am confident that my education and my experience qualify me in a special way for your position of computer systems coordinator. I am familiar with all of your present equipment and software.
I would very much like to join the professional staff at Cole Enterprises. Please let me know when you have made your decision.

Sincerely yours, / Timothy J. Robinson / 5816 Foxfire Road / Lawton, OK 73501

UNIT FOURTEEN ▶ Correspondence

Lesson 66 — Multipage Letters

GOALS: To type 41 wam/5'/5e; to format multipage letters.

A. Type 2 times.

A. WARMUP

```
1      We were quite dazzled when the plumber drove up in a      11
2  C-150 pickup truck!  She was joined by 26 young people (all    23
3  students) who gazed intently as she welded six of the rods.    35
```
| 1 | 2 | 3 | 4 | 5 | 6 | 7 | 8 | 9 | 10 | 11 | 12

SKILLBUILDING

B. PROGRESSIVE PRACTICE: ALPHABET

Turn to the Progressive Practice: Alphabet routine beginning on page SB-7. Take six 30-second timings, starting at the point where you left off the last time.

C. Type the paragraph 2 times. Change every singular noun to a plural noun, and change every plural noun to a singular noun.

C. TECHNIQUE PRACTICE: CONCENTRATION

```
4      The person at the desk with the computer will want to
5  help the owner.  The men and women prepared the contracts
6  for the sales of the buildings.  The secretaries prepared
7  the forms so that the children will be the beneficiaries.
```

D. Take two 5-minute timings. Determine your speed and errors.

Goal: 41 wam/5'/5e

D. 5-MINUTE TIMING

```
8       Imagine that you have just finished college and you       11
9   are starting a new job in human resources.  What are the      22
10  major qualities you will need to perfect in order to become    34
11  successful in your position?  While human resource experts     46
12  display a variety of skills, there are two competencies        57
13  that all need to get:  the ability to connect with their       68
14  clients and the knowledge to counsel them through crises.      80
15      Connecting is the process of building good relations       91
16  with a sizable range of contacts in your business unit.       102
17  When connecting with an employee, there are several things    114
18  to keep in mind.  A number one goal is to determine the       125
19  needs and wants of that other person and to work toward       136
20  meeting them.  Remember to aim for an end result that is      148
21  beneficial to both parties.  Another key factor is trying     159
22  to establish open communication.  A person must feel he or    171
23  she can trust you in order to build a foundation for an       182
24  open discussion.  Finally, there must be give-and-take.       194
25  Both parties must be given a chance to speak their minds.     205
```
| 1 | 2 | 3 | 4 | 5 | 6 | 7 | 8 | 9 | 10 | 11 | 12

E. MULTIPAGE LETTERS

To format a multipage letter:

1. Type the first page on letterhead stationery and continuing pages on plain paper that matches the letterhead.
2. Leave an approximate 2-inch top margin on page 1. Use the default top margin on continuing pages. Use the default bottom margin on all pages.
3. Add a header to all pages other than the first page that includes the addressee's name, the page number, and the date, aligned at the top left.

4. Be sure that widow/orphan protection is turned on to avoid leaving a single line of a paragraph at the bottom or at the top of a page.

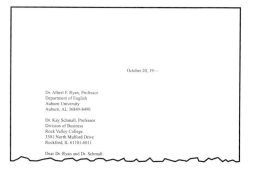

F. MULTIPLE ADDRESSEES

Often a letter may be sent to two or more people at the same or different addresses.

1. If a letter is addressed to two people at the same address, type each name on a separate line above the same inside address.
2. If a letter is addressed to two people at different addresses, type each name and address one under the other. Press Enter 2 times between the addresses.
3. If a letter is addressed to three or more people, type the names and addresses side by side, with one at the left margin, and another beginning at the centerpoint. Insert a blank line before typing the third name and address.

4. Include all addressees' names in the salutation and in the header for the continuing pages of a multipage letter. In the header, list the names one under another.

G. WORD PROCESSING: HEADERS AND FOOTERS

Study Lesson 66 in your word processing manual. Complete all of the shaded steps while at your computer. Then format the jobs that follow.

 **DOCUMENT PROCESSING**

Letter 42
Two-Page Letter With Multiple Addresses in Modified-Block Style

October 16, 19— / Miss Florence B. Glashan / Attorney-at-Law / 12406 Shadows Glade / Dayton, OH 45426-0348 / Mr. Michael D. Eiden / Attorney-at-Law / 2408 Ridgecrest Avenue / Dayton, OH 45416-0317 / Dear Miss Glashan and Mr. Eiden:

¶It was good to meet both of you at the convention in Detroit last week. In addition to the regular sessions, I find that the informal discussions with people like you are an added plus at these meetings.

(continued on next page)

Create a header for the second page. If necessary, turn widow/orphan protection on.
Use the numbering command for the numbered list. Remember to insert a blank line before and after the list.

¶You may recall that I told you I had just been appointed by the court to defend a woman here in Dayton who has been charged with embezzling large sums of money from her previous employer. She was in charge of accounts receivable at a large department store. Her previous employer, the plaintiff in the case, claims that she embezzled $18,634 in 1992, $39,072 in 1993, and $27,045 in 1994.

¶I recall that both of you mentioned that you had represented defendants in similar cases last year. As I prepare for this defense, perhaps you might help me in the following ways:

¶1. Please send me the appropriate citations for all similar trials in which each of you participated.

¶2. Also, please provide me with any other case citations that you think might be helpful to me in this case.

¶3. Arrange to meet with me soon so that I can benefit from your experience as I prepare for the trial.

¶A copy of the formal complaint is enclosed for your review. I shall call you in about a week to arrange a time and place for our meeting.

¶I have never been involved with anything like this before. Any help that you give me will be appreciated.

Sincerely, / Ms. Jeanne M. Hoover / Attorney-at-Law / {urs} / Enclosure

Letter 43
Two-Page Letter in Block Style

Set a tab at the center-point to begin typing the second address.
You may wish to review proofreaders' marks on page R-13 in the reference manual before typing this letter.

April 3, 19--

Mr. Michael Mc Ginty

District Manager

Starr & Morgan Company

One DuPont cicle

Washington, DC 2006-2133

Ms. Debra Ann Goode

Sales Representative

Starr & Morgan Company

7835 Virginia Avenue Northwest

Washington, DC 30037-2133

Mr. Albert R. Batson

Sales Representative

Starr & Morgan Company

3725 Stevens Road Southeast

Washington, DC 20020-2133

(continued on next page)

Dear Mike, Deb, and Al:

It was good to see all three of you at our sales conference last week. Your
winning ~~our~~ the "golden apple" award for the most sales for the ~~month~~ year was
well deserved. There is no doubt that Starr & Morgan is very well
represented in the metro Washington area. We particularly want to
commend you for obtaining the Westerminster Account. None of our
company's other sales representives have been able to ~~do~~ accomplish this feat. Just the
idea of a new account of over $500,000 is quite mind-boggling. How did
you do it? Did you:

1. spend considerable time with the President, Mr. Arch Davis, or the Director
   of Purchasing, Ms. Betsy Matin?
2. Conduct a series of "hands-on" workshops for the employees and
   managers?
3. Develope a special marketing campaign for Westerminster it self or use
   a regular campaign model?
4. Combine various strategies in your efforts to obtain this important
   account?

~~Can you~~ Please let me know what approaches were used to make this sale? If it
can be arranged, a presentation by the three of you at our next sales
conference would seem ~~very~~ appropriate. The other sales representatives
would benefit ~~much~~ greatly from your success story. Again, congratulations on
~~your receipt of~~ receiving this award.

All of us here in the home office are pleased greatly with the performance
of our entire sales team. Indications are that this will be a year when
records are broken and we will be in the media spotlight again.

Sincerely yours,

Robert D. Miley

Pres.

urs

c: R. Olson, Director of Sales

Letter 44
Two-Page Letter With Multiple Addresses in Modified-Block Style

Open the file for Letter 42 and make the following changes:

1. Add the following as an addressee (beginning at the centerpoint): Mr. Richard G. Snowden, Attorney-at-Law. His offices are at 8704 Renwood Drive, Dayton, OH 45429-1362.

2. Change the salutation and header as needed.

3. Change the word *both* to *all* in the first sentence of the first and third paragraphs.

4. Add this sentence at the end of the second paragraph: *The defendant is also being accused of embezzling $35,680 in 1995.*

Lesson 67   Special Letter Parts

GOALS: To improve speed and accuracy; to refine language-arts skills in capitalization; to format special letter parts.

A. Type 2 times.

A. WARMUP

```
1        Six citizens from 14th Avenue East joined 83 other        10
2   residents to discuss the #794 proposal* for a new swimming     22
3   pool.  Barry Kelm quoted numbers about current pool usage.     34
    |  1  |  2  |  3  |  4  |  5  |  6  |  7  |  8  |  9  |  10  |  11  |  12
```

SKILLBUILDING

B. DIAGNOSTIC PRACTICE: ALPHABET

Turn to the Diagnostic Practice: Alphabet routine beginning on page SB-2. Type one of the Pretest/Posttest paragraphs and identify any errors made. Then type the corresponding drill lines 2 times for each letter on which you made 2 or more errors and 1 time for each letter on which you made only 1 error. Finally, repeat the same Pretest paragraph and compare your performance.

C. PACED PRACTICE

Turn to the Paced Practice routine beginning on page SB-14. Take three 2-minute timings, starting at the point where you left off the last time.

D. Study the rules at the right.

≡ noun #

≡ comp

Edit the sentences to correct any errors in capitalization.

D. CAPITALIZATION

Rule: Capitalize nouns followed by a number or letter (except for the nouns *line*, *note*, *page*, *paragraph*, and *size*).

Danielle said that Report 8 would be sent on Friday, October 22.
But: The receiving department reported that all the dresses were size 12.

Rule: Capitalize compass points (such as *north*, *south*, or *northeast*) only when they designate definite regions.

When they retire, they will spend the winter months in the South.
But: The new warehouse is located about three blocks east of the stadium.

4 The officers of the firm have season tickets in Section 4.
5 My company's new address is 3718 Newcombe Street Southwest.
6 A professor called attention to the quotation on Page 249.
7 The valley is a main flyway for geese as they fly North.
8 A caravan of flood relief trucks drove east on highway 43.
9 Some of the computer firms are relocating in the northeast.

FORMATTING

E. INTERNATIONAL ADDRESSES

Type the name of a foreign country in all caps on a separate line at the end of the address.

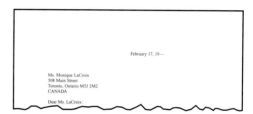

F. ON-ARRIVAL NOTATIONS

On-arrival notations (such as *Confidential*) should be typed on the second line below the date, at the *left* margin. Type the notation in all caps. Press Enter 2 times to begin the inside address.

G. SUBJECT LINES

A subject line indicates what a letter is about. It is typed below the salutation at the left margin, preceded and followed by 1 blank line. (The term *Re* or *In re* may be used in place of *Subject*.)

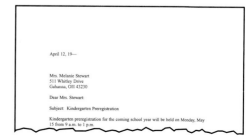

H. COMPANY NAME IN CLOSING LINES

Some business firms show the company name in the closing lines of a letter. It is typed in all caps on the second line below the complimentary closing, followed by 3 blank lines before the writer's name.

I. BC NOTATION

A blind copy (*bc:*) notation is used when the addressee is not intended to know that one or more other persons are being sent a copy of the letter. Type the *bc* notation on the file copy at the left margin on the second line after the last item in the letter.

When preparing a letter with a blind copy, print one copy of the letter; then add the blind copy notation and print another.

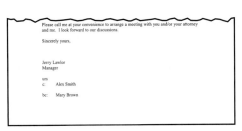

J. DELIVERY NOTATION

Type a delivery notation on the line below the enclosure notation (if used) or on the line below the reference initials. A delivery notation comes before a copy notation.

K. POSTSCRIPT

If a postscript is added to a letter, it is typed as the last item in the letter, preceded by 1 blank line. If the paragraphs in the letter are indented, the first line of the postscript should be indented as well.

DOCUMENT PROCESSING

Letter 45
Business Letter in Block Style

November 8, 19--

CONFIDENTIAL

Mrs. Katie Hollister

11426 Prairie View Rd.

(continued on next page)

Kearney, NE 68847

Dear Mrs. Holister:

Subject: Site For New Elementary School

≡ comp

As you are aware, your 160-acre farm, located in the |quarter| |northeast| of

Section 25 *60* in Tyro township, is a part of independent School District 17.

≡ noun #

three
Each of our elementary schools occupies ~~two~~ *2* acres and is adjoined by an

8-acre park. We are now in the early pla|nning stages for a ~~third~~ *fourth*

≡ noun #

elementary school. As you*r* ~~large~~ farm is centrally located, the District 17

Board has directed me to initiate discussions with you for the purchase of

10
~~8~~ acres of land.

(I look forward to our discussions.) Please call me at your convenience to

arrange a meeting with you and/or your attorney and me. ←

Yours truly,

Irvin J.Hagg

Superintendent of Schools

urs
c: District 17 Board

Letter 46
Business Letter in
Block Style

Open the file for Letter 45 and make the following changes:

1. Delete the on-arrival notation and the subject line.
2. Insert *Independent School District 17* as a company name in the closing lines.

3. A delivery notation is needed, as Mr. Hagg wants the letter sent by Priority Mail.
4. Add a blind copy notation; the copy is to be sent to Mrs. Allison B. Schlee/ Attorney-at-Law.

Letter 47
Personal-Business
Letter in Block Style

November 17, 19--

Dr. Arif Gureshi
8726 East Ridge Drive
Morehead, KY 40351-7268

(continued on next page)

Do not indent the paragraphs in a block-style letter.

Dear Dr. Gureshi:

Your new book, <u>The Middle East in the Year 2000</u>, has gotten excellent reviews. The citizens of Morehead are pleased that a respected member of one of our local colleges is receiving national attention.

Our book discussion group here in Morehead, composed of members of the AAUW (American Association of University Women), has selected your book for discussion at our May meeting. We would very much like you to be a participant; your attendance at the meeting would be a real highlight.

I shall call you next week. Our members are hoping that you will be able to attend and that an acceptable date can be arranged.

Sincerely,

Theresa A. Gorski
2901 Garfield Court
Morehead, KY 40351-2687

 **Lesson 68**

Letters With Tables

GOALS: To type 41 wam/5'/5e; to format letters with tables.

A. Type 2 times.

A. WARMUP

1   The 83 Lions Club members raised $6,690 (95% of the   11
2 requested sum) to resurface the tennis courts. Gayle was   22
3 amazed when sixteen jolly members picked up over 10% more.   34

| 1 | 2 | 3 | 4 | 5 | 6 | 7 | 8 | 9 | 10 | 11 | 12 |

SKILLBUILDING

Pretest
Take a 1-minute timing. Determine your speed and errors.

B. PRETEST: HORIZONTAL REACHES

4   Four famous adults gazed at a wren on our farm gate.   11
5 A group of gawking writers wrote facts about an additional   23
6 upward gain in wildlife numbers on their supply of pads.   34

| 1 | 2 | 3 | 4 | 5 | 6 | 7 | 8 | 9 | 10 | 11 | 12 |

Practice
Speed Emphasis: If you made no more than 1 error on the Pretest, type each *individual* line 2 times.
Accuracy Emphasis: If you made 2 or more errors, type each *group* of lines (as though it were a paragraph) 2 times.

Posttest
Repeat the Pretest timing and compare performance.

F. Take two 5-minute timings. Determine your speed and errors.

Goal: 41 wam/5'/5e

C. PRACTICE: IN REACHES

```
 7  wr wrap wren wreak wrist wrote writer unwrap writhe wreaths
 8  ou pout ours ounce cough fouls output detour ousted coupons
 9  ad adds dead adult ready blade advice fading admits adheres
```

D. PRACTICE: OUT REACHES

```
10  fa fact farm faith sofas fakes faulty unfair famous defames
11  up upon soup upset group upper upturn supply uplift upsurge
12  ga gate gave cigar gains legal gazing legacy gawked garbage
```

E. POSTTEST: HORIZONTAL REACHES

F. 5-MINUTE TIMING

```
13      All animals perform basic acts for survival.  Birds      11
14  gather twigs to make nests, while squirrels hunt for nuts    22
15  and berries.  People perform very basic acts too, but we     34
16  often disregard them in favor of such complex achievements   45
17  as reading, language, philosophy, and math.  Yet, despite a  57
18  truly amazing array of artifacts that we have developed,     69
19  devised, and built over the years, we can still observe      80
20  similar actions in people from a wide range of cultures.     91
21      There are two major types of actions.  The first is     102
22  called inborn actions.  The idea with an inborn action is   114
23  that the brain is programmed to link particular reactions   125
24  with specific stimuli.  The classic example is the newborn  137
25  baby who can drink milk from a bottle given to him or her.  149
26      The second type is all those actions we have to be      159
27  taught.  Trained actions are consciously acquired through   171
28  teaching or by self-studies and practice time.  Watching a  181
29  child first master winking provides a graphic reminder of   194
30  how hard some actions can be for both young and old.        205
```
```
| 1 | 2 | 3 | 4 | 5 | 6 | 7 | 8 | 9 | 10 | 11 | 12
```

FORMATTING

G. TABLES WITHIN DOCUMENTS

To format a table that is part of a letter, memo, or report:

1. In a single-spaced document, press Enter 2 times before and after the table. Be sure you are outside the table structure before pressing Enter.

2. In a double-spaced document, press Enter 1 time before and after the table.

3. Single-space the body of the table.

4. Adjust the column widths, and center the table within the margins of the document.

5. Never split a table between two pages. If a table will not fit at the bottom of the page on which it is first mentioned, place it at the top of the next page.

DOCUMENT PROCESSING

Letter 48
International Business Letter in Block Style With Open Table

Automatically adjust the column widths and center the table horizontally.

March 2, 19— / Ms. Maureen Testa / Austin Communications / 37 Portland Place / London WIN 4BB / ENGLAND / Dear Ms. Testa:

¶We are indeed interested in designing a new corporate logo and the corresponding stationery for your fine company. As I indicated in our recent telephone conversation, we have a design staff that has won many national awards for letterhead form design, and we consider it an honor to be contacted by you.

¶Within a couple of weeks, we will submit to you and your committee several basic designs. Based on your evaluation and suggestions, we can go from there. Here is a modified price list for the printed stationery:

Letterhead (550 sheets)	$80.00
Business cards (1,000 cards)	$39.50
Coated brochures (1,000 sheets)	$219.30
Envelopes	$92.00

¶In the meantime, please call me if we can be of further service.

Sincerely yours, / Samantha A. Steele / General Manager / {urs}

Letter 49
Business Letter in Block Style With Boxed Table

Open the file for Letter 48 from Ms. Steele and make the following changes:

1. Send the letter to Mr. Rodney Graae / Thompson Corporation / 42 Harris Court / Trenton, NJ 08648.
2. Change the word *company* in the first paragraph to *corporation*.
3. Revise the first two sentences of the second paragraph to say: *Within a month, we will submit several basic designs to you and your board of directors. At that time, please feel free to make any comments and suggestions that will help us finalize a design.*
4. Change the table to a *boxed* table.

Letter 50
Business Letter in Modified-Block Style

{Current Date} / Master Gyms, Inc. / 4201 Castine Court / Raleigh, NC 27613-5981 / Ladies and Gentlemen:

¶We have 494 apartments here at Fountain Ridge. As the recreation coordinator, I have concerns not only about the leisure-time activities of our residents but also about the health and physical fitness of the more than 1,100 people who call Fountain Ridge home.

¶Our recreation facilities are excellent. In addition to our two outdoor tennis courts and swimming pool, we also have the following indoor facilities: two racquetball courts, swimming pool, whirlpool bath, sauna, steam room, and two billiard tables. However, we have no workout equipment.

¶During the next few months we will be equipping a new gymnasium. The dimensions of the gym are shown on the enclosed sketch. There will be

(continued on next page)

exercise bicycles, treadmills, and rowing machines. In addition, we would like to install a muscle-toning machine that includes features such as the following: leg press, chest press, shoulder press, arm pull, leg pull, arm lift, leg lift, and sit-up board.

¶Do you have a sales representative serving this area who could meet with me within a week or ten days? As an alternative, perhaps you have some brochures, including prices, that could be sent to me.

Sincerely yours, / Rosa Bailey-Judd / Recreation Coordinator / {urs} / Enclosure / By fax

Lesson 69 Multipage Memos With Tables

GOALS: To improve speed and accuracy; to refine language-arts skills in spelling; to format multipage memos with tables.

A. Type 2 times.

A. WARMUP

```
1       Over 270 cars were backed up near the Baxter & Meintz    11
2  building after an 18-wheeler jackknifed at an icy junction.   23
3  About 1/3 to 1/2 of the cars were required to use a detour.   35
   |  1  |  2  |  3  |  4  |  5  |  6  |  7  |  8  |  9  |  10  |  11  |  12
```

 SKILLBUILDING

B. DIAGNOSTIC PRACTICE: NUMBERS

Turn to the Diagnostic Practice: Numbers routine beginning on page SB-5. Type one of the Pretest/Posttest paragraphs and identify any errors made. Then type the corresponding drill lines 2 times for each number on which you made 2 or more errors and 1 time for each number on which you made only 1 error. Finally, repeat the same Pretest paragraph and compare your performance.

C. Take three 12-second timings on each line. The scale below the last line shows your wam speed for a 12-second timing.

C. 12-SECOND SPEED SPRINTS

```
4  Pam knew that five girls in the other car were on the team.
5  The women drove eight blue autos when they made some trips.
6  All the girls in four other autos may go on the same trips.
7  Spring is the time of the year when they have a lot of pep.
   | | | |5| | | |10| | |15| | |20| | |25| | |30| | |35| | |40| | |45| | |50| | |55| | |60
```

D. Type this list of frequently misspelled words, paying special attention to any spelling problems in each word.

Edit the sentences to correct any misspellings.

D. SPELLING

8 personnel information its procedures their committee system
9 receive employees which education services opportunity area
10 financial appropriate interest received production contract
11 important through necessary customer employee further there
12 property account approximately general control division our

13 The revised systom was adopted by the finantial division.
14 Four employes want to serve on the new property commitee.
15 Approximatly ten proceedures were included in the contract.
16 Further informasion will be recieved from the customers.
17 Their was much interest shown by the production personal.
18 The services in that aria are necesary for needed control.

E. WORD PROCESSING: FIND AND REPLACE

Study Lesson 69 in your word processing manual. Complete all of the shaded steps while at your computer. Then format the jobs that follow.

Memo 16
Multipage Memo With Open Table

MEMO TO: L. B. Chinn, Station Manager / **FROM:** Mitzi Grenell, News Director / **DATE:** May 5, 19— / **SUBJECT:** FCC European Trip

¶As you requested, this memo is being sent to you as one in a series to keep you informed about my upcoming trip to Europe. I have been invited by the Federal Communications Commission to participate in a study of television news in European countries. The invitation came from Jill Andrews, FCC vice-chair; and I am, of course, delighted to take part in this challenging project.

¶One function of this study will be to compare the news in countries that have a long history of free-access broadcasting with the programming in newly democratic countries. I have been assigned to lead a study group to six European countries to gather firsthand information on this topic. We will be visiting England, France, Germany, Poland, Romania, and Latvia from August 24 through September 3. In addition to me, our group will consist of the following members:

Arkady Gromov	News Director National Public Radio	Washington, DC
Manuel Cruz	Executive Editor *Miami Herald*	Miami, FL
Katherine Grant	Station Manager WPQR-TV	Boston, MA

(continued on next page)

Richard Logan   Operations Manager   New York, NY
                       Cable News System

¶Our initial plans are to spend at least one full day in each of the countries, meeting with the news staff of one or two of the major networks, touring their facilities, viewing recent broadcasts, and becoming familiar with their general operations.

¶If you need to contact me during my absence, Barbara Brooks, our liaison at the Federal Communications Commission (1919 M Street, NW, Washington, DC 20554; phone: 202-555-3894), will be able to provide a location and phone number.

¶Arrangements will be made with several different staff members in the News Department to handle my responsibilities here at Channel 5 while I am gone. Dave Gislason will be the contact person for the department. As you can imagine, this is an exciting time for me. Thank you for supporting the project.

{urs}

PS: Thanks also for suggesting that this trip be combined with a vacation. My husband and I have discussed the possibility of his joining me for a two-week tour of the Scandinavian countries after the FCC trip has been completed. I shall let you know what our plans are by the end of May.

Memo 17
Multipage Memo With Open Table

Revise Memo 16 based on some changes you just learned about.

1. Jill Andrews has just been promoted to FCC chair.
2. Finland has been added as a seventh country.
3. The trip has been extended through September 5.

4. Each occurrence of *news* (lowercase) has to be changed to *news programming*. (Do not replace *News*.)
5. Reggie Jordan, Staff Assistant, FCC, Washington, DC, will replace Manuel Cruz on the trip.
6. Gil Friesen will replace Dave Gislason as contact person.

Memo 18
Memo With Boxed Table

MEMO TO: Terry Hackworth, Manager

FROM: Rosa Bailey-Judd, Recreation Coordinator

DATE: April 14, 19--

SUBJECT: Fitness room

The new Fitness Room will be ready for use in about 1 month. Your leadership in bringing this about is sincerely appreciated. After ~~much~~ extensive investigation (much reading and several interviews), I likely will be requesting approval soon to purchase the following equipment:

(continued on next page)

No.	Type
4	exercise bicycles
2̶ 4̶	treadmill~s~
1	muscle-toner~ing~ machine

Three other types of equipment wer~e~ considered seriously, but those listed above enable users to reach objectives with out excessive cost. I am not quite ready to recommend the specific brands or the suppiers for these machines. As we expect that there will be heavy usage, we are concerned with dur~a~bility, warranties, and the available ~ility~ of dependable service personnel. Thanks again for your full support and cooperation with this project.

Lesson 70   Memo Reports

GOALS: To type 41 wam/5'/5e; to format memo reports.

A. Type 2 times.

A. WARMUP

```
1      The sizable judge asked three questions:  "What's the    11
2  best time of the day for you to be in court?  Can you leave   23
3  your job at exactly 4 p.m.?  If not, 5 p.m. or 7 p.m.?"       34
   | 1 | 2 | 3 | 4 | 5 | 6 | 7 | 8 | 9 | 10 | 11 | 12
```

SKILLBUILDING

B. Take a 1-minute timing on the first paragraph to establish your base speed. Then take four 1-minute timings on the remaining paragraphs. As soon as you equal or exceed your base speed on one paragraph, advance to the next, more difficult paragraph.

B. SUSTAINED PRACTICE: SYLLABIC INTENSITY

```
4       Each of us has several bills to be paid on a monthly     11
5  basis.  For most of us, a checkbook is the tool that we use   23
6  to take care of this chore.  However, in this electronic      34
7  age, other ways of doing this have received rave reviews.     46

8       You likely will be surprised to learn that the most      11
9  basic way and the cheapest way to pay bills electronically    22
10 involves the use of a Touch-Tone phone.  The time required    34
11 is approximately a third of that used when writing checks.    46
   | 1 | 2 | 3 | 4 | 5 | 6 | 7 | 8 | 9 | 10 | 11 | 12
```

12	Several banking institutions offer or plan to offer	11
13	screen phones as a method for paying bills. It is possible	23
14	to buy securities, make transfers, and determine account	34
15	balances. You will save time by using a Touch-Tone phone.	46

16	A third type of electronic bill processing involves	11
17	using a microcomputer and a modem. Software programs have	22
18	on-screen checkbooks linked to bill-paying applications.	34
19	Other microcomputers use on-line services through a modem.	46

| 1 | 2 | 3 | 4 | 5 | 6 | 7 | 8 | 9 | 10 | 11 | 12

C. Take two 5-minute timings. Determine your speed and errors.

Goal: 41wam/5'/5e

C. 5-MINUTE TIMING

20	Have you ever observed what happens when two friends	11
21	meet and talk in an easy manner? They adopt similar body	22
22	postures. If they are really friendly and share the same	34
23	attitudes toward the subjects being discussed, the poses	45
24	in which they hold their bodies are liable to become even	57
25	more alike, to the point where they virtually become carbon	69
26	copies of each other. This is not a deliberate imitative	81
27	process. While not aware of it, the friends in question	92
28	are indulging in an unconscious act called postural echo.	104

29	The precision of the postural echo is quite amazing.	115
30	Two friends reclining in armchairs both have their legs	126
31	crossed the same way, and both have an arm relaxed across	137
32	their lap. Even more surprising is the fact that they may	149
33	synchronize their movements as they talk. When one person	161
34	uncrosses the legs, the other soon follows suit, and when	173
35	one leans back a little, so does the partner. If, for some	185
36	reason, one does not participate, a loss of synchrony will	196
37	occur. Both may feel testy and not know why.	205

| 1 | 2 | 3 | 4 | 5 | 6 | 7 | 8 | 9 | 10 | 11 | 12

FORMATTING

D. REPORT HEADINGS IN MEMOS

There are times when a memo report is used rather than preparing a cover memo to accompany a report. The documents are combined into one, and headings are formatted as they are in a report.

MEMO TO: All Employees / **FROM:** Franklin Coates, Director / **DATE:** February 24, 19— / **SUBJECT:** Security System

¶Beginning March 1, we will install a new security access system. Complete installation should occur by the end of March. The system will include new magnetic card readers at all entrances. It will also provide a more secure working environment, especially in the evenings and on weekends. Entrances will lock and unlock automatically each day during working hours. Please carefully read and follow the detailed instructions for using the new system.

RECEIVING A NEW ACCESS CARD

¶Once the new system is installed, you will need a new access identification card to enter the building during nonworking hours. Human Resources will begin taking pictures for new cards during the week of March 20. When you are called, report immediately. The cards will be issued as soon as they are ready. To receive your new card, you must turn in your old one.

ENTERING THE BUILDING

¶Entrances will automatically unlock each working day at 8 a.m. and lock at 5 p.m. To enter the building during nonworking hours, slide your access identification card (with the magnetic strip facing left) through the card reader at the right of the entrance door. When the green light comes on, open the door. Do not hold the door open longer than 30 seconds.

¶Once you enter the building during nonworking hours, please proceed immediately to the front desk and sign in. Record in the log book your name, department, extension number, and arrival time.

LEAVING THE BUILDING

¶Before leaving the building, you must sign out. Please record your departure time beside your name. Do not use the special latch handle to open the door, or the alarm will sound. Instead, use the push bar. Once you have opened the door, do not let it remain open longer than 30 seconds, or the alarm will sound. If you accidentally set off the alarm, return to the front desk and call the security company (the telephone number is at the top of the log book). Be prepared to provide them with your name, extension number, and access card number.

¶At times you may need to have the door held open for extended periods of time during nonbusiness hours. In these situations, please make arrangements with Building Maintenance by calling extension 4444.

¶If you have any questions about our new security access system and procedures, please contact me.

Memo 20
Memo Report

Mr. Coates has asked you to revise Memo Report 19 as follows:

1. Use February 25 as the date.
2. Change *nonworking* to *nonbusiness* throughout the report.
3. Add the following sentence at the end of the second paragraph: *New employees will be asked for a special form, to be provided by their supervisors.*
4. Change *Building Maintenance* to *Building Security.*

Memo 21

Progress Check
Memo Report

Do not indent paragraphs in a memo.

MEMO TO: All Employees
FROM: Adrienne Barzanov
DATE: March 2, 19--
SUBJECT: New Building Site

We have consulted with several architects and have finalized plans to build a new administrative center at 6400 Easton Plaza. This memo provides general information about plans for the center's exterior and interior development.

EXTERIOR PLANS

Exterior plans will maintain the historical integrity and beauty of the surrounding area and reflect the architecture of other buildings in the office park. Landscaping plans include a nature preserve, a picnic area, and a small pond.

INTERIOR PLANS FOR STAFF

Staff will be located within the new facility as follows:

1. Accounting will be located on the first floor in the west wing.
2. Sales and marketing will be located on the first floor in the east wing. All staff will be grouped according to product line.
3. All other staff will be located on the second floor.

Exact locations will be determined at a later date.

INTERIOR PLANS FOR SPECIAL FACILITIES

Conference rooms will be located in the center of the

(continued on next page)

building on the first floor to provide easy access for everyone. All rooms will be equipped with state-of-the-art technology.

Our new center will also include a full-service cafeteria, a copy center, a library, an athletic center, and an on-site day care center.

Construction of the new center will begin when we obtain the necessary permits.

Lesson 71   Formal Report Project

GOALS: To improve speed and accuracy; to refine language-arts skills in grammar; to format a formal report.

A. Type 2 times.

A. WARMUP

```
1       The jalopy quivered as it crossed over the 1/5-mile      11
2  long bridge on Route 67 about 14 miles south of Granite       22
3  City.  The axle on Richard's truck broke as he whizzed by.    33
   |  1  |  2  |  3  |  4  |  5  |  6  |  7  |  8  |  9  | 10 | 11 | 12
```

SKILLBUILDING

B. Take three 12-second timings on each line. The scale below the last line shows your wam speed for a 12-second timing.

B. 12-SECOND SPEED SPRINTS

```
4  There are many things to think about if you buy a used car.
5  Two of the main things are its age and the number of miles.
6  Take the car for a test drive in town and on the open road.
7  Pay a fee to an auto expert who will check it over for you.
   | | | |5| | | |10| | | |15| | |20| | |25| | |30| | |35| | |40| | |45| | |50| | |55| | |60
```

C. PROGRESSIVE PRACTICE: ALPHABET

Turn to the Progressive Practice: Alphabet routine beginning on page SB-7.

Take six 30-second timings, starting at the point where you left off the last time.

LANGUAGE ARTS

D. Study the rules at the right.

D. AGREEMENT

Rule: Some pronouns (*anybody, each, either, everybody, everyone, much, neither, no one, nobody,* and *one*) are always singular and take a singular verb. Other pronouns (*all, any, more, most, none,* and *some*) may be singular or plural, depending on the noun to which they refer.

agr pro

agr pro

Neither Charlie nor Bea is planning to apply for the vacant position.
Most of the people in Plant 12 are establishing excellent attendance records.

Rule: Disregard any intervening words that come between the subject and verb when establishing agreement.

agr inter

agr inter

The contract, including all attachments, was due in her office on October 23.
The retirees, as well as Miss Brown, have been honored at luncheons.

Edit the sentences to correct any errors in grammar.

```
8  Everybody who signed up for the trip are to be at Building 16.
9  All the tourists are sending cards to us from their hotels.
10 Everyone on the trip, including spouses, have been having fun.
```

(continued on next page)

11 Some of the postcards from their vacations are not arriving.
12 Two of the sales reps from Region 4 were given cash bonuses.
13 The fastest runner from all five teams are receiving a trophy.

E. WORD PROCESSING: STYLES

Study Lesson 71 in your word processing manual. Complete all of the shaded steps while at your computer. Then format the jobs that follow.

Report 41
Unbound, Single-Spaced Multipage Report

Business reports are often formatted according to the preferences of the business. For example, reports may be single-spaced and have different heading formats from standard reports. Format Report 41 as follows:

1. Begin the first page, the appendix page, and the references page approximately 2 inches from the top of the page. Use default top and bottom margins for all other pages.

2. Create a style named *Center* for the centered headings within the body of the report. Centered headings are typed in all caps and bold and are preceded and followed by 1 blank line.

3. Create a style named *Side* for the side headings. Side headings are typed in initial caps, bold, and italic, and are preceded and followed by 1 blank line.

4. Single-space the paragraphs, but insert a blank line between paragraphs.

5. Turn on widow/orphan protection.

6. Create a header for all pages except the first page. Use 10-point Times New Roman italic font. Type *Human Resources Department* at the left margin. At the right margin, type *Page* followed by 1 space, and insert automatic page numbering. Add a bottom border/line.

7. Create a footer for every page. Use 10-point Times New Roman italic font. Add a top border/line, then center and type *Intercultural Communication.*

Center and type this title line for line as shown.

SS **A PRELIMINARY PLAN FOR INTERCUTURAL**
SEMINARS AT DOMESTIC AND
INTERNATION SITES (INTERNATIONAL)

DS
Jordan D. Sylvester, Director
SS Department of Human Resources
DS
February 12, 19--
DS

The marketing department has been ~~doing~~ *conducting* surveys of our world wide offices, foreign customers, and prospective foreign customers over the last several months. Information received through the use of *mailed* questionnaires has made us aware of an urgent need to improve our communicating skills as we incre*a*singly conduct our operations *on* at the international level.

(continued on next page)

Apply the *Center* style.

THE PROBLEM

Numerous incidents ~~and cases~~ have been reported to us in which we have failed to negotiate contract**s** with foreign customers and prospective foreign customers because of serious break downs in communication.

agr pro

Some ~~Very few~~ of these setbacks have been the result of conscious negative acts on the part of our employees. However, The main culprit seems to be lack of

Your line breaks may differ from those shown here.

awareness of cultural differences and lack of ~~an~~ apreciation for the nuances that ~~which~~ reflect these cultural differences. Indeed there are almost unlimited possibilities for misunderstandings, insults, miscues, and avenues for people of good intent to miscommunicate.

INTERCULTURAL SEMINARS (center)

Three-day seminars designed to improve intercultural communication skills will be held at regional sites in the U.S. and in foreign cities where we have offices. It will be our intent that all employees who have direct contact with people from other countries will participate in these seminars over a four-month period.

It would be unreasonable to assume that a small team of people from our company would have the breadth of knowledge needed to conduct these seminars in 8 foreign countries.

However, Dale Dolder, Tanya Falness, and Jodi Farmen have agreed to work together as the coordinating team for this effort. They have been working over the past two months with the managers of our international offices as well as natives in specific countries to formulate a preliminary plan for these in-service programs. Their plan will utilize the expertise of our employees who have had negotiating experience in each country and who have knowledge of local customs as demonstrated by natives. We are confident that through this team approach, our seminar participants will gain an understanding of problems not only from the position of our company but also from the perspective of those with whom they conduct business.

INSTRUCTIONAL APROACH (center)

Smith and steward suggest a frame work of instruction with the following three components: (1995, pp. 26-27)

(continued on next page)

The affective ~~frame~~ *component* is the area in which attention is given to attitudes, emotions, and resulting behaviors as they are ~~e~~*a*ffected by human interaction in a multicultural environment.

The cognitive ~~frame is the~~ component ~~which~~ includes informational ~~aspects for~~ *about* communicating with people of other cultures.

The experiential ~~frame~~ *component* is the "hands-on" element which suggests different possibilities. Others have found that the ~~the~~ use of simulations is a natural for this type of experience. The writing of letters, memos, and reports to persons in other cultures also provides beneficial learning experiences. In addition, the use of tutors can be very helpful to workers unfamiliar with a particular culture.

Save this unfinished report. You will resume work on it in Lesson 72.

Lesson 72   Formal Report Project

GOALS: To type 42 wam/5'/5e; to format a formal report.

A. Type 2 times.

A. WARMUP

```
1       The path will be covered by approximately 30 pieces    11
2  of slate from Quarry #9.  Schreiner & Zimmer (the general    22
3  contractor) took the joint bid of $638, including delivery.  34
   |  1  |  2  |  3  |  4  |  5  |  6  |  7  |  8  |  9  |  10  |  11  |  12
```

SKILLBUILDING

Pretest
Take a 1-minute timing. Determine your speed and errors.

B. PRETEST: VERTICAL REACHES

```
4       The scents in the trunk scared the rest of the drama    11
5  class.  One judge drank juice and ate pecans as the cranky   23
6  coach scolded the best junior and bought the pink dresses.   34
   |  1  |  2  |  3  |  4  |  5  |  6  |  7  |  8  |  9  |  10  |  11  |  12
```

Practice
Speed Emphasis: If you made no more than 1 error on the Pretest, type each *individual* line 2 times.
Accuracy Emphasis: If you made 2 or more errors, type each *group* of lines (as though it were a paragraph) 2 times.

C. PRACTICE: UP REACHES

```
7  dr draft drank dryer drain drama dread dream drag drew drug
8  ju judge juice jumpy junks juror julep jumbo judo jump just
9  es essay nests tests bless dress acres makes uses best rest
```

D. PRACTICE: DOWN REACHES

```
10  ca cable caddy cargo scare decay yucca pecan cage calm case
11  nk ankle blank crank blink think trunk brink bank junk sink
12  sc scale scalp scene scent scold scoop scope scan scar disc
```

F. Take two 5-minute timings. Determine your speed and errors.

Goal: 42 wam/5'/5e

E. POSTTEST: VERTICAL REACHES

F. 5-MINUTE TIMING

13	There is only one total escape from the crazy demands	11
14	of our day-to-day lives: sleep. Every evening we take a	23
15	lengthy break, giving ourselves a well-deserved rest. In	34
16	many respects, sleep is even more essential to our mental	46
17	health than to our physical well-being. We can relax our	57
18	tired muscles by having a massage or sitting down for a	69
19	minute, but this does very little to recharge our mental	80
20	batteries. By the end of every day, we have amassed quite	92
21	a confusion of new ideas, concerns, and experiences; and we	104
22	need about eight hours of sleep to get this new material	115
23	filed away in our memory banks.	122
24	Our brains are busy not just filing but also sorting	132
25	through the various contradictions and conflicts that have	144
26	arisen during the day. This is what dreaming is all about.	156
27	What we remember afterwards as our dreams is merely the tip	168
28	of the nocturnal iceberg. Modern studies of sleepers have	180
29	revealed that we are actively dreaming in repeated bouts	192
30	every night, regardless of whether or not we can remember	203
31	the dreams after we have awakened.	210

| 1 | 2 | 3 | 4 | 5 | 6 | 7 | 8 | 9 | 10 | 11 | 12

DOCUMENT PROCESSING

Report 41
Continued

Continue working on Report 41.

SEMINAR CONTENT —center

The cognitive, affective, and experiential frames would be applied as *components*

appropriate for each of the topics included. The coordinating team

members have utilized the resources available to them at our ③ local

universities. Most colleges & universities now provide instruction in

international communication. While the content at times is integrated into several

business adminstration courses, there has been a trend in recent years to

provide a couse or courses specifically designed for business interaction

in an intercultural setting. The very nature of this type of study makes it

very difficult to segment the broad topical areas, as all elements are so

closely intertwined. However, the tentative seminar plan is to cover the

content as briefly described below.

¶ The seminars must reflect the broad involvement of our international

operations. There is need for many workers in our domestic offices to

(continued on next page)

develop an appreciation of the intercultural challenge. This is true not only for those in the marketing and sales areas. Those in our finance department and our legal department are increasingly involved not only with foreign companies but also with huge multi-national corporations that at times are as large as or larger than the biggest companies in the U.S.

Dolder, Falness, and Farmen suggest the following as tentative instructional topics:

Format the table as shown, with the title and column headings in bold.
Review the format for a table within a report on page R-8 in the reference manual.
Automatically adjust the column widths.

TABLE 1.   SEMINAR TOPICS center

Instructional Topic	**Time**
Concept of Culture	2 hours
Language	2 hours
Religion, Values, and Ethics	2 hours
Body Positions and Movements	2 hours
Male/Female Roles	2 hours
Punctuality, Time, and Space	2 hours
Intimacy in relationships	2 hours
Conflict Resolution	2 hours

Apply the *Side* style.

Concept of Culture

This session will be an overview of the various cultures in which we conduct our business affairs. Stanton et al. identify the need for varied marketing strategies within the different economical, political, and cultural environments:

International marketing is complicated because these environments--particularly in the cultural environment--often consists of elements unfamiliar to american marketing executives. A further complication is the tendency for people to use their own cultural values as a frame of reference when in a foreign environment. (1991, p. 527)

Case studies will be reviewed that are considered classics in the field of International Communication. In addition, summaries of some of our own successes and failures will be reported.

Save this unfinished report. You will resume work on it in Lesson 73.

Lesson 73 Formal Report Project

GOALS: To improve speed and accuracy; to refine language-arts skills in proofreading; to format a formal report.

A. Type 2 times.

A. WARMUP

```
1        The 16 young farmers (only 50% over 30 years of age)    11
2   gathered in Room 209 to begin discussing the earthquake      22
3   threat; an extra door prize was given as a "joke present."    34
```
| 1 | 2 | 3 | 4 | 5 | 6 | 7 | 8 | 9 | 10 | 11 | 12

SKILLBUILDING

B. Take three 12-second timings on each line. The scale below the last line shows your wam speed for a 12-second timing.

B. 12-SECOND SPEED SPRINTS

```
4   Spring is the time when bird songs fill the air with music.
5   It is also the time when many of us like to dig in gardens.
6   It is fun to plant seeds and then see those pretty flowers.
7   Spring is also the time to paint and clean up all the junk.
```
| | | |5| | | |10| | | |15| | | |20| | | |25| | | |30| | | |35| | | |40| | | |45| | | |50| | | |55| | | |60

C. PROGRESSIVE PRACTICE: NUMBERS

Turn to the Progressive Practice: Numbers routine beginning on page SB-11.

Take six 30-second timings, starting at the point where you left off the last time.

D. Type the columns 2 times. Use the Tab key to move from column to column.

D. TECHNIQUE PRACTICE: TAB KEY

```
8    M. E. Barnes    Julie Herden    Lynn Masica     Don Trueblood
9    Bonnie Bursh    Brett Jones     Lisa O'Keefe    Matthew Utbert
10   Lee Chinn       Rick Kenwood    J. E. Perry     Jill Voss-Walin
11   Beth Gardner    Lance King      Chun Taing      Robin Yager
```

LANGUAGE ARTS

E. Edit this paragraph to correct any typing or formatting errors.

E. PROOFREADING

```
12       Many home computer user like the challenge of haveing
13   the latest in both hardware and software technology.  Their
14   are those however, who's needs likely can be satisfied at
15   a very low costs.  A used 286-chip personnel computer with
16   color monitor and keyboard might be your's for under $ 300.
17   Check out th Yellow Page, or visit a used-computer store.
```

DOCUMENT PROCESSING

Report 41
Continued

Continue working on Report 41.

Language

It is obvious that language differences play a major part in business miscommunication. Whenever there is an interpreter or a written translation involved, the chances for error are increased. There are over 3,000 languages used on the earth. Just as with English, there are not only

(continued on next page)

grammar rules but also varied meanings as words are both spoken and written. Even with the English language, there are differences in usage between the English used in the United States and that used in England.

Although English is the language usually used in international communication, the topics identified in Table 1 above illustrate the complexity of the challenge to communicate accurately; and the problem continues to grow. For example, literal translations of American advertising and labeling have sometimes resulted in negative feelings toward products. As world trade increases, so does the volume of international communication. Lesikar underscores the challenge:

> Although we can take comfort from knowing that ours is the primary language of international business, we must keep in mind that it is not the primary language of many of those who use it. Since many of these users have had to learn English as a second language, they are likely to use it less fluently than we and to experience problems in understanding us.
> (1991, p. 551)

A good sense of humor is an asset not only in our personal lives but also in the business environment. However, it probably should be avoided in multicultural settings because the possibilities for misinterpretation are compounded.

Religion, Values, and Ethics

While we can recognize the difficult challenge presented by language differences, this category (religion, values, and ethics) is in some ways the area that can bring about the most serious breakdowns in relations with those from other cultures.

Religion.   The very nature of religious beliefs suggests that this is a delicate area for those involved in business transactions in foreign countries. Also, religious beliefs affect the consumption of certain products throughout the world. Examples are tobacco, liquor, pork, and coffee.

Values.   Values are a reflection of religious beliefs for most people. We often hear references to right and wrong as applied to the ideals and customs of a society. Values relate to a range of topics, such as cleanliness, education, health care, and criminal justice.

Ethics.   Ethics are standards of conduct that reflect moral beliefs as applied to both one's personal life and one's business life. One's ethical conduct should be exemplary because it reflects what one considers to be right. Stanton et al. suggest, however, that while the concept is beautiful, pragmatic considerations sometimes make things more complicated:

(continued on next page)

In most countries in the Middle East it is generally not possible for a foreign marketer to sell directly to a branch of the government or to local private firms. Invariably sales are made through local agents who have personal contacts (often family members) in the buying organizations. To make sales under these conditions, some foreign firms pay these agents commissions well beyond what is reasonable for the tasks they perform. If your firm wished to expand into international markets, would you consider it ethical to make such payments to agents? (1991, p. 542)

Body Positions and Movements

Body language—that is, facial expressions, gestures, and body movements—conveys messages about attitude and may be interpreted differently by people in different cultures. For example, firm handshakes are the norm in the United States; loose handshakes are the custom in some other countries. The way we stand, sit, and hold our arms may convey different messages in different cultural settings.

Save this unfinished report. You will resume work on it in Lesson 74.

Lesson 74   Formal Report Project

GOALS: To type 42 wam/5'/5e; to format a formal report.

A. Type 2 times.

A. WARMUP

```
1       The new schedule* has the Lynx at their home park on     11
2  July 27 with the zany Waverly Blackhawks.  The Lynx scored    23
3  five fourth-quarter goals in their last game to win 8 to 4!   34
   |  1  |  2  |  3  |  4  |  5  |  6  |  7  |  8  |  9  |  10  |  11  |  12
```

SKILLBUILDING

B. Take a 1-minute timing on the first paragraph to establish your base speed. Then take four 1-minute timings on the remaining paragraphs. As soon as you equal or exceed your base speed on one paragraph, advance to the next, more difficult paragraph.

B. SUSTAINED PRACTICE: NUMBERS AND SYMBOLS

```
4        There is a need at this time to communicate our new      11
5  pricing guidelines to our franchise outlets.  In addition,     22
6  they must be made aware of inventory implications.  They       34
7  will then be in a position to have a successful operation.     45

8        Franchise operators could be requested to use either     11
9  a 20% or a 30% markup.  A $50 item would be marked to sell     23
10 for either $60 or $65.  Depending on future prospects for      34
11 sales, half of the articles would be priced at each level.     46
   |  1  |  2  |  3  |  4  |  5  |  6  |  7  |  8  |  9  |  10  |  11  |  12
```

```
12        Ms. Aagard's suggestion is to assign items in Groups   11
13   #1470, #2830, and #4560 to the 20% category.  The Series 77   23
14   items* would be in the 30% markup category except for those   35
15   items with a base rate under $100.  What is your reaction?    46

16        Mr. Chavez's recommendation is to assign a 30% markup    11
17   to Groups #3890, #5290, #6480, and #7180.  About 1/4 of the   23
18   remainder (except for soft goods) would also be in the 30%    35
19   category.  Groups #8340 and #9560 would have a 20% markup.     46
     | 1 | 2 | 3 | 4 | 5 | 6 | 7 | 8 | 9 | 10 | 11 | 12
```

C. Take two 5-minute timings. Determine your speed and errors.

Goal: 42 wam/5′/5e

C. 5-MINUTE TIMING

```
20        You have moved into a new apartment, and everything     11
21   looks wonderful except for the walls.  That multicolored      22
22   rug and those old posters were just what you wanted when      33
23   you were living in your old home.  But now they look out of   45
24   place.  While you like the idea of making the rounds of art   57
25   galleries and purchasing about five original oil paintings    69
26   and watercolors, the budget says no.  Some art enthusiasts    81
27   say the problem can be solved without spending a fortune.      93
28        Many people now rent beautiful paintings to hang on     103
29   their walls.  And they put forth some very good reasons for  115
30   doing this.  First, of course, is that they can acquire      126
31   prize works of art for a small fraction of the purchase      138
32   price.  But there are other reasons as well.  Wouldn't it    149
33   be fun to have your own gallery at home by changing your     161
34   wall hangings every six months?  In doing this, you would    172
35   visit art museums and galleries frequently and get to know   184
36   the consultants at your favorite places.  You would become   196
37   much more knowledgeable about artists and their various      207
38   styles and works.                                            210
     | 1 | 2 | 3 | 4 | 5 | 6 | 7 | 8 | 9 | 10 | 11 | 12
```

DOCUMENT PROCESSING

Report 41
Continued

Continue working on Report 41.

Male/Female Roles

There are major contrasts in the ways male and female roles are perceived in different cultures. The right to vote is still withheld from women in countries all over the world. Opportunities for female employment in the business environment vary considerably. Pay differentials for men and women continue to exist even when they are performing the same tasks. Opportunities for advancement for men and women often are not the same.

(continued on next page)

Punctuality, Time, and Space

A meeting that is scheduled for 9 a.m. likely will start on time in the United States, but in some other cultures the meeting may not start until 9:30 or even 10 o'clock. Punctuality and time concepts vary with the customs and practices of each country. Patience really can be a virtue.

There is also the element of space—the distance one stands from someone when engaged in conversation. If a person stands farther away than usual, this may signal a feeling of indifference or even a negative feeling. Standing too close is a sign of inappropriate familiarity.

Intimacy in Relationships

The degree of physical contact that is acceptable varies considerably. Hugs and kisses are the standard, even in the business office, in some countries. By contrast, the act of touching a person is considered an extreme invasion of privacy in other places. The use of first names may or may not be acceptable. To ask a personal question is extremely offensive in some cultures. While socializing with business clients is to be expected in some countries, that would be highly inappropriate in others. These are only a few of the relationship concerns that will be explored.

Conflict Resolution

Whether in negotiating a contract, working together to remedy product quality issues, or resolving contract interpretations, the need for tact and skill is particularly important in the foreign setting. Many of the seminar topics discussed above have implications in the area of conflict resolution. While every effort should be made to prevent conflict, there is a need for guidance in resolving disagreements in foreign cultures.

TENTATIVE SEMINAR SCHEDULE

As indicated earlier, it is our intent that all employees who have direct contact with people in other cultures will participate in these seminars. For that reason there will be two identical three-day seminars scheduled at each foreign site. Only selected employees in our regional sites in the United States will participate. (See Appendix, Table A.) These people have been tentatively identified on the basis of the extent of their involvement with persons from other countries.

As all employees in our foreign offices will participate, a decision has been made to schedule these seminars through the summer. A tentative schedule for these seminars is shown in Table 2.

(continued on next page)

City	First Seminar	Second Seminar
Melbourne	May 2-4	July 5-7
Rio de Janeiro	May 9-11	July 11-13
Beijing	May 16-18	July 18-20
Hamburg	May 23-25	July 25-27
Tokyo	June 6-8	August 1-3
Warsaw	June 13-15	August 8-10
Oslo	June 20-22	August 15-17
Madrid	June 27-29	August 22-24

TABLE 2.   FOREIGN-CITY SEMINARS

The Marketing Department is to be commended for calling our attention to the seriousness of our international communication problem. Dale Dolder, Tanya Falness, and Jodi Farmen also deserve our sincere thanks for their planning efforts for our intercultural communication seminars. As can be seen, special attention is being given to the seminar topics for these in-service programs. Efforts are also being made to identify instructors and resource persons who will develop instructional strategies that will be effective, interesting, and well received by the participants. These seminars will help significantly in increasing our market share in the international market.

Save this unfinished report. You will resume work on it in Lesson 75.

Lesson 75 Formal Report Project

GOALS: To improve speed and accuracy; to refine language-arts skills in the use of abbreviations; to format a formal report.

A. Type 2 times.

A. WARMUP

```
1      Bev ordered the following:  24 #79 napkin boxes, 48      11
2  #265B quarts of ketchup, and 72 reams of 20-lb white print    22
3  paper.  Did you receive the prize jalapeno peppers I sent?    34
   |  1  |  2  |  3  |  4  |  5  |  6  |  7  |  8  |  9  |  10  |  11  |  12
```

B. DIAGNOSTIC PRACTICE: ALPHABET

Turn to the Diagnostic Practice: Alphabet routine beginning on page SB-2. Type one of the Pretest/Posttest paragraphs and identify any errors made. Then type the corresponding drill lines 2 times for each letter on which you made 2 or more errors and 1 time for each letter on which you made only 1 error. Finally, repeat the same Pretest paragraph and compare your performance.

C. PACED PRACTICE

Turn to the Paced Practice routine beginning on page SB-14. Take three 2-minute timings, starting at the point where you left off the last time.

LANGUAGE ARTS

D. Study the rules at the right.

D. ABBREVIATIONS

Rule: In technical writing, on forms, and in tables, abbreviate units of measure when they occur frequently; do not use periods.

abb meas

Then pour 3 qt and 6 oz of water into the container with the chemicals.
The outside dimensions are 2 ft 6 in wide, 3 ft 8 in deep, and 4 ft 4 in high.

Rule: In lowercase abbreviations made up of single initials, use a period after each initial but no internal spaces.

abb lc

The executive officers will be meeting at 8 a.m. in Conference Room 304.
The items on the order will be shipped f.o.b. destination on October 17.

Rule: In all-caps abbreviations made up of single initials, do not use periods or internal spaces. (Exception: Keep the periods in most academic degrees and in abbreviations of geographic names other than two-letter state abbreviations.)

abb ≡

On the basis of their recommendation, the FIFO inventory method is used.
Nikki will be receiving a B.S. degree in office systems on December 19.

Edit the sentences to correct any errors in the use of abbreviations.

4 A mixture of 25 lb of cement and 100 lb of gravel was used.
5 The desk height must be reduced from 2 ft. 6 in. to 2 ft 4 in.
6 The meeting has been changed to 1 p. m. because of a conflict.
7 Auditors said sales were understated in the eom statement.
8 She enlisted in the U.S.M.C. after she received her degree.
9 His research paper deals with the early history of NATO.

DOCUMENT PROCESSING

Report 41
Continued
Appendix Page

1. Begin the appendix on a new page.
2. Center and type *APPENDIX* in bold approximately 2 inches from the top of the page.
3. Press Enter 2 times and create the table. Type the table data in the format shown.
4. Be sure the header and footer appear on this page and all other pages except the title page and the table of contents.

APPENDIX

TABLE A. DOMESTIC REGIONAL PARTICIPANTS		
Regional Office	**Tentative Dates**	**No. of People**
Birmingham	September 12-14	18
Boston	September 19-21	34
Chicago	September 26-28	27
Denver	October 3-5	12
San Francisco	October 10-12	38

Intercultural Communication

Spell-check your report to check for errors. However, remember that you must also proofread carefully for omitted or repeated words, errors that form a new word, and formatting errors.

Reference Page

1. Begin the references on a new page.
2. Center and type the title *REFER-ENCES* in bold approximately 2 inches from the top of the page.
3. Press Enter 2 times to insert a blank line.
4. Type the first line of each entry at the left margin. Indent carryover lines 0.5 inch.
5. Be sure the header and footer appear on this page.

REFERENCES

Lesikar, Raymond V., *Basic Business Communication,* 5th ed., Richard D. Irwin, Inc., Homewood, Ill., 1991.

O'Brien, Tyler D., Personal Interview, January 4, 19—.

(continued on next page)

Smith, Marsha O., and James F. Steward, "Communication for a Global Economy," *Business Education Forum,* April 1995, pp. 25–28.

Stanton, William J., Michael J. Etzel, and Bruce J. Walker, *Fundamentals of Marketing,* 9th ed., McGraw-Hill, Inc., New York, 1991.

Volworth, Elaine R., Personal Interview, January 6, 19—.

Report 42
Table of Contents

Create a table of contents for Report 41 as a separate document named Report 42.

1. Center and type the title *CONTENTS* in all caps and bold approximately 2 inches from the top of the page; then press Enter 2 times to insert a blank line.
2. Type the entries (using the centered and side headings from the report.)

Type the centered headings in all caps at the left margin. Type the side headings in initial caps indented 0.5 inch.
3. Do not include the header and footer on the table of contents page.
4. Type the page numbers at the right margin, preceded by dot leaders. Use the page numbers for your report.

CONTENTS

THE PROBLEM 1

INTERCULTURAL SEMINARS 1

INSTRUCTIONAL APPROACH 2

SEMINAR CONTENT 2

Indent the side headings 0.5 inch.

     Concept of Culture 3
     Language 4
     Religion, Values, and Ethics 4
     Body Positions and Movements 5
     Male/Female Roles 5
     Punctuality, Time, and Space 5
     Intimacy in Relationships 6
     Conflict Resolution 6

TENTATIVE SEMINAR SCHEDULE 6

APPENDIX 8

REFERENCES 9

Create a title page for Report 41 as a separate document named Report 43. Use the copy in the illustration.

1. Center the page vertically and type all copy in bold.
2. Change to 14-point font, and center and type the title in all caps with a blank line between each line as shown.
3. Change to 12-point font and press Enter 10 times.
4. Center and type the company name and address in all caps, single-spaced.
5. Press Enter 10 times and center and type *Prepared by.* Insert a blank line, then center and type the name and title of the person who prepared the report, single-spaced. Insert a blank line, then center and type the date.
6. Select the company name and address and insert a heavy top and bottom border above and below it. Then, press Enter 2 times after the top border and 2 times before the bottom border.

A PRELIMINARY PLAN FOR INTERCULTURAL

SEMINARS AT DOMESTIC AND

INTERNATIONAL SITES

ARMSTRONG ELECTRONICS
2400 TREADWAY ROAD
BOSTON, MA 02125

Prepared by

Jordan D. Sylvester, Director
Human Resources Department

February 12, 19--

1. Proofread all pages for format and typing errors.
2. Assemble the pages in this order: title page, table of contents, body, appendix, references, and a blank page for a back cover sheet.
3. Staple the report at three places along the left edge.

Lesson 76 — Inserting and Deleting Rows and Columns

GOALS: To type 43 wam/5'/5e; to insert and delete rows and columns in tables.

A. Type 2 times.

A. WARMUP

```
1      Order #Z391 must be processed "quickly" and exactly        11
2   as specified!  In January several orders were sent out by     22
3   mistake; regrettably, one order worth $5,680 was canceled.    34
    |  1  |  2  |  3  |  4  |  5  |  6  |  7  |  8  |  9  |  10  |  11  |  12
```

SKILLBUILDING

B. PROGRESSIVE PRACTICE: ALPHABET

Turn to the Progressive Practice: Alphabet routine beginning on page SB-7.   Take six 30-second timings, starting at the point where you left off the last time.

C. Take two 5-minute timings. Determine your speed and errors.

Goal: 43 wam/5'/5e

C. 5-MINUTE TIMING

```
4        How many times during the day do you remind yourself      11
5    that you have to remember to do something later that day or   23
6    perhaps the next day?  Then something happens to distract     34
7    you, and soon after you forget an important appointment or    46
8    task.  If this scenario repeats itself more than once a       57
9    day, you might find yourself in some serious trouble on the   69
10   job.  Fortunately, many simple techniques are available to    81
11   help jog your memory.                                         86
12       One simple technique you can try is to twist your ring    97
13   or watch around so that it is backwards.  When you notice     108
14   that it feels uncomfortable, that will be your reminder to    120
15   take action.  If you prefer a technique that is a little      132
16   more sophisticated, try programming your computer to sound    143
17   an alarm or flash a message on the screen.                    152
18       You could also purchase a key ring that is equipped       163
19   with a miniaturized tape recorder; you could just record      174
20   a reminder while you are driving or walking and review it     186
21   later when you are by a calendar.  Once you realize how       197
22   many ways you can jog your memory, you should be able to      208
23   increase your ability to remember.                            215
     |  1  |  2  |  3  |  4  |  5  |  6  |  7  |  8  |  9  |  10  |  11  |  12
```

FORMATTING

D. WORD PROCESSING: TABLE—INSERT AND DELETE ROWS OR COLUMNS

Study Lesson 76 in your word processing manual. Complete all of the shaded steps while at your computer. Then format the jobs that follow.

DOCUMENT PROCESSING

Table 24
Boxed Table

Do not adjust the column widths.

1. Center the table vertically.
2. Create a boxed table with 3 columns and 4 rows.
3. Type the column headings at the left
4. Follow standard table format for the rest of this table.

in initial caps and bold.

Date	Location	Hotel
May 1	San Francisco	Hilton
July 17	Scottsdale	Mountain Shadows
August 1	Detroit	Westin

Table 25
Boxed Table

Open the file for Table 24 and make the following changes:

1. Insert this row of information before Row 3: *June 10, Dallas, Crowne Plaza.*
2. Delete the last row of the table.
3. Insert a row above Row 1, join the cells, and center and type the title *SOFTWARE DEMONSTRATIONS* in all caps and bold. Press Enter 1 time to insert a blank line after the title.

Table 26
Open Table

Your completed table will look different from the one shown here.

1. Center the table vertically.
2. Create an open table with 3 columns and 5 rows.
3. Center and type the column headings in Row 2 in initial caps and bold.
4. Follow standard table format for the rest of this table.
5. Insert this column of information
before the column headed "Credits": *Miles, 234, 733, 229.*
6. Delete the column headed "Credits."
7. Automatically adjust column widths.
8. Join the cells in Row 1; then center and type the title in all caps and bold. Press Enter 1 time after the title.
9. Center the table horizontally.

AIR MILEAGE

Origination	Destination	Credits
Los Angeles	Las Vegas	500
Chicago	New York	1,000
Detroit	Cincinnati	500

Table 27
Open Table

1. Open the file for Table 26.
2. Insert this row of information before the last row in the table: *Cleveland, Miami, 1,274.*
3. Change the title to: *FLIGHT FUND MILEAGE.*

Lesson 77   Joining and Splitting Cells

GOALS: To improve speed and accuracy; to refine language-arts skills in composing; to join and split cells; to format braced headings.

A. Type 2 times.

A. WARMUP

```
1        This VGA monitor (Model #JKQ-6GM) displays lines at     11
2   1280 x 1024 at 80 Hz.  It would be an excellent purchase!    22
3   Could delivery be guaranteed by 3:30 p.m. on Friday, 7/9?    34
       | 1 | 2 | 3 | 4 | 5 | 6 | 7 | 8 | 9 | 10 | 11 | 12
```

SKILLBUILDING

B. PACED PRACTICE

Turn to the Paced Practice routine beginning on page SB-14. Take three 2-minute timings, starting at the point where you left off the last time.

C. DIAGNOSTIC PRACTICE: NUMBERS

Turn to the Diagnostic Practice: Numbers routine beginning on page SB-5. Type one of the Pretest/Posttest paragraphs and identify any errors made. Then type the corresponding drill lines 2 times for each number on which you made 2 or more errors and 1 time for each number on which you made only 1 error. Finally, repeat the same Pretest paragraph and compare your performance.

LANGUAGE ARTS

D. COMPOSING

Compose a paragraph to explain how to insert and delete rows in tables. Use the following suggestions: Explain briefly that to insert or delete a row, you position the insertion point where you want the row inserted or deleted. You then issue the command from the menu to insert or delete a row.

E. BRACED COLUMN HEADINGS

A braced column heading is a heading that applies to more than one column (for example, *Retirement Account,* in the table shown below).

1. To create a braced heading, position the insertion point where you want the braced heading to appear.

2. You may either join cells to create space for the braced heading or split the cells below it into two or more columns.

F. WORD PROCESSING: TABLE—SPLIT CELLS

Study Lesson 77 in your word processing manual. Complete all of the shaded steps while at your computer. Then format the jobs that follow.

DOCUMENT PROCESSING

Table 28
Boxed Table

1. Center the table vertically.
2. Create a boxed table with 3 columns and 6 rows.
3. Center and type the braced and regular column headings in initial caps and bold. Right align the number columns.
4. Follow the standard table format for the rest of the table.
5. Join and split cells and columns as necessary.

INSURED ACCOUNT DEPOSITS For Melanie and Frank Rice					
First World Savings		**Individual Account**		**Retirement Account**	
Month	**Branch**	**M. Rice**	**F. Rice**	**M. Rice**	**F. Rice**
January	Reseda	$5,500	$2,350	$2,000	$10,000
February	Valencia	$7,950	$5,700	$5,500	$4,300
March	Van Nuys	$2,400	$7,300	$9,300	$2,550

Table 29
Boxed Table

1. Center the table vertically.
2. Create a boxed table with 2 columns and 6 rows.
3. Center and type the braced and regular column headings in initial caps and bold; right align the number columns.
4. Follow the standard table format for the rest of the table.
5. Join and split cells and columns as necessary.

CINEPLEX VIDEOS Sales Trends			
Western Region		**Total Sales**	
State	**Manager**	**Last Year**	**This Year**
California	George Lucas	$1,956,250	$2,135,433
Nevada	Marjorie Matheson	$859,435	$1,231,332
Washington	Valerie Harper	$737,498	$831,352

Table 30
Boxed Table

Open the file for Table 29 and make the following changes.

1. Change the column heading *Western Region* to *Eastern Region*.
2. Change the state names to *New York, New Jersey,* and *Delaware*.
3. Change the managers' names to

Robert DeLuca, Doris Lynch, and *Marcia Chisholm*.

4. Change last year's amounts to *$2,052,659, $534,958,* and *$894,211*.
5. Change this year's amounts to *$3,345,312, $2,311,478,* and *$925,138*.

Lesson 78 Calculations

GOALS: To type 43 wam/5'/5e; to format tables with footnotes; to perform calculations within a table.

A. Type 2 times.

A. WARMUP

```
1     This week order a monitor with a resolution of 1280 x      11
2  1024 that supports a 60-MHZ refresh rate from V & Q Inc.       23
3  It will cost $573* (*a 9% savings) if ordered before July!     34
   | 1 | 2 | 3 | 4 | 5 | 6 | 7 | 8 | 9 | 10 | 11 | 12
```

SKILLBUILDING

B. DIAGNOSTIC PRACTICE: ALPHABET

Turn to the Diagnostic Practice: Alphabet routine beginning on page SB-2. Type one of the Pretest/Posttest paragraphs and identify any errors made. Then type the corresponding drill lines 2 times for each letter on which you made 2 or more errors and 1 time for each letter on which you made only 1 error. Finally, repeat the same Pretest paragraph and compare your performance.

C. Take two 5-minute timings. Determine your speed and errors.

Goal: 43 wam/5'/5e

C. 5-MINUTE TIMING

4   There is no question that making sound and effective   11
5   decisions is a valuable skill in any job. Anyone who has   22
6   mastered this skill should prove to be a valuable asset in   34
7   any company. A person who is decisive has the ability to   46
8   think quickly and see the bottom line in a given situation.   58
9   This person can also recognize when a decision should be   69
10   delegated to someone else and when it should be delayed.   81

11   You can train yourself to make decisions quickly if   91
12   you will just follow a few simple rules. You must realize   103
13   that no decision will be perfect and then be willing to   114
14   accept the consequences. You need to give yourself enough   126
15   time for fact-finding so that your decision will be a sound   138
16   one. However, don't take more time than is needed.   149

17   Even though your decision might be the wrong one, at   159
18   times the mere fact that you took some action instead of   171
19   waiting will outweigh any negative effects. Don't waste   182
20   time second-guessing your choice. Remember that even if   194
21   things don't turn out as you had hoped, you can still gain   205
22   valuable insights and learn from the experience.   215

| 1 | 2 | 3 | 4 | 5 | 6 | 7 | 8 | 9 | 10 | 11 | 12

FORMATTING

D. TABLES WITH FOOTNOTES

To format tables with footnotes, follow these steps:

1. Include a separate row for the footnote reference at the bottom of the table when you are creating the table structure.

2. Place the insertion point inside the bottom row; then, join all the cells in this row.

3. Type an asterisk (or some other symbol) at the appropriate point within the table to indicate that there is a footnote.

4. Type the footnote.

E. WORD PROCESSING: TABLE—FORMULAS (ADVANCED)

Study Lesson 78 in your word processing manual. Complete all of the shaded steps while at your computer. Then format the jobs that follow.

DOCUMENT PROCESSING

Table 31
Boxed Table

1. Center the table vertically.
2. Create a boxed table with 5 columns and 7 rows.
3. Type the column headings in initial caps and bold, aligned as shown. Type the columns aligned as shown. Do not type the question marks.
4. Insert the formulas to calculate the necessary amounts in column E.

Format the numbers with dollar signs, thousands separator, and 2 places after the decimal point.
5. Automatically adjust the column widths.
6. Join cells as necessary, and type the title, TOTAL, and the footnote.
7. Center the table horizontally.

EQUIPMENT REQUISITION*				
Department	**Item**	**Unit Price**	**Quantity**	**Cost**
Desktop Publishing	Laser Printer	$975.00	2	?
Sales and Marketing	Keyboard	$95.00	5	?
Communications	Internal Modem	$105.00	3	?
TOTAL				?
*Please note that all requisitions are subject to approval by managers.				

Table 32
Boxed Table

1. Center the table vertically.
2. Create a boxed table with 5 columns and 7 rows.
3. Type the column headings in initial caps and bold, aligned as shown. Type the columns aligned as shown. Do not type the question marks.
4. Insert the formulas to calculate the necessary amounts in column E.

Format the numbers with dollar signs, thousands separator, and 2 places after the decimal point.
5. Automatically adjust the column widths.
6. Join the cells as shown and type the title, subtitle, TOTAL, and footnote as shown.
7. Center the table horizontally.

PC SOLUTIONS Price List*				
Item	**Description**	**Retail Price**	**Our Price**	**Savings**
PC-9400	Multimedia System	$2,350.00	$1,975.00	?
LPP-3299	Laser Pointer Pen	$75.00	$59.00	?
ICD-2335	CD-ROM Drive	$175.00	$155.00	?
TOTAL				?
*Prices are subject to change.				

Table 33
Open Table

Open the file for Table 31 and make the following changes:

1. Change it from a boxed table to an open table.

2. Delete the footnote reference symbol and the footnote.

3. Delete the *TOTAL* row.

Lesson 79   Formatting Options

GOALS: To improve speed and accuracy; to refine language-arts skills in spelling; to format table cells using fill options.

A. Type 2 times.

A. WARMUP

1 Please request this key item by June: a 486DX2-100   11
2 motherboard with 32-MB RAM. I don't expect delivery until   22
3 7/5; I realize this is a "great" investment for the money!   34

| 1 | 2 | 3 | 4 | 5 | 6 | 7 | 8 | 9 | 10 | 11 | 12

SKILLBUILDING

B. Take a 1-minute timing on the first paragraph to establish your base speed. Then take four 1-minute timings on the remaining paragraphs. As soon as you equal or exceed your base speed on one paragraph, advance to the next, more difficult paragraph.

B. SUSTAINED PRACTICE: ROUGH DRAFT

4 The possibility of aging and not being able to live as   11
5 independently as we want to is a prospect that no one wants   23
6 to recognize. One resource designed to counter some of the   35
7 negative realities of aging is called the Handyman Project.   47

8 This type of ~~project~~ *program* helps support elders and disabled   11
9 residents in their efforts to maintain the^ir homes. As the   23
10 name implies, "handy" volunteers perform minor home repairs   35
11 such as tightening leaky faucets and fixing broken windows.   47

12 Other types of work include: painting, plumbing, yard   11
13 work, and carpentery. The volunteers are all as diversified   23
14 as the word itself. You may find a retiree working next to   35
15 an executive or a student ~~helping~~ *assisting* a licensed electrician.   47

| 1 | 2 | 3 | 4 | 5 | 6 | 7 | 8 | 9 | 10 | 11 | 12

16   Their back grounds may vary, but ~~that~~ w̄hat they share is the   11
   desire
17 ~~hope~~ to put their ~~capabilities~~ to good use. Volunteers ~~take~~ find   23
                                                              finishing
18 a high level of personal satisfaction after ~~doing~~ a job   35
   and
19 ~~but~~ spending time with∧an elder who really needs the help.   47

       | 1 | 2 | 3 | 4 | 5 | 6 | 7 | 8 | 9 | 10 | 11 | 12

C. 12-SECOND SPEED SPRINTS

C. Take three 12-second timings on each line. The scale below the last line shows your wam speed for a 12-second timing.

20 You paid for the ruby that she owned when he was just five.
21 Toby wishes to thank all eight of the girls for their time.
22 Yale is a very fine place to learn about the world of work.
23 She has a theory that the icy roads will cause a bad wreck.

   | | | |5| | | |10| | | |15| | | |20| | | |25| | | |30| | | |35| | | |40| | | |45| | | |50| | | |55| | | |60

LANGUAGE ARTS

D. SPELLING

D. Type this list of frequently misspelled words, paying special attention to any spelling problems in each word.

24 assistance compliance initial limited corporation technical
25 operating sufficient operation incorporated writing current
26 advice together prepared recommend appreciated cannot based
27 benefit completing analysis probably projects before annual
28 issue attention location association participation proposed

Edit the sentences to correct any misspellings.

29 The complience by the corporation was sufficient to pass.
30 I cannot reccomend the project based on the expert advise.
31 The location of the proposed annual meeting was an issue.
32 Your assistance in completeing the project is appreciated.
33 Together we prepared an analysis of their current operation.
34 The writing was incorporated in the initial asociation bid.

FORMATTING

E. TABLES WITH FILL

1. Rows, columns, or cells in a table can be set apart from the rest of the table by using various fill options such as shading and patterns. Use fill options selectively.
2. Fill options may be set to a variety of intensities (light to heavy) and may have different patterns. Avoid using any fill with an intensity higher than 20% when there is text in a cell because usually it makes the text hard to read.

F. WORD PROCESSING: TABLE—FILL

Study Lesson 79 in your word processing manual. Complete all of the shaded steps while at your computer. Then format the jobs that follow.

DOCUMENT PROCESSING

Table 34
Boxed Table With Shading

1. Center the table vertically.
2. Create a boxed table with 4 columns and 7 rows.
3. Type the table as shown with centered column headings. Ignore any lines that wrap.
4. Follow standard table format for the rest of this table.
5. Automatically adjust column widths.
6. Apply a 20% fill intensity to Row 1 and a 10% fill intensity to Rows 3, 5, and 7.
7. Center the table horizontally.

COPIER USAGE			
Department	**Full Color**	**Oversize**	**Regular**
Public Information Services	329	35	235
Learning Resources	42	0	987
Student Services	22	129	760
Facilities Planning and Services	5	29	350
Personnel Services	17	2	530

Table 35
Open Table

1. Center the table vertically.
2. Create an open table with 6 columns and 10 rows.
3. Type the table data as shown with centered column headings in Rows 1, 2, 4, 6, 8, and 10.
4. Leave Rows 3, 5, 7, and 9 blank.
5. Follow standard format for the rest of this table.
6. Automatically adjust column widths.
7. Apply a 10% fill intensity to the entire table; apply a 30% fill intensity to Row 2; and apply a 60% fill intensity for the bars in Rows 4, 6, 8, and 10.

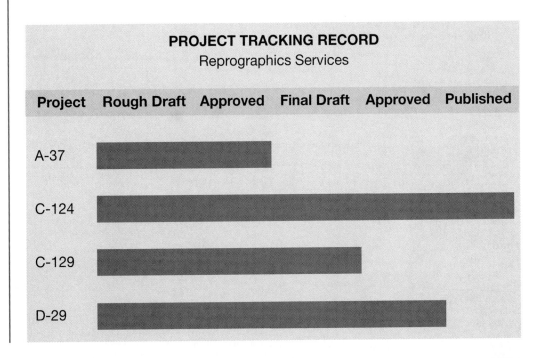

Table 36

1. Open Table 35 and change the project numbers to *B-48, C-27, C-125,* and *D-109.*

2. Select a different fill intensity or any pattern you prefer for the bars.

Lesson 80   Revising Tables

GOALS: To type 43 wam/5'/5e; to practice revising tables.

A. Type 2 times.

A. WARMUP

```
1       "Just when can we expect to realize a profit of 5% or      11
2   more?"  This kind of question will be important to 2/3 of      23
3   the shareholders; they own over 89% of the prime holdings.     34
    | 1 | 2 | 3 | 4 | 5 | 6 | 7 | 8 | 9 | 10 | 11 | 12
```

SKILLBUILDING

B. This paragraph is made up of very short words, requiring the frequent use of the space bar. Type the paragraph 2 times. Do not pause before or after pressing the space bar.

Pretest
Take a 1-minute timing. Determine your speed and errors.

B. TECHNIQUE PRACTICE: SPACE BAR

```
4       We will all go to the race if I win my event today.
5   Do you think that I will be able to finish the race at the
6   front of the pack, or do you think there are lots of really
7   fast runners out there who surely can finish ahead of me?
```

C. PRETEST: ALTERNATE- AND ONE-HAND WORDS

```
8       They both blame the fight on the visitor.  The girl      11
9   had no right to imply that the proxy was brave enough to     22
10  draw you into the unholy case.  The union will reward you.   34
    | 1 | 2 | 3 | 4 | 5 | 6 | 7 | 8 | 9 | 10 | 11 | 12
```

Practice
   Speed Emphasis: If you made no more than 1 error on the Pretest, type each *individual* line 2 times.
   Accuracy Emphasis: If you made 2 or more errors, type each *group* of lines (as though it were a paragraph) 2 times.

D. PRACTICE: ALTERNATE-HAND WORDS

```
11  also angle field bushel ancient emblem panel sight fish big
12  both blame fight formal element handle proxy signs girl and
13  city chair giant island visitor profit right their laid cut
```

E. PRACTICE: ONE-HAND WORDS

```
14  acts hilly award uphill average poplin refer jolly adds him
15  area jumpy based homily baggage you'll serve union beat ink
16  case brave extra limply greater unholy wages imply draw you
```

Posttest
Repeat the Pretest timing and compare performance.

F. POSTTEST: ALTERNATE- AND ONE-HAND WORDS

G. Take two 5-minute timings. Determine your speed and errors.

Goal: 43 wam/5'/5e

G. 5-MINUTE TIMING

17 The first three months on a new job are very important 11
18 for many reasons. This is a time in which a new employee 23
19 is being watched closely by both peers and supervisors; the 35
20 opportunity to make a second impression might never come if 47
21 the first impression is a bad one. People will begin to 58
22 form judgments about you and your work routine right away. 70
23 If you are prompt and conscientious, they will form a very 82
24 positive impression. If you are often late or turn into a 94
25 clock watcher, you are laying the foundation for a dismal 105
26 future instead of a long, profitable one. 114
27 Once a reputation has been established, either good or 125
28 bad, it is difficult to reverse it; your actions speak for 137
29 themselves. If your actions demonstrate positive habits 148
30 like working until the job is done, you will be rewarded. 160
31 Those employees who zip out the door as soon as they can 171
32 are not the ones who receive the promotions or the raises. 183
33 Offer help whenever you can. If you have any extra 194
34 time, take the initiative to find a productive way to use 205
35 it. In the long run, your acts will be rewarded. 215

| 1 | 2 | 3 | 4 | 5 | 6 | 7 | 8 | 9 | 10 | 11 | 12

DOCUMENT PROCESSING

Table 37
Boxed table

1. Open the file for Table 25.
2. Insert 2 rows in the table to include the information as shown.
3. Apply a 20% fill intensity to Rows 1, 3, 5, and 7.

SOFTWARE DEMONSTRATIONS		
Date	**Location**	**Hotel**
May 1	San Francisco	Hilton
May 20	Los Angeles	Biltmore
June 10	Dallas	Crowne Plaza
July 17	Scottsdale	Mountain Shadows
July 30	Seattle	Red Lion

Table 38
Boxed Table

1. Open the file for Table 28.
2. Insert a row at the end of the table as shown.
3. Use the appropriate commands to calculate the last row and format the row with a dollar sign and a thousands separator.
4. Apply a 20% fill intensity as shown and join cells as shown.
5. Center the table vertically and horizontally.

INSURED ACCOUNT DEPOSITS For Melanie and Frank Rice						
First World Savings		Individual Account		Retirement Account		
Month	Branch	M. Rice	F. Rice	M. Rice	F. Rice
January	Reseda	$5,500	$2,350	$2,000	$10,000
February	Valencia	$7,950	$5,700	$5,500	$4,300
March	Van Nuys	$2,400	$7,300	$9,300	$2,550
TOTAL		?	?	?	?

Table 39

Progress Check
Boxed Table

1. Center the table vertically and horizontally.
2. Apply a 20% fill intensity to the cells that are shaded.
3. Center the text in all cells.
4. Automatically adjust the column widths.

WESTERN PACIFIC COMMUNICATIONS NETWORK Fee Increase Effective January 1		
Per Visit Service	Charges Today	Charges January 1
Residence	$45 for the first 15 minutes	$95 flat rate
Business	$50 for the first 15 minutes	$110 flat rate
Private Line	$55 for the first 15 minutes	$250 flat rate

Ask your instructor for the General Information Test on Part 4.

Test 4-A
5-Minute Timing

1	More and more business firms and agencies are now	10
2	doing their own desktop publishing. This is because of the	22
3	new software which has been designed to make it easier to	34
4	place copy on the page. The big challenge now is to design	46
5	the page effectively so that the reader will want to read	57
6	the copy. After all, that is the sole reason for investing	69
7	time and money in the publication.	76
8	There are times when the reader is confused because	87
9	there are too many headlines and articles on the page. It	99
10	is much better to have only a few on each page. This makes	111
11	it possible to have both longer articles and larger print	122
12	size. A large headline will quickly draw the reader's eye	134
13	to the article. Place the most important article at the	146
14	top of the first page and lesser ones in the inside pages.	157
15	Subheadings and listings are excellent tools to guide	168
16	the reader through the copy. Pictures and other uses of	180
17	graphics may be just the touch that is needed. Including	191
18	white copy on a black background or highlighted text in a	203
19	box can be used most effectively to draw attention to copy.	215

| 1 | 2 | 3 | 4 | 5 | 6 | 7 | 8 | 9 | 10 | 11 | 12 |

Test 4-B
Memo 22
Memo Report With Boxed Table

MEMO

TO: All employees

FROM: Paula Sullivan

Date: January 15, 19--

SUBJECT: Capital Communication Co.

Capital Communciation Co. (CCC) operates the fourth largest network in the U.S. In addition, CCC owns 8 television stations, 3 radio stations, and 4 newspapers. HISTORY CCC was started in 1962 by a subsidary of Heartland Publications as a public service network. It began with three radio stations and added both radio and television stations until it went public in 1956. In 1987 it merged with Pacific Media Company and added 4 newspapers. CCC's largest newspaper, *The San Antonio Tribune,* won a pulitzer prize for feature writing last year.

(continued on next page)

EARNINGS With sales of $4.9 billion ~~dollars~~ for the most recent 12-month period and a net ~~,~~ income of $486 million, ~~it~~ CCC continues to lead the "buy" list of most stock brokers. The table shows a break down of ~~its~~ CCC's earnings. [following]

CAPITAL COMMUNICATION COMPANY Sales (in Billions)			*(center)*
Company	Last Year	This Year	Next Year ✳
Radio	$ #1.3	$1.4	$1.4
Television	$1.8	$2.0	$2.2
Newspapers	$1.4	$1.5	$2.0
*Projected			

Test 4-C
Letter 51
Modified-Block Style
With Indented
Paragraphs

{Current date} / Mr. Owen F. Austin / 1734 Perry Street / Flint, MI 48504 / Dear Mr. Austin:

¶I am sorry that time constraints shortened our telephone conversation yesterday. Given the circumstances as you presented them, you would be wise to consider drafting a General Durable Power of Attorney as described in Section 495 of the new act.

¶A Power of Attorney under the old law is effective only up to the time that a person is disabled or incompetent. Now the General Durable Power of Attorney, under the new statute, will remain in effect until a person either revokes it or passes away.

¶The new law will be very helpful to many elderly and infirm people.

Sincerely yours, / C. F. Storden / Attorney-at-Law / {urs} / bc: Peggy Austin / Walter Austin / PS: You may want to discuss this matter with your children before calling my office for an appointment.

Test 4-D
Table 40
4-Column Boxed
Table

Add 20% shading
to the title row and 10%
to column headings and
total rows.

AMERICAN TRADE (As a Percentage of Total)			
Exports		**Imports**	
Canada	22	Japan	20
Japan	12	Canada	19
Mexico	7	Mexico	6
United Kingdom	6	Germany	5
Germany	5	Taiwan	5
South Korea	4	South Korea	4
Other Countries	44	Other Countries	41
TOTAL	100	TOTAL	100

PART FIVE

Forms, Specialized Correspondence, Reports, and Tables

OBJECTIVES

KEYBOARDING
- To type 47 wam/5'/5e

LANGUAGE ARTS
- To refine proofreading skills and correctly use proofreaders' marks.
- To correctly capitalize, punctuate, and spell.
- To recognize subject/verb and pronoun agreement and refine composing skills.

WORD PROCESSING
- To use the word processing com-

mands necessary to complete the document processing activities.

DOCUMENT PROCESSING
- To format memos, purchase orders, invoices, press releases, and labels using templates; specialized correspondence; special reports; advanced tables.

TECHNICAL
- To answer correctly at least 90 percent of the questions on an objective test.

Lesson 81   Memos

GOALS: To improve speed and accuracy; to refine language-arts skills in proofreading; to format memos using a template.

A. Type 2 times.

A. WARMUP

```
1        Martin bought five chances for the contest.  He won    11
2    six prizes and was given a check for $2,350--these prizes  22
3    are equal to 1/4 of Jill's winnings for all of last year.  34
     |  1  |  2  |  3  |  4  |  5  |  6  |  7  |  8  |  9  |  10  |  11  |  12
```

SKILLBUILDING

B. Take three 12-second timings on each line. The scale below the last line shows your wam speed for a 12-second timing.

B. 12-SECOND SPEED SPRINTS

```
4    They saw the sun shine through after days and days of rain.
5    She hopes to get a much higher math score on the next test.
6    Jo did not study for the math exam she took late last week.
7    This time he spent at least ten days studying for the test.
     | | | |5| | | |10| | | |15| | | |20| | | |25| | | |30| | | |35| | | |40| | | |45| | | |50| | | |55| | | |60
```

C. PROGRESSIVE PRACTICE: ALPHABET

Turn to the Progressive Practice: Alphabet routine beginning on page SB-7.   Take six 30-second timings, starting at the point where you left off the last time.

D. Type the paragraph 2 times, concentrating on each letter typed.

D. TECHNIQUE PRACTICE: CONCENTRATION

```
8        El uso de la bicicleta es muy popular en Barranquilla.
9    Cuando el tiempo es bueno a toda la gente joven le gusta ir
10   a pasear en bicicletas.  Me gusta ir a montar en bicicleta,
11   especialmente cuando hace sol y el tiempo es agradable.
```

LANGUAGE ARTS

E. Compare this paragraph with the 5-minute timing on page 221. Edit the paragraph to correct any errors.

E. PROOFREADING

```
12       Business in our nation has seen many changes in the
13   last decade as a result of down sizing, acquisions and
14   the need too stay competative in a global market.  The last
15   decade have witnessed a dramatic increase in the number of
16   employees working in the larger companies in the country.
```

F. FILLING IN FORMS

Many business forms can be created by using templates that are provided within word processing software. When a template is opened, a "printed" form is displayed on the screen, enabling you to fill in the necessary information.

Template forms contain data fields that correspond to blank sections on printed forms. For example, a memo template may include the guide words *TO:*,

FROM:, *DATE:*, and *SUBJECT:*. Templates are designed so that you can quickly move to each data field, usually with a single keystroke. Templates also enable you to customize your work by having you fill in repetitive information (such as the company name and telephone number) before you use a template for the first time. Then, each time you open that template, the information automatically appears.

G. WORD PROCESSING: TEMPLATES—USING

Study Lesson 81 in your word processing manual. Complete all of the shaded steps while at your computer. Then format the jobs that follow.

DOCUMENT PROCESSING

Form 1
Memo

Select the first memo template listed in your word processing software.
   The sequence of the guide words in a memo may vary depending on the software you are using.

TO: Carol Newby / **FROM:** Allen Colley / **DATE:** July 10, 19— / **SUBJECT:** Software Clip Art

¶Our computer graphics department has reviewed the Office Gallery Graphics catalog and is impressed by the quality of the images available on the three CD-ROM disks. The quality of these images is superb, and the color selection is used well. The first disk is especially well-suited for our work.

¶We would like to order all three disks in this set because a complete order comes with a file conversion package. We will prepare a purchase order after receiving your authorization. / {urs}

Form 2
Memo

Select the first memo template listed in your word processing software.

TO: Alex R. Henson / **FROM:** Paige Pera / **DATE:** {Current Date} / **SUBJECT:** ID Card

¶Your new ID card may be picked up at this office on March 25 or 26 between the hours of 10 a.m. and 2 p.m. Please be sure to sign the card and carry it with you at all times. When you pick up your new card, you will be required to turn in your old ID card.

¶As we discussed at our last departmental meeting, your new card will be required for admission to the exercise room and the cafeteria, as well as for

(continued on next page)

cashing checks at the cashier's office. Finally, your new card will be required for access to Buildings A, B, and E, as well as for entrance at Gate C on weekends.

¶Please notify this office immediately if your card is lost or stolen. / {urs}

Form 3
Memo

Open the file for Form 1, and make the following changes:
1. Change the subject to *CD-ROM Clip Art.*
2. Change the total number of disks to seven.

3. Change the first sentence in the second paragraph to the following: *We would like to order only the first two clip art disks because they are the ones most appropriate for our graphics needs.*

Lesson 82   Invoices

GOALS: To type 44 wam/5'/5e; to format invoices using a template.

A. Type 2 times.

A. WARMUP

```
1      Jacqueline kept prize #2490 instead of #3761 because      11
2   it was worth 58% more value.  That was a great prize!  Last   23
3   year the law firm of Adams & Day donated all grand prizes.    34
    |  1  |  2  |  3  |  4  |  5  |  6  |  7  |  8  |  9  |  10  |  11  |  12
```

SKILLBUILDING

Pretest
Take a 1-minute timing. Determine your speed and errors.

B. PRETEST: COMMON LETTER COMBINATIONS

```
4      The insurance agent read the report before giving it     11
5   to the deputy director.  This weekly action showed that the   23
6   agent really knew the actual input on a daily basis.          33
    |  1  |  2  |  3  |  4  |  5  |  6  |  7  |  8  |  9  |  10  |  11  |  12
```

Practice
Speed Emphasis: If you made no more than 1 error on the Pretest, type each *individual* line 2 times.
Accuracy Emphasis: If you made 2 or more errors, type each *group* of lines (as though it were a paragraph) 2 times.

C. PRACTICE: WORD BEGINNINGS

```
7   re- repel renew remit relax refer ready react really reveal
8   in- inept inert inset input infer index incur inches insert
9   be- bears beams beach below being began befit beauty beside
```

D. PRACTICE: WORD ENDINGS

```
10  -ly truly madly lowly early daily apply hilly simply weekly
11  -ed sized hired dated cited based acted added opened showed
12  -nt plant meant giant front event count agent amount fluent
```

F. Take two 5-minute timings. Determine your speed and errors.

Goal: 44 wam/5′/5e

E. POSTTEST: COMMON LETTER COMBINATIONS

F. 5-MINUTE TIMING

13	Business in our country has seen great changes in the	11
14	last decade as a result of downsizing, acquisitions, and	23
15	the need to stay competitive in a global market. The last	35
16	decade has witnessed a dramatic decline in the number of	46
17	employees working in the largest companies in the nation.	58
18	The labor market turnover has caused many firms to rethink	70
19	their staffing standards in favor of a flexible work unit.	81
20	There are all sorts of ways to make the work setting	92
21	more flexible. Job sharing is just one example. In job	104
22	sharing, two employees split one full-time job with each	115
23	working a portion of the hours. Flextime is another work	127
24	schedule that grants a wide range of starting and quitting	138
25	times based on personal needs. A third way, telecommuting,	150
26	is an arrangement whereby employees work out of their homes	162
27	and are linked to their office via the phone or a computer.	174
28	More than almost any other benefit, a flexible work	185
29	schedule gives many people the power to adjust and balance	197
30	home with work. Many firms believe this type of flexible	208
31	scheduling for employees can pay off with large dividends.	220

| 1 | 2 | 3 | 4 | 5 | 6 | 7 | 8 | 9 | 10 | 11 | 12

FORMATTING

G. INVOICES

An invoice (or *bill*) is prepared by a seller for the buyer and shows an itemized list of the charges for goods purchased.

An invoice template may ask for information that is not necessary (such as a company slogan) or contain data fields for which you have no information. In these instances, delete any unnecessary information and leave the data fields blank.

H. WORD PROCESSING: TEMPLATES—MODIFYING

Study Lesson 82 in your word processing manual. Complete all of the shaded steps while at your computer. Then format the jobs that follow.

Form 4
Invoice

Select the first invoice template in your word processing software. Prepare Invoice 43227 from Benson Associates, 2859 Pacific Avenue, Atlantic City, NJ 08401. Benson's telephone number is 609-555-3949; its fax number is 609-555-3950. Send the invoice to Appleton Community College, 10432 Hot Springs Drive, Greeley, CO 80634. Use the current date, order no. 8070, date shipped of 3/5/—, and shipped via UPS. The items invoiced are as follows:

3 Brad mailer, Model G4681 @ 78.99; 15 Router pad, Part No. C3238 @ 7.95; 2 8″ × 72″ heavy-duty jointer, Model B1348 @ 625.75; 20 Polycrylic finish (1 gallon) @ 50.75; 5 Model 610 CFM dust collector, 1 1/2 hp, 110/220 volts @ 199.95.
   Sales tax = 181.12 (5%); shipping and handling = 55.00.

Form 5
Invoice

Use the first invoice template in your word processing software.

Prepare a second invoice (No. 43228) from Benson Associates. Send the invoice to Ms. Janice Voiss, Adams Construction Company, 865 Boston Boulevard, Portland, ME 04103-2762. Use the current date, order no. 8099, date shipped 7/2/—, and shipped via FedEx. The items invoiced are as follows:

4 Variable-speed scroll saw with 1.3-amp, 110-volt motor; cut depth, 2″; throat, 15″ deep; tilt to 45 degrees @ 189.99; 12 Adjustable steel bar clamp, 2 1/4″ × 24″ @ 9.75; 2 Drum sander with 38″ dual drum and 2-hp motor @ 1,275.75; 1 12″ contractor-style table saw (Model WSR-12) @ 425.05; 3 Portable planer (Model GT-50L) @ 349.75.
   Sales tax = 269.65 (5.5%); shipping and handling = 75.00.

Form 6
Invoice

Use the first invoice template in your word processing software.

Prepare Invoice 43250 from Benson Associates to Mr. James Akers, Home Products Inc., 2365 Cobb Parkway, Marietta, GA 30302-1239. Use the current date, order no. 9033, date shipped 2/16/—, and shipped via UPS. The items invoiced are as follows:

20 20-qt. double boiler @ 29.97; 15 Connors 16-pc. cookware set @ 139.97; 10 Connors "Excel" stainless-steel 13-pc. cookware set @ 189.97; 5 Tableware convection oven @ 189.96; 1 Connors toaster/oven/broiler @ 78.79.
   Sales tax = 281.36 (5%); shipping and handling = 15.00.

Form 7
Invoice

Use the first invoice template in your word processing software.

Prepare Invoice 43251 from Benson Associates to Mr. James Akers, Home Products Inc., 2365 Cobb Parkway, Marietta, GA 30302-1239. Use the current date, order no. 9045, date shipped 10/14/—, and shipped via UPS. The items invoiced are as follows:

(continued on next page)

5 18-qt. Sunshine roaster oven @ 78.77; 1 Sunshine 16-speed kitchen center @ 179.97; 3 Comfort deluxe food processor @ 283.55; 10 Comfort under-the-cabinet coffee maker @ 37.95; 4 Sunshine all-in-one bread maker @ 235.83.

Sales tax = 109.89 (4%); shipping and handling = 25.00.

Lesson 83　　Purchase Orders

GOALS: To improve speed and accuracy; to refine language-arts skills in composing; to format purchase orders using a template.

A. Type 2 times.

A.　WARMUP

```
1        Janet bought dozens of disks (5 or 6) to store her        10
2    article, "The Internet Sanction."  She quickly sent it to    22
3    her editor, Max Pavlow, on the 18th or 19th of September.     33
     |  1  |  2  |  3  |  4  |  5  |  6  |  7  |  8  |  9  |  10  |  11  |  12
```

SKILLBUILDING

B. Take three 12-second timings on each line. The scale below the last line shows your wam speed for a 12-second timing.

B.　12-SECOND SPEED SPRINTS

```
4   The main office wants to get this payment early next month.
5   On our way home from the bank, we may stop to see a friend.
6   Short words are very easy when you try to build your speed.
7   If you use the black pen, please take very good care of it.
    | | | |5| | | |10| | |15| | |20| | |25| | |30| | |35| | |40| | |45| | |50| | |55| | |60
```

C.　DIAGNOSTIC PRACTICE: ALPHABET

Turn to the Diagnostic Practice: Alphabet routine beginning on page SB-2. Type one of the Pretest/Posttest paragraphs and identify any errors made. Then type the corresponding drill lines 2 times for each letter on which you made 2 or more errors and 1 time for each letter on which you made only 1 error. Finally, repeat the same Pretest paragraph and compare your performance.

D.　PACED PRACTICE

Turn to the Paced Practice routine beginning on page SB-14. Take three 2-minute timings, starting at the point where you left off the last time.

E. COMPOSING

E. Answer each question with a brief paragraph.

8 How can your keyboarding skills help you in searching for a job?

9 What features do you like best about your word processing software package?

10 What career appeals to you the most and why?

F. PURCHASE ORDERS

A purchase order is prepared by a company to order the goods or services it needs from another firm.

A purchase order template may ask for information that is not necessary (such as a company slogan) or contain data fields for which you have no information. In these instances, delete any unnecessary information and leave the data fields blank.

DOCUMENT PROCESSING

Form 8
Purchase Order

Select the first purchase order template in your word processing software. Prepare Purchase Order 4832 from Metro Pool Company, 6831 Blake Street, Battle Creek, MI 49017. Metro's telephone number is 616-555-7256; its fax number is 616-555-7257. Send the purchase order to Copper's Pool Supplies, 186 Chase Road, Dearborn, MI 48126. Use the current date, and ship via UPS, FOB Detroit. The items ordered are as follows:

2 Patio end table, 16″ × 16″ × 14″ @ 28.75; 8 Woven, vinyl-coated, polyester umbrella, tubular aluminum frame, crank-lift handle, 3-position tilt @ 99.99; 2 High-back chair, 24″ × 28″ × 36″ @ 32.50; 2 Patio chaise lounge with 4-position backrest, 27″ × 74″ × 39″ @ 183.33.
Sales tax = 70.90 (5.5%); shipping and handling = 128.92.

Form 9
Purchase Order

Use the first purchase order template in your word processing software.

Prepare a second purchase order (No. 4833) from Metro Pool Company. Send the purchase order to SwimHouse Discount Center, 13843 Mackey Street, Shawnee Mission, KS 66210. Use the current date, and ship via UPS, FOB Detroit. The items ordered are as follows:

18 24-gauge, heavy-duty water tube @ 7.25; 10 18′ × 36′ pool cover with polyethylene coating @ 128.30; 2 Swimming pool pump, 1 3/4 hp @ 332.50; 15 10-gallon container of algicide (8 per box) @ 123.89.
Sales tax = 196.84 (5%); shipping and handling = 203.10.

Form 10
Purchase Order

Use the first purchase order template in your word processing software.

Prepare Purchase Order 4834 from Berkeley Associates, 9582 Pacific Avenue, Atlantic City, NJ 08402. Berkeley's telephone number is 609-555-6475; its fax number is 609-555-6480. Send the purchase order to McAdams Tool Supplies, 1618 Brandon Road, Lynchburg, VA 24505-0003. Use the current date, and ship via FedEx, FOB Newark. The items ordered are as follows:

(continued on next page)

3 3/8″ chuck hammer drill @ 134.95; 5 6″ dado blade @ 68.34; 1 Biscuit joiner @ 246.79; 4 Random orbit sander @ 310.75; 2 1 1/4-hp plunge router @ 169.95.

Sales tax = 103.05 (4%); shipping and handling = 110.00.

Form 11
Purchase Order

Use the first purchase order template in your word processing software.

Prepare a second purchase order (No. 4835) from Berkeley to McAdams. Use the current date, and ship via Airborne. The items ordered are as follows:

10 Box of 6″ × 5/8″ stainless-steel flathead screws @ 18.36; 15 #2 × 2″ 6-pack hex bits @ 4.25; 5 Adjustable C-style wood clamp, 40″ opening @ 45.75; 4 Box of 80-grit 5″, 8-hole sanding disks @ 2.25.

Sales tax = 20.52 (4%); shipping and handling = 28.00.

Lesson 84 Press Releases

GOALS: To type 44 wam/5′/5e; to format press releases using a template.

A. Type 2 times.

A. WARMUP

```
1     Zeke sharpened his ax so that he could quite easily    11
2  saw through 15 very large oak trees.  Each load will sell  22
3  for $175 (to Blake & James Inc.) at next Friday's auction.  34
   |  1  |  2  |  3  |  4  |  5  |  6  |  7  |  8  |  9  |  10  |  11  |  12
```

SKILLBUILDING

B. Take a 1-minute timing on the first paragraph to establish your base speed. Then take four 1-minute timings on the remaining paragraphs. As soon as you equal or exceed your base speed on one paragraph, advance to the next, more difficult paragraph.

B. SUSTAINED PRACTICE: CAPITAL LETTERS

```
4      A visit to Europe is a vacation that many people dream  11
5  of taking.  There are many countries to visit and hundreds  23
6  of sites to see if you can spend at least two weeks on the  35
7  continent.  A trip to Europe is one you will never forget.  46

8      If you decide to visit Europe, the months of June and   11
9  July would probably be the prettiest, but they would also   23
10 be the busiest.  England, France, and Germany are popular   34
11 countries to visit; Spain is popular for Americans as well.  46

12     In England you will want to visit St. Paul's Cathedral  11
13 and Big Ben.  And, of course, if you are in England, you    23
14 do not want to pass up the opportunity to see Buckingham    34
15 Palace.  Plan on staying a few days to see all the sites.   45
   |  1  |  2  |  3  |  4  |  5  |  6  |  7  |  8  |  9  |  10  |  11  |  12
```

```
16        France certainly is a highlight of any European visit..   11
17   Paris offers many sites such as the Arc de Triomphe, the       23
18   Louvre, the Eiffel Tower, and the Gothic Cathedral of Notre    35
19   Dame.  Other cities to see are Nice, Lyon, and Versailles.     46
     | 1 | 2 | 3 | 4 | 5 | 6 | 7 | 8 | 9 | 10 | 11 | 12
```

C. Take two 5-minute timings. Determine your speed and errors.

Goal: 44 wam/5′/5e

C. 5-MINUTE TIMING

```
20        The business of insurance is based on the concept of      11
21   sharing of loss.  This concept is very simple, and it also     23
22   has a very practical side.  If risks, defined as chances of    35
23   loss, can be split up among members of a certain group,        46
24   they need not jeopardize any single member of that group.      58
25   Hence misfortunes that could be punishing to one can be        69
26   made quite bearable for all.                                   75

27        The practice of sharing all risks first originated in     86
28   antiquity.  Some years ago, Chinese merchants devised an       97
29   ingenious way of protecting themselves against the chance     109
30   of a financially ruinous accident in the cold, swift river    120
31   rapids along the trade routes.  For example, they would       132
32   divide the cargoes among many of the boats.  If the rapids    143
33   claimed one of the boats, no merchant lost all his goods.     155
34   Each stood to lose only a very small portion.                 164

35        Although the ancient Chinese may not have thought of      175
36   the scheme as insurance, the principle they employed is       186
37   very much like all of our property and casualty insurance     198
38   of today.  Consumers can now buy a policy ranging from fire   210
39   to the damaging forces of storms and earthquakes.             220
     | 1 | 2 | 3 | 4 | 5 | 6 | 7 | 8 | 9 | 10 | 11 | 12
```

FORMATTING

D. PRESS RELEASES

A press release (also called a news release) is information sent to a newspaper or magazine for publication. Press releases usually contain a date, a title, the city and state of origin, the company name and address, and the actual copy that will appear in the publication. The placement of the information will vary depending on the software you are using as well as the template you select.

Form 12
Press Release

Do not indent the paragraphs in a press release, but do press Enter 2 times between paragraphs.

Select the first press release template in your word processing software. Prepare the template (using your name as the contact person) for the NCSA, 2368 Cornelia Avenue, Waukegan, IL 60083.

Your telephone number is 708-555-8923. Use the current date, and title the release *NCSA Conducts Computer Systems Meeting.* The text of the release is as follows:

The National Computer Systems Association held its annual meeting in Waukegan, Illinois, from April 15 through April 18. More than 1,000 participants attended the meeting, including representatives from all 50 states and 3 Canadian provinces.

At the meeting, computer hardware manufacturers and software vendors revealed their latest advances in CD-ROM technology and RAM chip storage. The most recent advancements made in read/write capabilities for CD-ROM drives attracted most of the participants' interest. Improvements in the past year have lowered considerably the cost of drives capable of writing data directly to the CD-ROM disks.

Next year's meeting will be held from April 18 through April 21 in Tallahassee, Florida. The theme for the meeting will be "Internet Use and Capabilities."

Form 13
Press Release

Use the first press release template listed in your word processing software.

Prepare a second NCSA press release. Use the current date, and title the release *Software Workshop.* The text of the release is as follows:

The Rockford chapter of the NCSA will conduct a software workshop for Northern Illinois and Southern Wisconsin members on October 10, 19--. The meeting will be held in the Chamber of Commerce Bldg, Room 107, from 5:30 p.m. to 9:03 p.m.

Ms. Sharon Tarkington from Computers Limited will be presenting Campbell Page, a groupware package designed to improve communication skills via a multisectional network environment. Ms. Tarkington has several years experience in writing and demonstrating network communications packages, and will provide each participant with a demo copy of the groupware package she is presenting.

If you are interested in attending this workshop, call 708-555-8932 to make your reservation. The preregistration fee is $55; the onsite registration fee is $65. The preregistration deadline is Oct. 7.

Form 14
Press Release

Open the file for Form 13, and make the following changes:
1. Change the meeting date to October 17.
2. The meeting time will be from 4:30 to 9:00 p.m.
3. Mr. Charles T. Madeira will make the presentation.

4. Each participant will be given a one-year subscription to *GroupWare Today.*
5. The preregistration fee is $50; the on-site registration fee is $55.
6. The deadline for preregistration is October 14.

Lesson 85　Labels

GOALS: To improve speed and accuracy; to refine language-arts skills in spelling; to format labels with a template.

A. Type 2 times.

A. WARMUP

```
1    Val Lopez and Jack Drew quickly bought six tickets for   11
2  the $24,600 collector's auto (a 1957 Chevrolet).  Over the   23
3  past month, its value increased by 1.5%.  That's fantastic!   35
       | 1 | 2 | 3 | 4 | 5 | 6 | 7 | 8 | 9 | 10 | 11 | 12
```

SKILLBUILDING

B. PROGRESSIVE PRACTICE: NUMBERS

Turn to the Progressive Practice: Numbers routine beginning on page SB-11.

Take six 30-second timings, starting at the point where you left off the last time.

C. PACED PRACTICE

Turn to the Paced Practice routine beginning on page SB-14. Take three 2-minute

timings, starting at the point where you left off the last time.

LANGUAGE ARTS

D. Type this list of frequently misspelled words, paying special attention to any spelling problems in each word.

D. SPELLING

```
4  means entry valve officer industry similar expenses patient
5  quality provisions judgment academic cooperation previously
6  foreign construction especially secretary indicated closing
7  manufacturing assessment continuing monitoring registration
8  accordance products presently policies implemented capacity
```

(continued on next page)

9 Every company offiser will have simaler expenses next week.
10 In my judgement, we must insist on co-operation from all.
11 My secretery said that she traveled to a foriegn country.
12 We must continue monitering the progress for assesment.
13 The new policeis must be implimented for all products.

FORMATTING

E. LABELS

The label feature simplifies the task of preparing a variety of labels. Different label definitions enable you to print a full sheet of labels or a single label.

When preparing labels, test the label settings by printing your labels on a blank page before you print them on the actual label form.

F. WORD PROCESSING: LABELS

Study Lesson 85 in your word processing manual. Complete all of the shaded steps while at your computer. Then format the jobs that follow.

DOCUMENT PROCESSING

Form 15
Mailing Labels

The addresses are shown in alphabetic order from left to right.

1. Select an address label definition large enough to fit a 4-line address (the label should be at least 1-inch deep).

2. Prepare address labels for the names and addresses that follow.

Purchasing Dept. Abbott Laboratories Abbott Park Chicago, IL 60064	Purchasing Dept. Acuson 1220 Charleston Rd. Mtn. View, CA 94034	Purchasing Dept. Adobe Systems 1585 Charleston Rd. Mtn. View, CA 94039
Purchasing Dept. Advanced Micro 901 Thompson Pl. Sunnyvale, CA 94088	Purchasing Dept. Aetna Life 151 Farmington Ave. Hartford, CT 06156	Purchasing Dept. Affiliated Publishing 135 Morrisey Blvd. Boston, MA 02107

Form 16
File Folder Labels

1. Select a file folder label definition.
2. Prepare file folder labels for the categories that follow.

3. Type each label in 16-point Times New Roman bold and all caps.

COMPANY PROCEDURES
PROJECT NOTES

CORRESPONDENCE
SCHEDULES

1. Select a rotary index card definition.
2. Prepare rotary index cards for the names and addresses that follow.
3. Type each card in 13-point Times New Roman.

American Brands
1700 East Putnam
Greenwich, CT 06870
203-555-1212

Alexander & Alexander
1211 West 48th Street
New York, NY 10036
212-555-2000

Holleran, Richard S.
2505 Dickerson Road
Manchester, NH 03103
603-555-1010

Roberts, Richard
1512 Woodsedge Drive
Victoria, MN 55836
612-555-6669

Ryerson, Incorporated
500 Border Street
New Bedford, MA 02740
508-555-7100

Specter Industries, Inc.
4050 North 480 East
Provo, UT 84604
801-555-2221

Select the first press release template in your word processing software. The press release is being prepared by you as an employee of National Office Supplies Company, 8054 Broadway, New York, NY 10040. Your telephone number is 212-555-2834. Use the current date, and title the release *25th Annual Office Supplies Show*. The text of the release is as follows:

The 25th Annual Office Supplies Show will be held at Madison Square Garden for four days beginning May 10. Over 300 manufacturers and suppliers will be presenting the latest innovations in office equipment and supplies.

Members will have hands-on demonstrations on various desktop and notebook computers. All companies marketing computer software and supplies will have booths adjacent to the computer demonstration areas. Sample copies of selected software programs will be available for a limited number of exhibit visitors.

Some of the outstanding sessions to be held will be concerned with the computer workforce of tomorrow, Web documents, and computer skills for tomorrow. Mr. Martin Hightower, president of Computers International, will deliver the opening address.

UNIT EIGHTEEN ▸ Correspondence

Lesson 86   Different-Sized Stationery

GOALS: To type 45 wam/5'/5e; to format letters on different-sized stationery.

A. Type 2 times.

A. WARMUP

```
1      The lynx at the zoo fought wildly and had to be moved    11
2  quickly to a new cage (#248-A or #357-A).  These adjoining   23
3  cages place the lynx (all of them) into individual areas.    35
   |  1  |  2  |  3  |  4  |  5  |  6  |  7  |  8  |  9  |  10  |  11  |  12
```

SKILLBUILDING

B. PACED PRACTICE

Turn to the Paced Practice routine beginning on page SB-14. Take three 2-minute timings, starting at the point where you left off the last time.

C. Take two 5-minute timings. Determine your speed and accuracy.

Goal: 45 wam/5'/5e

C. 5-MINUTE TIMING

```
4      A country innkeeper may have an idyllic life.  Many     11
5  people often think of leaving their demanding jobs to open   22
6  a country inn far from the crazy pace of the cities.  They   34
7  dream of a spot where they can be independent, creative,     46
8  and peaceful, a place where they might live in financial     57
9  comfort and security and enjoy the quieter pleasures of      68
10 life.  How accurate is this portrait?  Owning an inn is      79
11 a business; and just like any other business, it is filled   91
12 with many and various problems and joys, heartaches and      102
13 challenges, and anxieties and rewards.                       110
14     What are some qualities successful innkeepers share?     121
15 Although they all have a unique personality, there are a     133
16 few common attributes.  Innkeepers should enjoy meeting,     144
17 working with, and being near a lot of people.  They should   156
18 like to seek out challenges and should enjoy taking risks.   168
19 They should be stubborn enough to hold onto a dream in the   180
20 face of adversity and flexible enough to step in if a job    191
21 needs to be done and there is no one else to do it.  Also,   203
22 a solid bank account might be essential for a few related    215
23 expenses like repairs, landscaping, and furnishings.         225
   |  1  |  2  |  3  |  4  |  5  |  6  |  7  |  8  |  9  |  10  |  11  |  12
```

FORMATTING

D. Refer to the illustrations of executive and half-size stationery on page R-4 in the reference manual.

D. SPECIAL STATIONERY SIZES

Although most letters are typed on 8½-by 11-inch stationery, other paper sizes are sometimes used.

Executive Stationery. This stationery measures 7¼-inches wide by 10½-inches long. Use 1-inch side margins for a 5¼-inch line length. If the modified-block style is used, set a tab 2.62 inches from the left margin for the date and closing lines.

Half-Page Stationery. This stationery measures 5½-inches wide by 8½-inches long. Use 0.75-inch side margins for a 4-inch line length. If the modified-block style is used, set a tab 2.0 inches from the left margin for the date and closing lines.

E. MODIFIED-BLOCK STYLE WITH INDENTED PARAGRAPHS

In a modified-block style letter, paragraphs may be indented (usually 0.5 inch) or blocked at the left margin. However, in a block-style letter, paragraphs should never be indented.

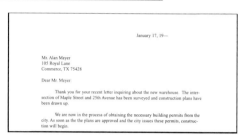

F. WORD PROCESSING: PAPER SIZE

Study Lesson 86 in your word processing manual. Complete all of the shaded steps while at your computer. Then format the jobs that follow.

DOCUMENT PROCESSING

Letter 52
Modified-Block Style With Indented Paragraphs

1. Format the letter for executive-size stationery.
2. Type the letter in modified-block style.
3. Indent the paragraphs 0.5 inch.

{Current Date} / Mr. Raymond R. Kemp / 6021 Glenmar Street / Waynoka, OK 73860 / Dear Mr. Kemp:

Your fiancee's engagement ring is being sent today by American Delivery. It will be delivered to you by 9 a.m. tomorrow.

You were wise to include both Janet and yourself in the selection of the diamond. Although the dollar amount of this ring represents a significant investment, the sentimental aspect should also be considered. Janet will treasure the ring all the more because both of you were involved in its selection.

I was impressed with the background information you had gathered about the selection of a quality diamond ring. Many people think that size alone is the only criterion to consider when making a purchase. However,

(continued on next page)

we both know that cut, color, and clarity are just as critical. Your knowledge of these ring characteristics allowed Janet and you to make a wise choice.

Thank you for choosing Danyell's for this important purchase. We look forward to helping Janet and you with your jewelry selections in years to come.

Sincerely, / Pauline R. Champion, C.G. / {urs}

Letter 53
Modified-Block Style
With Indented
Paragraphs

1. Format the letter for half-page stationery.

2. Type the letter in modified-block style with indented paragraphs.

November 7, 19-- / Mr. Kevin Cantrell, Engineer / City of Fall Creek / 342 Elm Street / Fall Creek, WI 54742 / Dear Mr. Cantrell:

Thank you for allowing me to examine your city's municipal wastewater installation. My visit has given me a clearer picture of your wastewater needs, and Collins Inc. is now ready to draw up plans for your new facility.

Please suggest a date and time that our engineers could get together to discuss the preliminary blueprints for this project. We should be able to begin the project within two weeks after the blueprints have been finalized.

Collins Inc. looks forward to assisting the City of Fall Creek in building its new wastewater treatment plant.

Sincerely yours, / Paul Blanchard / Chief Engineer / {urs}

Letter 54
Modified-Block Style
With Indented
Paragraphs

1. Format the letter for executive-size stationery.

2. Type the letter in modified-block style with indented paragraphs.

{Current Date} / Ms. Sharon Gray / 427 James Drive / Greenville, SC 29605 / Dear Ms. Gray:

After a lengthy search through our ~~monthly~~ current listings, we have found the home you requested. Enclosed are 5 photographs and a floor plan for you to review. The house has 10 rooms and 3 baths. There are six rooms and two baths on the main level and four rooms and one bath on the ~~next~~ second level. The house was built by Bench Craft in 1987, and the exterior was painted last in 1969. The ~~inside~~ interior is in excellent condition; the bathrooms

(continued on next page)

were wall papered in 1994.

The asking price is $250,000, but I believe an offer of $220,000 would [25]
be accepted. Please let me know ^as soon as possible if you are interested in this house. If you
are, I will make arrangements to show it ^to you.

Sincerely, / Marty Lopez / Agent / {urs} / Enclosure^s

Lesson 87 Letters for Window Envelopes

GOALS: To improve speed and accuracy; to refine language-arts skills in punctuation; to format and fold business letters for window envelopes.

A. Type 2 times.

A. WARMUP

1   On 1/10/96 Jamie exercised by "power walking" on the   11
2   athletic track.   She also zipped along the city's favorite   23
3   route (Ash Street & Bell Avenue).   It was a quick walk!   34

| 1 | 2 | 3 | 4 | 5 | 6 | 7 | 8 | 9 | 10 | 11 | 12

SKILLBUILDING

Pretest
Take a 1-minute timing. Determine your speed and errors.

B. PRETEST: CLOSE REACHES

4   Uncle Bert chased a fast, weary fox into the weeds of   11
5   the swamp.   He hoped to grab the old gray fox under the   22
6   bridge with a rope as he darted swiftly from his cold lair.   34

| 1 | 2 | 3 | 4 | 5 | 6 | 7 | 8 | 9 | 10 | 11 | 12

Practice
   Speed Emphasis: If you made no more than 1 error on the Pretest, type each *individual* line 2 times.
   Accuracy Emphasis: If you made 2 or more errors, type each *group* of lines (as though it were a paragraph) 2 times.

C. PRACTICE: ADJACENT KEYS

7   as asked asset based basis class least visas ease fast mass
8   op opera roped topaz adopt scope troop shops open hope drop
9   we weary wedge weigh towed jewel fewer dwell wear weed week

D. PRACTICE: CONSECUTIVE FINGERS

10   sw swamp swift swoop sweet swear swank swirl swap sway swim
11   un uncle under undue unfit bunch begun funny unit aunt junk
12   gr grade grace angry agree group gross gripe grow gram grab

Posttest
Repeat the Pretest timing and compare performance.

E. POSTTEST: CLOSE REACHES

F. Take three 12-second timings on each line. The scale below the last line shows your wam speed for a 12-second timing.

F. 12-SECOND SPEED SPRINTS

13 A good time to read is right when you get home after class.
14 Read for a while each day, and get rid of all your worries.
15 Their cat wants to lie down where it is warm when it rests.
16 Sam put the box in the corner when it was sent to us today.

| | | |5| | | |10| | | |15| | | |20| | | |25| | | |30| | | |35| | | |40| | | |45| | | |50| | | |55| | | |60

G. Type the paragraph 2 times. Use the caps lock key when typing in all caps.

G. TECHNIQUE PRACTICE: SHIFT/CAPS LOCK

17   Raymond and Karen must travel through TENNESSEE and
18 KENTUCKY on TUESDAY and WEDNESDAY. Raymond will speak in
19 NASHVILLE on the topic of COMPUTER AWARENESS; Karen will
20 speak in LOUISVILLE, and her talk is on INTERNET ACCESS.

LANGUAGE ARTS

H. Study the rules at the right.

H. COLON, DASH, AND PERIOD

Rule: Use a colon to introduce explanatory material that follows an independent clause. (An independent clause is one that can stand alone as a complete sentence.)

:expl

Your move to Albuquerque offers many benefits: good climate, reasonable housing costs, and a metropolitan environment.
Acceptable typing skills include the following ingredients: speed, accuracy, and production.

Rule: Use a dash instead of a comma, semicolon, colon, or parenthesis when you want to convey a more forceful separation of words within a sentence. (If your keyboard has a special dash character, use it. Otherwise, form a dash by typing two hyphens, with no space before, between, or after.)

—emph

My reason for wanting to buy a new car is simple--repair costs on my old car are more than that car is worth.
I need assistance from three people to complete my book--a proofreader, an editor, and a publisher.

Rule: Use a period to end a sentence that is a polite request. (Consider a sentence a polite request if you expect the reader to respond by doing as you ask rather than by giving a yes-or-no answer.)

.req

Would you please mail the computer back to us by Friday.
But: Are you going to mail the computer back to us by Friday?

Edit the sentences to correct any errors in the use of colons, dashes, and periods.

21 We need the following items, pens, pencils, and paper.
22 Call Sam Morris-he is the president of the college.
23 May I suggest that you send the report by Tuesday?
24 Would you please pay my bills when I am on vacation?
25 These are some of your colleagues: Bill, Mary, and Ann.
26 I drove three cars, a Chevy, a Ford, and a Chrysler.

I. WINDOW ENVELOPES

Letters for Window Envelopes. No. 10 window envelopes are often used to eliminate the need for addressing envelopes. Letters are prepared so that the inside address shows through the window.

To format a letter for a window envelope, type the date 2 inches from the top of the page followed by 2 blank lines (press Enter 3 times to insert 2 blank lines). Next, type the inside address, followed by 2 blank lines.

Folding Letters for Window Envelopes. To fold a letter for a window envelope so that the inside address appears through the window:

1. Place the letter *face down,* and fold the bottom third of the letter up toward the top.
2. Fold the top third down so that the address shows.

3. Insert the letter into the envelope with the address facing the window, and check to be sure it is visible.

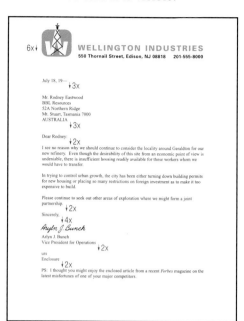

DOCUMENT PROCESSING

Letter 55
Modified-Block Style for a Window Envelope

—emph

After formatting Letter 55, fold it for insertion into a window envelope.

September 17, 19-- / Mr. Darin McCollum / 741 Margo Street / Omaha, NE 68147-3248 / Dear Mr. McCollum:

On October 25, 19--, our firm will conduct an eight-hour, one-day seminar in Lincoln on a topic that is relatively new to builders in the area -- compaction grouting.

A complete program for the seminar will be sent to you in about one week, but you may want to reserve this date on your calendar now. The seminar fee will be only $125; and we expect a large turnout from the Lincoln Builders Association, so make your reservation early.

Please feel free to share the enclosed flyer with other builders in your area. All of us at Builders' Presentations Inc. look forward to

(continued on next page)

seeing you in Lincoln on October 25.
Yours truly, / Alexa J. Sanchez / Consulting Engineer

Letter 56
Modified-Block Style
for a Window
Envelope

1. Use the current date for this letter.
2. Send the letter to Ms. Charlene Alford / 3247 Trawood Drive / Fort Worth, TX 79936-3782.
3. Provide a salutation and an enclosure notation.
4. The letter is from Tom R. Walsh, Store Manager. Use the closing *Sincerely,*.

We are pleased that you have decided to have Aqua Pools install the pool in your new home. As our brochures clearly illustrate, the construction techniques used in Aqua Pools are by far the finest of all pool builders in the Dallas/Fort Worth Metroplex. As you indicated in your order, we will install the 18′ × 36′ pool in your back yard with the following special

:expl

features: textured tile decking, an 8′ step entrance on the shallow end, a 1 1/2-hp circulating water pump, and an Aqua Pool automatic pool cleaning system. Please let us know if there are any additional features you wanted to add to your pool. Construction will begin 10 days from the date of this letter, and we should be placing the final touches on your pool within an additional 10 days. Would you please return the enclosed card

.req

to confirm this schedule. We'll not need final payment on the construction
you
until 30 days after completion. Thanks for bringing your pool business
very
to aqua pool. We have a special reason for wanting to build the finest
for many years to come.
—emph
pool for you--we want to provide your pool needs ~~in the coming years.~~
you
Thank for your business.

Letter 57
Modified-Block Style
for a Window
Envelope

—emph

{Current Date} / Ms. Brenda T. Hallock / Office Manager / Southland Wire Corp. / 1832 Evergreen Street / Longview, TX 75605 / Dear Ms. Hallock:
¶We are pleased to announce the program for the Annual Secretarial Conference, to be held on March 16, 19--, at the Ranger Inn in Texarkana, Texas. This conference is special—we will celebrate our 25th year.

:expl

¶Because of all the changes that have taken place in the past 25 years in office technology, this year's conference will highlight sessions on the following topics: multimedia presentations, Internet, CD-ROM graphics, and desktop publishing. Would you please identify those topics of special

.req

interest to you by returning the enclosed card no later than January 15.

(continued on next page)

¶Also enclosed is a registration form that you should return as soon as possible. This conference is special for many of us, and we anticipate a large attendance. We hope you will be able to join us for this 25th anniversary.

Sincerely, / Marjorie D'Angelo / Program Chair / {urs} / Enclosures

Lesson 88 Special Letterheads

GOALS: To type 45 wam/5′/5e; to format letters on special letterheads.

A. Type 2 times.

A. WARMUP

```
1      On May 4, 1996, Jeff gave a dazzling talk on graphics;    11
2  it was quite fantastic!  He is also writing an excellent    23
3  book about graphics with text.  It will sell for $23.85.    34
   | 1 | 2 | 3 | 4 | 5 | 6 | 7 | 8 | 9 | 10 | 11 | 12
```

SKILLBUILDING

B. Take a 1-minute timing on the first paragraph to establish your base speed. Then take four 1-minute timings on the remaining paragraphs. As soon as you equal or exceed your base speed on one paragraph, advance to the next, more difficult paragraph.

B. SUSTAINED PRACTICE: PUNCTUATION

```
4      One of the strengths you must have if you are going to   11
5  be a success in business is good writing skills.  You must   23
6  practice your writing skills every day if you want them to   35
7  improve.  Perfection of writing skills takes much practice.  47

8      You must always strive to write clearly, concisely,      11
9  and accurately.  Remember always that your writing can be    22
10 examined by more people than just the one to whom you have   34
11 written.  It's often looked at by other people as well.      45

12     You want to be sure that your letters always convey a     11
13 positive, helpful attitude.  Don't forget, you represent     22
14 more than yourself when you write--you also represent your   34
15 company!  This is an important, useful rule to remember.      45

16     Try to stay away from negative words like "can't" or     11
17 "won't."  Readers also do not like phrases such as "because  23
18 of company policies" or "due to unforeseen circumstances."   35
19 Using these words and phrases never help resolve problems.   46
   | 1 | 2 | 3 | 4 | 5 | 6 | 7 | 8 | 9 | 10 | 11 | 12
```

C. Take two 5-minute timings. Determine your speed and errors.

Goal: 45 wam/5'/5e

C. 5-MINUTE TIMING

20 When any holiday approaches, it becomes important to   11
21 plan all events with care. This is when gifts might be   22
22 exchanged and when special food may be prepared. To get   33
23 ready for these days, experts tell us that we can reduce   45
24 stress and enjoy the holidays more if we make lists and   56
25 manage our time. This will provide us with time to relax.   68
26 Lists of duties among family members and houseguests   79
27 shape the basic plan of action. When planning a strategy,   90
28 include cooking, baking, shopping, and wrapping. The most   102
29 important task to remember, and the one that most people   114
30 forget, is to plan to relax during these very busy days.   125
31 Psychologists warn us of the dangers of cutting out   136
32 personal pleasures. We all need time out to recharge and   147
33 diffuse developing stress. Nourish yourself with walks,   159
34 exercise classes, gardening, religious services, or a quiet   171
35 evening in with an old movie or a good novel. Do whatever   182
36 it takes to pacify your own spirit.   190
37 When the next holiday is on the horizon, don't be a   200
38 person who gets all stressed out. Remember to plan all the   212
39 activities carefully and to enlist the help of the entire   224
40 family.   225

| 1 | 2 | 3 | 4 | 5 | 6 | 7 | 8 | 9 | 10 | 11 | 12

FORMATTING

D. SPECIAL LETTERHEADS

Special letterheads may be used in an office. They often require different margin settings at the top or left side of the paper.

Deep-Letterhead Stationery. A short letter typed on deep-letterhead stationery can be centered vertically. However, if the letter length "pushes" the date line into the letterhead at the top of the page, delete the vertical centering command and type the date 0.5 inch below the letterhead, as shown in the illustration at the right.

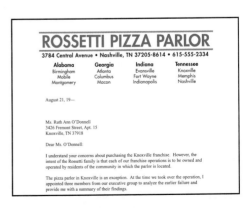

Deep-Letterhead Stationery

(continued on next page)

Left-Weighted Stationery. Some business stationery includes officers' names or divisional branch names along the left side of the paper, as shown in the illustration at the right. When left-weighted stationery is used, the left margin should be set 0.5 inch to the right of the widest item in the left column of the letterhead.

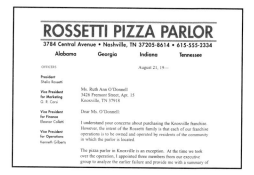

Left-Weighted Stationery

Letter 58
Block-Style on Deep-Letterhead Stationery

1. Set a top margin of 2.5 inches for this letter to be typed on deep-letterhead stationery.

2. Type the letter in block style.

{Current Date} / Mr. Bryan S. Denton / 248 Hill Avenue / Bowling Green, KY 42101 / Dear Mr. Denton:

¶I received your letter inquiring about the opening of a Rossetti Pizza Parlor in Bowling Green. According to our franchise guidelines, population size is the primary consideration in determining the number of parlors that will be authorized in a particular city.

¶The application of this guideline has been to award only one Rossetti Pizza Parlor franchise in a city with a population of less than 100,000. As I am sure you are aware, Bowling Green's population is much less than that.

¶I will keep your request on file in the event this policy should change. Sincerely yours, / Sheila Rossetti, President / {urs}

Letter 59
Modified-Block Style on Left-Weighted Stationery

Open the file for Letter 58 and revise it as follows:
1. Set a left margin at 2 inches to type this letter on left-weighted stationery.
2. Set a left tab at 2.75 inches for the date and complimentary closing.
3. Delete the 2.5-inch top margin, and vertically center the letter.

4. Address the letter to Ms. Maria Kennedy / 2210 Elm Street / Jackson, TN 38301.
5. Remember to change the salutation.
6. Change *Bowling Green* to *Jackson* in both the first and second paragraphs.
7. Change the complimentary closing to *Sincerely.*

Letter 60
Block-Style on Left-Weighted Stationery

Set a left margin at 2 inches.

March 25, 19-- / Mr. Danny Devereaux / 173 Covert Avenue / Evansville, IN 47713-3948 / Dear Mr. Devereaux:

Thank you for your inquiry regarding the

(continued on next page)

establishment of a Rossetti Pizza franchise in Evansville. Our marketing research team has determined that Evansville's population will support a second franchise.

Kenneth Gilberts, vice president for operations, will meet with you next week to discuss start-up activities and answer any specific questions you have about our franchise.

We are convinced that this second franchise in Evansville will be as successful as the first site. I look forward to meeting you soon.

Sincerely yours, / Sheila Rossetti, President / {urs}

Lesson 89 Form Letters

GOALS: To improve speed and accuracy; to refine language-arts skills in punctuation; to format form letters.

A. Type 2 times.

A. WARMUP

```
1      Did Jacqueline get 62% of the vote in the election on     11
2  9/04/96?  I think Buzz* (*Kelly) voted for her at 7:35 p.m.   24
3  that evening, and she was really excited when Jackie won.     34
   |  1  |  2  |  3  |  4  |  5  |  6  |  7  |  8  |  9  |  10  |  11  |  12
```

 SKILLBUILDING

B. DIAGNOSTIC PRACTICE: ALPHABET

Turn to the Diagnostic Practice: Alphabet routine beginning on page SB-2. Type one of the Pretest/Posttest paragraphs and identify any errors made. Then type the corresponding drill lines 2 times for each letter on which you made 2 or more errors and 1 time for each letter on which you made only 1 error. Finally, repeat the same Pretest paragraph and compare your performance.

C. PACED PRACTICE

Turn to the Paced Practice routine beginning on page SB-14. Take three 2-minute timings, starting at the point where you left off the last time.

D. PROGRESSIVE PRACTICE: ALPHABET

Turn to the Progressive Practice: Alphabet routine beginning on page SB-7. Take six 30-second timings, starting at the point where you left off the last time.

E. SEMICOLON

E. Study the rules at the right.

Rule: Use a semicolon to join two closely related independent clauses that are not connected by a conjunction (such as *and, but,* or *nor*).

;noconj

Douglas will graduate in June; Michelle will graduate in August.
We bought the computer on Monday; the printer was purchased last week.

Rule: Use a semicolon to separate three or more items in a series if any of the items already contain commas.

;ser

The meetings are in Buffalo, NY; Trenton, NJ; and Scranton, PA.
I'll be in my office on April 5, Tuesday; April 8, Friday; and April 11, Monday.

Edit the sentences to correct any errors in the use of semicolons.

4 Paul will travel to Madrid, Spain; Lisbon, Portugal, and
5 Nice, France.
6 Mary's gift arrived yesterday, Margie's did not.
7 Bring your textbook to class; I'll return it tomorrow.
8 The best days for the visit are Monday, May 10, Tuesday,
9 May 18, and Wednesday, May 26.
10 Jan is the president; Peter is the vice president.

F. FORM LETTERS

A form letter is a standard letter that can be customized by inserting information that may be different for each person receiving the letter.

To create a form letter, you must create two files and then merge these files. The data source or data file contains the variable information (such as names and addresses). The main document or form file contains the correctly formatted text of the letter.

As you create the form letter, you will need to insert field names where you want the variable information to appear within the letter. When the data files and the form files are merged, the field names will be replaced with the correct information.

The illustrations at the right show how a form letter may look when the field names are inserted.

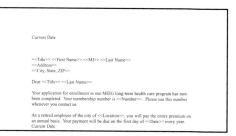

Main Document Codes

Form File Codes

G. WORD PROCESSING: MAIL MERGE

Study Lesson 89 in your word processing manual. Complete all of the shaded steps while at your computer. Then format the jobs that follow.

Letters 61, 62, 63, 64
Block Style

1. Create data files for each of the people whose records follow.
2. Create the form letter, inserting the appropriate fields where necessary.
3. Merge the data files and the form letter to create a customized letter for each person.

First Record
Title:	Mr.
First Name:	Randy
MI:	R.
Last Name:	Sorells
Address:	8342 Campbell Lane
City, State, ZIP:	Concord, CA 94523
Member No:	S1783
Location:	Concord
Month:	February

Second Record
Title:	Mr.
First Name:	Eric
MI:	
Last Name:	Shoohah
Address:	1274 Lucerne Avenue
City, State, ZIP:	Modesto, CA 95350
Member No:	S9348
Location:	Modesto
Month:	August

Third Record
Title:	Ms.
First Name:	Karen
MI:	
Last Name:	Sisson
Address:	1428 Apple Avenue
City, State, ZIP:	Hayward, CA 94546
Member No:	S2036
Location:	Hayward
Month:	May

Fourth Record
Title:	Ms.
First Name:	Amelia
MI:	T.
Last Name:	Doran
Address:	534 Spruce Street
City, State, ZIP:	Oakland, CA 94606
Member No:	D1946
Location:	Oakland
Month:	October

{Current Date}

<<Title>> <<First Name>> <<Middle Initial>> <<Last Name>>
<<Address>>
<<City, State, ZIP>>

Dear<<Title>> <<Last Name>>:

¶Welcome to the Holiday Travel Club. Your membership number is <<Member No.>>. Please use this number whenever you call or write to us at the home office.

¶As a member from the city of <<Location>>, you will pay your premiums on a quarterly basis. Your first payment will be due on the first day of <<Month>>.

¶We know that you will be pleased with the services provided by the Holiday Travel Club. The enclosed brochure explains all of your member

(continued on next page)

benefits. Welcome aboard!

Sincerely yours, / A. R. Wells / Policy Administrator / {urs} / Enclosure

Letters 65, 66, 67, 68
Modified Block Style

1. Use the same form letter you created for Letters 61–64.
2. Change the format of the letter to modified-block style.
3. Create data files for each of the people whose records follow.
4. Merge the new data files and the form letter to create a customized letter for each person.

First Record
Ms. Lucia Yates / 7325 Southern Heights Avenue / Oklahoma City, OK 73501-3890 / Y1384 / June

Second Record
Mr. Jose Camacho / 384 Fred Jones Avenue North / Oklahoma City, OK 73106-0320 / C1849 / December

Third Record
Ms. Audra L. Hernandez / 1484 Pennsylvania Avenue North / Oklahoma City, OK 73107-8900 / H8932 / September

Fourth Record
Mr. Gregory R. Pierce / 209 Smithsonian Avenue / Broken Arrow, OK 74013-4890 / P8234 /September

Lesson 90   Form Letters

GOALS: To type 45 wam/5'/5e; to reinforce the typing of form letters.

A. Type 2 times.

A. WARMUP

```
1        Jordan used a dozen of Harold's power trucks to quickly   11
2   move over 17 large boxes on 5/30/96.  I think these trucks     23
3   (just the diesels) may need maintenance work on 8/24/96.       34
      |  1  |  2  |  3  |  4  |  5  |  6  |  7  |  8  |  9  | 10  | 11  | 12
```

SKILLBUILDING

Take three 12-second timings on each line. The scale below the last line shows your wam speed for a 12-second timing.

B. 12-SECOND SPEED SPRINTS

```
4   The auto will now have to turn off on the lane to the lake.
5   Mark must type these lines fast and press for a high speed.
6   We had a lunch at the lake and went for a walk in the park.
7   Take this disk to have it fixed by the end of your workday.
    | | | 5 | | | 10| | | 15| | | 20| | | 25| | | 30| | | 35| | | 40| | | 45| | | 50| | | 55| | | 60
```

C. DIAGNOSTIC PRACTICE: NUMBERS

Turn to the Diagnostic Practice: Numbers routine beginning on page SB-5. Type one of the Pretest/Posttest paragraphs and identify any errors made. Then type the corresponding drill lines 2 times for each number on which you made 2 or more errors and 1 time for each number on which you made only 1 error. Finally, repeat the same Pretest paragraph and compare your performance.

D. 5-MINUTE TIMING

D. Take two 5-minute timings. Determine your speed and errors.

Goal: 45 wam/5'/5e

8	Business plays a major role today in the daily lives	11
9	of all of us, whether or not we are business employees.	22
10	All citizens must understand the role of business in our	34
11	society. It is part of all of our daily lives. Business	45
12	provides us with goods and services which are important for	57
13	all citizens. We could not maintain our high standard of	69
14	living if we did not have business to make the goods we buy	81
15	and sell. If business did not provide us with insurance	92
16	and banking, our lifestyles would be rather different from	104
17	what they are today. Business is a part of all aspects of	116
18	our lives and will play that role for years to come.	126
19	Businesses can be defined as commercial or industrial.	138
20	They are made up of people who work to provide us with the	150
21	goods and services we need and want. Most businesses are	161
22	managed by units that exert leadership to combine labor,	173
23	resources, and capital needed to satisfy both our needs and	185
24	our wants. Businesses are involved with lots of groups.	196
25	These groups encompass workers and the public as well as	208
26	some local, state, and federal agencies. Business affects	219
27	our lives in many, many ways.	225

| 1 | 2 | 3 | 4 | 5 | 6 | 7 | 8 | 9 | 10 | 11 | 12 |

DOCUMENT PROCESSING

Letters 69, 70, 71, 72
Modified-Block Style

1. Create data files for each of the people whose records follow.
2. Create the form letter in modified-block style, inserting the appropriate fields where necessary.
3. Merge the data files and the form letter to create a customized letter for each person.

(continued on next page)

First Record		Second Record	
Title:	Ms.	Title:	Mr.
First Name:	Shelly	First Name:	Leon
MI:	T.	MI:	R.
Last Name:	Cole	Last Name:	McCoy
Position:	Customer Relations	Position:	Marketing Dept.
Company:	Apex, Inc.	Company:	Redmond Industries
Address:	489 Lloyd Street	Address:	9327 Dillerville Road
City, State, ZIP:	Altoona, PA 16602	City, State, ZIP:	Lancaster, PA 17601
Model:	Model A-24Z	Model:	Model R-18M
Location:	Harrisburg	Location:	Scranton

Third Record		Fourth Record	
Title:	Mr.	Title:	Ms.
First Name:	Allen	First Name:	Barbara
MI:		MI:	
Last Name:	Ferguson	Last Name:	Searcy
Position:	Customer Relations	Position:	Sales Manager
Company:	Chester Products, Inc.	Company:	Don's Sales & Service
Address:	780 Chestnut Street	Address:	2002 Jacob Street
City, State, ZIP:	Chester, PA 19014	City, State, ZIP:	Pittsburgh, PA 15226
Model:	Model R-18M	Model:	Model A-24Z
Location:	Scranton	Location:	Harrisburg

{Current Date}

(Title) (First Name) (MI) (Last Name)
(Position)
(Company)
(Address)
(City, State ZIP)

Dear (Title) (Last Name):

　　Customers in the Pennsylvania service area have recently informed us that two of our television models (Model A-24Z and Model R-18M) have malfunctioned when the unit warms up--usually after 30 minutes of operation.

—emph

　　Our records indicate that (Company) purchased two dozen of (Model) from the (Location) plant. If you still have

(continued on next page)

these sets in your warehouse, we need to have them repaired. If any of the units have already been sold, we need to contact the customers so that the replacement part can be installed in their sets. Please send us the names, addresses, and telephone numbers of these customers; we will contact them directly.

Thank you for your assistance. / Sincerely, / Brad Chilton / Regional Manager / {urs}

Letters 73, 74, 75, 76
Progress Check
Block Style

1. Create data files for each of the people whose records follow. Use the following field names: *Title; First Name; MI; Last Name; Address; City, State, ZIP; Time; Room; Topics.*
2. Create the form letter in block style for left-weighted stationery (use a 2-inch left margin).
3. Use the current date for the letter.
4. Merge the data files and the form letter to create a customized letter for each person.

First Record
Mr. Raymond L. Meadows / 248 Masonboro Loop Road / Wilmington, NC 28403 / 9:00-11:00 a.m. / Room B / CD-ROM, Multimedia, Internet

Second Record
Ms. Darlene P. Honneycutt / 904 Lafayette Place / High Point, NC 27263 / 3:00-5:00 p.m. / Room C / PASCAL Programming, Internet, Mosaic

Third Record
Ms. Mandy Swafford / 1483 Claremont Avenue / Winston-Salem, NC 27105 / 1:00-3:00 p.m. / Room A / Windows, Desktop Publishing, Presentation Management

Fourth Record
Ms. Sheila Chu / 1210 Cumberland Road / Winston-Salem, NC 27105 / 9:00-11:00 a.m. / Room B / CD-ROM, Multimedia, Internet

:expl

(Title) (First Name) (MI) (Last Name)
(Address)
(City, State, ZIP)
Dear (Title) (Last Name):

¶Thank you for your registration for our computer workshop. You have been assigned to the (Time) session in (Room). This session will discuss the following topics: (Topics).

¶After the final session of the day, (Title) (Last Name), we would like you to complete the enclosed evaluation card so that we will know how effective the presentation was for the participants.

¶We hope you enjoy your conference.

Sincerely yours, / Pat Reynolds / Conference Director / {urs} / Enclosure

Lesson 91 — Meeting Reports

GOALS: To improve speed and accuracy; to refine language-arts skills in proofreading; to format agendas and minutes of meetings.

A. Type 2 times.

A. WARMUP

```
1      Rex Yantz was calm before quitting his job at the zoo    11
2  on 7/10/96.  On 8/23/96 he applied for a job at Vance &     22
3  Walton, "specialists" in corporate law and bankruptcies.    33
   |  1  |  2  |  3  |  4  |  5  |  6  |  7  |  8  |  9  |  10  |  11  |  12
```

SKILLBUILDING

B. Take three 12-second timings on each line. The scale below the last line shows your wam speed for a 12-second timing.

B. 12-SECOND SPEED SPRINTS

```
4  This is not the person who is my first choice for this job.
5  The day was bright as the sun shone on the clear blue lake.
6  All of you should take a long walk when the sun sets today.
7  This line has many easy words in it to type your very best.
  | | | |5| | |10| | |15| | |20| | |25| | |30| | |35| | |40| | |45| | |50| | |55| | |60
```

C. Take a 1-minute timing on the first paragraph to establish your base speed. Then take four 1-minute timings on the remaining paragraphs. As soon as you equal or exceed your base speed on one paragraph, advance to the next, more difficult paragraph.

C. SUSTAINED PRACTICE: ALTERNATE-HAND WORDS

```
8       A downturn in world fuel prices signals a lower profit   11
9   for giant oil firms.  In fact, most downtown firms will      22
10  see the usual sign of tight credit and other problems.  The  34
11  city must get down to business and make plans in the fall.   46

12      The hungry turkeys ate eight bushels of corn that were   11
13  given to them by our next door neighbors.  They also drank   23
14  the five bowls of water that were left in the yard.  All in  35
15  all, the birds caused quite a bit of chaos early that day.   47

16      A debate on what to do about that extra acreage in the   11
17  desert dragged on for two hours.  One problem is what the    23
18  effect may be of moving the ancient ruins to a much safer    35
19  place.  City officials must always protect our environment.  46

20      Molly was dressed in a plain pink dress at the annual    11
21  meeting that was taking place at the hotel in Tempe later    23
22  that last week in September.  The agenda included two very   34
23  controversial topics that have often generated much debate.  46
   |  1  |  2  |  3  |  4  |  5  |  6  |  7  |  8  |  9  |  10  |  11  |  12
```

D. Edit this paragraph to correct any typing or formatting errors.

D. PROOFREADING

24   The idea and practise of sharing risk originated in
25 antiquety. Many years ago, Chinese merchants deviced an
26 injenious way of protecting themselves against the chance
27 of a financialy ruinous accadent in the dangerous river
28 along the trade routtes when they were delivring goods.

E. AGENDAS

An agenda is a list of topics to be discussed at a meeting. It may also include a formal program of a meeting consisting of times, rooms, speakers, and other related information. Follow these steps to format an agenda:

1. Press Enter 6 times to leave an approximate 2-inch top margin.
2. Center and type the name of the company or committee in all caps and bold.
3. Press Enter twice and center and type *Meeting Agenda* in initial caps.
4. Press Enter twice and center and type the date in initial caps.
5. Press Enter twice and type the first item in the agenda. Number each item using the numbering command.

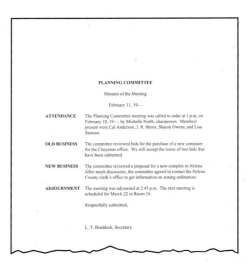

F. MINUTES OF MEETINGS

Minutes of a meeting are a record of items discussed during a meeting. To format meeting minutes, follow these steps:

1. Press Enter 6 times to leave an approximate 2-inch top margin.
2. Center and type the name of the company or committee in all caps and bold.
3. Press Enter twice, then center and type *Minutes of the Meeting* in initial caps.
4. Press Enter twice, then center and type the date in initial caps.
5. Press Enter twice, then at the left margin type the side heading *ATTENDANCE* in all caps and bold.
6. Align the remaining text for the section approximately 1.5 inches from the left margin. Press Enter twice between sections.

7. After the last section, press Enter twice and type the closing at the indent. Press Enter 4 times and type the secretary's name and title.

G. WORD PROCESSING: HYPHENATION AND SOFT HYPHEN

Study Lesson 91 in your word processing manual. Complete all of the shaded steps while at your computer. Then format the jobs that follow.

Report 44
Agenda

↓6X **ALLIANCE CORPORATION STAFF MEETING** ↓2X

Meeting Agenda ↓2X

November 17, 19— ↓2X

1. Approval of minutes of October 15 meeting
2. Progress reports of new district offices
3. Discussion of attendance at the National Hardware Association's annual meeting
4. Multimedia installation update: B. Harris
5. Annual fund drive: T. Henderson

Report 45
Agenda

APEX MULTIMEDIA CORPORATION
Meeting Agenda
October 13, 19--

1. Call to order
2. Approval of minutes of September 10 meeting
3. Progress report on Sherman contract (Julia Adams)
4. Upgrading of 4.0 presentation media
5. CD-ROM development program (Ray Sanchez)
6. Internet configuration (JoAnn Hubbard)
7. Adjournment

Report 46
Minutes of a Meeting

Turn on hyphenation.

↓6X **PLANNING COMMITTEE** ↓2X

Minutes of the Meeting ↓2X

February 10, 19— ↓2X

(continued on next page)

ATTENDANCE	The Planning Committee meeting was called to order at 1 p.m. on February 10, 19--, by Michelle North, chairperson. Members present were Cal Anderson, L. T. Braddock, Lisa Samson, Sharon Owens, and J. R. Stems. ↓2X
OLD BUSINESS	The committee reviewed bids for the purchase of a new computer for the Cheyenne office. We will accept the lower of two bids that have been submitted.
NEW BUSINESS	The committee reviewed a proposal for a new complex in Helena. After much discussion, the committee agreed to contact the Helena county clerk's office to get information on zoning ordinances.
ADJOURNMENT	The meeting was adjourned at 2:45 p.m. The next meeting is scheduled for March 22 in Room 16. ↓2X

Respectfully submitted, ↓4X

L. T. Braddock, Secretary

Report 47
Minutes of a Meeting

Turn on hyphenation.

PERSON̄EL COMMITTEE

Minutes of the Meeting

May 14, 19--

ATTENDĒNCE A special meeting of the Personnel Committee was held in on May 14, 19--, the office of Mr. Cameron. Members All present were except Richard Dixon, who was repre/sented by Monica Zick man. The meeting was called to order at 2 p. m.

-num

Old Business A copy of the survey is attached. Eighty-eight employees participated in a survey that had been completed by Andrea Fields. The minutes of the last monthly meeting were read.

(continued on next page)

NEW BUSINESS   Ms. ~~Samuels~~ Daniels discussed the need for planning a campaign for job applicants letting know about vacancies that occur within the company. Frank Lundquist will draft a flyer to be sent to the Park view sentinel. Programs for the N P A Convention to be held in Des Moines were *(italic)* distributed to all members. Each committee member ~~were~~ was asked to distribute copies to all employees in his or her department.

ADJOURNMENT   The meeting was adjourned at 3:25 P a.m. The next meeting has been scheduled for July 10 in the conference center.

Respectfully submitted,

Brandon Stinson, Secretary

Lesson 92   Procedures Manual

GOALS: To type 46 wam/5'/5e; to format a procedures manual.

A. Type 2 times.

A. WARMUP

1　　Zach sharpened the ax for Quinn just to help him win　　11
2　the $100 tree-cutting event to be held in Kildeer on May 18　23
3　(if it doesn't rain). The prize will be $250--fantastic!　34

　| 1 | 2 | 3 | 4 | 5 | 6 | 7 | 8 | 9 | 10 | 11 | 12

SKILLBUILDING

B. PACED PRACTICE

Turn to the Paced Practice routine beginning on page SB-14. Take three 2-minute timings, starting at the point where you left off the last time.

C. Take two 5-minute timings. Determine your speed and errors.

Goal: 46 wam/5'/5e

C. 5-MINUTE TIMING

4	Recycling is a process we can neglect no longer. Many	11
5	of the products we use each day are made up of materials	23
6	that can be recycled. Glass, steel, paper, plastics, and	34
7	aluminum are very good candidates for recycling. Each of	46
8	us discards several pounds of trash each day, and much of	57
9	this trash can be recycled to make other products we need.	69
10	Here are some unique thoughts as to how our waste can	80
11	be used effectively through the process of recycling. Used	92
12	coffee filters can be recycled to make soles for new shoes.	104
13	Burned-out lightbulbs and other similar glass products can	116
14	be used to resurface streets, and yard waste might be used	128
15	to power generators for supplying electricity. Half of the	140
16	papers that are thrown away every day can be recycled as	151
17	cardboard boxes, magazines, and other paper products. Much	163
18	of the office paper that is discarded can be recycled to	175
19	make tissue paper and paper towels. Most plastic that is	186
20	used in soda bottles can be recycled into car interiors and	198
21	jacket insulation. The plastic from shampoo bottles can be	210
22	recycled into milk jugs, and there is even talk that soon	222
23	we will be using plastic wood in the home.	230

| 1 | 2 | 3 | 4 | 5 | 6 | 7 | 8 | 9 | 10 | 11 | 12 |

FORMATTING

D. PROCEDURES MANUAL

Organizations often prepare procedures manuals to identify the steps or methods that employees must follow to accomplish particular tasks. To format a procedures manual:

1. Type the manual as a single-spaced report.
2. Place a header on every page except the first page. The header may include such items as the title of the manual (at the left margin) and the company name and page number (at the right margin).
3. Place a footer on every page including the first page. The footer may include the same information as the header or it may identify the content of that page (for example, *Training Program*).

Employee Training Manual   Kramer, Inc., Page 2

    This procedures manual, therefore, is designed to assist those managers who are responsible for developing training programs. All new employees hired in any of the five regional branches of Kramer, Inc., should be provided with a set of training guidelines and the opportunity to attend training sessions during normal workdays. The following sections outline the basic content of Kramer's training program.

INTRODUCTION

    This section explains the content of the manual and provides specific suggestions for using the manual within the company. It provides answers to the following questions:

1. Who is the training manual designed for, and what information is contained with the manual?
2. Where does the training manual fit within the training program?
3. How should the training manual be used?
4. Can the manual be used in a classroom setting?
5. Can the manual be used as self-paced instructional material?
6. Can managers provide study guides to accompany the manual?

PROGRAM PHILOSOPHY AND GOALS

    The philosophy of Kramer, Inc., is to provide training to new employees during the first six months of employment. We believe that by providing our employees with supervised training programs as well as on-the-job training, we develop employees' potential to contribute to the good of the company.

    We also feel that well-trained employees quickly become assets to the company as they assume additional job responsibilities. We also believe training programs help to develop each employee's full potential and, in the long run, create a more pleasant work environment. Both managers and employees work in cooperation with one another and develop a team spirit that has proven to be in the best interests of the company.

GOALS

    The goals of the training program are many and varied. Through a formal training program we hope to accomplish the following:

- Prepare new employees to take on additional job responsibilities once they learn their particular jobs.
- Prepare managers to assist new employees in making the transition into the company and into a new position.
- Develop new employees' full potential; that is, enable employees to learn about and perform all aspects of a job.

Training Program

1. Turn on hyphenation.
2. In page numbering, change the page number to 7, then create a header as follows: Type *Employees' Manual* at the left margin. Type *Chandler* *Industries, Page 7* flush right.
3. Create a footer by typing *Training Program* in italic and flush right.
4. Type the following portion of the procedures manual that follows.

Employees' Manual   Chandler Industries, Page 7

The purpose of this procedures manual is to assist managers who are responsible for developing training programs for new employees who have been hired in any of the seven regional branches of Chandler Industries. The basic content of this training program is outlined in the following paragraphs.

INTRODUCTION

This section identifies specific ways the manual should be used at Chandler Industries as well as the content of the manual. Answers are provided to the following questions:

1. Where does the training manual fit within the training program?
2. For whom is the manual designed, and what does it contain?
3. How should the manual be used?
4. Can the manual be used in a classroom setting?
5. Can the manual be used as self-paced instructional material?
6. Can study guides accompany the manual?

PROGRAM PHILOSOPHY AND GOALS

This section reveals the nature of the training program. The statements below provide the context for all courses within Chandler Industries. The focus of the section is as follows:

- Why does this program exist, and who benefits from it?
- What company needs are satisfied by this program?
- What goals, tasks, and competencies are satisfied by this program?
- What specific skills does this training program develop?

Training Program

Report 49
Procedures Manual

1. Turn on hyphenation.
2. In page numbering, change the page number to 2.
3. Create a header as follows: Type *Presentation Software Guide* at the left margin. Type *Cartwright Services, Page 2* flush right.
4. Create a matching footer.

(continued on next page)

FORMATTING SLIDES

Once you have written your presentation, you can place your key points on slides using presentation software. Follow these steps to prepare your presentation slides.

- Select a template or background that is appropriate for every slide.
- Select a layout such as text copy, bulleted or numbered lists, etc.
- Use the edit, copy, paste commands to add text to your presentation slides.

FORMATTING THE PRESENTATION

After you finished preparing the slides for your presentation, you may want to change the method by which each slide appears on the screen or the way individual points are displayed on the screen. In presentation software, known as Transition, moving from one slide to another is transition, it is accomplished by following these steps:

- Select those slides you want to controlled by the transition method.
- Select a transition method such as Cover Right or Wipe Left.
- Run through the slide show to determine whether or not you are satisfied with the transition.

A slide presentations can also be formatted so that each point you make on an individual slide appears individually on the screen. To structure your slides this way, follow these steps:

- Select those slides to be controlled by a build effect.
- Select a build effect style such as Fly From Left.
- Run through the slide show again to determine whether or not you are satisfied with the build effect that you selected.

Report 50
Procedures Manual

1. Open the file for Report 49.

2. Add the following sections to the end of the report.

ADDING CLIP ART

Clipart # can enhances the appearance of a slide, and it can be easily added

(continued on next page)

to selected slides or to every other slide in your presentation. Several clip art images are included in this presentation package, and any one of them can be used in slides that you prepare. If you choose, however, you can insert clip art images from other packages. To insert a clip art image from your presentation package, follow these steps:

- Select the slide on which you want the clip art to appear.
- Click the icon for adding a clip art image. ~~This icon is found on he~~ ~~menu bar.~~
- Select the image from the software clip art library. ~~The slide can come~~ ~~from the presentation package or you can retrieve it from another clip~~ ~~art package.~~
- Size and move the image to its correct location on the ~~presentation~~ page.
- Copy the image to the master slide if it is to appear on all slides.

You can also change the appearance of the clip art image by (1) changing the colors used in the image; (2) flipping the image so that its horizontal or vertical position is reversed (mirror image); (3) changing the contrast or brightness of the image; and (4) cropping the image so that unwanted sections are eliminated from view.

Lesson 93 Manuscript Reports

GOALS: To improve speed and accuracy; to refine language-arts skills in proofreading; to format magazine articles.

A. Type 2 times.

A. WARMUP

```
1       On 12/30/96 Jim gave Alex and Pam a quiz--it was quite    11
2  difficult!  Neither scored higher than 82%; their average    23
3  was 79.  They should retake the quiz by the 4th or 5th.      34
   | 1  | 2  | 3  | 4  | 5  | 6  | 7  | 8  | 9  | 10 | 11 | 12
```

B. Take three 12-second timings on each line. The scale below the last line shows your wam speed for a 12-second timing.

B. 12-SECOND SPEED SPRINTS

4 You do not have to worry at all about the problem they had.
5 Mary can type fast on the short words found in these lines.
6 We would like to have these people on our panel as we work.
7 We must write our notes on this paper that was given to us.
| | | |5| | | |10| | | |15| | | |20| | | |25| | | |30| | | |35| | | |40| | | |45| | | |50| | | |55| | | |60

C. PROGRESSIVE PRACTICE: ALPHABET

Turn to the Progressive Practice: Alphabet routine beginning on page SB-7.

Take six 30-second timings, starting at the point where you left off the last time.

D. Study the rules at the right.

D. HYPHEN, ADJECTIVE, AND ADVERB

Rule: Hyphenate compound numbers (between twenty-one and ninety-nine) and fractions that are expressed in words.

-num

Seventy-five of the participants voted to repeal the law--this represents nearly two-fifths of the total membership.
Thirty-five letters were sent to Mr. Alexander to thank him for his excellent service.

Rule: Hyphenate words that are divided at the end of a line. Do not divide one-syllable words, contractions, or abbreviations; divide other words only between syllables.

-div

We will attend the next meeting in Toronto. However, if it is determined that this site is not suitable, another city will be selected.
All those who exceeded their monthly sales quota will receive a commission for their efforts.

Rule: Use comparative adjectives and adverbs (-er, more, and less) when referring to two nouns; use superlative adjectives and adverbs (-est, most, and least) when referring to more than two.

adj/adv

Of the two players, Sam is more skillful at free-throw shooting.
She is looking for the most beautiful state to visit this summer.

Edit the sentences to correct any errors in the use of the hyphen, adjectives, and adverbs.

8   Two thirds of the membership must be present for a quorum.
9   Thirty-nine students qualified for the math competition.
10 After adding all the numbers in the column, we must then calculate the percentage of increase.
11 I worked all day preparing the transparencies for my demonstration next week.
12 Both of the mountains had fantastic ski slopes; however, I preferred the slopes on the highest one.
13 Of the two computers, the one that is networked is the newest.

E. MAGAZINE ARTICLES

Magazine articles can be formatted as two-column reports. Follow these steps:

1. Change to double-spacing and full justification; then turn on hyphenation.
2. Create a header to identify the author's name and the page number at the top right of every page. Use only the author's last name and the page number in the header (for example, *Mysweski—2*). Suppress the header on page 1.
3. Press Enter 3 times, then center and type the article title in all caps and bold.
4. Press Enter once, then center and type the byline in initial caps.
5. Press Enter once, then type the article in a two-column format.

Magazine Article, page 1

Magazine Article, page 2

F. WORD PROCESSING: COLUMNS

Study Lesson 93 in your word processing manual. Complete all of the shaded steps while at your computer. Then format the jobs that follow.

Report 51
Magazine Article

1. Type the following magazine article in a two-column format.
2. Format the columns so that those on the second page will end evenly.

MEMBER BUYING SERVICES / By Brenda T. Mysweski

Policyholders of AICA (and their dependents) are eligible for a wide range of discount services. These services provide you with a variety of items you can purchase, from automobiles to computers to jewelry. Here are some examples of the merchandise and services that are available to all AICA members.

AUTO PRICING

You can order the most sophisticated auto information guide on the market. The guide will give you information on retail prices, vehicle specifications, safety equipment, and factory-option packages.

(continued on next page)

When you are ready to place your order for an automobile, a team of company experts will work with you and with the prospective dealer to ensure that you are getting the best possible price through a network of nationwide dealers. You are guaranteed to get the best price for the automobile you have chosen.

Once you have purchased your automobile, AICA will provide all your insurance needs. Discounts on policy rates are provided for completion of a driver-training program, for installed antitheft devices, and for installed passive restraint systems such as air bags.

Finally, we can make your purchase decision an easy one by always providing a low-rate finance plan for you. You can be certain that you are getting the most competitive interest rate for the purchase of your automobile when you finance with AICA.

CAR RENTAL DISCOUNTS

When you need to rent an automobile while traveling, special rates are available to you from five of the largest car rental agencies.

ROAD AND TRAVEL SERVICES

You can enjoy the security of emergency road service through the AICA Road and Travel Plan. This plan also includes discounts on hotels and motels.

As an AICA traveler, you can take advantage of our exclusive discounts and bonuses on cruises and tours. Our travel plan provides daily and weekend trips to over 100 destinations. Take advantage of this wonderful opportunity to let AICA serve all your travel needs.

MERCHANDISE BUYING

Each quarter a buying services catalog will be sent to you. This catalog includes a variety of items that can be purchased through AICA--and you'll never find better prices! Through the catalog you can purchase jewelry, furniture, sports equipment, electronics, appliances, and computers. To place an order, all you have to do is call AICA toll-free at 1-800-555-3838. Your order will arrive within 10 to 15 days.

INTERVIEW TECHNIQUES / By Paul Sanford

The interview process ~~allows~~ enables a company to gather information about you that ~~has~~ was not ~~been~~ provided on your resume or application form. This information may include such items as your career goals, appearance, personality, poise, attitudes, and ability to express yourself verbally.

APPEARANCE

There are several things you should keep in mind when going ~~for~~ to an interview. You should plan your wardrobe ~~well~~ carefully, because first impressions are lasting ones when you walk into the interviewer's office. If you are not quite certain as to what you should wear, dress conservatively. Whatever you ~~select~~ choose, be sure that your clothing is clean, neat, and comfortable. You should also pay attention to important details such as clean hair, shined shoes, well-groomed nails, and appropriate jewelry and other accessories.

MEETING THE INTERVIEWER

Be sure to arrive at the interview site a few minutes early. Stand when you meet the interviewer for the first time. If ~~a handshake is offered~~ the interviewer offers to shake hands, shake hands in a confident, firm manner. It is also a good idea not to smoke or chew gum during the interview.

THE INTERVIEW PROCESS

Maintain ~~good~~ direct eye contact with the interviewer when you respond to his or her questions. Listen intently to everything that is said. Be aware of ~~the~~ any movements you make with your eyes, your hands, and other parts of your body during the interview. Too much movement may be a signal to the interviewer that you are nervous, that you lack confidence, or that you are not certain of your answers.

During the interview ~~process~~, the interviewer will judge not only what you say but also how you say it. As you ~~speak~~ answer questions, you will be judged on grammar, articulation, vocabulary, and tone of voice. The nonverbal skills

(continued on next page)

the interviewer

that may be judged are your attitude, enthusiasm, listening abilities, and

promptness in responding to questions.

ENDING THE INTERVIEW

Let the interviewer determine when it is time to close the interview.

When this time arrives, ask the interviewer when he or she expects to

make a decision on hiring for this position and when you can expect to

hear about the job. Thank the interviewer for taking the time to meet with

you, and express a positive desire to work for the company.

After the interview, send a follow-up letter to remind the interviewer of

your name and your continued interest in the company. Let that person

know how to contact you by providing the telephone number where you

can be reached, either at home or at your current work location.

Report 53
Magazine Article

Open the file for Report 51, and make the following changes:

1. Make yourself the author of the article.
2. Make the *MERCHANDISE BUYING* section the second paragraph in the article.
3. Replace all instances of *AICA* with *UAIC*. (**Note:** Any "a/an" changes?)
4. Replace all instances of *auto* or *automobiles* with *car* or *cars*. **Note:** You may also have to change the article *a*

or *an* if it precedes any of these changes.

5. Add the following section to the end of the article: *MISCELLANEOUS SERVICES / In addition to the above services, UAIC provides permanent life insurance, pension plan funding, cash management, and credit card programs. At your request, detailed catalogs will be sent to you that explain each of these services.*

Lesson 94 Miscellaneous Reports

GOALS: To type 46 wam/5'/5e; to format itineraries.

A. Type 2 times.

A. WARMUP

```
1       Had Phil been given a quiz on a subject that had been    11
2   reviewed by Max and Kay?  Frank scored 89 on that quiz; Sue    23
3   scored 93 (*math only).  Both tests were taken on 10/25/96.    35
    |  1  |  2  |  3  |  4  |  5  |  6  |  7  |  8  |  9  |  10  |  11  |  12
```

B. Type each sentence on a separate line. Type 2 times.

B. TECHNIQUE PRACTICE: ENTER KEY

4 Decorate the room. Attend the seminar. Go to the theater.
5 Watch the inauguration. Go to the rally. See the recital.
6 Run in the marathon. Bake the bread. Vacuum the bedrooms.
7 Visit the nursing home. Sell the ticket. Drive the truck.

C. DIAGNOSTIC PRACTICE: ALPHABET

Turn to the Diagnostic Practice: Alphabet routine beginning on page SB-2. Type one of the Pretest/Posttest paragraphs and identify any errors made. Then type the corresponding drill lines 2 times for each letter on which you made 2 or more errors and 1 time for each letter on which you made only 1 error. Finally, repeat the same Pretest paragraph and compare your performance.

D. Take two 5-minute timings. Determine your speed and errors.

Goal: 46 wam/5'/5e

D. 5-MINUTE TIMING

8   Making a successful presentation to an audience is a   11
9 skill that is absolutely essential in your career. The   22
10 art of speaking before a group requires planning and very   34
11 hard work. Although each speaker makes preparation in a   45
12 different manner, here are some rules to be followed.   56
13   As a speaker, you are quite visible to your listeners.   67
14 Therefore, you must make a good first impression on the   78
15 group. Dress well, maintain good posture, and exhibit a   90
16 confident manner when you approach the speaker's podium.   101
17 Always stand up to your full height, but try to maintain a   113
18 natural stance when speaking to the group. Remind yourself   125
19 to stand erect, with shoulders back and stomach in. Such   137
20 posture will no doubt improve on the quality of your voice.   148
21   Be careful how you use your eyes, face, and hands to   159
22 emphasize points. Eye contact is essential, and you should   171
23 never look away from your audience for any extended period   183
24 of time. When you speak to a large group, just move your   195
25 eyes over the audience; do not focus on one person. Facial   207
26 expressions and hand movements can convey meaning to your   218
27 listeners, and they should be used frequently as you speak.   230

| 1 | 2 | 3 | 4 | 5 | 6 | 7 | 8 | 9 | 10 | 11 | 12 |

E. ITINERARIES

An itinerary is a proposed outline of a trip that provides a traveler with information such as flight times and numbers, meeting times, travel dates, and room reservations. An itinerary may also include notes of special interest to the traveler.

 **DOCUMENT PROCESSING**

Report 54
Itinerary

Follow these steps to format Report 54.

1. Press Enter 6 times to leave an approximate 2-inch top margin.
2. Insert a blank line between each centered line of the heading.
3. After the last heading line, press Enter twice and type the day and date at the left margin in bold.
4. Press Enter twice and type the destination at the left margin. Type the flight information flush right with dot leaders.
5. Indent the flight details 0.5 inch.
6. Insert a blank line between each new section of the itinerary.
7. Type the word *NOTES* in all caps and bold at the left margin. Press Enter twice, and automatically number the entries.

↓6X **PORTLAND SALES MEETING**
↓2X

Itinerary for Arlene Gilsdorf
↓2X

March 12-15, 19--
↓2X

Thursday, March 12
↓2X

Detroit/Minneapolis . . . . Northwest 83
    Depart 5:10 p.m.; arrive 5:55 p.m.
    Seat 8D; nonstop
    ↓2X

Minneapolis/Portland . . . . Northwest 2363
    Depart 6:30 p.m.; arrive 8:06 p.m.
    Seat 15C; nonstop; dinner
    ↓2X

Sunday, March 15

Portland/Minneapolis . . . . Northwest 360
    Depart 7:30 a.m.; arrive 12:26 p.m.
    Seat 15H; one stop; breakfast

Minneapolis/Detroit . . . . Northwest 748
    Depart 1 p.m.; arrive 3:32 p.m.
    Seat 10D; nonstop; snack
    ↓2X

(continued on next page)

NOTES

↓2X

1. Jack Weatherford, assistant western regional manager, will meet your flight on Thursday and return you to the airport on Sunday.
2. All seat assignments are aisle seats; smoking is not allowed on any of the flights.

Report 55
Itinerary

INTERCO SEMINAR
Itinerary for Mrs. Helen Kyslowsky
September 25-27, 19--

Wednesday, September 25
Columbus / Boston . . . . America West 2053
   Depart 6:50 p.m.; arrive 9:10 p.m.
   Seat 13F; nonstop
Friday, September 27
Boston / Columbus . . . . America West 3242
   Depart 4:40 p.m.; arrive 6:35 p.m.
   Seat 9A; nonstop
NOTES
1. Marcia Chisholm, Interco human resources manager, will meet your flight and return you to Logan Airport on Friday.
2. All seat assignments are window seats; no meals or snacks will be served.
3. On Thursday, the seminar will begin at 8:30 a.m. and end at 4:30 p.m. Dinner will be served at 6 p.m.
4. On Friday, the seminar will begin at 8:30 a.m. and end at 12:30 p.m. Lunch will be on your own.

Report 56
Itinerary

CALIFORNIA PLANNING MEETING / Itinerary for Nancy Perkins / July 8-10, 19-- / **Monday, July 8** / Houston to Los Angeles; United Flight 834 / leave at 2:45 p.m.; arrive at 4:05 p.m.; seat 10C; nonstop / **Tuesday, July 9** / Los Angeles to Sacramento; American Flight 206 / leave at 10 a.m.; arrive at 11:15 a.m.; seat 4A; nonstop / **Wednesday, July 10** / Sacramento to Houston; United Flight 307 / leave at 7 p.m.; arrive at 11:15 p.m.; seat

(continued on next page)

7B; nonstop; dinner / **NOTES** / 1. Adam Broderick, chief engineer for Natural Gas Division, will meet you at the airport in Los Angeles. / 2. At 7 p.m. on July 8 you will have dinner with C. J. Brantley and Adam Broderick at the Hollywood & Vine Restaurant. / 3. You will have a 9 a.m. tour of the wastewater treatment plants in northern California on Wednesday, July 10. / 4. At 12 noon on Wednesday, July 10, you will have lunch with Assemblyman O. J. Walton at J. C. Crawford's. Topic: Senate Bill 4501-68.

Lesson 95   Report Review

GOALS: To improve speed and accuracy; to refine language-arts skills in composing; to review report formats.

A. Type 2 times.

A. WARMUP

```
1       Felix Quayle sat in Seat #14 when he won the jackpot;     11
2  Van Gill sat in Seat #23 but did not win a prize.  Do you     23
3  think Row 19 (Seats #1560 and #1782) will be lucky for me?     34
   |  1  |  2  |  3  |  4  |  5  |  6  |  7  |  8  |  9  | 10  | 11  | 12
```

SKILLBUILDING

B. PROGRESSIVE PRACTICE: NUMBERS

Turn to the Progressive Practice: Numbers routine beginning on page SB-11.

Take six 30-second timings, starting at the point where you left off the last time.

C. PRETEST: DISCRIMINATION PRACTICE

Pretest
Take a 1-minute timing. Determine your speed and errors.

```
4       Did the new clerk join the golf team?  John indicated     11
5  to me that Beverly invited her prior to last Wednesday.  He     23
6  believes she must give you a verbal commitment at once.        34
   |  1  |  2  |  3  |  4  |  5  |  6  |  7  |  8  |  9  | 10  | 11  | 12
```

D. PRACTICE: LEFT HAND

Practice
  Speed Emphasis: If you made no more than 1 error on the Pretest, type each *individual* line 2 times.
  Accuracy Emphasis: If you made 2 or more errors, type each *group* of lines (as though it were a paragraph) 2 times.

```
7  vbv bevy verb bevel vibes breve viable braves verbal beaver
8  wew went week weans weigh weave wedges thawed weaker beware
9  ded dent need deals moved ceded heeded debate edging define
```

E. PRACTICE: RIGHT HAND

```
10 klk kale look kilts lakes knoll likely kettle kernel lacked
11 uyu buys your gummy dusty young unduly tryout uneasy jaunty
12 oio oils roil toils onion point oriole soiled ration joined
```

Posttest
Repeat the Pretest timing and compare performance.

F. POSTTEST: DISCRIMINATION PRACTICE

G. PROGRESSIVE PRACTICE: ALPHABET

Turn to the Progressive Practice: Alphabet routine beginning on page SB-7.

Take six 30-second timings, starting at the point where you left off the last time.

LANGUAGE ARTS

H. COMPOSING

Compose a two-paragraph personal-business letter that summarizes the content of the 5-minute timing on page 253. Address the letter to your instructor; provide a suitable inside address and salutation for your letter. Also provide a complimentary closing, and sign the letter yourself.

In the letter, discuss the following:

Paragraph 1: Inform your instructor of the various materials that can be recycled.

Paragraph 2: Provide examples of how coffee filters, lightbulbs, and paper can be used in the recycling process.

DOCUMENT PROCESSING

Report 57
Agenda

Crandall First National Bank / Meeting Agenda / May 15, 19--

1. Call to Order

2. Approval of minutes of April 1̶7̶⁶ meeting

3. Mortgage loans (J. William Hokes)

4. Installment loans (Lorraine Hagen)

5. Series EE bonds (Joni Ellickson)

6. Club memberships

7. Certificates of deposit (Louise Abbey)
   (Robert Hunt)

8. Closing remarks

9. Adjournment

Report 58
Minutes of a Meeting

Turn on hyphenation.

LITTLETON WATER COLOUR SOCIETY
Minutes of Meeting
Oct. 23, 19--

(continued on next page)

CALL TO ORDER The meeting was called ^to order^ by Sandra Garvy at 8 ~e~ ^p.m.^ in the

Littleton library confrence^e^ room.

OLD BUSINESS susan Firtz furnished each member with a list of

artists and the name^s^ of the wtercolor^a^ paintings each

artist is entering in the Fall Arts Fair.

NEW BUSINESS John Cahmpion informed members ^that^ a new supply of

canvas and oil paint ^has^ arrived. Members can check out ^any^

items they need to begin ^their^ winter projects. ^He reminded everyone that^ Winter Fair

will be held December 14 ^at the Expo^.

ADJOURMENT^N^ The meeting ^was^ adjourned at 9:45 ^p.m.^. The next meeting is ^will be held on^

November 12⊙

Respecfully^t^, ^submitted^

Catherine Argetes

**Report 59
Progress Check**
Magazine Article

1. Type the following article in two columns. Turn hyphenation on and balance the columns.

2. Double-space the article and create a header for page 2.

PERFORMING SUCCESSFULLY

By Ginger Nichols

¶We have been involved in giving performances since our very early years when we played a part in a class play or participated in competitive sporting events at our school. The most terrifying part of each performance was probably the fear that we would "freeze" when it came our turn to perform. Whenever we find ourselves in this predicament, the best thing to do is to accept that fear and learn to let it work for us, not against us. We need to recognize that nervousness or fear may set in during our performance. Then, when it does happen (if it does), we will be ready to cope with it and overcome it.

¶If you forget some of your lines in a recitation, try to remember other lines and recite them. Doing so may help those forgotten lines to "pop back" into your memory so that you can put them in at a later time, if possible.

¶You always want to leave your audience with the idea that you have

(continued on next page)

given them something worthwhile that they can use or apply to their own lives. For maximum impact on your audience and to make sure that they remember what you say, use audiovisual aids to reinforce your message. Remember, however, that audiovisual aids are nothing more than aids. The real message should come in the words you choose when giving your presentation.

¶Study your speech well; even rehearse it if necessary. However, do not practice it to the extent that it appears that you are merely reading what is written down on the paper in front of you. Much of your personality should be exhibited while you are giving your speech. If you are an enthusiastic, friendly person who converses well with people face-to-face, then that same persona should be evident during your speech. A good piece of advice is to just go out there and be yourself—you will be much more comfortable by doing so, and your audience will relate to you better than if you try to exhibit a different personality when at the podium.

¶No matter how rapidly you speak in general, slow down when you are in front of a group. The fact that you are nervous can cause your speech rate to increase. The best way to slow down your speaking is to breathe deeply. Doing so also causes your nervous system to relax, allowing you to proceed with your speech calmly.

¶Finally, possibly the best advice for giving a successful speech is to be prepared. You will be more confident if you are thoroughly prepared. Do your research, rehearse your speech, and make notes where you want to give emphasis or use an audiovisual aid.

Lesson 96 Tables With Font Changes

GOALS: To type 47 wam/5′/5e; to format tables with font changes.

A. Type 2 times.

 *SKILLBUILDING*

C. Take two 5-minute timings. Determine your speed and errors.

Goal: 47 wam/5′/5e

A. WARMUP

```
1    Jeremiah coaxed eight squawking birds out of the green    11
2  shed on April 23, 1996.  He was concerned that they would    23
3  freeze (and quickly!) if they weren't moved immediately.     34
   |  1  |  2  |  3  |  4  |  5  |  6  |  7  |  8  |  9  |  10  |  11  |  12
```

B. PACED PRACTICE

Turn to the Paced Practice routine beginning on page SB-14. Take three 2-minute timings, starting at the point where you left off the last time.

C. 5-MINUTE TIMING

```
4     Listening skills are often considered in the top three    11
5   of those executives consider most critical for people they   23
6   hire.  Listening is different from most of the skills that   35
7   are learned in school in that no one typically spends time   47
8   teaching us to become better listeners.  Many people often   58
9   think that listening is automatic and, therefore, we don't  70
10  have to improve this acquired skill.  To become better at   82
11  listening, we should follow these half-dozen rules daily.   93
12     First, screen out all the distracting sounds that may    104
13  interfere with your ability to hear all that is being said. 117
14  Second, avoid doing other things when someone is talking to 129
15  you.  Third, pay close attention when someone is talking    140
16  to you.  This task includes concentrating on the message    151
17  and finding something interesting about what is being said. 164
18  Fourth, ask questions if something is not too clear to you. 176
19  Doing so will prevent a communication breakdown.  Fifth, be 188
20  sure not to interrupt the speaker until he or she is done   199
21  talking.  If you interrupt, you might miss a vital part of  211
22  the message.  Sixth, never let a speaker's looks or habits  223
23  affect your ability to listen to and evaluate the message.  235
    |  1  |  2  |  3  |  4  |  5  |  6  |  7  |  8  |  9  |  10  |  11  |  12
```

Table 41
Boxed Table With
Braced Headings

1. Center the table vertically.
2. Create a boxed table with 5 columns and 10 rows.
3. Type the table as shown with centered column headings. Type the column heading for the first column in Row 3. Then remove the border between Rows 2 and 3 in Column 1.
4. Follow standard table format for the rest of the table.
5. Apply a 10% fill intensity to Rows 2, 3, and 10.
6. Change the font in Rows 1, 2, and 3 to Impact.
7. Insert the formula to calculate the total amounts and format the numbers with a thousands separator.
8. Center the table horizontally.

SEMIANNUAL SALES TOTALS Western and Eastern Regions				
	Western Region		Eastern Region	
Month	Est. Sales ($)	Actual Sales ($)	Est. Sales ($)	Actual Sales ($)
January	246,500	238,225	384,200	395,775
February	257,200	265,835	405,500	410,535
March	265,800	277,200	410,000	398,500
April	295,000	286,255	435,000	442,765
May	285,000	285,500	395,500	395,475
June	276,500	291,250	392,600	401,385
TOTAL	?	?	?	?

Table 42
Open Table

1. Center the table vertically.
2. Create an open table with 5 columns and 8 rows.
3. Type the table as shown with centered column headings.
4. Follow standard table format for the rest of the table. Do not type the question marks.
5. Insert the formula to calculate the total amounts.
6. Automatically adjust the column widths.
7. Center the table horizontally.
8. Choose a different font for title, subtitle, and column headings.

FINAL MEDAL COUNT FOR TOP 5 NATIONS
(1996 Centennial Olympic Games)

Country	Gold	Silver	Bronze	Total
United States	44	32	25	?
Germany	20	18	27	?

(continued on next page)

Russia	26	21	16	?
China	16	22	12	?
Australia	9	9	23	?
TOTAL	?	?	?	?

Table 43
Open Table

Open the file for Table 41, and make the following changes.

1. Change the table to an open table.
2. Change the font for Rows 1, 2, and 3 to Arial 11 point.
3. Change the estimated sales for the Western Region as follows: January,

247,300; February, 257,500; March, 268,500.

4. Change the estimated sales for the Eastern Region as follows: April, 435,800; May, 395,580; June, 396,500.
5. Recalculate the totals.

Lesson 97   Directories

GOALS: To improve speed and accuracy; to refine language-arts skills in using pronouns; to format directories.

A. Type 2 times.

A. WARMUP

1   Did Zach get 47 quart jugs of hot apple cider to take   11
2 to the Barnes & Bailey circus on 5/31/96? We should take   23
3 in $240* (12% more than in '95) this year. That's great!   34

| 1 | 2 | 3 | 4 | 5 | 6 | 7 | 8 | 9 | 10 | 11 | 12

 SKILLBUILDING

B. Take three 12-second timings on each line. The scale below the last line shows your wam speed for a 12-second timing.

B. 12-SECOND SPEED SPRINTS

4 I did not think I should have to pay the bill at this time.
5 The four of them will take their time when they drive home.
6 He is sure the sun will be up all the way when they arrive.
7 Add the numbers to see if you get the same totals as I did.

| | | 5 | | | 10 | | | 15 | | | 20 | | | 25 | | | 30 | | | 35 | | | 40 | | | 45 | | | 50 | | | 55 | | | 60

Pretest
Take a 1-minute timing. Determine your speed and errors.

C. PRETEST: HORIZONTAL REACHES

8   Art enjoyed his royal blue race car. He bragged about   11
9 how he learned to push for those speed spurts that helped   23
10 him win many races. The car had a lot of get-up-and-go.   34

| 1 | 2 | 3 | 4 | 5 | 6 | 7 | 8 | 9 | 10 | 11 | 12

Practice

Speed Emphasis: If you made no more than 1 error on the Pretest, type each *individual* line 2 times.

Accuracy Emphasis: If you made 2 or more errors, type each *group* of lines (as though it were a paragraph) 2 times.

Posttest

Repeat the Pretest timing and compare performance.

D. PRACTICE: IN REACHES

11 oy toy ahoy ploy loyal coyly royal enjoy decoy annoy deploy
12 ar fare arch mart march farms scars spear barns learn radar
13 pu pull push puts pulse spurt purge spuds pushy spurs pupil

E. PRACTICE: OUT REACHES

14 ge gear gets ages getup raged geese lunge pages cagey forge
15 da dare date data dance adage dazed sedan daubs cedar daily
16 hi high hick hill hinge chief hires ethic hiked chili hitch

F. POSTTEST: HORIZONTAL REACHES

G. Type line 17. Then type lines 18–20 (as a paragraph), reading the words from right to left. Type 2 times.

G. TECHNIQUE PRACTICE: CONCENTRATION

17   When typing, always strive for complete concentration.
18 concentration. complete for strive always typing, When
19 errors. your on down cut may rate typing your in decrease A
20 errors. of number the reduce to rate reading your down Slow

LANGUAGE ARTS

H. Study the rules at the right.

H. PRONOUNS

Rule: Use nominative pronouns (such as *I, he, she, we,* and *they*) as subjects of a sentence or clause.

pro nom

I wonder if she is going to participate in the contest next month.
We saw that they were very well prepared for the test.

Rule: Use objective pronouns (such as *me, him, her, us,* and *them*) as objects in a sentence or clause.

pro obj

Diane will give her car to them on Friday for the meeting next week.
Alex is grateful to them for the assistance given to him last month.

Edit the sentences to correct any errors in the use of pronouns.

21 We hope they will take all of them to the concert tomorrow.
22 John gave the gift to she on Monday; her was very pleased.
23 If them do not hurry, Mary will not finish her work on time.
24 The book was proofread by her; the changes were made by he.
25 It is up to them to give us all the pages they read today.
26 Me cannot assure they that it will not rain for the picnic.

FORMATTING

I. WORD PROCESSING: SORT

Study Lesson 97 in your word processing manual. Complete all of the shaded steps while at your computer. Then format the jobs that follow.

DOCUMENT PROCESSING

Table 44
Directory

Format the table as follows:

1. Center the table vertically.
2. Create a boxed table with 4 columns and 8 rows.
3. Center and type the title in all caps and bold. Center and type the subtitle and the date on separate lines in initial caps.
4. Left-align the column headings and type them in bold.
5. Automatically adjust the column widths.
6. Center the table horizontally.

PERSONNEL DIRECTORY
Management Department
June 19--

Name	Address	City	ZIP
Traylor, Karen	4365 Highland Circle	Austell	30001
Melton, Jane	6549 Brown Street	Austell	30001
Landrum, Bill	3325 Lauada Drive	Douglasville	30134
Hennington, Marylee	2901 Bakers Bridge Court	Douglasville	30135
Hodge, George	4027 Golfview Drive	Douglasville	30135
Wagner, Sam	6628 Windwood Court	Mableton	30059

Table 45
Directory

1. Open the file for Table 44 and add the following two entries: *Sue Ballentine / 6823 Creekwood Drive / Mableton / 30059; Barbara Chaffin / 4101 Yaeger Road / Marietta / 30060.*
2. Sort the table by employees' last names.

Table 46
Directory

1. Open the file for Table 45.
2. Sort the table by ZIP Codes in descending order.

Lesson 98   Tables Formatted Sideways

GOALS: To type 47 wam/5'/5e; to format tables in landscape page orientation.

A. Type 2 times.

A. WARMUP

```
1      The size of my quarter horse was judged by experts.  I    11
2  do not think judges #17, #28, and #36 looked at my horse      23
3  after 7:45 p.m. when the arena was "vented" for the night.    34
   |  1  |  2  |  3  |  4  |  5  |  6  |  7  |  8  |  9  | 10  | 11  | 12
```

B. DIAGNOSTIC PRACTICE: ALPHABET

Turn to the Diagnostic Practice: Alphabet routine beginning on page SB-2. Type one of the Pretest/Posttest paragraphs and identify any errors made. Then type the corresponding drill lines 2 times for each letter on which you made 2 or more errors and 1 time for each letter on which you made only 1 error. Finally, repeat the same Pretest paragraph and compare your performance.

C. PROGRESSIVE PRACTICE: ALPHABET

Turn to the Progressive Practice: Alphabet routine beginning on page SB-7. Take six 30-second timings, starting at the point where you left off the last time.

D. Take two 5-minute timings. Determine your speed and errors.

Goal: 47 wam/5′/5e

D. 5-MINUTE TIMING

```
 4        Preparing for group meetings is a challenge for most    11
 5    people.  If you are in charge of conducting such a meeting,  23
 6    there are some rules you should follow to make certain that  35
 7    it is successful.  If the size of the group may be large,    46
 8    put some extra time into preparation.  Set the starting      57
 9    time and length of the meeting, select a meeting site and    69
10    date, and send an agenda to those who will be joining you    81
11    at the meeting.                                              84
12        In the meeting room, be sure that all equipment and      94
13    facilities are available and ready to use.  Before the      105
14    meeting starts, check the equipment to make sure it is      116
15    working properly.  To take care of this, arrive early at    128
16    the meeting site.                                           131
17        The person in charge of the meeting sets the tone for   142
18    the meeting.  If you start the meeting late, people might   154
19    lose their interest or enthusiasm quickly.  When discussion 166
20    begins, keep it on track.  Encourage those in attendance    177
21    to participate in the discussion.  Learn to ask pointed     188
22    questions so that you can keep the discussion going in the  200
23    right direction.  While you may have to prompt some people  212
24    to talk, others may have to be discouraged.  You should try 224
25    to avoid letting a few participants dominate a meeting.     235
     |  1  |  2  |  3  |  4  |  5  |  6  |  7  |  8  |  9  |  10  |  11  |  12
```

E. WORD PROCESSING: PAGE ORIENTATION

Study Lesson 98 in your word processing manual. Complete all of the shaded steps while at your computer. Then format the jobs that follow.

Table 47
Boxed Table in
Landscape Format

1. Format the table in landscape orientation.
2. Use 0.5-inch side margins for the table.
3. Create a boxed table with 7 columns and 10 rows.
4. Center the table vertically and horizontally.
5. Type the following column headings in bold: *Customer, Address, City, ZIP, Telephone No., Item, Stock No.* Align the headings over text columns at the left. Align the headings over number columns at the right.
6. In Column 1, type the customer's last name followed by a comma; then type the first name.

CUSTOMER DATABASE INFORMATION

(Ohio District)

August 31, 19--

Jack Nuttre / 3309 Aaron Place ~~Avenue~~ Street / Kenton / 44426 / 419-555-2384 / 486 computer / 4-238-cw

John Stewart / 20604 Lucile Rd. South / Columbus / 43230 / 614-555-2074 / laser printer / 3-895-LP

Darrell Davis / 322 W. Lyons Road / Mansfield / 44902 / 216-555-2002 / ~~Color~~ Laser Printer / 3-895-LP

Mark Jaderstrom / 5914 Bay Oaks Place / Chillicothe / 45610 / 614-555-1399 / Color Ink-Jet Printer / 2-550-cij

Barbara Stevens / 10386 power Dr. / Steubenville / 43952 / 614-555-7821 / 568 Pentium Computer / 5-987-PC

Bill McGraw / Box 365 / Youngstown / 44502 / 216-555-3885 / 486 computer / 4-238-CW

Tony Hodge / 6823 Creekwood ~~Lane~~ Drive / Columbus / 43085 / 614-555-2934 / 586 Pentium Computer / 5-987-PC

Fred Obernberger / 26044 Manzano Court / Youngstown / 44505 / 216-555-1777 / FlatBed Color Scanner / 6-8820-CSc

(continued on next page)

Tom McGraw / 936 East wind Drive / Cleveland / 44121 / 216-555-2839 / Lasser Printer / 3-895-LP

Table 48
Boxed Table in Landscape Format

Open the file for Table 44, and make the following changes:

1. Use landscape orientation.
2. Change the date to August 19, 19--.

3. Sort the table alphabetically by the employees' last names.
4. Change the font for the column headings to Century Schoolbook and shade them with a 10% fill.

Table 49
Boxed Table

Open the file for Table 47, and make the following changes:

1. Add the following information to the table: *Dupres, James / 5507 Foxhound Lane / Westerville / 43081 / 614-555-8803 / Pentium Computer / 5-897-PC;*

Windrift, Lorraine / 514 Whitley Drive / Columbus / 43230 / 614-555-4181 / Laser Printer / 3-895-LP.

2. Sort the table by the customers' last name.

Lesson 99   Multipage Tables

GOALS: To improve speed and accuracy; to refine language-arts skills in spelling; to format multipage tables typed in landscape page orientation.

A. Type 2 times.

A. WARMUP

```
1      Seven unique prizes were won by a boxer named Jake      10
2  Gray.  He gave the prizes (all of them) to the club*; the   22
3  contents--coupons, CDs, and cash--were worth over $500.     33
     |  1  |  2  |  3  |  4  |  5  |  6  |  7  |  8  |  9  |  10  |  11  |  12
```

SKILLBUILDING

B. PACED PRACTICE

Turn to the Paced Practice routine beginning on page SB-14. Take three 2-minute timings, starting at the point where you left off the last time.

C. SUSTAINED PRACTICE: SYLLABIC INTENSITY

```
 4        People continue to rent autos for personal use and for      11
 5   their work, and the car-rental business continues to grow.        23
 6   When you rent a car, look carefully at the insurance costs.       34
 7   You might also have to pay a mileage charge for the car.          46

 8        It is likely that a good deal of insurance coverage is       11
 9   part of the standard rental cost.  But you might be urged         23
10   to procure extra medical, property, and collision coverage.       35
11   If you accept, be ready to see your rental charge increase.       47

12        Perhaps this is not necessary, as you may already have       11
13   the kind of protection you want in a policy that you have         23
14   at the present time.  By reviewing your own auto insurance        35
15   policy, you may easily save a significant amount of money.        46

16        Paying mileage charges could result in a really large       11
17   bill.  This is especially evident when the trips planned          22
18   involve destinations that are many miles apart.  Complete a       34
19   total review of traveling plans before making a decision.         46

     | 1 | 2 | 3 | 4 | 5 | 6 | 7 | 8 | 9 | 10 | 11 | 12
```

LANGUAGE ARTS

D. SPELLING

D. Type this list of frequently misspelled words, paying special attention to any spelling problems in each word.

```
20   distribution executive extension requested specific carried
21   recommended alternative programs access budget issued seize
22   objectives indicated calendar family could these until your
23   administrative accommodate possibility students fiscal past
24   transportation employee's categories summary offered estate
```

Edit the sentences to correct any misspellings.

```
25   The execitive requested an extention on spicific programs.
26   I have recomended alternitive programs for early next week.
27   These objectives were indacated for the new calender year.
28   These passed administrative goals will accomodate the team.
29   These catagories could be included in the employee summery.
```

FORMATTING

E. MULTIPAGE TABLES

Tables should generally be formatted to fit on one page. However, if a table extends to another page, follow these formatting rules:

1. Repeat the column headings at the top of each new page.
2. Number all pages in the upper right-hand corner.

(continued on next page)

2

30 LARGEST STATES (Ranked by Square Miles)				
State	**Nickname**	**Sq. Mi.**	**Rank**	**Capital**
Illinois	Prairie State	57,918	25	Springfield

F. WORD PROCESSING: MULTIPAGE TABLES

Study Lesson 99 in your word processing manual. Complete all of the shaded steps while at your computer. Then format the jobs that follow.

Table 50
Multipage Boxed Table

Follow these steps to create a multipage table:

1. Change the page orientation to landscape.
2. Create a boxed table with 5 columns and 32 rows.
3. Type the table as shown with centered column headings.
4. Include column headings on all pages.
5. Apply a 10% fill intensity to the column headings row.
6. Automatically adjust the column widths.

30 LARGEST STATES (Ranked by Square Miles)				
State	**Nickname**	**Sq. Mi.**	**Rank**	**Capital**
Alaska	The Last Frontier	656,424	1	Juneau
Texas	Lone Star State	268,601	2	Austin
California	Golden State	163,707	3	Sacramento
Montana	Treasure State	147,046	4	Helena
New Mexico	Land of Enchantment	121,598	5	Santa Fe
Arizona	Grand Canyon State	114,006	6	Phoenix
Nevada	Sagebrush State	110,567	7	Carson City
Colorado	Centennial State	104,100	8	Denver
Oregon	Beaver State	98,386	9	Salem
Wyoming	Equality State	97,818	10	Cheyenne
Michigan	Great Lakes State	96,705	11	Lansing
Minnesota	North Star State	89,943	12	St. Paul
Utah	Beehive State	89,904	13	Salt Lake City

(continued on next page)

Idaho	Gem State	83,574	14	Boise
Kansas	Sunflower State	82,282	15	Topeka
Nebraska	Cornhusker State	77,358	16	Lincoln
South Dakota	Coyote State	75,896	17	Pierre
Washington	Evergreen State	71,302	18	Olympia
North Dakota	Peace Garden State	70,704	19	Bismarck
Oklahoma	Sooner State	69,903	20	Oklahoma City
Missouri	Show Me State	69,709	21	Jefferson City
Florida	Sunshine State	65,756	22	Tallahassee
Wisconsin	Badger State	65,499	23	Madison
Georgia	Peach State	59,441	24	Atlanta
Illinois	Prairie State	57,918	25	Springfield
Iowa	Hawkeye State	56,276	26	Des Moines
New York	Empire State	54,471	27	Albany
North Carolina	Tar Heel State	53,821	28	Raleigh
Arkansas	Land of Opportunity	53,182	29	Little Rock
Alabama	Camellia State	52,423	30	Montgomery

Table 51
Multipage Boxed
Table

Open the file for Table 50, and make the following changes:

1. Delete the column headings from each continuation page of the table so that they are not included in the sort.

2. Sort the table alphabetically by state in ascending order.

3. When the sort is complete, reinsert the column headings on each continuation page of the table.

Lesson 100 Table Review

GOALS: To type 47 wam/5'/5e; to reinforce the formatting of tables.

A. Type 2 times.

A. WARMUP

```
1      Buzz exhibited 10 quaint games at the Kansas fair on      11
2  3/31/96.  In Booths #27 and #45 we had the biggest crowds--  23
3  close to 100 people!  Jill and Vi will exhibit next year.    34
     | 1 | 2 | 3 | 4 | 5 | 6 | 7 | 8 | 9 | 10 | 11 | 12
```

B. PROGRESSIVE PRACTICE: ALPHABET

Turn to the Progressive Practice: Alphabet routine beginning on page SB-7. Take six 30-second timings, starting at the point where you left off the last time.

C. DIAGNOSTIC PRACTICE: NUMBERS

Turn to the Diagnostic Practice: Numbers routine beginning on page SB-5. Type one of the Pretest/Posttest paragraphs and identify any errors made. Then type the corresponding drill lines 2 times for each number on which you made 2 or more errors and 1 time for each number on which you made only 1 error. Finally, repeat the same Pretest paragraph and compare your performance.

D. Take two 5-minute timings. Determine your speed and errors.

Goal: 47 wam/5'/5e

D. 5-MINUTE TIMING

4   The importance of speaking skills is stressed by   10
5 many employers who hire graduates with business degrees.   22
6 These skills are used extensively on the job, and they will   34
7 often continue to grow in importance as years pass. Most   45
8 people do not realize just how essential these skills are   57
9 to job success. The following paragraphs summarize some   68
10 basic applications of speech in a business office.   78
11   If you major in sales or marketing in college, there   89
12 is no doubt that you will be using your speaking skills   100
13 each day. Someone who prepares for a teaching career also   112
14 relies on speaking skills, whether it is to teach a class   124
15 or to conduct a training session. In either of these roles   136
16 you will be using your speaking skills in individual or   147
17 group sessions. Regardless of your rank or position in a   159
18 company, you will always be required to communicate with   170
19 your subordinates, your peers, or your superiors. As one   182
20 who represents your company, you will be asked on occasion   193
21 to give a speech to a local group. Another use of speaking   205
22 skills might be to converse during social meetings. You   217
23 might also have to use your speaking skills to purchase   228
24 goods or services from businesses.   235

| 1 | 2 | 3 | 4 | 5 | 6 | 7 | 8 | 9 | 10 | 11 | 12

DOCUMENT PROCESSING

Table 52
Open Table

1. Center the table vertically.
2. Create an open table with 5 columns and 10 rows.
3. Type the table as shown. Left-align column headings over text; right-align column headings over numbers.
4. Sort the table in ascending order by number of square feet.

BUILDING DIRECTORY
Paulding Meeting Facility

No.	Room Name	Seating	Square Feet	AV
102	Alabama	35	400	Yes
104	Colorado	150	1,600	Yes
106	Delaware	25	350	No
108	Georgia	50	600	Yes
202	Montana	35	400	No
204	Nevada	50	600	No
206	New Jersey	300	3,200	Yes
208	Pennsylvania	350	3,600	Yes

Table 53
Open Table

Open the file for Table 52 and make the following changes.
1. Add the following rooms to the building directory list: *302 / Florida / 100 / 1,200 / Yes; 304 / Minnesota / 28 / 375 / No; 306 / Tennessee / 75 / 1,000 / Yes; 308 / Virginia / 275 / 3,000 / Yes.*
2. After you add the new information to the table, resort the table in descending order by room size.

Table 54
Progress Check
Boxed Table

1. Vertically center the table.
2. Create a boxed table with 4 columns and 15 rows.
3. Type the table with the column headings aligned as shown.
4. Sort the table by area (size of the states) in descending order.

ORIGINAL 13 COLONIES			
Statistical Data			
State	**Admission**	**Area**	**Rank**
Delaware	Dec. 7, 1787	2,490	12
Pennsylvania	Dec. 12, 1787	46,060	4

(continued on next page)

New Jersey	Dec. 18, 1787	8,720	10
Georgia	Jan. 2, 1788	59,440	1
Connecticut	Jan. 9, 1788	5,544	11
Massachusetts	Feb. 6, 1788	10,560	8
Maryland	Apr. 28, 1788	12,410	7
South Carolina	May 23, 1788	32,010	6
New Hampshire	June 21, 1788	9,350	9
Virginia	June 25, 1788	42,780	5
New York	July 26, 1788	54,470	2
North Carolina	Nov. 21, 1789	53,820	3
Rhode Island	May 28, 1790	1,550	13

Ask your instructor for the General Information Test on Part 5.

Test 5-A
5-Minute Timing

1	Computer technology is changing every day. What was	11
2	considered to be on the cutting edge today will be ancient	23
3	history only a few years from now. It is difficult to keep	35
4	abreast of exactly what will happen five years from now.	46
5	Here is a quick look at what we expect to see in just the	59
6	next few years.	61
7	Computers will be very fast and will be able to store	72
8	much more information than they do today. A disk that now	84
9	can store millions of bytes will easily store trillions of	96
10	bytes in the near future. Floppy disks will be replaced by	108
11	disks that are no larger than the size of a credit card and	120
12	capable of holding a trillion bits of data. Computers will	132
13	be popular in all homes and we will talk to them to turn on	144
14	the air conditioning or furnace, turn on or off the lights,	156
15	or activate the security system.	162
16	We will do our weekly grocery shopping by activating a	173
17	virtual cart on the screen. This cart will display all the	185
18	groceries in the store. As we choose a particular item, we	197
19	can read the nutritional labels, compare prices on various	209
20	brands, and total our bill. Our account will automatically	221
21	be charged, and the groceries will be delivered right away	233
22	to homes.	235

| 1 | 2 | 3 | 4 | 5 | 6 | 7 | 8 | 9 | 10 | 11 | 12 |

Test 5-B
Form 19
Press Release

Use the first press release template in your word processing software. The press release is being prepared by you as Office Manager for Tera Computers, Inc., 2456 Patterson Street, Nashville, TN 37203. The company telephone number is 615-555-9045. Use the current date and title the release *6th Generation Enters the Market*. The text of the release is as follows:

The 6th Generation has arrived! During the week of May 21, Tera Computers will introduce the first 6th-generation computer during an open house at its Patterson Street store. See this new computer marvel demonstrated by Tera representatives.

(continued on next page)

The 6th-generation computers process information at dazzling speeds. All models enable you to process data with 32-bit capability.

A special feature of the 6th-generation computers is the tera-byte hard drive that enables you to store up to a trillion bits of data. No longer will you have to worry about having space to store memory-hungry software programs.

Make your reservations today! A drawing will be held after the opening session, and some lucky person will take home a new Tera 6th-generation computer.

Test 5-C
Letters 77, 78, 79, 80

1. Create data files for each of the people whose records follow.
2. Create the form letter in modified-block style. Use the current date for the letter.
3. Merge the data files and the form letter to create a customized letter for each person.

First Record

Title:	Mr.
First Name	Todd
Last Name:	Nesbit
Address:	405 Delta Way
City, State, Zip:	Knoxville, TN 37919
Room:	Elizabeth Room
Time:	9:00 a.m.
Date:	October 22
Speaker:	Ms. Marianne Singleton

Second Record

Title:	Ms.
First Name:	Sheryl
Last Name:	Ho
Address:	4023 Woodmont Blvd.
City, State, Zip:	Nashville, TN 37205
Room:	Sweetbriar Room
Time:	9:00 a.m.
Date:	October 23
Speaker:	Ms. Eva Stanton

Third Record

Title:	Ms.
First Name:	Darlene
Last Name:	Kennedy
Address:	1384 Annendale Street
City, State, Zip:	Nashville, TN 37215
Room:	Baywood Room
Time:	10:00 a.m.
Date:	October 23
Speaker:	Mr. Wayne Landwether

Fourth Record

Title:	Mr.
First Name:	Karl
Last Name:	Tallant
Address:	2401 North Royal Street
City, State, Zip:	Jackson, TN 38305
Room:	Woodberry Room
Time:	11:00 a.m.
Date:	October 22
Speaker:	Mr. Wayne Caston

(continued on next page)

[Current Date]
(Title) (First Name) (Last Name)
(Address)
(City, State, Zip)

Dear (Title) (Last Name):

¶Thank you for volunteering to assist with the upcoming Southern Computer Users' Conference to be held in Nashville, Tennessee, from October 21 through October 25. I appreciate your willingness to work at one of the sessions of the conference.

¶You are assigned to the (Room) at (Time) on (Date) as session recorder. Your session speaker will be (Speaker). A speaker introduction will be sent to you prior to the conference.

¶I look forward to working with you to make the Southern Computer Users' Conference a success for all of us.

Sincerely, / Paul Armstrong / Program Coordinator / {urs}

Test 5-D
Table 55
Boxed Table

1. Create a 4-column, 10-row table from the information that follows.
2. Center the column headings.
3. Shade the row with the column headings with a 10% fill.
4. When you finish typing the table, sort the table by the largest to the smallest lake.

MAJOR LAKES OF THE WORLD / Statistical Data

Column Headings: **Lake / Continent / Area / Depth**

Aral Sea / Asia / 24,900 sq mi / 220 ft
Baykal / Asia / 12,160 sq mi / 5,320 ft
Caspian Sea / Asia / 143,240 sq mi / 3,360 ft
Great Bear / North America / 12,100 sq mi / 1,460 ft
Huron / North America / 23,000 sq mi / 750 ft
Michigan / North America / 22,300 sq mi / 923 ft
Superior / North America / 31,700 sq mi / 1,330 ft
Victoria / Africa / 26,830 sq mi / 270 ft

PART SIX

Designing Forms and Publications; Specialized Applications; and In-Basket Exercise

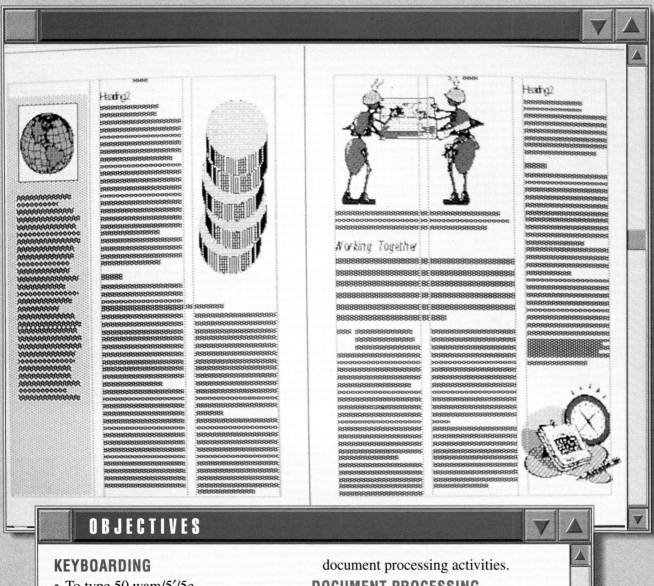

OBJECTIVES

KEYBOARDING
- To type 50 wam/5′/5e

LANGUAGE ARTS
- To refine proofreading skills and correctly use proofreaders' marks.
- To correctly capitalize, punctuate, and spell.
- To recognize subject/verb agreement and refine composing skills.

WORD PROCESSING
- To use the word processing commands necessary to complete the document processing activities.

DOCUMENT PROCESSING
- To design office forms and publications; to prepare documents for specialized applications; to apply high-level formatting skills while completing an integrated office project.

TECHNICAL
- To answer correctly at least 90 percent of the questions on an objective test.

Lesson 101 Designing Letterhead Forms

GOALS: To improve speed and accuracy; to refine language-arts skills in grammar; to design letterheads.

A. Type 2 times.

A. WARMUP

```
1      The secretary made a reservation on Flight #847; it      11
2  departs at exactly 3:05 on July 6.  A sizable number of     22
3  key executives (about 1/2) requested seats in Rows G to M.  33
   |  1  |  2  |  3  |  4  |  5  |  6  |  7  |  8  |  9  |  10  |  11  |  12
```

 **SKILLBUILDING**

B. PROGRESSIVE PRACTICE: ALPHABET

Turn to the Progressive Practice: Alphabet routine beginning on page SB-7. Take six 30-second timings, starting at the point where you left off the last time.

C. Take three 12-second timings on each line. The scale below the last line shows your wam speed for a 12-second timing.

C. 12-SECOND SPEED SPRINTS

```
4  Bob will lend all the keys to you if you will fix the leak.
5  Ruth wanted to thank you for all of the work you did today.
6  Both of the boxes will have to be sent to her by next week.
7  Dick paid her half of the money when she signed the papers.
   | | | |5| | | |10| | |15| | |20| | |25| | |30| | |35| | |40| | |45| | |50| | |55| | |60
```

 **LANGUAGE ARTS**

D. AGREEMENT

D. Study the rules at the right.

Rule: If two subjects are joined by *or, either/or, neither/nor,* or *not only/but also,* the verb should agree with the subject nearer to the verb.

agr near

Either Mr. Lee or the custodians have the key to the office.
Not only the report but also the letters are ready for duplication.

Rule: The subject *a number* takes a plural verb; *the number* takes a singular verb.

agr num

The number of employees has increased gradually over the years.
A number of employees have volunteered for the project.

Edit the sentences to correct any errors in grammar.

```
8   A number of secretaries are planning to attend the meeting.
9   Not only the manager but also the employees wants to attend.
10  The number of computers in need of repairs are excessive.
11  Neither the printer nor the monitors is in working order.
12  Either Mr. Cortez or his assistants have to sign the order.
```

(continued on next page)

13 Cake or cookies is available for the afternoon session.
14 Not only the printer but also the cables were supplied.
15 Not only the manual but also the software were mailed.

FORMATTING

E. BASIC DESIGN GUIDELINES

Use the following guidelines to design an attractive, effective document:

1. Keep all elements of your design simple and balanced.
2. Limit the number of typefaces (fonts), attributes (bold, italics, etc.), and sizes. Using two typefaces is a good rule of thumb.
3. Use white space liberally to separate and open up text and graphics.
4. Use different alignments (left, center, right, and full) to add interest and emphasis.
5. Experiment and change—word processing software makes this easy.

F. WORD PROCESSING: SPECIAL CHARACTERS AND SMALL CAPS

Study Lesson 101 in your word processing manual. Complete all of the shaded steps while at your computer. Then format the jobs that follow.

DOCUMENT PROCESSING

Form 20
Letterhead Form

Create the following letterhead form. Remember to make any font changes at the start of a new line.

1. Change the top margin to 0.5 inch.
2. Create an open table with 2 columns and 1 row.
3. In the first cell, change the font to Wingdings 48 point, and type the letter *Q* to create the jet airplane.
4. In the second cell, change the font to Arial Bold Italic 18 point, center and type *Jet Set Resorts, Ltd.;* then press Enter.
5. Change the font to Arial Regular 10 point small caps, and center and type the remaining lines in initial caps.
6. Automatically adjust the column widths.
7. Center the table horizontally.

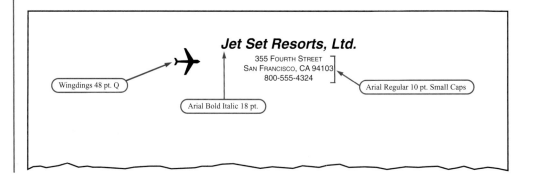

Form 21
Letterhead Form

Create the letterhead form as illustrated below. Remember to make any font changes at the start of a new line.

1. Change the top margin to 0.5 inch.
2. Create a boxed table with 3 columns and 1 row.
3. In the first cell, change the font to Symbol 36 point, and type *Wpb* to create the Greek letters.
4. In the middle cell, change the font to Times New Roman Bold Italic 24 point, and center and type *It's All Greek to Me.*
5. Change the font to Arial Regular 10 point small caps, and type the remaining lines in the middle column. *Note:* The tilde (~) is to the left of the 1 key.
6. In the third cell, change the font to Symbol 36 point, and type *xvS* to create the Greek letters.
7. Automatically adjust the column widths.
8. Center the table horizontally.

Form 22
Letterhead Form

1. Use the Wingdings or Symbol fonts to create a letterhead design of your own—for you personally, for your school, or for an organization.
2. Try using other fonts that you have not yet applied—experiment with point sizes and attributes.

Lesson 102 Designing Memo Forms

GOALS: To type 48 wam/5'/5e; to design memo forms.

A. Type 2 times.

A. WARMUP

SKILLBUILDING

B. PACED PRACTICE

Turn to the Paced Practice routine beginning on page SB-14. Take three 2-minute timings, starting at the point where you left off the last time.

C. Take two 5-minute timings. Determine your speed and errors.

Goal: 48 wam/5′/5e

C. 5-MINUTE TIMING

4   Setting long-term goals for your professional career   11

5 can mean the difference between success and failure. When   23

6 you set specific goals for your future, you allow yourself   34

7 the freedom to reach for them because you have taken time   46

8 out to devise a plan. Quite often people find that they   57

9 are just getting through their workday without any solid   69

10 thought about their future. If this sounds familiar, you   80

11 may find that you don't have a future.   88

12   Begin by writing down an exact list of very specific,   99

13 realistic goals. You will find that setting smaller goals   111

14 first will provide you with a sense of accomplishment when   123

15 you realize these goals. These smaller successes will pave   135

16 the way for long-term goals.   141

17   Give yourself some time limits when you outline your   151

18 prospects. Setting limits will help you to judge whether   163

19 you have been effective in reaching your goal. If a task   175

20 has taken more time than you think is needed, you should   186

21 decide whether or not your goal is realistic and whether   197

22 it warrants more time and energy. Perhaps you just need   209

23 to analyze your plan of action, or perhaps the time limit   220

24 is not realistic; most goals are attainable if you follow   232

25 a strategy and maintain a good attitude.   240

| 1 | 2 | 3 | 4 | 5 | 6 | 7 | 8 | 9 | 10 | 11 | 12

FORMATTING

D. USING LINES AND BORDERS

1. Using a variety of line styles and borders in designing a form can add interest and make the form easier to use.

2. You can create many interesting effects by using a table as a tool for your design. Conceivably, every side of every cell could be formatted differently. Of course, you must remember the basic rule of any good design: *Keep it simple.*

E. WORD PROCESSING: LINES/BORDERS

Study Lesson 102 in your word processing manual. Complete all of the shaded steps while at your computer. Then format the jobs that follow.

Form 23
Memo Form

Create the memo form below:

1. Create an open table with 1 column and 1 row.
2. Format the bottom of the cell using a heavy line style (2 1/4 point).
3. Change the font to Arial Regular 20 point, and type *MEMO,* leaving 1 space between each letter.
4. Move to the next line below the table, and change to right justification.
5. Change the font to Times New Roman Regular 10 point small caps, and type *Data Research & Development, Inc.*
6. Press Enter 3 times, change to left justification, and change the font to Times New Roman Bold Regular 12 point.
7. Type the guide word *TO:* in all caps, and press Enter twice to begin the next guide word.
8. Repeat Step 7 for the remaining guide words.

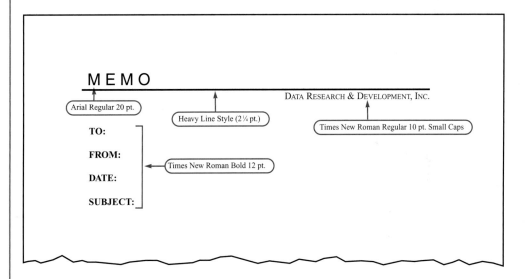

Form 24
Memo Form

Create the memo form that follows:

1. Create an open table with 1 column and 1 row.
2. Format the top and bottom of the row using a heavy line style (2 1/4 point).
3. Change the font to Arial Regular 26 point small caps, and type *MEMO,* leaving 1 space between each letter and 5 spaces after the last letter (O).
4. Change the font to Wingdings 36 point, and type an *!* to create the pencil.
5. Adjust the column width, and center the table horizontally.
6. Move to the first line below the table.
7. Change to Times New Roman Bold 12 point, and press Enter 3 times.
8. Type the guide word *TO:* in all caps, and press Enter twice to begin the next guide word.
9. Repeat Step 8 for the remaining guide words.

(continued on next page)

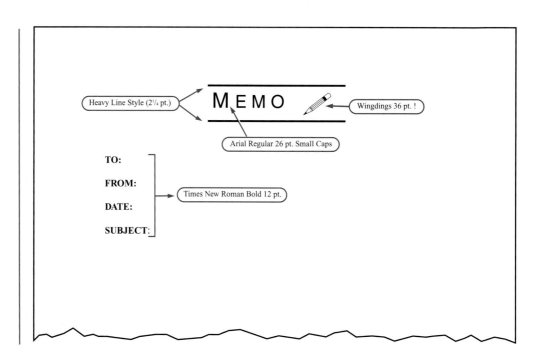

Heavy Line Style (2¼ pt.)

MEMO

Wingdings 36 pt. !

Arial Regular 26 pt. Small Caps

TO:

FROM:

DATE:

SUBJECT:

Times New Roman Bold 12 pt.

Lesson 103 · Designing Notepad Forms

GOALS: To improve speed and accuracy; to refine language-arts skills in proofreading; to design notepad forms.

A. Type 2 times.

A. WARMUP

```
1        Was the printer expected on 5/30, or did she keep it      11
2   until June?  A shipping charge of 12% will be added to any     23
3   order mailed to Zone 9; direct any questions to "Vinnie."      34
```
| 1 | 2 | 3 | 4 | 5 | 6 | 7 | 8 | 9 | 10 | 11 | 12

SKILLBUILDING

B. DIAGNOSTIC PRACTICE: ALPHABET

Turn to the Diagnostic Practice: Alphabet routine beginning on page SB-2. Type one of the Pretest/Posttest paragraphs and identify any errors made. Then type the corresponding drill lines 2 times for each letter on which you made 2 or more errors and 1 time for each letter on which you made only 1 error. Finally, repeat the same Pretest paragraph and compare your performance.

C. Type the columns 2 times. Press Tab to move from column to column.

C. TECHNIQUE PRACTICE: TAB KEY

```
4   third       beard       horde       gourd       board
5   vague       value       about       label       table
6   award       straw       drawn       await       drawl
7   track       paced       races       knack       above
```

D. 12-SECOND SPEED SPRINTS

D. Take three 12-second timings on each line. The scale below the last line shows your wam speed for a 12-second timing.

8 Ryan will pay for the six pens that they left on the shelf.
9 Rod was in a rush to sign all the papers and send them off.
10 Toby works in town and will spend the day fixing the signs.
11 The man must pay all the duty tax before he can take title.

| | | |5| | | |10| | | |15| | | |20| | | |25| | | |30| | | |35| | | |40| | | |45| | | |50| | | |55| | | |60

E. PROOFREADING

E. Compare this paragraph with the second paragraph of the 5-minute timing on page 290. Edit the paragraph to correct any errors.

12   Begin by writing down an exact list of every specific
13 realistic goals. You will find that setting small goals
14 first will provide you with a sense of accomplishment if
15 you realize these goals. These smaller successes will pave
16 the way for long term goals.

DOCUMENT PROCESSING

Form 25
Notepad Form

Create the notepad form below:

1. Create a boxed table with 1 column and 1 row and change the font to Times New Roman Bold Italic 24 point.
2. Type *From the Desk of.* Fill in your own name and follow it with three periods leaving a space between them.
3. Apply a 20% fill.
4. Move outside the table structure and create a footer.

5. Change the font to Wingdings 16 point, type the letter *q* to create the check box, and space once.
6. Change the font to Times New Roman Bold Italic 16 point, type *Urgent,* and press Enter once.
7. Repeat Steps 5 and 6 for the remaining lines, then close the footer.

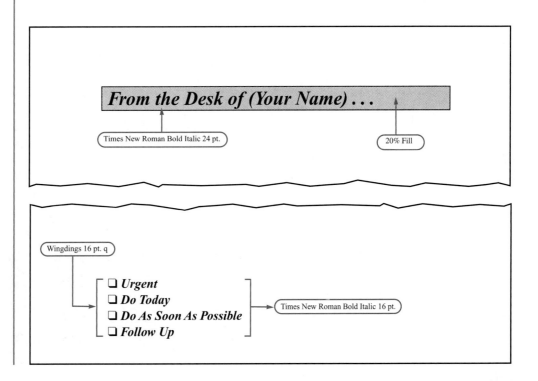

Form 26
Notepad Form

Create the following notepad form:

1. Use 1¼-inch left and right margins.

2. Create a boxed table with 1 column and 3 rows; apply a 20% fill to the first row.

3. Clear all tabs, and set tabs at 4½ inches and 5 inches from the left margin.

4. Change the font to Arial Bold 20 point, type *From*, and press CTRL+TAB to move to the first tab stop.

5. Change the font to Wingdings 14 point, and type a number *1* to create the file folder.

6. Press CTRL+TAB, then change the font to Arial Bold 14 point and type *File*.

Then, press Enter.

7. Repeat Steps 4–6 for the remaining words and symbols. Type a (for the telephone, a $ for the glasses, and the letter *M* for the bomb.

8. In the second row, press Enter repeatedly until the insertion point is positioned at approximately 8.9 inches.

9. Move the insertion point into the bottom row, and apply a 20% fill.

10. Change the font to Wingdings 18 point, space once, and type the < to create the disk. Space once between each disk. Type as many disks as needed to fill the row.

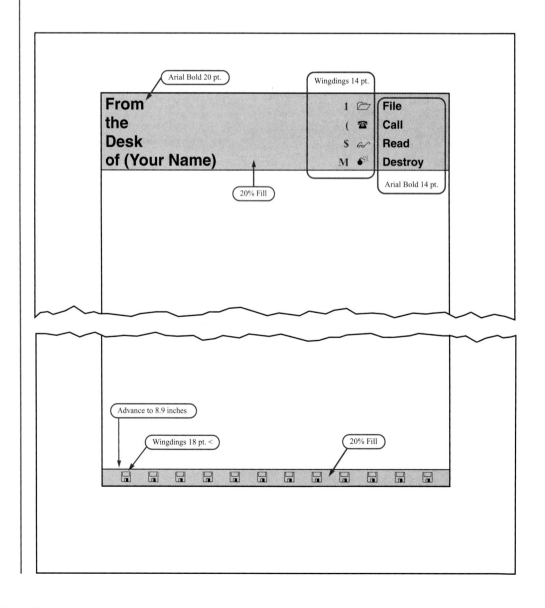

Form 27
Notepad

1. Design a customized notepad form for your personal use.
2. Experiment with different lines such as thick, dashed, dotted, and so forth.
3. Experiment with the various fill patterns such as horizontal, diagonal, vertical, and so forth.
4. Use some fonts you have never applied before.
5. Try different font attributes to create a variety of effects.
6. Remember that it is simple to undo your mistakes, so enjoy undoing and redoing until you are satisfied with your design.

Lesson 104 Designing Fax Cover Forms

GOALS: To key 48 wam/5'/5e; to design fax covers.

A. Type 2 times.

A. WARMUP

1 Quail & Jones requested a check for $897. Once they   11
2 got it (Check #61), they were most anxious to leave. They   23
3 realized the bank closed at 5 p.m., and it was almost 4:50!   34

| 1 | 2 | 3 | 4 | 5 | 6 | 7 | 8 | 9 | 10 | 11 | 12

SKILLBUILDING

B. Take a 1-minute timing on the first paragraph to establish your base speed. Then take four 1-minute timings on the remaining paragraphs. As soon as you equal or exceed your base speed on one paragraph, advance to the next, more difficult paragraph.

B. SUSTAINED PRACTICE: NUMBERS AND SYMBOLS

4 Shopping in the comfort and convenience of your own   11
5 living room has never been more popular than it is right   22
6 now. Shopping clubs abound on cable channels. You can   33
7 buy anything from exotic pets to computers by mail order.   45

8 Sometimes you can find discounts as high as 20% off   11
9 the retail price; for example, a printer that sells for   22
10 $565 might be discounted 20% and be sold for $452. You   33
11 should always investigate quality before buying anything.   44

12 Sometimes hidden charges are involved; for example,   11
13 a printer costing $475.50 that promises a discount of 12%   22
14 ($57.06) has a net price of $418.44. However, if charges   34
15 for shipping range from 12% to 15%, you did not save money.   46

16 You must also check for errors. Several errors have   11
17 been noted so far: Invoice #223, #789, #273, and #904 had   23
18 errors totaling $21.35, $43.44, $79.23, and $91.23 for a   34
19 grand total of $235.25. As always, let the buyer beware.   45

| 1 | 2 | 3 | 4 | 5 | 6 | 7 | 8 | 9 | 10 | 11 | 12

C. Take two 5-minute timings. Determine your speed and errors.

Goal: 48 wam/5'/5e

C. 5-MINUTE TIMING

20   Getting a raise in pay at work may seem out of reach   11
21 at times; but with some clever strategy, you will realize   22
22 it is not quite as difficult as you may think. Attaining   34
23 this goal will require patience and planning, but in time   46
24 you can expect results. You must begin by analyzing the   57
25 needs of your employer. Try to judge whether or not your   69
26 accomplishments on the job are meeting those needs.   79
27   Define your job responsibilities very specifically   90
28 and find out what other companies are paying their workers   101
29 for comparable jobs. This knowledge gives you a definite   113
30 edge when it comes to the bargaining table. If you don't   125
31 know what your skills are worth, you won't be prepared to   136
32 ask for an appropriate raise in pay.   144
33   If your boss is cold to the idea, don't just give up.   155
34 Prove you can do the job; wait for an opportune time to   166
35 ask for your well-deserved raise. The best time might be   178
36 right after you have landed that new account or perhaps   189
37 right after your employer has received a raise. Timing   200
38 is critical in these situations.   207
39   If you ask a second time and are refused, it might be   218
40 wise to start looking for another position. Who knows--a   229
41 wonderful opportunity might be just around the corner.   240

| 1 | 2 | 3 | 4 | 5 | 6 | 7 | 8 | 9 | 10 | 11 | 12

DOCUMENT PROCESSING

Form 28
Fax Cover Form

Create the fax cover form that follows:

1. Create a boxed table with 2 columns and 6 rows, change the font to Arial Bold 36 point, and type *Fax*. Press Enter and type *Cover*.
2. Move to Row 1, Column B, and change to right justification.
3. Change the font to Wingdings 48 point, and type a *:* to create the computer.
4. Press Enter, change the font to Arial Bold 16 point, and type *Data Resources, Inc.*
5. Move to Row 2, Column A. In Arial Bold 12 point, type the remaining lines, joining and splitting cells as needed.
6. Join the cells in Row 6. Continue pressing Enter until the insertion point is positioned at approximately 9.4 inches.

(continued on next page)

Form 29
Fax Cover Form

Create the following fax cover form on page 298:

1. Create a boxed table with 1 column and 3 rows.
2. Change the font to Times New Roman Bold 36 point, and center and type *Fax Cover Page.*
3. Move to Row 2, and change the font to Times New Roman Bold 12 point.
4. Type *Total Pages:*, press Enter twice, then type *Comments.*
5. In Row 2, continue pressing Enter until the insertion point is positioned at approximately 7.5 inches.

6. Move to Row 3 and split it.
7. In Column A, change the font to Arial 48 point, 36 point, 28 point, and 20 point respectively, to type *ABC Incorporated.* Press Enter once, change the font to Arial 12 point, and type the remaining lines of the column.
8. In Column B, change the font to Times New Roman Bold 12 point, and type the remaining lines. Press Enter twice after *Subject:*.

(continued on next page)

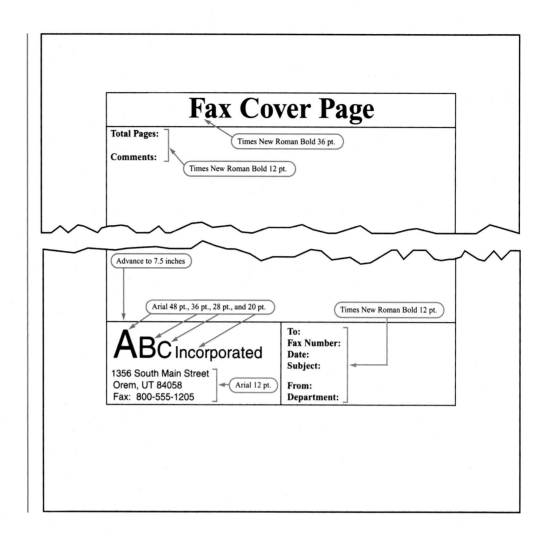

Lesson 105 Designing Miscellaneous Forms

GOALS: To improve speed and accuracy: to refine language-arts skills in composing; to design miscellaneous forms.

A. Type 2 times.

A. WARMUP

```
1      Jack was in charge of ordering several new keyboards.      11
2    When you find Serial #Z312, #Q459, and #X867, please send    23
3    them to the manufacturer; all costs are 100% reimbursable.   34
     |  1  |  2  |  3  |  4  |  5  |  6  |  7  |  8  |  9  |  10  |  11  |  12
```

B. PROGRESSIVE PRACTICE: NUMBERS

Turn to the Progressive Practice: Numbers routine beginning on page SB-11.

Take six 30-second timings, starting at the point where you left off the last time.

C. PRETEST: VERTICAL REACHES

```
4        The man knelt on the lawn and used a knife with skill    11
5   to raise the valve away from the brace.  His back ached in    23
6   vain as he crawled over the knoll to fix the flawed valve.    34
    |  1  |  2  |  3  |  4  |  5  |  6  |  7  |  8  |  9  |  10  |  11  |  12
```

Practice
    Speed Emphasis: If you made no more than 1 error on the Pretest, type each *individual* line 2 times.
    Accuracy Emphasis: If you made 2 or more errors, type each *group* of lines (as though it were a paragraph) 2 times.

D. PRACTICE: UP REACHES

```
7   aw away award crawl straw drawn sawed drawl await flaw lawn
8   se self sense raise these prose abuse users serve send seem
9   ki kind kites skill skier skims skips skits kilts king skid
```

E. PRACTICE: DOWN REACHES

```
10  ac ache track paced brace races facts crack acute back aces
11  kn knob knife kneel knows knack knelt known knoll knot knew
12  va vain vague value valve evade naval rival avail vats vase
```

F. POSTTEST: VERTICAL REACHES

LANGUAGE ARTS

G. COMPOSING

Compose the body of a memo to explain basic design guidelines. Refer to page 288—Section E, Basic Design Guidelines—frequently. Use the following suggestions for each paragraph:

Paragraph 1. Explain that a simple, balanced design is essential and that typefaces, attributes, and sizes should be limited.

Paragraph 2. Explain that white space should be used to make text easier to read and graphics easier to see.

Paragraph 3. Explain that word processing software is a powerful tool that makes experimenting easy.

DOCUMENT PROCESSING

Form 30
Routing Slip Form

Create the following routing slip form on page 300:

1. Vertically center the page.
2. Create a boxed table with 1 column and 4 rows.
3. Change to Times New Roman Bold Italic 28 point, center and type *Routing Slip* with spaced periods, and press Enter twice.
4. Change to Times New Roman Bold 14 point, center and type *FROM: Colleen Laroquette,* and press Enter twice.
5. Center and type the directions for the routing slip, and press Enter twice.
6. Move to Row 2, and apply a diagonal fill pattern.
7. Move to Row 3, split the cell, then press Enter once.
8. Change to Wingdings 20 point, type the letter *q* to create the check box, and space once.
9. Change to Times New Roman 14 point, type the names, and press Enter twice.

(continued on next page)

10. Repeat Steps 8 and 9 for the remaining lines in the column. Leave 2 blank lines after the last name.

11. Move to Column B, Row 3, and press Enter once.

12. Change to Times New Roman Bold 14 point, and center and type *Comments:*.

13. Move to Row 4, and apply a diagonal fill pattern.

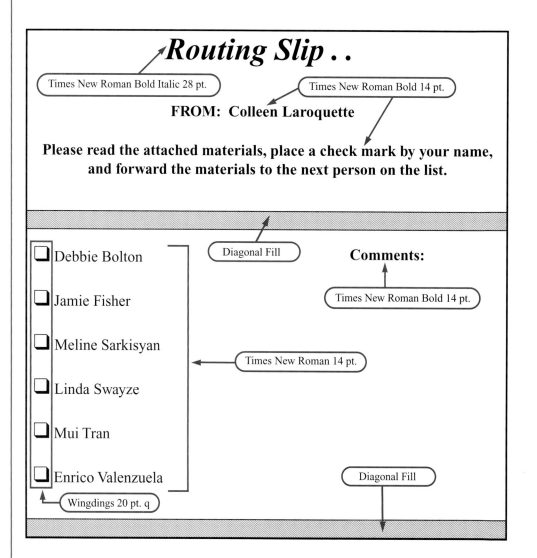

Form 31
Survey Form

Create the following survey form on page 301:

1. Clear all tabs, and set a tab 1 inch from the left margin.

2. Create a boxed table with 1 column and 5 rows.

3. Change the font to Times New Roman Bold Italic 36 point, center and type the heading, and apply a 20% fill.

4. Move to Row 2, and change the font to Times New Roman Regular 14 point.

5. Type the line *Please rate* . . . , press Enter twice, then type the paragraph.

6. Move to Row 3, and split the cell. Type the headings in Times New Roman Bold 14 point.

(continued on next page)

7. Move to Row 4, and press Enter once.

8. Change to Wingdings 28 point, and type the letter *o* to create the box.

9. Move to the tab stop, change the font to Times New Roman Bold 14 point, and type the sentence. Press Enter twice.

10. Repeat Steps 8 and 9 for the remaining lines. After the last line with a box, press Enter 3 times.

11. Type the question, and press Enter 5 times.

12. Type the lines *If there were . . . ,* then press Enter 5 times.

13. In Row 5, change the font to Times New Roman Bold Italic 36 point, center and type *Thank You!,* and apply a 20% fill.

What Do You Think?

Please rate your visit to our business today: — Times New Roman Regular 14 pt.

A rating of 5 means excellent, and a rating of 1 means poor. You can use any number from 1 through 5—the higher the number, the more positive the rating. Use the check box to fill in your rating.

Date: ◄— | **Time:**

Times New Roman Bold 14 pt.

☐ **Please rate the service you received.**

☐ **Please rate the friendliness of the employees.**

☐ **Please rate the appearance of the office.**

Wingdings 28 pt. o

What can we do to make your next visit better?

If there were any employees who were particularly helpful to you, please feel free to write their names here:

Times New Roman Bold Italic 36 pt.
20% Fill

Thank You!

Create the following directory form:

1. Use left and right margins of 1 inch.
2. Vertically center the page.
3. Create a boxed table with 4 columns and 23 rows.
4. Join the cells in Row 1, change to Times New Roman Bold Italic 36 point, center and type *Directory at a Glance,* then space 3 times.
5. Change the font to Wingdings 36 point, and type the (to create the telephone.
6. Move to Row 2, and center and type the headings in Arial Bold 14 point.
7. Move to Row 3, Column A, and apply a 10% fill to all but the last row.
8. Move to Row 3, Column C, and apply a 10% fill to all but the last row.
9. Move to Row 23 and join the cells.
10. Change the font to Wingdings 18 point, space once, and type the) to create the telephone in a circle. Type additional characters, inserting a space between each to fill the line.

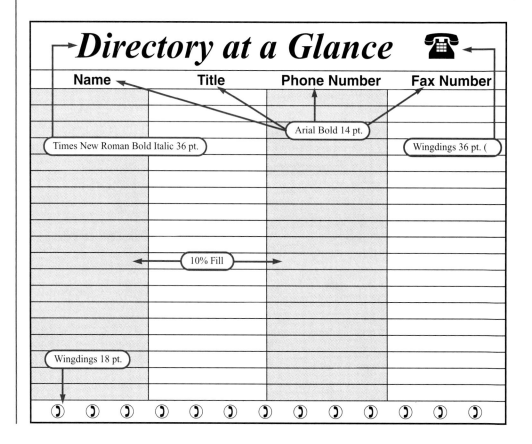

UNIT
TWENTY-TWO ▶ Designing Office Publications

Lesson 106 Designing Cover Pages

GOALS: To type 49 wam/5'/5e; to design cover pages.

A. Type 2 times.

A. WARMUP

1   Buzz told us that Flight #7864 got into Phoenix just   11
2   3 minutes before Vick's! This is quite remarkable when   22
3   you realize that we never planned for such a "coincidence."   34

| 1 | 2 | 3 | 4 | 5 | 6 | 7 | 8 | 9 | 10 | 11 | 12

SKILLBUILDING

B. PROGRESSIVE PRACTICE: ALPHABET

Turn to the Progressive Practice: Alphabet routine beginning on page SB-7. Take six 30-second timings, starting at the point where you left off the last time.

C. Take two 5-minute timings. Determine your speed and errors.

Goal: 49 wam/5'/5e

C. 5-MINUTE TIMING

4   Joining professional organizations in your own field   11
5   will enrich your life personally and on the job. These   22
6   groups sponsor a wide range of activities, and they also   33
7   schedule conferences through the year. You can meet the   45
8   people who are dealing with issues you are interested in   56
9   and who are finding some good solutions. Networking with   68
10 these leaders can be the key to finding the answers to a   79
11 number of tough problems that you might be facing.   89
12   If you are looking for the chance to move up in your   100
13 professional career track, you will be privy to some very   112
14 valuable information by simply conversing informally with   123
15 the people you will meet in these organizations. Clearly,   135
16 many of the good jobs are never announced because there   146
17 usually is not a need to do so. These jobs are quickly   157
18 filled through contacts and word of mouth.   166
19   If keeping abreast of the ever-changing technology in   177
20 your field is important in your job, the seminars will be   189
21 a great asset to you. These meetings are often led by very   201
22 experienced people who have chosen to specialize in one   212
23 given area. Their expertise will make it much simpler for   224
24 you to keep abreast of the sizable leaps in technology as   235
25 they happen. The results can be quite remarkable.   245

| 1 | 2 | 3 | 4 | 5 | 6 | 7 | 8 | 9 | 10 | 11 | 12

D. WORD PROCESSING: TEXT BOXES

Study Lesson 106 in your word processing manual. Complete all of the shaded steps while at your computer. Then format the jobs that follow.

Report 60
Cover Page

When creating, sizing, or positioning text box, change to a full-page document view. Switch to a normal view when entering text.

Follow these steps to create the cover page that is illustrated.

1. Create a text box about the size and in the same position of the first one shown in the illustration.

2. If necessary, format the top and bottom borders using a thick line style (4½ point), and apply a 10% fill.

3. Inside the box, press Enter twice, change to Arial Regular 28 point, and center and type *Health and Wellness Benefits Program* as shown.

4. Press Enter twice, change to Arial Regular 16 point, type the next three lines as shown, and press Enter twice.

5. Move out of the box, and create another text box large enough to fit the text in the lower part of the illustration.

6. If necessary, remove the borders from the box.

7. Change to Arial Regular 28 point, center and type *Classic America Plan,* then press Enter.

8. Change to Times New Roman Regular

16 point, and center and type *for all salaried employees of.* Change to Times New Roman Regular 24 point, and center and type *Crest Corporation;* then move out of the text box.

9. Position and size the boxes as necessary to match the illustration.

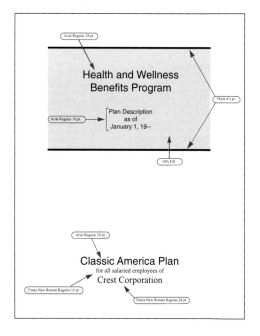

Report 61
Cover Page

Follow these steps to create the cover page that is illustrated on page 305.

1. Create a text box about the same size as the one shown in the illustration. Position it on the top half of the page.

2. If necessary, format the top and bottom borders using a thick line style (4½ point).

3. Inside the box, press Enter once, change to center justification, change to Arial Regular 48 point, and type *Fantasy Vacations.*

4. Press Enter once, change to Times New Roman Italic 24 point, and type *presents the vacation values of a lifetime!* as illustrated.

5. Press Enter 2 times, change to Times New Roman Regular 16 point, and type the remaining lines as illustrated. Press Enter 2 times after the last line.

6. Drag and size the image as necessary to match the illustration.

(continued on next page)

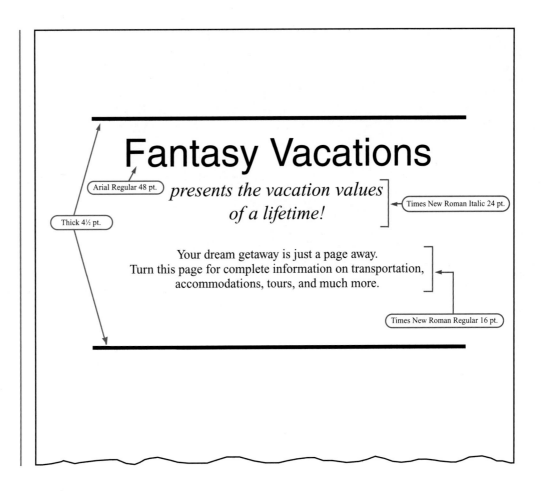

Fantasy Vacations

Arial Regular 48 pt.

Thick 4½ pt.

presents the vacation values of a lifetime!

Times New Roman Italic 24 pt.

Your dream getaway is just a page away.
Turn this page for complete information on transportation, accommodations, tours, and much more.

Times New Roman Regular 16 pt.

Lesson 107 Designing Announcements

GOALS: To improve speed and accuracy; to refine language-arts skills in capitalization; to design announcements.

A. Type 2 times.

A. WARMUP

```
1      On 9/2 XYZ Inc. announced that as of 10/15, they will    11
2   be merging with another company (Q & F Limited).  Sales in  23
3   July were so low that the company was virtually bankrupt!   34
    |  1  |  2  |  3  |  4  |  5  |  6  |  7  |  8  |  9  |  10  |  11  |  12
```

SKILLBUILDING

B. Take three 12-second timings on each line. The scale below the last line shows your wam speed for a 12-second timing.

B. 12-SECOND SPEED SPRINTS

```
4   Rico will rush to tidy the big room that held the supplies.
5   Yale is a very fine school that has some very strict rules.
6   Helen will audit the books of one civic leader in the city.
7   The man had a name that was hard for the small girl to say.
    | | | |5| | | |10| | | |15| | | |20| | | |25| | | |30| | | |35| | | |40| | | |45| | | |50| | | |55| | | |60
```

C. TECHNIQUE PRACTICE: SPACE BAR

C. This paragraph is made up of very short words, requiring the frequent use of the space bar. Do not pause before or after pressing the space bar. Type the paragraph twice.

```
 8      He had the car in the shop and knew that the cost for
 9   the work might be high.  If the bill for the work was to be
10   more than he could pay, he knew that he would skip it.  It
11   did not make any sense to put more money into the old car.
```

D. DIAGNOSTIC PRACTICE: NUMBERS

Turn to the Diagnostic Practice: Numbers routine beginning on page SB-5. Type one of the Pretest/Posttest paragraphs and identify any errors made. Then type the corresponding drill lines 2 times for each number on which you made 2 or more errors and 1 time for each number on which you made only 1 error. Finally, repeat the same Pretest paragraph and compare your performance.

LANGUAGE ARTS

E. CAPITALIZATION

E. Study the rules at the right.

Rule: Capitalize common organizational terms (such as *advertising department* and *finance committee*) when they are the actual names of the units in the writer's own organization and when they are preceded by the word *the*.

≡ org

The Advertising Department here at Hi-Tech Resources is quite large.
But: Our competitor's advertising department is quite small in comparison.

Rule: Capitalize the names of specific course titles but not the names of subjects or areas of study.

≡ course

She enrolled in Computer Literacy 105 and Algebra 120.
But: I am taking a computer literacy course and algebra.

Edit the sentences to correct any errors in capitalization.

```
12   I think I am going to pass Keyboarding 1 with flying colors!
13   The finance committee will make a recommendation today.
14   The proposal must first be sent to the Marketing Department.
15   I have always wanted to learn more Business English rules.
16   You must attend your Sociology class three times a week.
17   The other company's marketing committee will meet today.
```

FORMATTING

F. MORE DESIGN GUIDELINES

Follow these guidelines to design attractive, effective office publications:

1. Make choices that enhance the purpose of your document—to announce, sell, inform, and so forth.

2. Choose a consistent design that will

(continued on next page)

provide flow and unity; use graphics to attract the eye, emphasize a key point or theme, or illustrate an idea.

3. Use sans serif fonts (such as Arial 48 point or larger) for headlines and serif fonts (such as Times New Roman 9 to 12 point) for body text.

4. Main topic headings usually are in 18-point font (minimum) and bold or italic.

5. Subheadings of main topics may be in 12- to 14-point font and bold or italic.

G. SIZING AND POSITIONING TECHNIQUES

1. Learn to move efficiently between a full-page view and a normal view; use the scroll bars to position the pointer.

2. Graphics are usually positioned more efficiently in full-page view.

3. Graphics are usually sized more easily in a normal view, since the handles and two-sided arrows can be seen clearly.

4. Experiment with the zoom feature to find the choice that works the best.

H. WORD PROCESSING: GRAPHICS/PICTURES

Study Lesson 107 in your word processing manual. Complete all of the shaded steps while at your computer. Then format the jobs that follow.

Report 62
Announcement

Follow these steps to create the announcement that is illustrated on page 308.

1. At the top margin, insert a clip art image that relates to businesswomen.

2. Size the image as shown in the illustration, and drag to center it horizontally.

3. Create a text box, and format the top and bottom of the box using a thick line style (4½ point).

4. Change to center justification, and press Enter once.

5. Change to Arial Bold 18 point, and type *WOMEN IN THE WORKPLACE.*

6. Press Enter twice, change to Arial Bold 14 point, type *Presented by Inmac International,* and press Enter twice.

7. Type *Tuesday, April 7, 10 a.m.,* press Enter once, type *Los Angeles Convention Center,* and press Enter twice.

8. Change to Arial Bold 12 point, and type *Learn how to:.* Press Enter twice.

9. Change to left justification, and type the bulleted list in Arial Bold 12 point as shown:
   • *Manage your time effectively.*
   • *Deal with difficult personalities.*
   • *Promote yourself on the job.*
   • *Project a positive image.*

10. Press Enter after the last item, and end the bulleted list.

11. Size the box to match the illustration.

(continued on next page)

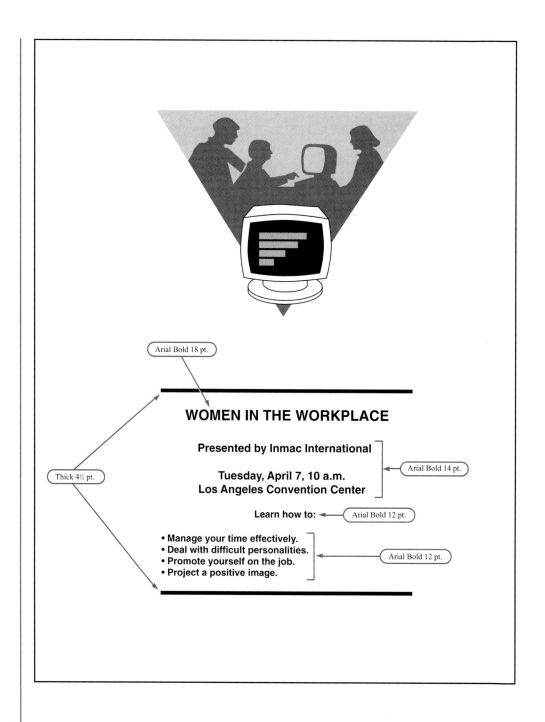

Report 63
Announcement

Follow these steps to create the announcement illustrated on page 309.

1. Center the page vertically.
2. Create an open table with 1 column and 1 row, and format the left side of the cell using a heavy double line style (2¼ point).

3. Change to Arial Bold 48 point, space twice, and type *N;* change to Arial Bold 12 point and type the rest of the letters in the word. Space once, and repeat these steps for the next two words, *Business* and *Consortium.*

(continued on next page)

4. Space 3 times, change to Arial Bold 20 point, type *PRESENTS,* and press Enter 4 times.

5. Change to center justification, change to Arial Bold Italic 20 point, center and type *The Information Highway . . . ,* and press Enter once.

6. Press the space bar 8 times; then type *Your Gateway to the World.*

7. Press Enter repeatedly until the insertion point is positioned at approximately 8 inches.

8. Change to right justification, change to Times New Roman Bold 24 point, type *Playa Del Sol Hotel,* and press Enter once.

9. Change to Times New Roman Regular 18 point, type the remaining lines, and press Enter once after the last line.

10. Move into the space below *Your Gateway . . . ,* and insert a clip art image that relates to the world or the continents.

11. Drag and size the image so that it looks like the one in the illustration.

Report 64
Announcement

1. Create an announcement of your own.

2. Use any clip art image that enhances the purpose of your announcement.

Lesson 108   Designing Flyers

GOALS: To type 49 wam/5′/5e; to design flyers.

A. Type 2 times.

A. WARMUP

```
 1        Does Pamela know if Region 29* (*Ventura) has met the      11
 2  sales quota?  Their exact target zone is just not clear;         22
 3  they don't have to submit their totals until 4:30 on 5/7.        34
```
| 1 | 2 | 3 | 4 | 5 | 6 | 7 | 8 | 9 | 10 | 11 | 12

SKILLBUILDING

B. PACED PRACTICE

Turn to the Paced Practice routine beginning on page SB-14. Take three 2-minute timings, starting at the point where you left off the last time.

C. Take two 5-minute timings. Determine your speed and errors.

Goal: 49 wam/5′/5e

C. 5-MINUTE TIMING

```
 4        Buying by mail order is a trend that is enjoying more      11
 5  and more success because it saves time and money for the        22
 6  consumer.  Most of us tend to feel somewhat apprehensive         34
 7  when we buy an item through the mail because we are never        45
 8  quite sure we will actually receive what we have ordered.        57
 9  We also might wonder about the reliability of the company        69
10  in the event that the item ordered is defective.  If these       81
11  kinds of doubts seem familiar, you aren't alone.                 90
12        There are many ways to protect yourself from some of      101
13  the problems you might encounter by ordering through the        113
14  mail.  As always, read the terms for payment, warranties,       124
15  shipment, and support very carefully.  Find out exactly         135
16  what will happen if you receive an item that is defective.      147
17  Very often you never know how good a company is until you       159
18  have a problem with an item that you ordered.                   168
19        It is also a good idea to find out what type of local     179
20  service is available if you need it.  Some companies have       191
21  established service zones to support their customers in         202
22  case some help is needed.  If you have to pay a fee for         213
23  shipping an item out for service, you might find that mail      225
24  order is not a bargain at all; however, if you shop with        236
25  care, you just might find some great buys.                      245
```
| 1 | 2 | 3 | 4 | 5 | 6 | 7 | 8 | 9 | 10 | 11 | 12

DOCUMENT PROCESSING

Report 65
Flyer

Follow these steps to create the flyer that is illustrated below.

1. Center the page vertically, and create a boxed table with 2 columns and 3 rows.

2. Join the cells in Row 1. Change to Times New Roman Bold 48 point, and center and type *The Los Angeles Zoo.*

3. In Column A, Row 2, drag the inside column border to the right, as shown in the illustration, and press Enter once.

4. Change to right justification.

5. Change to Times New Roman Regular 20 point, and type the lines be-ginning with *Cordially* as illustrated.

6. Press Enter repeatedly until the insertion point is positioned at approximately 7 inches.

7. In Column A, Row 3, change to Times New Roman Bold Italic 28 point, and type *We need your help . . . .*

8. In the next cell, type the lines as illustrated using Times New Roman Bold Italic 20 point and 14 point. Press Enter once between the pairs of lines.

9. Move outside the table, and choose an image of an animal, and position it approximately as shown.

10. Drag and size the image as shown.

Follow these steps to create the flyer illustrated below.

1. Center the page vertically, create an open table with 3 columns and 2 rows, and join the cells in Row 1.

2. Change to center justification, change to Arial Italic 48 point, type *Summerset Homes,* and press Enter once.

3. Change to Arial Italic 24 point, type the remaining lines in the cell as shown, and press Enter 5 times.

4. Change to Times New Roman Bold 22 point. Type the lines in Row 2 as shown, and insert 1 blank line between each line.

5. In Row 2, right-align the text in Column C.

6. In Row 2, drag the inside column borders so that the information will be positioned as shown in the illustration.

7. If necessary, adjust the blank lines in each column of Row 2 so that all columns align horizontally.

8. Move to the area where the image is shown, and insert a clip art image similar to the one shown.

9. Drag and size the image as shown in the illustration.

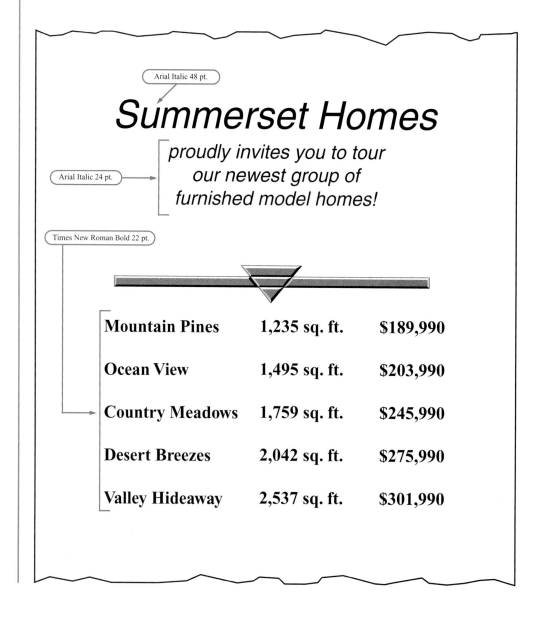

Designing Newsletters

GOALS: To improve speed and accuracy; to refine language-arts skills in spelling; to format a newsletter.

A. Type 2 times.

A. WARMUP

```
1       Approximately 90% of the weekly budget was just used    11
2  to buy equipment.  A very sizable amount totaling $12,654    22
3  was spent on "necessities" as requested by the department!   34
   | 1 | 2 | 3 | 4 | 5 | 6 | 7 | 8 | 9 | 10 | 11 | 12
```

SKILLBUILDING

B. DIAGNOSTIC PRACTICE: ALPHABET

Turn to the Diagnostic Practice: Alphabet routine beginning on page SB-2. Type one of the Pretest/Posttest paragraphs and identify any errors made. Then type the corresponding drill lines 2 times for each letter on which you made 2 or more errors and 1 time for each letter on which you made only 1 error. Finally, repeat the same Pretest paragraph and compare your performance.

Pretest
Take a 1-minute timing. Determine your speed and errors.

C. PRETEST: ALTERNATE- AND ONE-HAND WORDS

```
4       A great auditor is eager to spend a minimum of eighty   11
5  hours to amend a problem.  If he assessed a penalty that     22
6  exceeded the usual fee, I reserve the right to correct it.   34
   | 1 | 2 | 3 | 4 | 5 | 6 | 7 | 8 | 9 | 10 | 11 | 12
```

Practice
    Speed Emphasis: If you made no more than 1 error on the Pretest, type each *individual* line 2 times.
    Accuracy Emphasis: If you made 2 or more errors, type each *group* of lines (as though it were a paragraph) 2 times.

D. PRACTICE: ALTERNATE-HAND WORDS

```
7  also amend maps thrown blame city problem panel formal down
8  snap rigid lens social visit with penalty right height half
9  chap usual such enrich shape dish auditor spend eighty kept
```

E. PRACTICE: ONE-HAND WORDS

```
10 was only great pupil regret uphill scatter homonym assessed
11 bed join water nylon target pompon savages minimum exceeded
12 age hook eager union teased limply reserve opinion attracts
```

Posttest
Repeat the Pretest timing and compare performance.

F. POSTTEST: ALTERNATE- AND ONE-HAND WORDS

G. Type this list of frequently misspelled words, paying special attention to any spelling problems in each word.

G. SPELLING

13 operations health individual considered expenditures vendor
14 beginning internal pursuant president union written develop
15 hours enclosing situation function including standard shown
16 engineering payable suggested participants providing orders
17 toward nays total without paragraph meetings different vice

Edit the sentences to correct any misspellings.

18 The participents in the different meetings voted for hours.
19 The presdent of the union is working toward a resolution.
20 The health of each individal must be seriously considered.
21 Engineering has suggested providing orders for the vendor.
22 One expanditure has been written off as part of oparations.
23 He is inclosing the accounts payible record as shown today.

FORMATTING

H. NEWSLETTER DESIGN

1. Newsletters have become increasingly important in the business world as a forum for communicating information on a wide range of subjects to clients, employees, and the general public.

2. A well-planned newsletter will employ all the basic principles of good design. However, because newsletters usually include information on a wide variety of topics, they are generally more complex in their layout.

3. Most newsletters have certain elements in common, such as: main headings and subheadings; text arranged in flowing newspaper-column format using a variety of column widths to add interest; text boxes to emphasize and summarize; graphic images to draw reader attention and interest to a topic; a variety of borders and fills.

DOCUMENT PROCESSING

Report 67
Newsletter

Follow these steps to create the first part of the newsletter shown on page 315. (You will complete the newsletter in Lesson 110.)

1. Set all margins at 0.75 inch, clear all tabs, and set one tab at 0.25 inch from the left margin.

2. Create an open table with 2 columns and 2 rows; drag the middle column border to the left so the first column is about 1.75 inches wide.

3. Change alignment in Column B to right.

4. In Column B, Row 1, change to Times New Roman Bold 36 point, and type *Health Connection.*

5. Press Enter twice, change to Arial Regular 16 point, type *A Newsletter From Office Temporaries,* and then press Enter once.

6. Move to Column A, Row 2. Change to Arial Regular 12 point, and type *Vol. XX, Issue No. 7.* Move to Column B, and type *January 19--* in Arial Regular 12 point.

(continued on next page)

Reminder: You will finish the newsletter in the next lesson.

7. Change the line styles in the table to those shown. Set the bottom of Row 1 for a thick line style (4½ point) and the bottom of Row 2 for a single line style (¾ point).

8. In Column A, Row 1, insert a decorative image such as the one shown. Size and position the image as shown.

9. Move outside the table below Column A, press Enter twice, change to Times New Roman Bold 12 point, and type *From the President:*.

10. Press Enter once, change to Times New Roman Bold 24 point, type *Stress Reduction Seminar,* and press Enter twice.

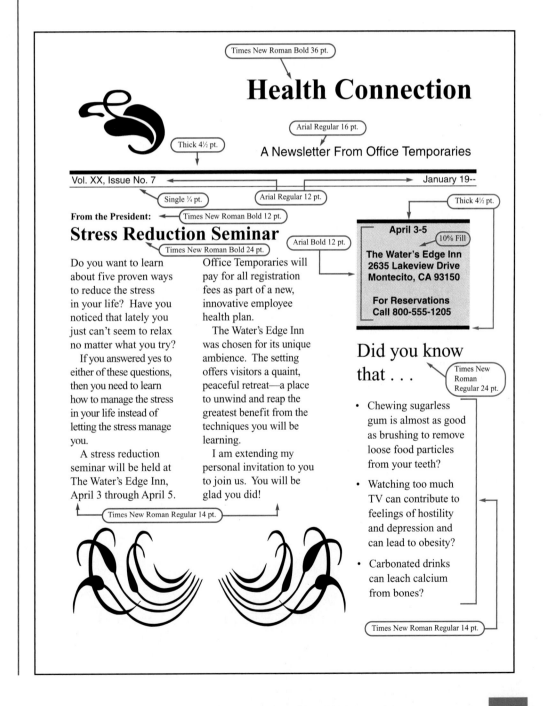

Times New Roman Bold 36 pt.

Health Connection

Arial Regular 16 pt.

Thick 4½ pt.

A Newsletter From Office Temporaries

Vol. XX, Issue No. 7   January 19--

Single ¼ pt.   Arial Regular 12 pt.   Thick 4½ pt.

From the President: Times New Roman Bold 12 pt.

Stress Reduction Seminar

Times New Roman Bold 24 pt.   Arial Bold 12 pt.

April 3-5   10% Fill

The Water's Edge Inn
2635 Lakeview Drive
Montecito, CA 93150

For Reservations
Call 800-555-1205

Do you want to learn about five proven ways to reduce the stress in your life? Have you noticed that lately you just can't seem to relax no matter what you try?

If you answered yes to either of these questions, then you need to learn how to manage the stress in your life instead of letting the stress manage you.

A stress reduction seminar will be held at The Water's Edge Inn, April 3 through April 5.

Office Temporaries will pay for all registration fees as part of a new, innovative employee health plan.

The Water's Edge Inn was chosen for its unique ambience. The setting offers visitors a quaint, peaceful retreat—a place to unwind and reap the greatest benefit from the techniques you will be learning.

I am extending my personal invitation to you to join us. You will be glad you did!

Times New Roman Regular 14 pt.

Did you know that . . .

Times New Roman Regular 24 pt.

- Chewing sugarless gum is almost as good as brushing to remove loose food particles from your teeth?

- Watching too much TV can contribute to feelings of hostility and depression and can lead to obesity?

- Carbonated drinks can leach calcium from bones?

Times New Roman Regular 14 pt.

Report 68
Newsletter

1. Create a newsletter masthead of your own, similar to the one presented in Report 67.
2. Use any clip art images that enhance the purpose of your newsletter.
3. Do not prepare the body of the newsletter.

Lesson 110 Designing Newsletters (Continued)

GOALS: To type 49 wam/5′/5e; to design newsletters.

A. Type 2 times.

A. WARMUP

```
1      At exactly 8:30 a.m., Quigley & Co. will host a wide      11
2  variety of roundtable discussions that you should enjoy.      22
3  Organizational skills will be discussed in Rooms K5 and P6.   34
   | 1 | 2 | 3 | 4 | 5 | 6 | 7 | 8 | 9 | 10 | 11 | 12
```

SKILLBUILDING

B. Take a 1-minute timing on the first paragraph to establish your base speed. Then take four 1-minute timings on the remaining paragraphs. As soon as you equal or exceed your base speed on one paragraph, advance to the next, more difficult paragraph.

B. SUSTAINED PRACTICE: ROUGH DRAFT

```
4      The pattern of employment in our country is undergoing      11
5  some major changes.  Companies are slowly decreasing their     23
6  permanent staff to just a core group of managers and other     35
7  high-powered people and are using temporaries for the rest.    47

8      This trend is creating an accordion aftermath in many       11
9  firms:  the ability to expand and contract as the time and     23
10 the balance sheets dictate.  Having this bit of flexibility    35
11 will be a key ingredient in the competitive fight to come.     47

12 All of these changes will make it tough for the unions         11
13 to stay afloat.  They do not have a satisfactory method of     23
14 organizing such employees.  Unions could try to change into    35
15 social agencies providing aid to members outside of work.      47

16     Such services as elder or child care, counseling, debt      11
17 management, and even health care may be of great assistance    23
18 as employers find it more and more difficult to offer these    35
19 benefits. Unions may find their niche by filling this gap.     47
   | 1 | 2 | 3 | 4 | 5 | 6 | 7 | 8 | 9 | 10 | 11 | 12
```

C. Take two 5-minute timings. Determine your speed and errors.

Goal: 49 wam/5'/5e

C. 5-MINUTE TIMING

20   A vital skill for anyone living along the coast is   10

21 being prepared for an earthquake. Fault lines tend to be   22

22 most active in cities by the shore. However, this does not   34

23 mean that those cities in the Midwest or in the central   45

24 part of the United States are immune. Some experts believe   57

25 that many parts of the country, including places like New   68

26 York City, are long overdue for a major earthquake. The   80

27 key to living through such a disaster is being prepared.   92

28   There are many ways to prepare yourself. One of the   102

29 most important items is a supply of water. Camping stores   114

30 often stock kits that include first-aid supplies and dried   126

31 foods, flashlights, thermal blankets, and other important   138

32 items. These items could be kept in your car in the event   149

33 that you are at work when an earthquake hits. At home you   161

34 should always keep a flashlight and warm clothing within   173

35 easy reach and sturdy shoes under the bed.   181

36   As in any emergency, you must remain calm. If you   192

37 are at work, you should know where all emergency exits   204

38 are located. You should also know your responsibility is   216

39 for helping others in the event of an emergency, including   228

40 fires or power outages. Being prepared and organized will   239

41 help you survive any disaster.   245

| 1 | 2 | 3 | 4 | 5 | 6 | 7 | 8 | 9 | 10 | 11 | 12 |

DOCUMENT PROCESSING

Report 69
Newsletter (cont.)

Open the file for Report 67 shown on page 314. Complete the newsletter following these steps:

1. Move to the end of the document, and define 3 columns to apply from this point forward. Use the default settings.

2. Type the information as shown using Times New Roman Regular 14 point in Columns 1 and 2.

3. Press Tab to indent the paragraphs as shown, and force a column break at the end of each column as shown.

(continued on next page)

4. At the top of Column 3, create a text box about the size of the one shown, and drag it into position as shown.

5. If necessary, format the top and bottom borders using a thick line style (4½ point), and apply a 10% fill.

6. Inside the box, change to Arial Bold 12 point, and center and type the lines as shown. Adjust the box size, if necessary, so that all text is visible.

7. Move outside the text box, and position the insertion point below the text box to type the rest of the column as shown.

8. Change to Times New Roman Regular 24 point, and type the heading *Did you know that* . . . .

9. Press Enter once. Change to Times New Roman Regular 14 point, and type the bulleted list as shown using any bullet style.

10. If the bulleted list extends to a new page, drag the text box in Column 3 up until all of the Column 3 text fits on the first page.

11. Below the first two columns, insert a clip art image of a relaxing setting or a decoration.

12. Size and drag the image under the first two columns as shown in the illustration.

Report 70
Progress Check
Flyer

Follow these steps to create the flyer shown on page 319.

1. Create a table with 1 column and 1 row.

2. Format all sides of the cell using a heavy double-line style (2¼ point), and apply a 10% fill.

3. Change to Times New Roman Bold 36 point, and center and type *Paradise Ranch Equestrian Center* on two lines as shown.

4. Move outside and below the table, press Enter twice, and increase the left margin 0.5 inch.

5. Change to Arial Bold Italic 24 point, type *We specialize in:*, and press Enter twice.

6. Change to Arial Bold 16 point, and type the bulleted list using any bullet style, and insert a blank line between each item in the list.

7. Create a text box about the size and position of the one shown in the lower left corner, and change to right justification.

8. Change to Times New Roman Bold 14 point, type the name of the center, and press Enter once.

9. Change to Times New Roman Regular 14 point, and type the two lines of the address as shown.

10. If necessary, remove any borders from the box, and move out of the box.

11. To the right of this text box, insert an equestrian clip art image. Size and drag all boxes to appear as they do in the illustration.

(continued on next page)

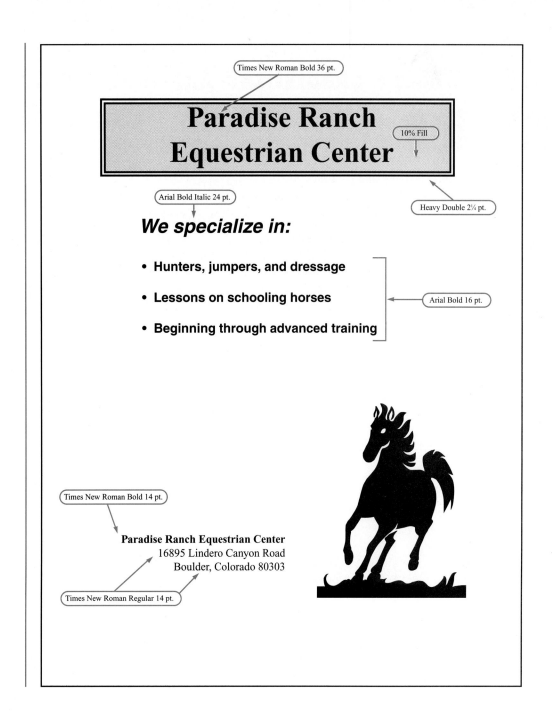

Times New Roman Bold 36 pt.

Paradise Ranch Equestrian Center

10% Fill

Heavy Double 2¼ pt.

Arial Bold Italic 24 pt.

We specialize in:

- **Hunters, jumpers, and dressage**

- **Lessons on schooling horses**

- **Beginning through advanced training**

Arial Bold 16 pt.

Times New Roman Bold 14 pt.

Paradise Ranch Equestrian Center
16895 Lindero Canyon Road
Boulder, Colorado 80303

Times New Roman Regular 14 pt.

UNIT
TWENTY-THREE ▶ Specialized Applications

Lesson 111 Legal

GOALS: To improve speed and accuracy; to refine language-arts skills in subject-verb agreement; to format legal documents.

A. Type 2 times.

A. WARMUP

```
1      The taxes* were quickly adjusted upward by 20 percent    11
2  because of the improvements to her house (built in 1901).    23
3  A proposed law will not penalize good homeowners like this.  35
   |  1  |  2  |  3  |  4  |  5  |  6  |  7  |  8  |  9  |  10 |  11 |  12
```

SKILLBUILDING

B. Take three 12-second timings on each line. The scale below the last line shows your wam speed for a 12-second timing.

B. 12-SECOND SPEED SPRINTS

```
4  Their home is on a lake that is right south of the prairie.
5  They have a boat and motor and spend a lot of time fishing.
6  Kay caught so many fish that she gave some to the old lady.
7  She was so pleased that a young girl would do this for her.
   | | | 5 | | | |10| | | |15| | |20| | |25| | | |30| | |35| | | |40| | | |45| | | |50| | | |55| | | |60
```

C. PROGRESSIVE PRACTICE: ALPHABET

Turn to the Progressive Practice: Alphabet routine beginning on page SB-7. Take six 30-second timings, starting at the point where you left off the last time.

LANGUAGE ARTS

D. Study the rules at the right.

D. AGREEMENT

Rule: Subjects joined by *and* take a plural verb unless the compound subject is preceded by *each, every,* or *many a (an).*

agr comp

Margaret and Adam are eligible to compete in the state math contest.
Each girl and boy who competes is likely to win a scholarship award.

Rule: Verbs that refer to conditions that are impossible or improbable (that is, verbs in the *subjunctive* mood) require the plural form.

agr subj

If I were she, I would counsel all students to enroll in a keyboarding course.
If it were not raining today, they would be playing golf in the afternoon.

Edit the sentences to correct any errors in the use of agreement.

```
8  The receptionist and her replacement were both sick on Tuesday.
9  Every printer and copy machine were purchased new last year.
10  Many a man and woman have lost a job because of absenteeism.
11  I wish I was more involved in the decision-making process.
12  Even if I were he, I would still want the same procedures used.
13  If the deadline was on Friday, we would still finish on time.
```

E. WORD PROCESSING: LINE NUMBERING

Study Lesson 111 in your word processing manual. Complete all of the shaded steps while at your computer. Then format the jobs that follow.

Situation: You are a legal secretary in the office of Ms. Jeanne M. Hoover, attorney-at-law. You are responsible for all administrative duties and the preparation of correspondence and various legal documents.

Report 71
Last Will and Testament

Follow these steps to format the will:

1. Type the title of the will approximately 2 inches from the top of the page in bold, 14-point Times New Roman.
2. As legal documents are bound at the top, leave a 1.5-inch top margin on continuation pages.
3. Use the default side margins, double spacing, and 1-inch paragraph indentions.
4. Legal documents (even one page) are usually numbered at the bottom center in this format: *Page 1 of 4.* Create a footer in 10-point Times New Roman for every page of the will. Once you know the total number of pages in the complete document, insert the page numbering command.
5. Use line numbering for the document, beginning with the first paragraph. End line number before the signature line.

Legal documents are sometimes printed on ruled stationery. A vertical double line is printed the length of the stationery on the left; a vertical single line is printed on the right. Margins are set a space or two inside the ruled lines.

↓2″ **LAST WILL AND TESTAMENT**

OF

LAURA J. MACKLIN

1   Being of sound mind and disposing memory for the

2 purpose of making disposition upon my death of my entire estate, real,

3 personal, and mixed, wherever situated, whether owned by me me at the

4 date of execution hereof, or acquired by me after such date, I hereby do make

5 ~~hereby~~ publish, and declare this to be my Last Will and Testament. My

6 present domicile is at 807 Carver St, Fenton, Michigan 48430

7   **ARTICLE I**

8   I hereby expressly revoke and cancel any and all Wills,

9 Codicils, or ~~other~~ testamentary dispositions at any time heretofore made

10 by me.

11   **ARTICLE II**

12   I direct my Personal Representative to pay before making

A female Personal Representative, the person appointed to execute a will, is often referred to as an *Executrix.* A male is often referred to as an *Executor.*

(continued on next page)

13 any distributions: [#] (1) all of the expenses of my last illness, funeral, and

14 burial; (2) all of the expenses of administering my estate; (3) all estate,

15 inheritance, and other taxes that may be payable by reason of my death;

16 and (4) all of my just debts.

17 *double space*   **ARTICLE III**

18   I give and bequeath all of my remaining property, real and

19 intangible and wheresoever situated, after payment of taxes and other

20 payments required by Article II as follows:

21   (A) Fifty percent (50%) to my beloved daughter, JUDITH

22 MACKLIN COSGROVE, or her surviving issue, per stirpes;

23   (B) Fifty percent (50%) to my beloved son, WILLIAM L.

24 MACKLIN, or his surviving issue, per stirpes;

25   (C) In the event either of my beloved children predeceases

26 me leaving no issue surviving, I hereby give, devise, and bequeath said

27 share of my estate to my surviving child, or her/his surviving issue, per

28 stirpes.

29   **ARTICLE IV**

30   I appoint JUDITH MACKLIN COSGROVE as Personal

31 Representative of this, my Last Will and Testament. In the event my

32 Personal Representative shall predecease me, or, for any reason, is

33 unable or unwilling to accept the office of Personal Representative, then I

34 appoint WILLIAM L. MACKLIN as Alternate Personal Representative.

35   I hereby give my said Personal Representative all powers

36 provided by the Michigan Revised Probate Code, as amended, and any

37 other conferred by statute and, in addition, the full power to sell,

38 mortgage, hypothecate, invest, reinvest, exchange, manage, and control

39 and in any way use and deal with any and all of my estate, both real and

40 personal, without making notice or application to any court for leave.

41   IN WITNESS WHEREOF, I subscribe my name to this, my

42 Last Will and Testament, consisting of (three (3)) printed pages, this day of [12th]

43 March, 19--.   *please check*

_____

LAURA J. MACKLIN

In legal documents, important numbers are typed in both figures and words.

An attorney might use the line numbers as referral points when discussing the draft of a will with a client. The numbers would be removed from the final copy.

After completing this page, go back to the beginning of Page 1 and insert page numbers.

Use a table with a top cell border to create the signature line.

Memo 23
Memo on Plain Paper

MEMO TO: Justen Busiahn / **FROM:** Jeanne M. Hoover / **DATE:** March 12, 19-- / **SUBJECT:** Change in Will for Alfred T. Braxton

When you were out of the office this morning, I took a call from Alfred T. Braxton concerning the revision of his will. His wish is that each of his sons and daughters is to receive an equal share of his estate at the time of his death.

agr comp

agr subj

Mr. Braxton asked that I tell you that if the will were not modified to reflect this change, neither his desires nor those of his late wife would be heeded. He will expect a call from you when the draft is ready for review.

Lesson 112   Insurance

GOALS: To type 50 wam/5′/5e; to format insurance documents.

A. Type 2 times.

A. WARMUP

```
1      Missy examined these items:  the #426 oil painting, a      11
2  Bowes & Elkjer porcelain vase, and the 86-piece collection     23
3  of glazed antique pitchers.  There were 337 people present.    33
   |  1  |  2  |  3  |  4  |  5  |  6  |  7  |  8  |  9  |  10  |  11  |  12
```

SKILLBUILDING

Pretest
Take a 1-minute timing. Determine your speed and errors.

B. PRETEST: COMMON LETTER COMBINATIONS

```
4      He did mention that they are sending a lawful taping       11
5  of the comedy format to a performing combo.  A motion to       22
6  commit a useful option forced a fusion of forty persons.       33
   |  1  |  2  |  3  |  4  |  5  |  6  |  7  |  8  |  9  |  10  |  11  |  12
```

Practice
Speed Emphasis: If you made no more than 1 error on the Pretest, type each *individual* line 2 times.
Accuracy Emphasis: If you made 2 or more errors, type each *group* of lines (as though it were a paragraph) 2 times.

C. PRACTICE: WORD BEGINNINGS

```
7  for forty forth format former forget forest forearm forbear
8  per peril perky period permit person peruse perform persist
9  com combo comic combat commit common combed compose complex
```

D. PRACTICE: WORD ENDINGS

```
10  ing doing mixing living filing taping sending biking hiding
11  ion onion nation lotion motion option mention fusion legion
12  ful awful useful joyful earful lawful helpful sinful armful
```

Posttest
Repeat the Pretest timing and compare performance.

E. POSTTEST: COMMON LETTER COMBINATIONS

F. Take two 5-minute timings. Determine your speed and errors.

Goal: 50 wam/5'/5e

F. 5-MINUTE TIMING

13   Some firms help make it possible for their employees   11

14 to enhance their education in various ways. Some workers   22

15 are able to attend courses held during and after work hours   34

16 in their place of work. Such courses often provide the   46

17 latest news there is of new systems and related new ways   57

18 for completing tasks. These courses can help equip workers   69

19 with new technical skills while also helping their firms   80

20 become more competitive. Many times the instructors are   92

21 those workers who enrolled in such courses earlier and are   104

22 being rewarded for doing so.   109

23   Some firms pay their employees for some or all of   120

24 their tuition costs if they have enrolled in a recognized   131

25 educational program. Workers at times enroll in college   143

26 programs to obtain degrees which will help them find more   154

27 rewarding jobs in their firms. When technical change has   166

28 affected their work or the competitive edge of the firm,   177

29 improving the workers' efficiency is well worth the time   189

30 and money invested in the workers.   196

31   Many firms also provide workers with the time and the   207

32 money for them to attend a workshop or a session conducted   219

33 by known experts in the field. Such programs are often   230

34 held away from the firm. Then those who attend can keep   241

35 their minds on the topic without distractions.   250

| 1 | 2 | 3 | 4 | 5 | 6 | 7 | 8 | 9 | 10 | 11 | 12

DOCUMENT PROCESSING

Situation: You are employed in the office of Fidelity Insurance Company at 8504 Gunnison Avenue, NW, in Grand Rapids, Michigan 49504. Fidelity handles automobile, homeowner's, and life insurance coverage throughout the state of Michigan. You work for E. H. Kosowicz, Executive Vice President. Mr. Kosowicz prefers the block-style letter and *Sincerely* as the complimentary closing.

Memo 24

MEMO TO: Sandra Gearhart, Sales Director

FROM: E. H. Kosowicz, Executive Vice President

DATE: August 2, 19--

SUBJECT: Nondiscriminatory Employment Practices

(continued on next page)

While Fidelity has not been the subject of lawsuits in its hiring practices, there have been six complaints from rejected candidates for positions in recent months. I am therefore requesting that each department head begin planning in-service programs for all ~~employees~~ personnel who are involved with the hiring of employees new to the firm. Specifically, we need to be concerned with any thing in our hiring practices that may violate the provisions of the Elliott-Larsen Civil Rights act:

> An employer, labor organization, or employment agency
> shall not indicate a preference, limitation, specification, or
> discrimination, based on religion, race, color, national origin,
> age, sex, height, weight, or marital status.

Operationally we need to be certain that we do not use written or oral inquiries which attempt to elicit information in these areas. I am confident that past offenses by management ~~employees~~ personnel have not been intentional. We have no verified cases in our files that are the result of ~~purposeful~~ intentional discriminatory hiring practices. However, we must make every effort to ensure that there are no ~~other~~ inadvertent offenses in the employment process. The need for specific instruction in this area can be demonstrated with two illustrations:

1. It is lawful to ask a candidate if he or she has ever been convicted of a crime; it is unlawful to ask if he or she has ever been arrested.

2. It is lawful to ask about an applicant's military experience in the Armed Forces of the U.S.; it is unlawful to inquire into an applicant's general military experience.

Joy Lynn Rose from the Department of Human Resources will contact you and the other Department Heads soon about this important project. She will ~~will~~ work with you in organizing the instructional content.

Letter 81
Block Style With
Open Punctuation

Mr. Kosowicz has dictated the following letter for you to transcribe. Correct paragraphing is shown, but you will have to punctuate and capitalize correctly.

{Current Date} / Mr. J. W. Dawson / Executive Director / Fidelity Insurance Company / 708 Eighth Avenue / Lansing, MI 48906 / Dear Mr. Dawson ¶in a recent issue of your newsletter . . . i read of the continuing education

(continued on next page)

course that will be offered beginning on thursday . . . september 15 . . .
¶since we have a claims adjuster who recently joined our staff . . . i would like more information on that course so that i might enroll him . . . please send me complete details on class meeting times . . . the cost of enrollment . . . an application for admission . . . and the complete course description . . . in addition . . . please provide me with the name of the individual who will be teaching the course and the name of the textbook that will be used . . .

¶every time we have arranged for one of our employees to attend one of your continuing education courses . . . we have been extremely pleased with the growth we have noted when the individual returns to the job . . .

Table 56
Boxed Table

FIDELITY SECOND-QUARTER NEW POLICIES			
Sales Representative	**Homeowner's**	**Auto**	**Life**
Cornish, Richard	17	24	32
DeVries, Maureen	15	20	24
Principi, Mario	14	18	21
Ruiz, Matilda	25	32	38
Sek, Victoria	18	30	28
Thompson, Ernest	21	22	26

Lesson 113 Hospitality

GOALS: To improve speed and accuracy; to refine language-arts skills in proofreading; to format documents used in the hospitality industry.

A. Type 2 times.

A. WARMUP

```
 1      Did you hear the excellent quartet of junior cadets?     11
 2  Everybody in the crowd (estimated at over 500) applauded     22
 3  "with gusto."  The sizable crowd filled the 3/4-acre park.   34
    | 1  | 2  | 3  | 4  | 5  | 6  | 7  | 8  | 9  | 10 | 11 | 12
```

B. Take three 12-second timings on each line. The scale below the last line shows your wam speed for a 12-second timing.

B. 12-SECOND SPEED SPRINTS

4 Henry knew for years that he would work at a big golf club.
5 He labored at the local golf shop on weekdays after school.
6 There were times when he also helped the busy ground crews.
7 Now he is going to manage the golf club two days each week.

| | | |5| | | |10| | | |15| | | |20| | | |25| | | |30| | | |35| | | |40| | | |45| | | |50| | | |55| | | |60

C. PROGRESSIVE PRACTICE: ALPHABET

Turn to the Progressive Practice: Alphabet routine beginning on page SB-7. Take six 30-second timings, starting at the point where you left off the last time.

D. Type the paragraph 2 times. Use the A finger to tap the Shift key and the Caps Lock key.

D. TECHNIQUE PRACTICE: SHIFT/CAPS LOCK

8   A CLASSIFIED AD in the AMES JOURNAL was for two jobs.
9 Later Carrie and Amy saw the WELCOME mat at JAHN'S CAFE on
10 Copeland Avenue. After reading YOUR FIRST JOB by Madeline
11 H. Prestholdt, they began working on Tuesday at JAHN'S.

LANGUAGE ARTS

E. Edit this paragraph to correct any keyboarding or formatting errors.

E. PROOFREADING

12   Suprising as it may seem, their has been a good deal
13 of interest in comunicating with a computer thruogh the
14 human voice for about fourty years. Researchers haev spent
15 millions ofdollars in hteir efforts to improve voice input
16 tecknology. It is likly that in the next decade we will
17 see many use ful applications in busness and in education.

DOCUMENT PROCESSING

Situation: You are the administrative assistant to Mr. Arvid D. Beamann, president of Beamann & Associates, and you also serve as the program director. Beamann & Associates is a service company that was created for the purpose of planning and coordinating conventions, seminars, and other retreat-type activities for business firms and other organizations. You work with various agencies in providing for travel arrangements, lodging, meeting rooms, formal meal functions, and entertainment.

Letter 82
Block Style

August 3, 19-- / Mrs. Andrea Kamehemaha / Ritz-Champlin Hotel / 2407 Nohonani Street / Honolulu, HI 96815 / Dear Mrs. Kamehemaha / Subject: Norline Industries Program

I have been unable to contact you by telephone. Would you please call me at 502-555-4444 as soon as possible, as I would like to discuss menu selections and costs for the Norline Industries program scheduled at your

(continued on next page)

hotel on September 24-29, 19--. I look for ward to haering ~~from you~~ and working with you on the program.

sincerely

{Your Name}
Program Director
By Fax

Memo 25

MEMO TO: Service Representatives
FROM: Arvid D. Beamann
DATE: August 3, 19--
SUBJECT: New Code of Ethics

While this memo is about a proposed new Code of Ethics for our company, I do want to use the opportunity to congratulate all of you for the continued growth in both the number of programs and new clients. All of the employees at Beamann & Associates are aware that the success of the firm depends largely on your success in the field.

At the last meeting of regional managers, there was discussion about the need for developing a new Code of Ethics for our employees. I want to stress that this in no way reflects on the performance of any of our service representatives. As agents for Beamann's in both soliciting new clients and conducting on-site coordination, you have demonstrated exemplary ethical conduct. However, as the firm continues to grow, with the resulting addition of new service representatives, we want to take steps to ensure that all of our employees understand the ethical framework under which we operate.

Our board members and executive officers believe that we must operate in a fashion that is socially responsible by responding to community needs, by showing concern for the environment, and by interacting with clients and other

(continued on next page)

business contacts in a manner which reflects high ethical standards. The guiding philosophy is that we should operate in such a way that we never try to "get away with anything."

We must conduct our affairs so that our communications are clear and we make no misleading claims. In the rush to secure a contract, it would be too easy to convey a message that is not completely accurate. In contracts with multinational people, we must ensure that mutual feedback (both oral and written) results in clear and accurate messages. Rather than exaggerating the quality of our services (facilities, lodging, food, etc.), our goal will be to deliver the very best programs that the industry can provide.

It is true that the long-range success of Beamann & Associates depends on our reputation of integrity and performance. However, we also want to conduct our business affairs at the highest ethical level for the reason that it is the right thing to do.

Report 72
Menu

SUGGESTED DINNER MENU

The Olde Fort Myers Inn
Fort Myers, Florida
7 p.m., October 24, 19--

Mixed Green Salad
With House Dressing

Cannelloni
Stuffed with Veal and Chicken in a Red Sauce

CHOICE OF

Scallopini al Marsala
Sliced Veal Sauteed with Dry Marsala Wine and Mushrooms
OR

(continued on next page)

Pollo Alla Ligure
Breast of Chicken with Sun-dried Tomato, Artichoke, and Zucchini
OR
Sogliola Dorata
Petrale Sole with Lemon Butter

Chocolate Mousse

Freshly Brewed Coffee or Tea

Lesson 114   Retail

GOALS: To type 50 wam/5′/5e; to format retail documents.

A. Type 2 times.

A. WARMUP

```
 1      Mr. Baxter will move to 1749 Larkin Street; his old      11
 2  home is in Gray's Woods, just east of the corner of Parson   22
 3  and 167th Avenue.  The house sizes are quite different!      33
```
| 1 | 2 | 3 | 4 | 5 | 6 | 7 | 8 | 9 | 10 | 11 | 12

SKILLBUILDING

B. Take a 1-minute timing on the first paragraph to establish your base speed. Then take four 1-minute timings on the remaining paragraphs. As soon as you equal or exceed your base speed on one paragraph, advance to the next, more difficult paragraph.

B. SUSTAINED PRACTICE: CAPITALIZATION

```
 4      Even though he was only about thirty years old, Jason    11
 5  knew that it was not too soon to begin thinking about his    23
 6  retirement.  He soon found out that there were many things   34
 7  involved in his plans for an early and long retirement.      45

 8      Even without considering the uncertainty of social       10
 9  security, Jason knew that he should plan his career moves     22
10  so that he would have a strong company retirement plan.  He  34
11  realized that he should have an Individual Retirement Plan.   46

12      When he became aware that The Longman Company, the       10
13  firm that employed him, would match his contributions to a   22
14  supplemental retirement account, he began saving even more.  34
15  He used the Payroll Department funds from the Goplin Group.   46

16      He also learned that The Longman Company retirement      11
17  plan, his Individual Retirement Plan, and his supplemental   22
18  retirement account are all deferred savings.  With those     34
19  tax-dollar savings, Jason bought New Venture Group mutuals.  46
```
| 1 | 2 | 3 | 4 | 5 | 6 | 7 | 8 | 9 | 10 | 11 | 12

C. Take two 5-minute timings. Determine your speed and errors.

Goal: 50 wam/5'/5e

C. 5-MINUTE TIMING

20   You have almost finished a course in which you gained   11

21 sound skills needed for seeking a good job in the business   23

22 world today. You have worked to acquire sound competencies   35

23 in language arts, formatting business documents, editing,   46

24 following directions, setting priorities, and working under   58

25 pressure. All of these skills were refined while you were   70

26 mastering your keyboarding and document processing skills.   82

27 They are required in every phase of business by both office   94

28 workers and managers for the processing of information.   105

29   Now you need to maintain and strengthen these skills.   117

30 In doing so, you will find that changes will continue to   128

31 occur over the years. No one expected that the typewriter   140

32 would be largely replaced by the personal computer over the   152

33 last decade. And now there are times when we think that   163

34 there is no way that the machines and the software we use   175

35 can be improved. But that is not true. Certainly, we can   187

36 expect that there will be amazing new ways to do things in   198

37 the future. In order to advance on the job, there will be   210

38 a need to keep up to date by continuing your education in   222

39 various ways. As technology changes over time, businesses   234

40 will want workers who have sharp minds and who want to   245

41 help their company succeed.   250

| 1 | 2 | 3 | 4 | 5 | 6 | 7 | 8 | 9 | 10 | 11 | 12

Situation: You are working as the administrative assistant to Richard E. Paluch, Manager, Star Hardware Company. You and Mr. Paluch work in the Willmar store. As his assistant, you are responsible for sending memos, letters, and other correspondence. You are also responsible for typing the minutes of the monthly staff meeting.

Memo 26

MEMO TO: All Employees / **FROM:** Richard E. Paluch, Manager / **DATE:** April 14, 19— / **SUBJECT:** Employee Right-to-Know Program

¶The Willmar store of Star Hardware will again be holding meetings for all employees on May 2-3 concerning the handling of hazardous substances

(continued on next page)

and agents. This is in compliance with the Employee Right-to-Know Act passed by the Minnesota Legislature in 1983.

¶A publication of The Minnesota Department of Labor & Industry dated August 1994 lists the following as requirements for the program:

- An inventory of hazardous substances and/or agents that exist in the workplace.
- Identification of employees who are routinely exposed to those substances or agents.
- A system for obtaining and maintaining written information on the substances and agents employees may be exposed to in the workplace.
- Methods for making ERTK (Employee Right-to-Know) information readily accessible to employees in their work areas.
- A plan for providing initial, preassignment, and annual training of employees.
- Implementation and maintenance of a labeling system or other warning methods.

¶All employees are encouraged to review the list and bring any concerns, suggestions, or questions to the meetings. A list containing the names of participants for each of the two sessions will be posted within a few days.

Letter 83
Block Style

_____ June 2, 19--

Simmons ~~Supply~~ *Mower* Company

12500 Indiana Avenue

Chicago, IL 60604

Ladies and Gentlemen:

We are ~~intersteded~~ in stocking a line of mowers for ~~resale~~ in the Willmar Area. Our customers have indicated an interest in the Landrover mower. We are particularly interested in models that have 4-cycle engines with solid-start ignition and a ~~wheelbase~~ *#size* from 7.0 × 1.5 to 8.0 × 2.0. Our customers have also indicated an interest in mowers that have the following features:

1. Pressurized lubrication, which helps prevent heat buildup.
2. Mechanical governors that help maintain blade speed in tall grass and weeds.

(continued on next page)

3. No-rust tranks that will not chip or corrode.

4. No-adjust carburetors that supply the exact fuel and air mixture for fast starting.

If you have models with these features, please send me a catalog listing further specifications.

Sincerely,

STAR HARDWARE

Richard E. Paluch

Manager

Report 73
Meeting Agenda

STAR HARDWARE, WILLMAR STORE
Meeting Agenda
June 7, 19--, 1 p.m.

1. *Call to order*
2. *Approval of minutes of May 5 meeting*
3. *Progress report on building addition (Viola Burkowitz)*
4. *Discussion of attendance at the National Hardware Association's annual meeting*
5. *Computer operations update (Ronald Peete)*
6. *Home office visit (Jan Byerly)*
7. *Adjournment*

Lesson 115 · Government

GOALS: To improve speed and accuracy; to refine language-arts skills in composing; to format government documents.

A. Type 2 times.

A. WARMUP

```
1     The extra black vacuum cleaners with the large-sized     11
2  grips were just lowered to $160 from $240 (a 33 1/3% mark-   22
3  down).  Jay's #55 quilts were marked down to $88 from $99.   34
   | 1 | 2 | 3 | 4 | 5 | 6 | 7 | 8 | 9 | 10 | 11 | 12
```

B. DIAGNOSTIC PRACTICE: ALPHABET

Turn to the Diagnostic Practice: Alphabet routine beginning on page SB-2. Type one of the Pretest/Posttest paragraphs and identify any errors made. Then type the corresponding drill lines 2 times for each letter on which you made 2 or more errors and 1 time for each letter on which you made only 1 error. Finally, repeat the same Pretest paragraph and compare your performance.

C. PACED PRACTICE

Turn to the Paced Practice routine beginning on page SB-14. Take three 2-minute timings, starting at the point where you left off the last time.

LANGUAGE ARTS

D. Using correct format and April 16 as the date, compose a memo to Mr. Richard E. Paluch, Manager, from you concerning the hazardous substances and agents meetings scheduled for May 2-3.

D. COMPOSING

Paragraph 1. Inform Mr. Paluch that you will not be able to attend either of the meetings because you will be in Milwaukee to attend your brother's wedding. Explain that the vacation dates had been approved in early March.

Paragraph 2. Suggest the possibility of the meeting being videotaped for later viewing. If this is not feasible, perhaps an audiotape would suffice.

Paragraph 3. Be sure to tell him that you are sorry the conflict occurred. You should also tell him that if the taping would not be a satisfactory alternative, you would be willing to attend a similar meeting at another Willmar Star Hardware store in the area.

DOCUMENT PROCESSING

Report 74
Rough Draft

Situation: You are an assistant in the office of Alice K. Slade, director of the Public Aviation Safety Agency, a government agency in Washington, D.C. Your supervisor is Terry Wilson, Ms. Slade's executive assistant.

Double-space the entire document.

D R A F T   u/ℓ

POLICY ON SEXUAL HARASSMENT

The 1964 Civil Rights Act (federal) prohibits discrimination because of sex in employment and in the utilization of (govt.) facilities. Sexual harassment is included in the discrimination area. Sexual harassment is defined as unwelcome sexual advances, requests for sexual favors, and other verbal or physical conduct or communication of a sexual nature when:

1. A. Submission to such conduct or communication is made a term or condition, either explicitly or implicitly, to obtain employment.

(continued on next page)

2. B. Submission to or rejection of such conduct or communication by an individual is used as a factor in decisions affecting such individual's employment.

3. C. Such conduct or communication has the purpose or effect of unreasonably interfering with an individual's employment or creating an intimidating, hostile, or offensive employment environment.

The Public Aviation Safety agency reaffirms its desire to create a work environment for all employees that is fair, humane, and responsible. Sexual harassment is inconsistent with the above environment and is absolutely prohibited. Upon receipt and verification of information that such harassment has occurred, the agency will take action corrective up to and including discharge. All complaints of alleged sexual harassment are to be reported to the Personnel Department.

Table 57
Boxed Table

TEN BUSIEST U.S. AIRPORTS Total Takeoffs and Landings	
Airport	**Total**
Chicago O'Hare (ORD)	883,062
Dallas/Ft. Worth (DFW)	854,406
Atlanta Hartsfield (ATL)	715,920
Los Angeles International (LAX)	689,888
Miami (MIA)	557,680
Denver Stapleton (DEN)	530,839
Las Vegas (LAS)	495,940
Phoenix Sky Harbor (PHX)	490,015
Detroit (DTW)	485,306
St. Louis (STL)	479,943

Report 75
Transparencies

Ms. Slade would like two transparencies prepared for use with a speech that she is scheduled to deliver in Las Vegas. You are to prepare paper originals of the transparencies; they will be photocopied onto transparency film later.

Use 18-point, bold Arial font. As you can see from this sample transparency she used in another speech, Ms. Slade likes a border above and below the PASA heading at the top of the page, and a heavy border at the bottom of the page. Center the material attractively on the page, leaving wide margins all around and plenty of space.

Public Aviation Safety Agency

SAFETY PRECAUTIONS

FOR

CARGO LOADING

- Metal detectors
- Chemical detectors
- X-ray equipment
- Dogs
- Other

CAUSES OF AIRLINE ACCIDENTS
—Weather Conditions
—Wind Shear
—Pilot Error
—Engine Failure
—Runway Length
—Cargo Loading
—Terrorism

AIRPORT SECURITY
—Security Personnel
—Airline Personnel
—Airport Personnel
—Passengers
—Facilities
—Equipment

Lesson 116 Monday: Desktop Publishing Project

GOALS: To type 50 wam/5′/5e; to create a letterhead form, memo form, and fax cover form.

A. Type 2 times.

A. WARMUP

1　　He realized that exactly 10% of the budget ($62,475) 　11
2　was questionable. Several key people reviewed it; most of 　23
3　them wanted to reject about 1/3 of the proposed line items! 　34

| 1 | 2 | 3 | 4 | 5 | 6 | 7 | 8 | 9 | 10 | 11 | 12 |

B. PROGRESSIVE PRACTICE: ALPHABET

Turn to the Progressive Practice: Alphabet routine beginning on page SB-7. Take six 30-second timings, starting at the point where you left off the last time.

C. Take two 5-minute timings. Determine your speed and errors.

Goal: 50 wam/5′/5e

C. 5-MINUTE TIMING

4　　It is clear why some of us might be very distracted by 　11
5　noise at work. Keyboards tapping, phones ringing, office 　23
6　machines running, air vents blowing, and loud voices all 　34
7　may interfere with our concentration. We realize that all 　46
8　of us were hired with a purpose in mind: to perform tasks 　58
9　that help our company function in a more productive way. 　69
10　Distractions can reduce our ability to perform well, but 　81
11　what can we do to try to quiet things down in an office? 　92
12　　The first step is to examine our work environment in 　103
13　order to identify the trouble spots. Equipment noise can 　115
14　sometimes be reduced with proper maintenance or by calling 　126
15　the equipment dealer or sales agent to see what might be 　138
16　done about loud, irritating, or distracting sounds. The 　149
17　telephone ring can be regulated by adjusting the volume 　160
18　control, usually located on the side or the bottom of the 　172
19　phone. Just be sure not to turn the volume down so low 　183
20　that you miss calls when you are away from your desk. 　194
21　　Other distracting noises and voices can be reduced 　204
22　with specially padded room dividers. Although this may 　216
23　become expensive, the consequences of not fixing a noisy 　227
24　office can be worse. Dealing with a hearing loss can be 　238
25　stressful and have a negative impact on job performance. 　250

| 1 | 2 | 3 | 4 | 5 | 6 | 7 | 8 | 9 | 10 | 11 | 12 |

In-Basket Exercise
Orientation to Chandler Air Traffic Control School

Situation: Today is Monday, April 23, 19--. You are working as an administrative assistant for Ms. Marsha D. Ebert, director of the Chandler Air Traffic Control School, located in San Jose, California. Ms. Ebert is on a business trip to Washington, D.C., and has left the following jobs in your in-basket for you to complete during her absence.

Use all of the word processing commands you have learned thus far to prepare the documents. Ms. Ebert prefers her letters in block style with standard punctuation and this closing:

Sincerely yours,

Marsha D. Ebert
Director

Please prepare new standard office forms to replace our old letterhead form, memo form, and fax cover. Use the thumbnail sketches as a guide for positioning your text, graphics boxes, and text boxes. Begin the letterhead design 0.5 inch from the top edge of the paper and the memo and fax designs 1 inch from the top edge of the paper.

Form 33
Letterhead Form

> Insert Decorative Image
>
> *Chandler Air Traffic Control School*
> *5241 Lincoln Avenue, Suite 203*
> *San Jose, California 95121*
> *408-555-2769*

Form 34
Memo Form

> *MEMO*
>
> TO:
> FROM:
> DATE:
> SUBJECT:

Form 35
Fax Cover Form

FAX TRANSMISSION
Chandler Air Traffic Control School
5241 Lincoln Avenue, Suite 203
San Jose, California 95121
Fax: 408-555-2235
408-555-2769

To:
Fax Number:
From:
Subject:
Date:
Pages: _____

COMMENTS:

Lesson 117   Tuesday: Correspondence Project

GOALS: To improve speed and accuracy; to refine language-arts skills in word usage; to format a letter, an envelope, a memo, and the minutes of a meeting.

A. Type 2 times.

A. WARMUP

```
1       The executive meeting won't begin until 8:15; please     11
2   notify just the key people.  Do you know if they realize     22
3   that quite a large group* (*234) is expected by 9 o'clock?   34
    |  1  |  2  |  3  |  4  |  5  |  6  |  7  |  8  |  9  |  10  |  11  |  12
```

SKILLBUILDING

B. Take three 12-second timings on each line. The scale below the last line shows your wam speed for a 12-second timing.

B. 12-SECOND SPEED SPRINTS

```
4   Half of the space was going to be used for seven new desks.
5   She will soon know if all their goals have been met or not.
6   You must learn to focus on each one of your jobs every day.
7   The group will meet in the new suite that is down the hall.
    | | | |5| | |10| | |15| | |20| | |25| | |30| | |35| | |40| | |45| | |50| | |55| | |60
```

C. Type each sentence on a separate line. Type the lines twice.

C. TECHNIQUE PRACTICE: ENTER KEY

```
8   Find the printer.  Change those ribbons.  Buy the supplies.
9   Always be on time.  Attend the seminar.  Sign the petition.
10  Prepare your report.  Sign the contract.  Mail the letters.
11  Read that note.  Post the results.  Call all the employees.
```

D. DIAGNOSTIC PRACTICE: NUMBERS

Turn to the Diagnostic Practice: Numbers routine beginning on page SB-5. Type one of the Pretest/Posttest paragraphs and identify any errors made. Then type the corresponding drill lines 2 times for each number on which you made 2 or more errors and 1 time for each number on which you made only 1 error. Finally, repeat the same Pretest paragraph and compare your performance.

LANGUAGE ARTS

E. Study the rules at the right.

E. WORD USAGE

Rule: Do not confuse the following pairs of words:

• *Accept* means "to agree to"; *except* means "to leave out."

word   The Shipping Department agreed to accept the order except for two items.

• *Affect* is most often used as a verb meaning "to influence"; *effect* is most often used as a noun meaning "result."

word   Our office was greatly affected by budget cuts; we will feel the effect for months.

• Farther refers to distance; *further* refers to extent or degree.

word   If the printer is moved farther away, further adjustments are needed.

• *Personal* means "private"; *personnel* means "employees."

word   All office personnel have been instructed to eliminate all personal phone calls.

• *Principal* means "primary"; *principle* means "rule."

word   The principal reason for her dismissal was that she violated a basic principle of office conduct.

Edit the sentences to correct any errors in word usage.

12   The company cannot accept any collect calls, except for his.
13   The affect of the speech was dramatic; everyone was affected.
14   Further discussion by office personal was not appropriate.
15   Comments made during any meeting should never be personal.
16   If the meeting is held any further away, no one will attend.
17   The principle reason for the decision was to save money.
18   Office ethics is a basic principle that should be practiced.
19   He cannot except the fact that the job was delegated to Jack.
20   Any further effects on office personnel will be evaluated.

DOCUMENT PROCESSING

Letter 84
Block Style

Type this letter. Prepare an envelope, but do not append/add it to the letter.

(continued on next page)

April 24, 19--

Ms. Brenda J. Boettcher
Office for Compliance Review
State of California
3902 Bacchini Avenue
Sacramento, CA 95828

Dear Ms. Boettcher:
A table summarizing the ethnic composition of our January 19-- entering class is enclosed.
You will note that exactly half of our students are female. Also, 12 of the 28 students are in the nonwhite categories.
Please let me know if you need further information.
M. Ebert.
PS: Our detailed report, which analyzes the ethnic composition for all applicants for the July 19-- class, will be forwarded by August 1.

Memo 27

Open the file for Form 34, the memo form you created on Monday. Type this memo on the form.

MEMO

TO: All Faculty

FROM: Marsha D. Ebert, Director

DATE: April 42 19--

SUBJECT: Meeting on April 30
^Faculty

A meeting for all instructional personnel has been scheduled for 8 a.m. on April 30, 19--. We will further review the following items as they related to the new course entitled advanced radar principals, which will begin in
les

January. The minutes of our last meeting have been attached for your review.

Course
• Program description. A program description that reflects course
course   new
objectives will be developed.

(continued on next page)

UNIT TWENTY-FOUR Lesson 117   341

- Test and References. Brad Danielson and Fran Hybert will submit their recommendations at the meeting.
- Course Objectives. The committee will distribute a ~~revised~~ list on (Apr.) 26; please review this list before the meeting.

Report 76
Minutes of a Meeting

CHANDLER AIR TRAFFIC CONTROL SCHOOL
Minutes of the Faculty Meeting
April 15, 19--, 8 a.m.

ATTENDANCE — The CATCS faculty met on April 15, 19--. Faculty present were Brad Danielson, Carlos Garcia, Fran Hybert, Thomas Lee, and Judy Painter. Marsha D. Ebert, Chairperson, called the meeting to order at 8 a.m.

OLD BUSINESS — Brad Danielson and Fran Hybert are reviewing further textbooks for the Advanced Radar Principles course.

NEW BUSINESS — There was agreement that all basic radar course objectives should be achieved by all enrollees in the advanced radar course. There was agreement to accept the following principles for inclusion: aircraft emergency procedures and safety alerts.

ADJOURNMENT — The meeting was adjourned at 9:35 a.m.; the next faculty meeting will be held in two weeks.

Respectfully submitted,
(Your Name)
Administrative Assistant

word

word

Lesson 118   Wednesday: Correspondence Project (Continued)

GOALS: To type 50 wam/5'/5e; to format a multipage letter (with a table) and a flyer.

A. Type 2 times.

A. WARMUP

```
 1        Ms. Ebert was just scheduled for Flight #9867 on 4/3.    11
 2   She has been detained quite unexpectedly!  A sizable fee      22
 3   will be charged if the agency won't "forgive" the mistake.    34
     |  1  |  2  |  3  |  4  |  5  |  6  |  7  |  8  |  9  | 10  | 11  | 12
```

SKILLBUILDING

B. PACED PRACTICE

Turn to the Paced Practice routine beginning on page SB-14. Take three 2-minute timings, starting at the point where you left off the last time.

C. Take two 5-minute timings. Determine your speed and errors.

Goal: 50 wam/5'/5e

C. 5-MINUTE TIMING

```
 4        One of the biggest dilemmas for graduating students     11
 5   is how to find and keep that first job.  The first obstacle   23
 6   is often the fact that these students typically don't have    34
 7   any practical experience.  They also tend to look for a job   46
 8   by using the classified ads in the paper as a main source     58
 9   of information on job openings.  Both of these mistakes can    70
10   be serious ones in the race to find that first job.  Many     82
11   steps can be taken to overcome these obstacles.               91
12        The first step is to get practical work experience.     102
13   Most colleges offer internship programs where the students   114
14   can work on campus in an office and receive college credit   126
15   at the same time.  If you will pursue this approach, you     137
16   just might find that the second step in landing that first   149
17   job will take care of itself.  You might receive an offer    160
18   to continue working even after your internship is over, or   172
19   you might make valuable contacts that could lead you to a    184
20   different job opening that you might like even better.       195
21        You must believe that there is no problem that does     205
22   not have a solution and that you can accomplish anything      217
23   you decide to do.  Usually, the difference between those     228
24   who succeed and those who fail comes down to determination   240
25   and attitude; recognize your power and never quit.           250
     |  1  |  2  |  3  |  4  |  5  |  6  |  7  |  8  |  9  | 10  | 11  | 12
```

Type this letter for Tom Panian. Be sure to use a header for the second page.

April 25, 19--

Ms. Charlene Helbert 2307 Reeves Avenue
Ogden, Ut 84401

Thank you for your letter ~~in which you inquired~~ asking about the air traffic control program here at Chandler Air Traffic Control School. You first asked me to describe what an air traffic controller does. Air traffic controllers are responsible for the safe, methodical, and expeditious movement of air traffic. They are men and women with special skills who can handle complex and precise tasks and yet remain alert in pressure situations.

You also ~~inquired~~ asked about job opportunities. ~~Qualified~~ graduates from CATCS continue to be in high demand. Almost all ~~of~~ our graduates obtain positions with the Federal Aviation Administration (FAA), which is in the Dept. of Transportation. Most of them work at en route centers, where air traffic is controlled along established air ways in the ~~geographic area~~ location served by each center. Others work at FAA airport traffic control towers. The table below details the placement of our December 19-- graduates.

add a 10% fill

GRADUATE PLACEMENT December 19--		
Sex	**En Route Center**	**Airport Tower**
Male	8	6
Female	8	3

Our Instructors are ~~particularly~~ well qualified; and Our ~~instructionale~~ facilities are excellent, equipped with the latest in instructional media and technology. Our advanced students spend ~~some~~ much of thier time in a simulated lab setting. The instructional media are programmed so that the learner encounters very real air traffic control situations.

I have enclosed a flyer that will provide you with details about an open house we are hosting. Several of our instructors will be there. You will be

(continued on next page)

able to tour our facilities and have some hands-on experience with some of the equipment. I hope you can attend.

If you have other questions or if I can help you in any way, please ~~do~~ let me know.

Yours truly,

CHANDLER AIR TRAFFIC CONTROL SCHOOL

Thomas V. Panian
Admissions Director

Please prepare a flyer to publicize our open house.

Report 77
Flyer

Chandler Air Traffic Control School

We proudly invite you to attend our open house!

► Find out what it means to be an air traffic controller.

► Explore job opportunities.

► Use state-of-the-art equipment.

When: Saturday, May 12

Where: Chandler Air Traffic Control School
5241 Lincoln Avenue, Suite 203
San Jose, California 95121
408-555-2769

Insert image you used in letterhead

Lesson 119 Thursday: Merge Letters Project

GOALS: To improve speed and accuracy; to refine language-arts skills in spelling; to create merged letters and an itinerary.

A. Type 2 times.

A. WARMUP

```
1      Turner & Finch will charge us $10,234 to complete the    11
2  job.  Do they realize that they quoted us an initial fee of   23
3  exactly $9,876?  Kelly will call them very soon to verify.    35
   |  1  |  2  |  3  |  4  |  5  |  6  |  7  |  8  |  9  |  10  |  11  |  12
```

SKILLBUILDING

Pretest
Take a 1-minute timing. Determine your speed and errors.

B. PRETEST: CLOSE REACHES

```
4      Sadly, the same essay was used to oppose and deny the    11
5  phony felony charge.  After the weapon was located in his     23
6  pocket, the jury was left to cast the joint ballot anyway.    34
   |  1  |  2  |  3  |  4  |  5  |  6  |  7  |  8  |  9  |  10  |  11  |  12
```

C. PRACTICE: ADJACENT KEYS

```
7  po post spot pours vapor poker powder oppose weapon pockets
8  sa sash same usage essay sadly safety dosage sample sailing
9  oi oily join point voice doing choice boiled egoist loiters
```

Practice
Speed Emphasis: If you made no more than 1 error on the Pretest, type each *individual* line 2 times.
Accuracy Emphasis: If you made 2 or more errors, type each *group* of lines (as though it were a paragraph) 2 times.

D. PRACTICE: CONSECUTIVE FINGERS

```
10  ft left soft often after shift gifted crafts thrift uplifts
11  ny onyx deny nylon vinyl phony anyway skinny felony canyons
12  lo loss solo loser flood color locate floral ballot loaders
```

Posttest
Repeat the Pretest timing and compare performance.

E. POSTTEST: CLOSE REACHES

F. DIAGNOSTIC PRACTICE: ALPHABET

Turn to the Diagnostic Practice: Alphabet routine beginning on page SB-2. Type one of the Pretest/Posttest paragraphs and identify any errors made. Then type the corresponding drill lines 2 times for each letter on which you made 2 or more errors and 1 time for each letter on which you made only 1 error. Finally, repeat the same Pretest paragraph and compare your performance.

LANGUAGE ARTS

G. Type this list of frequently misspelled words, paying special attention to any spelling problems in each word.

G. SPELLING

```
13  practice continue regular entitled course resolution assist
14  weeks preparation purposes referred communication potential
15  environmental specifications original contractor associated
16  principal systems client excellent estimated administration
17  responsibility mentioned utilized materials criteria campus
```

(continued on next page)

18 It is the responsability of the administration to assist.
19 The principle client prepared the excellent specifications.
20 He mentioned that the critiria for the decision were clear.
21 The contractor associated with the project referred them.
22 He estamated that the potential for resolution was great.
23 I was told that weeks of reguler practice were required.

DOCUMENT PROCESSING

Letters 86, 87, 88, 89
Block Style

Please send this letter from me to the following four members of our Advisory Board:

Record 1
Naomi Siedler
Assistant Secretary
U.S. Department of Transportation
6025 Lee Highway
Arlington, VA 22205
Naomi
ten

Record 2
Margaret M. O'Connor
Dean of Students
Arizona Aviation Center
10026 Black Canyon Drive
Phoenix, AZ 85051
Ms. O'Connor
five

Record 3
Enrique J. Hernandez
Air Traffic Controller
South California Center
2608 43d Street
Los Angeles, CA 90008
Mr. Hernandez
two

Record 4
Thomas A. Johnson
Vice President for Operations
California Coastal Airlines
22 Oakmont Circle
Cupertino, CA 95014
Tom
eight

Date

Name
Title
Company
Address
City, State, ZIP

Dear _____ :

¶On behalf of our entire administration, I want to take this opportunity to thank you for your service as a regular member of our Advisory Board for the past ____ years. The principal reason our campus continues to receive funding is the specifications for equipment that are mentioned by our Advisory Board. Your input is excellent! Please continue to assist us.

(continued on next page)

¶I look forward to meeting with you in a few weeks at the symposium in Nevada on May 18. Please look over the copy of my enclosed itinerary so that we can coordinate our schedules. I'll call soon to confirm a time.

Report 78
Itinerary

AIR TRAFFIC CONTROLLERS' SYMPOSIUM
Itinerary for Marsha D. Ebert
May 18-19, 19—

Monday, May 18

San Jose/Las Vegas .... Southwest 2677
    Depart 7:10 a.m.; arrive 8:50 a.m.
    Seat 7E; nonstop; breakfast

Las Vegas/Reno .... Nevada-Utah 1824
    Depart 7:30 p.m.; arrive 9:35 p.m.
    Seat 5A; one stop

Tuesday, May 19

Reno/San Jose .... Cal Coastal 1372
    Depart 2:00 p.m.; arrive 2:50 p.m.
    Seat 4C; nonstop

Lesson 120   Friday: Miscellaneous Projects

GOALS: To type 50 wam/5'/5e; to format an agenda and a news release.

A. Type 2 times.

A. WARMUP

```
1      Order extra color cartridges very soon!  G & K Supply    11
2  just announced a 15% discount on orders for the following    23
3  cartridges:  QB728 and ZM436* (*for the ink-jet printers).   34
   |  1  |  2  |  3  |  4  |  5  |  6  |  7  |  8  |  9  |  10  |  11  |  12
```

SKILLBUILDING

B. Take a 1-minute timing on the first paragraph to establish your base speed. Then take four 1-minute timings on the remaining paragraphs. As soon as you equal or exceed your base speed on one paragraph, advance to the next, more difficult paragraph.

B. SUSTAINED PRACTICE: PUNCTUATION

```
4      Have you ever noticed that a good laugh every now and    11
5  then really makes you feel better?  Research has shown that  23
6  laughter can have a very healing effect on our bodies.  It   35
7  is an excellent way to relieve tension and stress all over.  47

8      When you laugh, your heart beats faster, you breathe     11
9  deeper, and you exercise your lungs.  When you laugh, your   23
10 body produces endorphins--a natural painkiller that gives    34
11 you a sense of euphoria that is very powerful and pleasant.  46
   |  1  |  2  |  3  |  4  |  5  |  6  |  7  |  8  |  9  |  10  |  11  |  12
```

12	Someone said, "Laugh in the face of adversity." As it	11
13	happens, this is first-rate advice. It's a great way to	23
14	cope with life's trials and tribulations; it's also a good	34
15	way to raise other people's spirits and relieve tension.	46

16	Finding "humor" in any situation takes practice--try	11
17	to make it a full-time habit. We're all looking for ways	22
18	to relieve stress. Any exercise--jogging, tennis, biking,	34
19	swimming, or golfing--is a proven remedy for "the blues."	46

| 1 | 2 | 3 | 4 | 5 | 6 | 7 | 8 | 9 | 10 | 11 | 12 |

C. Take two 5-minute timings. Determine your speed and errors.

Goal: 50 wam/5'/5e

C. 5-MINUTE TIMING

20	Interruptions while you are working either at school	11
21	or on the job can be a major source of stress. Therefore,	23
22	it is extremely important that you learn how to cope with	34
23	and adjust to these interruptions. Something as simple as	46
24	an inexpensive answering machine or as automated as voice	58
25	mail can make a dramatic impact on the number of times you	69
26	must stop your work or break a train of thought.	79

27	Most phone calls do not require a response at all; you	90
28	will find that many of your callers just need to leave a	102
29	short message and don't really need to talk to anyone at	113
30	all. However, you must also understand that there will be	125
31	times when a caller needs and expects to talk to someone.	137

32	The nature of your job will help you recognize if and	148
33	when it is appropriate to activate voice mail or switch on	159
34	the answering machine. If your job is to provide service	171
35	to customers or clients, you should probably not rely much	183
36	on voice mail. There is nothing more annoying than to be	194
37	forced to listen to a series of recorded messages only to	206
38	discover that you cannot get through to an individual you	218
39	truly need to reach. Let your callers know the best time	229
40	to call. They will appreciate being able to contact you,	241
41	and you will be able to increase productivity.	250

| 1 | 2 | 3 | 4 | 5 | 6 | 7 | 8 | 9 | 10 | 11 | 12 |

DOCUMENT PROCESSING

Report 79
Agenda

Form 36
Progress Check
Press Release

Use the first press
release template in your
software.

CATCS FACULTY
Meeting Agenda
April 30, 19—, 8 a.m.

1. Call to order
2. Approval of minutes of April 15 meeting
3. Progress report on recruitment efforts (Carlos Garcia and Judy Painter)
4. Unfinished business: Course description; texts and references; course objectives
5. New business: Open house to be held on Saturday, May 12; press release for open house
6. Announcements
7. Program: "Technological Advances in Radar Tracking Systems"
8. Adjournment

From Marsha D. Ebert
Chandler Air Traffic Control School
5214 Lincoln Avenue; Suite 203
San Jose, CA 95121
Immediate
For Release ~~Tuesday, May 1, 19—~~

CATCS SPONSORS OPEN HOUSE

~~San Jose, CA, Apr. 23—~~The Chandler Air Traffic Control School will host an open house on Saturday, May 12, from 10 a.m. to 3 p.m. The public is invited to attend. A complimentary buffet luncheon will be served from 12 to 1 p.m.

Several instructors will be giving a series of presentations on the course offerings and certification requirements of the various programs. The public is also ~~will be~~ invited to participate in a series of hands-on demonstrations ~~exercises~~ using state-of-the-art equipment.

Several tours of the facilities will be conducted throughout the day beginning at 10 a.m., 11 a.m., and 1 p.m. The tours will last approximately one ~~an~~ hour. Registration for summer classes will be available for any interested students.

For more information, please call 408-555-2769. Chandler Air Traffic Control School is located at 5241 Lincoln Avenue, Suite 203, in San Jose.

Progress Test on Part 6

Ask your instructor for
the General Information
Test on Part 6.

Test 6-A
5-Minute Timing

1   Have you ever tried to accomplish a task only to find   11
2   that you just couldn't concentrate? Many factors in your   23
3   work environment directly affect your body and your ability   35
4   to focus on your tasks. When you are working, it is best   46
5   if distractions are minimal. When you are able to focus   58
6   your attention and fully concentrate on your job duties,   69
7   you are operating at maximum efficiency.   77

8   Experts agree that the largest amount of information   88
9   you receive from your environment is gathered through your   100
10 eyes. Therefore, proper lighting is high on the priority   111
11 list of a good work environment. Inadequate lighting makes   123
12 it difficult for your eyes to focus, and it takes more time   135
13 for the appropriate facts to be deciphered by your brain.   147
14 This extra effort can cause fatigue and eyestrain. As the   159
15 day gets later, it becomes more difficult to perform.   170

16 Room lighting should also not be so bright that you   180
17 must squint your eyes to see. The total effects of always   192
18 shifting your body, neck, and head to avoid bright lights   204
19 or reflections can cause enough stress or strain to produce   216
20 or aggravate other symptoms such as neck pain, back pain,   227
21 muscle tension, and fatigue. Manage your tasks with zest   239
22 each and every day and invest in a good lighting system.   250

| 1 | 2 | 3 | 4 | 5 | 6 | 7 | 8 | 9 | 10 | 11 | 12

36

Test 6-B
Report 80
Bound Report
Page 36

that the operation be closed if, in their judgment, the hazards could result in
severe injury or death to employees.

(continued on next page)

AUTOMOTIVE

All ~~workers~~ _employees_ working with in the scope of their duties are coverde by the company's professional liability self-insured funds.

Company-Owned Vehicles. The company ~~holds~~ _carries_ bodily injury and properaty insurance damage to cover the companys legal responsibility and liaility for the operation of motor ~~cars~~ _vehicles_. The company and it's authorized ~~employees~~ _drivers_ are covered for claims of negligence that ~~could~~ result in the damage too property of others, or bodily injury to 3rd parties within the limits of the michigan no-Fault Act.

The ~~firm~~ _Company_ does not carry collision insurance to cover damage to company-owned ~~cars~~ _vehicles_. Damage to vehicles company owned, rented, or leased by a division is the responsbility of the division.

Privately Owned Vehicles. The ~~firm~~ _Company_ does carry property dmage or personal liability insurance for the protection of ~~all~~ _the_ private owners of ~~autos~~ _vehicles_. Those using privately owned vehicles on company's business should have insureance in an amount that will cover there legal responsibility.

Test 6-C
Table 58
Boxed Table

Use a 10% fill, and automatically adjust the column widths.

INSURANCE BENEFITS		
Category	Salaried Employees	Hourly Employees
Medical Plans	159	230
Dental Plans	105	151
Vision Plans	105	151
Life Insurance	159	230

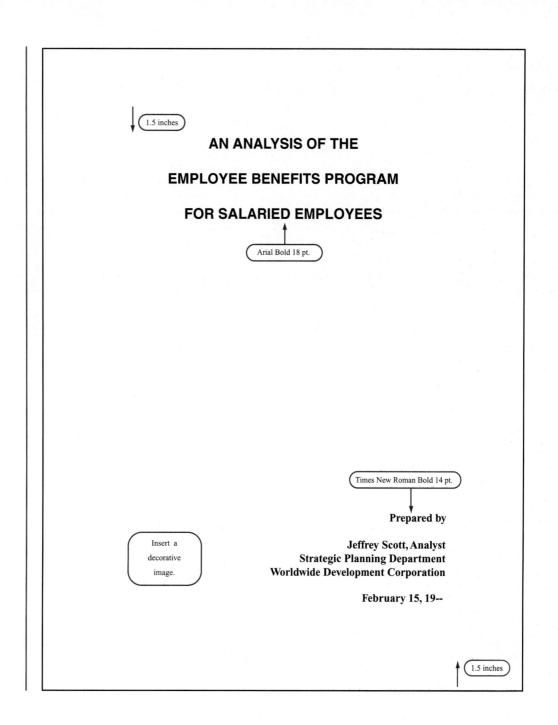

1.5 inches

AN ANALYSIS OF THE

EMPLOYEE BENEFITS PROGRAM

FOR SALARIED EMPLOYEES

Arial Bold 18 pt.

Times New Roman Bold 14 pt.

Prepared by

Jeffrey Scott, Analyst
Strategic Planning Department
Worldwide Development Corporation

February 15, 19--

Insert a decorative image.

1.5 inches

Skillbuilding

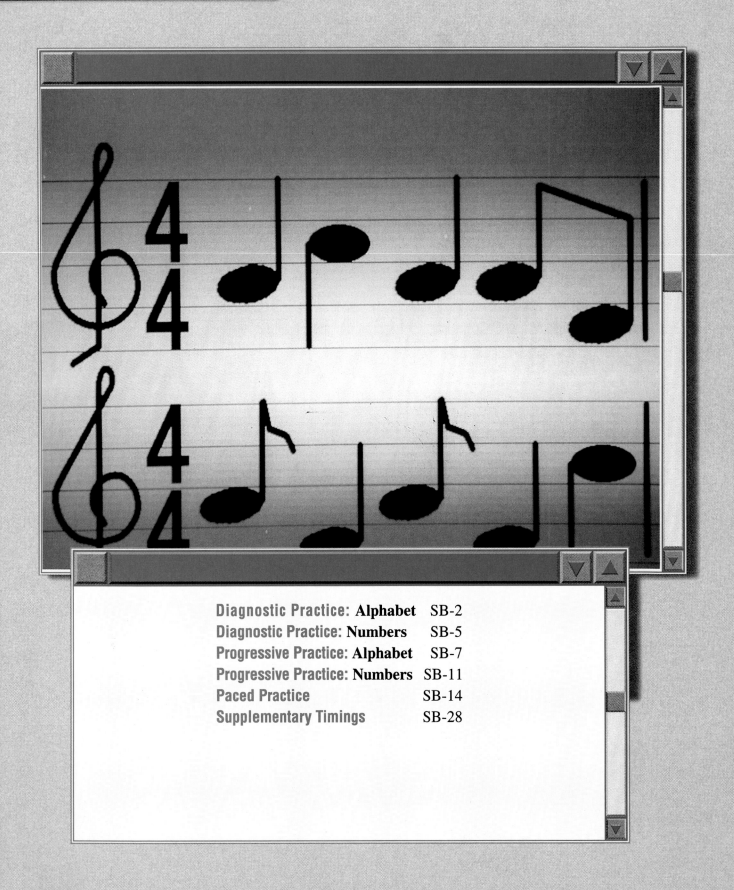

Diagnostic Practice: Alphabet

The Diagnostic Practice: Alphabet program is designed to diagnose and then correct your keystroking errors. You may use this program at any time throughout the course after completing Lesson 9.

Directions

1. Type one of the 3 Pretest/Posttest paragraphs once, pushing *moderately* for speed. Identify your errors.
2. Note your results—the number of errors you made on each key and your total number of errors. For example, if you typed *rhe* for *the,* that would count as 1 error on the letter *t.*
3. For any letter on which you made 2 or more errors, select the corresponding drill lines and type them twice. If you made only 1 error, type the drill once.
4. If you made no errors on the Pretest/Posttest paragraph, type one 3-line set of the Troublesome Pairs on page SB-4.
5. Finally, retype the same Pretest/Posttest, and compare your performance with your Pretest.

PRETEST/POSTTEST

Paragraph 1

Sylvia and Julia made six quilts that were sold at the bazaar. Several kinds of new craft projects were judged to be quite complex and were given five kinds of prizes. Most sizable quarterly taxes were backed by both boys and girls.

Paragraph 2

Jacob and Zeke Koufax quietly enjoyed jazz music on my new jukebox. My six or seven pieces of exquisite equipment helped both create lovely music by Richard Wagner; I picked five very quaint waltzes from Gregg Ward's jazz recordings.

Paragraph 3

A quiet girl seized the black vase and gave it to five judges who examined it carefully. Two quickly gave it high marks. Forty people in the adjoining zone were quite vexed at some lazy judges who were lax about keeping on schedule.

PRACTICE: INDIVIDUAL REACHES

Note that each letter drill provides practice in typing that letter combination with as many other letters as possible. For example, in the A drill, the first word (Isaac) practices *aa,* the second word (badge) practices *ba,* the third word (carry) practices *ca,* and so on, through *za* in Zaire.

```
aa Isaac badge carry dared eager faced gains habit dials AA
aa jaunt kayak label mamma Nancy oasis paint Qatar rapid AA
aa safer taken guard vague waves exact yacht Zaire Aaron AA

bb about ebbed ebony rugby fiber elbow amber unbar oboes BB
bb arbor cubic oxbow maybe abate abbot debit libel album BB
bb embed obeys urban tubes Sybil above lobby webby bribe BB

cc acted occur recap icing ulcer emcee uncle ocean force CC
cc scale itchy bucks excel Joyce acute yucca decal micro CC
cc mulch McCoy incur octet birch scrub latch couch cycle CC
```

```
dd admit daddy edict Magda ideal older index oddly order DD
dd outdo udder crowd Floyd adapt added Edith Idaho folds DD
dd under modem sword misdo fudge rowdy Lydia adept buddy DD

ee aegis beach cents dense eerie fence germs hence piece EE
ee jewel keyed leads media nerve poems penny reach seize EE
ee teach guest verse Wendy Xerox years zesty aerie begin EE

ff after defer offer jiffy gulfs infer often dwarf cuffs FF
ff awful afoul refer affix edify Wolfe infra aloof scarf FF
ff bluff afoot defer daffy fifty sulfa softy surfs stuff FF

gg again edges egged soggy igloo Elgin angel ogled Marge GG
gg outgo auger pygmy agape Edgar Egypt buggy light bulge GG
gg singe doggy organ bugle agree hedge began baggy Niger GG

hh ahead abhor chili Nehru ghost Elihu khaki Lhasa unhat HH
hh aloha phony myrrh shale Ethan while yahoo choir jihad HH
hh ghoul Khmer Delhi hoard photo rhino shake think while HH

ii aired bides cider dices eight fifth vigil highs radii II
ii jiffy kinds lives mired niece oiled piped rigid siren II
ii tired build visit wider exist yield aimed binds cigar II

jj major eject fjord Ouija enjoy Cajun Fijis Benjy bijou JJ
jj banjo jabot jacks jaded jails Japan jaunt jazzy jeans JJ
jj jeeps jeers jelly jerks jibed jiffy jilts joint joker JJ

kk Akron locks vodka peeks mikes sulky links okras larks KK
kk skins Yukon hawks tykes makes socks seeks hiker sulks KK
kk tanks Tokyo jerky pesky nukes gawks maker ducks cheek KK

ll alarm blame clank idled elope flame glows Chloe Iliad LL
ll ankle Lloyd inlet olive plane burly sleet atlas Tulsa LL
ll yowls axles nylon alone blunt claim idler elite flute LL

mm among adman demit pigmy times calms comma unman omits MM
mm armor smell umber axmen lymph gizmo amass admit demon MM
mm dogma imply films mommy omits armed smear bumpy adman MM

nn ankle Abner envoy gnome Johns input knife kilns hymns NN
nn Donna onion apnea angle snore undid owned cynic angle NN
nn entry gnash inset knoll nanny onset barns sneer unfit NN

oo aorta bolts coats dolls peony fouls goofs hoped iotas OO
oo jolts kooky loins moral noise poled Roger soaks total OO
oo quote voter would Saxon yo-yo zones bombs colts doles OO

pp apple epoch flips alpha ample input droop puppy sharp PP
pp spunk soups expel typed April Epsom slips helps empty PP
pp unpin optic peppy corps spite upset types apply creep PP
```

```
qq Iraqi equal pique roque squad tuque aquae equip toque QQ
qq squab squat squid squaw quail qualm quart queen quell QQ
qq query quest quick quiet quilt quirk quota quote quoth QQ

rr array bring crave drive erode freak grain three irate RR
rr kraft honor orate Barry tramp urges liver wrote lyric RR
rr rears armor broth crown drawl erect freer grade throw RR

ss ashen bombs specs binds bares leafs bangs sighs issue SS
ss necks mills teams turns solos stops stirs dress diets SS
ss usury Slavs stows abyss asked stabs cords mares beefs SS

tt attic debts pacts width Ethel often eight itchy alter TT
tt until motto optic earth stops petty couth newts extra TT
tt myths Aztec atone doubt facts veldt ether sight Italy TT

uu audio bumps cured dumps deuce fuels gulps huffy opium UU
uu junta kudos lulls mumps nudge outdo purer ruler super UU
uu tulip revue exult yucca azure auger burns curve duels UU

vv avows event ivory elves envoy overt larva mauve savvy VV
vv avant every rivet Elvis anvil coves curvy divvy avert VV
vv evict given valve ovens serve paves evade wives hover VV

ww awash bwana dwarf brews Gwenn schwa kiwis Elwin unwed WW
ww owner Irwin sweet twins byway awake dwell pewee tower WW
ww Erwin swims twirl awful dwelt Dewey owlet swamp twine WW

xx axiom exile fixed Bronx toxin Sioux Exxon pyxie axman XX
xx exert fixes foxes oxbow beaux calyx maxim exact sixth XX
xx proxy taxes excel mixed boxer axing Texas sixty epoxy XX

yy maybe bylaw cynic dying eying unify gypsy hypos Benjy YY
yy Tokyo hilly rummy Ronny loyal pygmy diary Syria types YY
yy buyer vying Wyatt epoxy crazy kayak ready cycle bawdy YY

zz azure Czech adzes bezel dizzy Franz froze Liszt ritzy ZZ
zz abuzz tizzy hazed czars maize Ginza oozes blitz fuzzy ZZ
zz jazzy mazes mezzo sized woozy Hertz fizzy Hazel Gomez ZZ
```

**PRACTICE:
TROUBLESOME PAIRS**

```
B/V Beverly believes Bob behaved very bravely in Beaverton.
F/G Griffin goofed in figuring their gifted golfer's score.
H/J Joseph joshed with Judith when John jogged to Johnetta.

M/N Many women managed to move among the mounds of masonry.
O/P A pollster polled a population in Phoenix by telephone.
Q/A Quincy acquired one quality quartz ring at the banquet.

U/Y Buy your supply of gifts during your busy July journey.
X/C The exemptions exceed the expert's wildest expectation.
Z/A Liza gazed as four lazy zebras zigzagged near a gazebo.
```

Diagnostic Practice: Numbers

The Diagnostic Practice: Numbers program is designed to diagnose and then correct your keystroking errors. You may use this program at any time throughout the course after completing Lesson 14.

Directions

1. Type one of the 3 Pretest/Posttest paragraphs once, pushing *moderately* for speed. Identify your errors.
2. Note your results—the number of errors you made on each key and your total number of errors. For example, if you typed *24* for *25* that would count as 1 error on the number *5*.
3. For any number on which you made 2 or more errors, select the corresponding drill lines and type them twice. If you made only 1 error, type the drill once.
4. If you made no errors on the Pretest/Posttest paragraph, type one set of the drills that contain all numbers on page SB-6.
5. Finally, retype the same Pretest/Posttest, and compare your performance with your Pretest.

Paragraph 1

The statement dated May 24, 1995, listed 56 clamps, 14 batteries, 160 hammers, 358 screwdrivers, 1,208 pliers, and 2,475 files. The invoice numbered 379 showed 387 hoes, 406 rakes, 92 lawn mowers, 63 tillers, and 807 more lawn items.

Paragraph 2

My inventory records dated May 31, 1994, revealed that we had 458 pints, 2,069 quarts, and 8,774 gallons of paint. We had 2,053 brushes, 568 scrapers, 12,063 wallpaper rolls, 897 knives, 5,692 mixers, 480 ladders, and 371 step stools.

Paragraph 3

Almost 270 hot meals were delivered to the 15 shut-ins in April, 260 in May, and 280 in June. Several workers had volunteered 7,534 hours in 1996, 6,348 hours in 1995, 5,438 in 1994, and 6,277 in 1993. About 80 people were involved.

PRACTICE: INDIVIDUAL REACHES

1 aq aq1 aq1qa 111 ants 101 aunts 131 apples 171 animals a1
They got 11 answers correct for the 11 questions in BE 121.
Those 11 adults loaded the 711 animals between 1 and 2 p.m.
All 111 agreed that 21 of those 31 are worthy of the honor.

2 sw sw2 sw2ws 222 sets 242 steps 226 salads 252 saddles s2
The 272 summer tourists saw the 22 soldiers and 32 sailors.
Your September 2 date was all right for 292 of 322 persons.
The 22 surgeons said 221 of those 225 operations went well.

3 de de3 de3ed 333 dots 303 drops 313 demons 393 dollars d3
Bus 333 departed at 3 p.m. with the 43 dentists and 5 boys.
She left 33 dolls and 73 decoys at 353 West Addison Street.
The 13 doctors helped some of the 33 druggists in Room 336.

4 fr fr4 fr4rf 444 fans 844 farms 444 fishes 644 fiddles f4
My 44 friends bought 84 farms and sold over 144 franchises.
She sold 44 fish and 440 beef dinners for $9.40 per dinner.
The '54 Ford had only 40,434 fairly smooth miles by July 4.

5 fr fr5 fr5rf 555 furs 655 foxes 555 flares 455 fingers f5
They now own 155 restaurants, 45 food stores, and 55 farms.
They ordered 45, 55, 65, and 75 yards of that new material.
Flight 855 flew over Farmington at 5:50 p.m. on December 5.

6 jy jy6 jy6yj 666 jets 266 jeeps 666 jewels 866 jaguars j6
Purchase orders numbered 6667 and 6668 were sent yesterday.
Those 66 jazz players played for 46 juveniles in Room 6966.
The 6 judges reviewed the 66 journals on November 16 or 26.

7 ju ju7 ju7uj 777 jays 377 jokes 777 joists 577 juniors j7
The 17 jets carried 977 jocular passengers above 77 cities.
Those 277 jumping beans went to 77 junior scouts on May 17.
The 7 jockeys rode 77 jumpy horses between March 17 and 27.

8 ki ki8 ki8ik 888 keys 488 kites 888 knives 788 kittens k8
My 8 kennels housed 83 dogs, 28 kids, and 88 other animals.
The 18 kind ladies tied 88 knots in the 880 pieces of rope.
The 8 men saw 88 kelp bass, 38 kingfish, and 98 king crabs.

9 lo lo9 lo9ol 999 lads 599 larks 999 ladies 699 leaders 19
All 999 leaves fell from the 9 large oaks at 389 Largemont.
The 99 linemen put 399 large rolls of tape on for 19 games.
Those 99 lawyers put 899 legal-size sheets in the 19 limos.

0 ;p ;p0 ;p0p; 100 pens 900 pages 200 pandas 800 pencils ;0
There were 1,000 people who lived in the 300 private homes.
The 10 party stores are open from 1:00 p.m. until 9:00 p.m.
They edited 500 pages in 1 book and 1,000 pages in 2 books.

All numbers   ala s2s d3d f4f f5f j6j j7j k8k 191 ;0; Add 6 and 8 and 29.
That 349-page script called for 10 actors and 18 actresses.
The check for $50 was sent to 705 Garfield Street, not 507.
The 14 researchers asked the 469 Californians 23 questions.

All numbers   ala s2s d3d f4f f5f j6j j7j k8k 191 ;0; Add 3 and 4 and 70.
They built 1,200 houses on the 345-acre site by the canyon.
Her research showed that gold was at 397 in September 1994.
For $868 extra, they bought 15 new books and 62 used books.

All numbers   ala s2s d3d f4f f5f j6j j7j k8k 191 ;0; Add 5 and 7 and 68.
A bank auditor arrived on May 26, 1994, and left on May 30.
The 4 owners open the stores from 9:30 a.m. until 6:00 p.m.
After 1,374 miles on the bus, she must then drive 185 more.

Progressive Practice: Alphabet

This skillbuilding routine contains a series of 30-second timings that range from 16 wam to 104 wam. The first time you use these timings, take a 1-minute timing on the Entry Timing paragraph. Note your speed.

Select a passage that is 2 words a minute higher than your current speed.

Then take six 30-second timings on the passage.

Your goal each time is to complete the passage within 30 seconds with no errors. When you have achieved your goal, move on to the next passage and repeat the procedure.

Entry Timing

Bev was very lucky when she found extra quality in the	11
home she was buying. She quietly told the builder that she	23
was extremely satisfied with the work done on her new home.	35
The builder said she can move into her new house next week.	47

| 1 | 2 | 3 | 4 | 5 | 6 | 7 | 8 | 9 | 10 | 11 | 12 |

16 wam The author is the creator of a document.

18 wam Open means to access a previously saved file.

20 wam A byte represents one character to every computer.

22 wam A mouse may be used when running Windows on a computer.

24 wam Soft copy is text that is displayed on your computer screen.

26 wam Memory is the part of the word processor that stores information.

28 wam A menu is a list of choices to direct the operator through a function.

30 wam A sheet feeder is a device that will insert sheets of paper into a printer.

32 wam An icon is a small picture that illustrates a function or an object in software.

34 wam A window is a rectangular area with borders that displays the contents of open files.

36 wam To execute means to perform an action specified by an operator or by the computer program.

38 wam Output is the result of a word processing operation. It is in either printed or magnetic form.

40 wam Format refers to the physical features which affect the appearance and arrangement of your document.

42 wam   A font is a style of type of one size or kind which includes all letters, numbers, and punctuation marks.

44 wam   Ergonomics is the science of adapting working conditions or equipment to meet the physical needs of employees.

46 wam   Home position is the starting position of a document; it is typically the upper left corner of the display monitor.

48 wam   The mouse may be used to change the size of a window and to move a window to a different location on the display screen.

50 wam   An optical scanner is a device that can read text and enter it into a word processor without the need to type the data again.

52 wam   Hardware refers to the physical equipment used, such as the central processing unit, display screen, keyboard, printer, or drives.

54 wam   A peripheral device is any piece of equipment that will extend the capabilities of a computer system but is not required for operation.

56 wam   A split screen displays two or more different images at the same time; it can, for example, display two different pages of a legal document.

58 wam   When using Windows, it's possible to place several programs on a screen and to change the size of a window or to change its position on a screen.

60 wam   With the click of a mouse, one can use a Button Bar or a toolbar for fast access to features that are frequently applied when using a Windows program.

62 wam   An active window can be reduced to an icon when you use Windows, enabling you to double-click another icon to open a new window for formatting and editing.

64 wam   Turnaround time is the length of time needed for a document to be keyboarded, edited, proofread, corrected if required, printed, and returned to the originator.

66 wam   A local area network is a system that uses cable or another means to allow high-speed communication among many kinds of electronic equipment within particular areas.

68 wam   To search and replace means to direct the word processor to locate a character, word, or group of words wherever it occurs in the document and replace it with newer text.

70 wam   Indexing is the ability of a word processor to accumulate a list of words that appear in a document, including page numbers, and then print a revised list in alphabetic order.

72 wam   When a program needs information from you, a dialog box will appear on the desktop. Once the dialog box appears, you must identify the option you want and then choose that option.

74 wam   A facsimile is an exact copy of a document, and it is also a process by which images, such as typed letters, graphs, and signatures, are scanned, transmitted, and then printed on paper.

76 wam   Compatibility refers to the ability of a computer to share information with another computer or to communicate with some other machine. It can be accomplished by using hardware or software.

78 wam   Some operators like to personalize their desktops when they use Windows by making various changes. For example, they can change the screen colors and the pointer so that they will have more fun.

80 wam   Wraparound is the ability of a word processor to move words from one line to another line and from one page to the next page as a result of inserting and deleting text or changing the size of margins.

82 wam   It is possible when using Windows to compare the contents of different directories on the screen at the very same time. You can then choose to copy or move a particular file from one directory to another.

84 wam   List processing is an ability of a word processor to keep lists of data that can be updated and sorted in alphabetic or numeric order. A list can also be added to any document that is stored in one's computer.

86 wam   A computer is a wondrous device which accepts data that are input and then processes the data and produces output. The computer performs its work by using one or more stored programs which provide the instructions.

88 wam   The configuration is the components that make up your word processing system. Most systems include a keyboard that is used for entering data, a central processing unit, at least one disk drive, a monitor, and a printer.

90 wam   Help for Windows can be used whenever you see a Help button in a dialog box or on a menu bar. Once you finish reading about a topic that you have selected, you may see a list of some related topics from which you can choose.

92 wam   When you want to look at the contents of two windows when using Windows, you will want to reduce the window size. Do this by pointing to a border or a corner of a window and dragging it until the window is the size that you want.

94 wam   Scrolling means to display a large amount of text by rolling it horizontally or vertically past the display screen. As the text disappears from the top section of the monitor, new text will appear at the bottom section of the monitor.

96 wam   The Windows Print Manager is used to install and configure printers, join network printers, and monitor the printing of documents. Windows requires that a default printer be identified, but you can change the designation of it at any time.

98 wam   A stop code is a command that makes a printer halt while it is printing to permit an operator to insert text, change the font style, or change the kind of paper in the printer. To resume printing, the operator must use a special key or command.

100 wam   A computerized message system is a class of electronic mail that enables any operator to key a message on any computer terminal and have the message stored for later retrieval by the recipient, who can then display the message on his or her terminal.

102 wam   Many different graphics software programs have been brought on the market in recent years. These programs can be very powerful in helping with a business presentation. If there is a need to share data, using one of these programs might be quite helpful.

104 wam   Voice mail has become an essential service that many people in the business world use. This enables anyone who places a call to your phone to leave a message if you cannot answer it at that time. This special feature helps many workers to be more productive.

Progressive Practice: Numbers

This skillbuilding routine contains a series of 30-second timings that range from 16 wam to 80 wam. The first time you use these timings, take a 1-minute timing on the Entry Timing paragraph. Note your speed.

Select a passage that is 4 to 6 words a minute *lower* than your current alphabetic speed. (The reason for selecting a lower speed goal is that sentences with numbers are more difficult to type.) Take six 30-second timings on the passage.

Your goal each time is to complete the passage within 30 seconds with no errors. When you have achieved your goal, move on to the next passage and repeat the procedure.

Entry Timing

Their bags were filled with 10 sets of jars, 23 cookie   11
cutters, 4 baking pans, 6 coffee mugs, 25 plates, 9 dessert   23
plates, 7 soup bowls, 125 recipe cards, and 8 recipe boxes.   35
They delivered these 217 items to 20487 Mountain Boulevard.   47

| 1 | 2 | 3 | 4 | 5 | 6 | 7 | 8 | 9 | 10 | 11 | 12

16 wam   There were now 21 children in Room 2110.

18 wam   Fewer than 12 of the 121 boxes arrived today.

20 wam   Maybe 12 of the 21 applicants met all 15 criteria.

22 wam   There were 34 letters addressed to 434 West Cranbrooke.

24 wam   Jane reported that there were 434 freshmen and 43 transfers.

26 wam   The principal assigned 3 of those 4 students to Room 343 at noon.

28 wam   Only 1 or 2 of the 34 latest invoices were more than 1 page in length.

30 wam   They met 11 of the 12 players who received awards from 3 of the 4 trainers.

32 wam   Those 5 vans carried 46 passengers on the first trip and 65 on the next 3 trips.

34 wam   We first saw 3 and then 4 beautiful eagles on Route 65 at 5 a.m. on Tuesday, June 12.

36 wam   The 16 companies produced 51 of the 62 records that received awards for 3 of 4 categories.

38 wam   The 12 trucks hauled the 87 cows and 65 horses to the farm, which was about 21 miles northeast.

40 wam She moved from 87 Bayview Drive to 657 Cole Street and then 3 blocks south to 412 Gulbranson Avenue.

42 wam My 7 or 8 buyers ordered 7 dozen in sizes 5 and 6 after the 14 to 32 percent discounts had been bestowed.

44 wam There were 34 men and 121 women waiting in line at the gates for the 65 to 87 tickets to the Cape Cod concert.

46 wam Steve had listed 5 or 6 items on Purchase Order 241 when he saw that Purchase Requisition 87 contained 3 or 4 more.

48 wam Your items numbered 278 will sell for about 90 percent of the value of the 16 items that have code numbers shown as 435.

50 wam The managers stated that 98 of those 750 randomly selected new valves had about 264 defects, far exceeding the usual 31 norm.

52 wam Half of the 625 volunteers received over 90 percent of the charity pledges. Approximately 83 of the 147 agencies will have funds.

54 wam Merico hired 94 part-time workers to help the 378 full-time employees during the 62-day period when sales go up by 150 percent or more.

56 wam Kaye only hit 1 for 4 in the first 29 games after an 8-game streak in which she batted 3 for 4. She then hit at a .570 average for 6 games.

58 wam The mail carrier delivered 98 letters during the week to 734 Oak Street and also took 52 letters to 610 Faulkner Road as he returned on Route 58.

60 wam Pat said that about 1 in 5 of the 379 swimmers had a chance of being among the top 20. The best 6 of those 48 divers will receive the 16 best awards.

62 wam It rained from 3 to 6 inches, and 18 of those 20 farmers were fearful that 4 to 7 inches more would flood about 95 acres along 3 miles of the new Route 78.

64 wam   Those 7 sacks weighed 48 pounds, more than the 30 pounds that I had thought. All 24 believe the 92-pound bag is at least 15 or 16 pounds above its true weight.

66 wam   They bought 7 of the 8 options for 54 of the 63 vehicles last month. They now own over 120 dump trucks for use in 9 of the 15 new regions in the big 20-county area.

68 wam   Andy was 8 or 9 years old when they moved to 632 Glendale Street away from the 1700 block of Horseshoe Lane, which is about 45 miles directly west of Boca Raton, FL 33434.

70 wam   Doug had read 575 pages in the 760-page book by March 30; Darlene had read only 468 pages. Darlene has read 29 of those optional books since October 19, and Doug has read 18.

72 wam   That school district has 985 elementary students, 507 middle school students, and 463 high school students; the total of 1,955 is 54, or 2.84 percent, over last year's grand total.

74 wam   Attendance at last year's meeting was 10,835. The goal for this year is to have 11,764 people. This will enable us to plan for an increase of 929 participants, a rise of 8.57 percent.

76 wam   John's firm has 158 stores, located in 109 cities in the West. The company employs 3,540 males and 2,624 females, a total of 6,164 employees. About 4,750 of those employees work part-time.

78 wam   Memberships were as follows: 98 members in the Drama Guild, 90 members in Zeta Tau, 82 members in Theta Phi, 75 in the Bowling Club, and 136 in the Ski Club. This meant that 481 joined a group.

80 wam   The association had 684 members from the South, 830 members from the North, 1,023 members from the East, and 751 from the West. The total membership was 3,288; these numbers increased by 9.8 percent.

Paced Practice

The Paced Practice skillbuilding routine builds speed and accuracy in short, easy steps, using individualized goals and immediate feedback. You may use this program at any time after completing Lesson 9.

This section contains a series of 2-minute timings for speeds ranging from 16 wam to 96 wam. The first time you use these timings, take the 1-minute Entry Timing.

Select a passage that is 2 wam higher than your current typing speed. Then use this two-stage practice pattern to achieve each speed goal—first concentrate on speed, and then work on accuracy.

Speed Goal. Take three 2-minute timings in total. Your goal each time is to complete the passage in 2 minutes without regard to errors.

When you have achieved your speed goal, work on accuracy.

Accuracy Goal. To type accurately, you need to slow down—just a bit. Therefore, to reach your accuracy goal, drop back 2 wam to the previous passage. Take consecutive timings on this passage until you can complete it in 2 minutes with no more than 2 errors.

For example, if you achieved a speed goal of 54 wam, you should then work on an accuracy goal of 52 wam. When you have achieved 52 wam for accuracy, you would then move up 4 wam (for example, to the 56-wam passage) and work for speed again.

Entry Timing

The judge quietly spoke to the attorneys before asking   11
them to begin. The defendant was in the courtroom, and the   23
court reporter was already there to record the proceedings.   35
The jury was anxious to hear about any evidence discovered.   47

| 1 | 2 | 3 | 4 | 5 | 6 | 7 | 8 | 9 | 10 | 11 | 12

16 wam

We often do not think about the amount of time and
effort spent doing a task. If we did, we would realize
that many of us work hard even while we are playing.

18 wam

For example, people sweat, strain, and even suffer
from discomfort when playing sports. People seem to do
this for fun. If someone made them do it, they might not
be so willing.

20 wam

Spending time on a job is work. For many people, work
is something that they do to stay alive. Today, work means
more than merely staying alive. People expect different
rewards from their careers.

22 wam   Work can be interesting, and more and more workers are now emphasizing that their work should be interesting. Yes, there are some very boring jobs, and every job has some aspects that are not exciting and more routine.

24 wam   Today, there are many different types of jobs from which you might choose. These range from the routine to the exotic. If you begin the planning early, you can work at many different types of jobs and learn much from each job experience.

26 wam   Workers tend to identify with their careers, and their careers in a real sense give them a feeling of importance and of belonging. People's jobs also help determine how people spend their spare time, who their friends are, and sometimes even where they live.

28 wam   Work can take place in school, in a factory, in an office, at home, or outside; it can be done for money or experience or even voluntarily. It should be quite clear that work can be an activity that involves responsibility of some type. That same thing can be said about a job.

30 wam   A career relates to work that is done for pay. But it means much more than a particular job; it is the pattern of work done throughout your lifetime. A career deals with looking ahead, planning, setting goals, and then reaching goals. The well-planned career becomes part of a person's lifestyle.

32 wam   Whichever career path you select, the degree of pride shown in your work has to be at a very high level. Others will judge you by how well you do the work. Your image is affected by what you believe other people think of you as well as what you think of yourself. The quality of your efforts impacts on both of them.

34 wam   If a matter is important to a supervisor or to a firm, it should also be important to the employee. The competent person can be depended on to place priorities in order. The higher your job-satisfaction level, the greater is the likelihood that you will be pleased with all aspects of your life. Positive attitudes will produce rewards.

36 wam   Whenever people work together, attention has to be given to human relations factors. A quality organization will concern itself with interpersonal skills needed by all workers. Respect, courtesy, and patience are examples of the many words that can blend together to bring about positive human relationships in the office as well as in different situations.

38 wam   My alarm didn't go off. The road was detoured. The baby-sitter was sick. The car wouldn't start. And for some, the list of excuses goes on and on. Be thankful that this list is not yours. You will keep the tardy times to a minimum by planning and anticipating. You will realize that those people who jump the gun to quit work early at the end of each day have a bad habit.

40 wam   Some people take forever to become acquainted with the office routines. Some must have every task explained along with a list of things to be done. Some go ahead and search for new things to do. Initiative is a trait that managers must look for in people who will get promoted while on the job. A prized promotion and a pay raise can be a reward for demonstrating that a person has unique ideas.

42 wam   Newly employed workers are quite often judged by their skills in informal verbal situations. A simple exchange of greetings when being introduced to a customer is an example that illustrates one situation. A new employee might have a very good idea at a small-group meeting. However, unless that idea can be verbalized to other members in a clear, concise manner, the members will not develop a special appreciation.

44 wam   Many supervisors state that they want their workers to use what they refer to as common sense. Common sense tells a person to answer the telephone, to open the mail, and to lock the door at the end of every working day. It is easy to see that this trait equates with the use of sound judgment. The prized employee should desire to capitalize on each new experience that will help him or her to use better judgment when making decisions.

46 wam   Every person should set as a goal the proper balancing of the principal components in one's life. Few people will disagree with the conviction that the family is the most important of the four major ingredients in a human life. Experts in the career education field are quick to say that the family must be joined with leisure time, vocation, and citizenship in order to encompass a full "career." The right balance will result in satisfaction and success.

48 wam   As we increasingly become an information society, there is an ever-increasing awareness of high office costs. Such costs are labor intensive, and those who justify them are very concerned about their workers' use of time management principles. Researchers in the time management field have developed several techniques for examining office tasks and analyzing routines. The realization that time is money is only the beginning and must be followed with an educational program.

50 wam

We all want to work in a pleasant environment where we are surrounded with jovial people who never make a mistake. The realities of the real world tell us, however, that this likely will not happen; the use of corrective action may be required. For the very reason that this quality is so difficult to cultivate, all of us should strive to improve the manner in which we accept constructive criticism. By recognizing the positive intent of a supervisor, each of us will accumulate extra benefits.

52 wam

The worker and the firm might be compared in some ways with a child and the family unit. Just as a child at times disagrees with a parent, the worker might question policies of the organization. In both cases, policies must exist for conflict resolution. One option for a vexed child is to run away from home; an employee may offer a letter of resignation. A much better option in both situations is the discussion of differences. The child remains loyal to the family, and the worker remains loyal to the company.

54 wam

Those people who aspire to a role in management must be equal to the challenge. Individuals who have supervisory responsibilities must make fine judgments as decisions are formed that affect the entire organization. The challenge of managing is trying and lonely. While other labels are sometimes used to explain some of the basic management functions, the concepts remain the same. The four main functions involve actuating, organizing, planning, and controlling of such components as personnel, production, and the sales of products.

56 wam
Going to work has always been a major part of being an adult. Of course, many adolescents also have jobs that can keep them extremely busy. The work one does or the job one holds is a critical factor in determining many other things about the way a person is able to live. Various work habits are as crucial to one's success as the actual job skills and knowledge that one brings to that job. If a person is dependable, organized, accurate, efficient, cooperative, enthusiastic, and understanding, he or she will be quickly recognized by most supervisors.

58 wam
Being dependable is a desirable trait to have. When a worker says that something will be done by a specific time, it is quite assuring to a manager to know that a dependable worker is assigned to it. Workers who are dependable learn to utilize their time to achieve maximum results. This trait is also apparent with workers who have a good record for attendance. If a company is to be productive, it is essential to have workers who are on the job. Of course, the trustworthy employee not only is on the job but also is the worker that can be counted on to be there on time.

60 wam
The ability to organize is one other quality that is necessary to exhibiting good work habits. A worker must have a sense of being able to plan the work that is to be done and then to be able to work that plan to be organized. It is commonly understood that competent workers are well organized. If office workers are organized, requests are handled promptly, letters are answered quickly, and projects do not accumulate on the desk. In addition, the organized office worker returns all phone calls without delay and makes a list of those activities that are to be accomplished on a daily basis.

62 wam   Another trait or work habit essential for success on a job is accuracy. Accurate workers are in much demand. The worker who tallies numbers checks them very carefully to be sure that there are no errors. When reviewing documents, the accurate worker has excellent proofreading skills to locate all errors. Since accuracy is required on all jobs, it is critical that a person possess this trait. Accurate workers are careful in all the work that they undertake or complete. If a worker checks all work that is done and analyzes all steps that are taken, it is likely that a high level of accuracy will be attained.

64 wam   Efficiency is another work habit that is much admired. This means that a worker is quick to complete an assignment and to begin work on the next job. Efficient workers think about saving steps and time when working. For example, one should plan to make one trip to the copier versus going for each individual job. Being efficient means having all the right tools to do the job right. An efficient worker is able to zip along on required jobs, concentrating on doing the job right. Being efficient also means having all needed supplies for every job within reach. This means that a worker can produce more work in a little less time.

66 wam   Cooperation is another desired work habit. This means that an employee is thinking of all the team members when a decision is made. A person who cooperates is willing to do something for the benefit of the entire group. As a member of a work unit or team, it is absolutely essential that you take extra steps to cooperate. Cooperation may mean being a good sport if you have to do something you would rather not do. It could also mean a worker helps to correct an error made by someone else in the office. If a worker has the interests of the organization at heart, it should be a little bit easier to resolve to cooperate with endeavors of the company.

68 wam   Enthusiasm is still another work trait that is eagerly sought by most employers. Being enthusiastic means that an employee has lots of positive energy. This is reflected in actions toward the work as well as toward the employer. It has been noted that enthusiasm can be catching. If workers have enthusiasm, they can reach for the gold. It might pay to examine your own level of enthusiasm for a given job or project. Analyze whether you help to build up people or whether you seem to project a negative or a pessimistic attitude. There will always be lots of job opportunities for workers who are known to possess a wealth of enthusiasm for the work they are assigned to.

70 wam   Understanding is another work habit or trait that is a requirement to be an excellent worker. In this society, the likelihood of working with people who have differences is quite probable. It is essential to have workers who can understand and accept all the differences that are evident in all the other employees who are in a unit or division. On the job, it is imperative that workers realize that employees will have different aptitudes and abilities. The chances are also good that differences in race, ethnicity, religion, work ethic, cultural background, and attitude can be found. With so many possible differences, it is clear that a very high degree of mutual understanding is needed.

72 wam   Reviewing the seven previous Paced Practice exercises, it can be concluded that specific work habits or traits can play a major role in determining the success of a worker at a given job or task. Most managers would be quick to agree on the importance of these traits. These habits would most likely be evaluated on any performance appraisal forms you might see. Of course, while these work habits are critical to the success of an individual on the job, there is also the need for specific competencies and abilities for a given job. A new worker must size up the needed blend of these traits in addition to those required competencies. As will be noted, a worker needs various skills to become a success at work.

74 wam

A major part of an office job is deciding what kinds of equipment will best meet company objectives. One should analyze several systems, checking for easy and flexible usage. The next step is then defining the requirements of each job in terms of work volume, space requirements, and overall budget restrictions. The different function types must then be categorized. An itemized checklist of every task should be used to identify the various tasks performed by every employee. Data may be obtained through the use of interviews, questionnaires, or observation. Some subjects covered may include document creation, worker interaction, scheduling, typing, filing, and telephoning. Technology must then be selected to match job needs.

76 wam

While technology has quite dramatically changed nearly all office procedures in the last decade, the attention to changing human interaction at the workplace because of all of these changes has been largely neglected. Some people have a great deal of enthusiasm for working with different kinds of computers, while others view computers as a great threat, a fearsome complexity. It is expected that most people's jobs will in time be affected by computers. It is imperative to ease employees' qualms about learning to use the new equipment. A good method is to nurture a positive attitude toward the computer by convincing employees of two things. First, office work is made much easier. Second, the workers are much more apt to become highly organized.

78 wam   The ergonomics experts stress the major role furniture plays in the well-being of office workers. Many years ago, we paid little attention to whether our chairs and desks suited our utility and comfort needs. But now we know that various styles, sizes, shapes, and colors have quite an impact on our quality and quantity of work. An informed manager must carefully plan workers' surroundings. Colors in a workplace may produce major effects on one's moods. Studies show that the cool colors, such as blue and green, are quiet and relaxing. Cool colors should be used in offices that are located in warm areas such as south or west sections of the building. The warm colors, such as red, yellow, and orange, are cheerful and add zip to a job, which may help improve morale.

80 wam   Today we hear a great deal about how important human relations are in management. Job-related human interaction is a comparatively new concern. This can be easily seen if we look at the history of leadership theories as they apply to management practice. When people first started to study leadership, it was expected that certain qualities, such as height, could predict effective leaders. Next, exceptional leaders were studied to see if they had similar qualities. However, that proposal was not any more successful than the earlier approaches. Now, it is generally known that many elements combine to make a person an effective leader. A specific leader's proficiency varies from one situation to another. Leaders must develop a personal style that will serve them well while on the job.

82 wam

     Do you enjoy your work most of the time? Do you look forward to going to work each day? Though some people say that their work is unpleasant, the majority of both men and women usually will say that they find their work generally satisfying. If it isn't, the problem may be that there is a poor fit between the job and the worker. Quality of life at work is a major concern of both management and labor. When jobs become boring and routine, workers often become less productive because they do not feel challenged. The concept of job enrichment greatly enhances the types of experiences an employee deals with every day by upgrading the responsibilities of the job. Opportunity for growth is the key to job enrichment. All organizations should have some jobs that have great potential for enrichment and growth.

84 wam

     More and more women are moving into executive levels in business and industry. Many women who pursue careers in management today have moved into their positions after having gained experience as office support personnel. This background gives them a real appreciation for those myriad contributions made by such workers as file clerks, word processors, and other office support staff members who work in a firm. Some women have acquired their managerial roles after earning degrees and acquiring experience through jobs in such fields as finance, marketing, accounting, and law. But the measure of success as a manager, no matter what the degrees or past experiences are, is how well one identifies goals and problems and then drives toward the realization of those goals and the resolution of those problems for the good of a company.

86 wam

Most of us have had occasion to write business letters from time to time whether to apply for a job, to comment on a product or service, or to place an order. Often it seems to be an easy task to sit and let our thoughts flow freely. In other cases we seem to struggle over the proper wording, trying to say what we want to say in just the right way. Writing is a skill that can come with practice and, most of all, with study. One can learn. There are many writing principles that must be studied to ensure good letters. Some of these principles are as follows: Use language in letters that you would be comfortable using face-to-face. Use words that are simple and direct. Choose words that will not offend others. Try to be positive. Emphasize the bright side of a situation when possible. Be kind. Write the way you would like people to talk.

88 wam

One of the most important areas for a business student to study is report writing. Many persons who are working in business organizations indicate that one of the areas they feel the least prepared for is report writing. Most people in college do not know that they probably will be asked to write reports on the job. However, most colleges are aware of this problem today and are striving to correct the situation. They are succeeding. There has been quite a large increase in the range of report writing courses in business curriculums in recent years. Reports may fall into categories such as horizontal, radial, and vertical. Horizontal reports move from person to person or from department to department and are informational. Radial reports may be publicized research. Vertical reports go up and down in the company and include status reports or policy statements.

Almost everyone has experienced interviewing for a job during his or her life. For some persons, the interview is[1] a traumatic time. But when a candidate adequately prepares for this interview, it doesn't have to be very frightening.[2] A person should apply only for those jobs for which he or she is professionally prepared. Before an interview one[3] should obtain detailed information about the company with which he or she is seeking employment. [4]You should always learn the name of the person who will conduct the interview and use the name during the interview.[5] It's also best to take a neat copy of your resume. It goes without saying that suitable business attire is[6] required. As a candidate, you will be judged on personality, appearance, and poise as well as competence. At[7] the finish of every interview, it would be prudent to stand up, shake hands, and address the interviewer by name.[8]

Are you an active listener? Listening is a skill that few people possess. It is one important way to bring about[1] change in people. Listening is not a passive activity, and it is the most effective agent for personality development.[2] Quality listening brings about change in people's attitudes toward themselves and others' values. People who have been[3] listened to become more open to their experiences, less defensive, more fair, and less authoritative. [4]Listening builds positive relationships and tends to constructively change the perspective of the listener. Active[5] listening on the job is extremely important whether an employee is in the top levels of management or works at the[6] lower end of the hierarchy. Every worker should try to analyze his or her listening habits to see whether some improvements in[7] listening can be made. Pleasant human interaction will often bring about even more job satisfaction.[8]

94 wam   Listening is a skill that is an essential component of the communication process. A great many experts have found that lack of good listening skills is a major cause for the breakdown in effective communications. In the first place, there must be understanding. If ideas given by a speaker are not completely understood, it is most likely that there will be problems. In addition, a listener must attempt to keep an open mind for any new, bright ideas which might be considered. A good listener must be active. Three steps should take place. Think about what the speaker is saying. The ideas and facts that you hear should be compared to information that you already know. Second, try to analyze what the person is saying, and try to read between the lines. Third, show empathy toward the speaker. This can be achieved by putting yourself in the speaker's place. You should make an attempt to establish a bond with the speaker.

96 wam   Speech is a major factor in the communication process. In evaluating the quality of your voice, you should analyze the four factors of pitch, tempo, tone, and volume in order to determine whether or not some improvements must be made. Pitch refers to the sound of a voice. A shrill voice would turn people off. If a voice has a very low pitch, it might be too dull or too hard to hear. The voice which is the most pleasing is the one which has a moderate pitch. The tone of a voice might help reveal the attitude and feelings of the speaker. You should hope to project a tone that is both cheerful and pleasant. You should always adapt the tone of your voice to the meaning of the words that you are speaking. Volume is also a critical factor in evaluating a voice. Your voice should carry to every person in a room. Using good breath control, you can enhance your ability to increase or decrease the volume of your speech to satisfy all audiences.

Supplementary Timings

Spacing: Double

Since the early settlers first came to this land, our | 11
people have always had a strong interest in the actions of | 23
our government. When you speak of our national, state, or | 35
local government, you can be sure that a lively debate will | 47
start. This is most true when election time comes and the | 58
candidates speak to the issues. Media reports of debates | 70
and of election issues tend to be quite broad and can serve | 82
as a gauge of what voters seem to want. | 90

Of course, economic issues are bound to start a major | 101
debate on the part of those who pay taxes. Raising taxes | 113
or changing the tax laws will often start a debate. One | 124
other topic that causes much debate deals with our defense | 136
plans. Many candidates have used this issue to put forth | 147
their own campaign. If you look at the past history of our | 159
nation, you will see that issues of defense will always be | 171
a chief concern. | 175

In addition to economic and defense issues, you will | 185
be amazed at how quickly a lively debate can start over | 197
social issues. For instance, crime, education, and privacy | 209
are topics that have been of special interest in recent | 220
years. There has also been a good deal of debate about the | 232
environment, as well as many questions about our welfare | 243
system. A lot of people have a profound interest in the | 255
actions of our judicial groups and the way in which they | 266
respond to social issues that face our nation. It is easy | 278
to see that issues debated by government are sure to be of | 290
concern in years to come. People must be concerned. | 300

| 1 | 2 | 3 | 4 | 5 | 6 | 7 | 8 | 9 | 10 | 11 | 12

More and more people are retiring at a younger age as 11
new retirement programs are being offered by business firms 23
and by the government. A good number of the people who 34
retire early may even be starting in a new career or a new 46
job. This is happening at a time when the life expectancy 58
for adults has been quickly rising in our changing society. 70

With the increase in life expectancy and the early 80
retirement plans, it can be seen that adults must be sure 92
to plan carefully for their retirement years. If planning 104
is not done, many people who are in good health could find 115
themselves at this point in their lives with plenty of free 127
time and not much to do. As one ages, it is important to 139
look at the activities that one enjoys and to strengthen 150
one's interest in those things. At the same time, it is 162
important to find new interests and hobbies so that the 173
time in retirement will be enjoyed to the very fullest. It 185
should be noted that the financial part of retirement must 197
also be planned in a careful way. One should be sure to 208
check all investments. 213

Of course, some retirees enjoy visiting with family 223
and friends. Others plan to travel as much as they can to 235
many parts of the country or of the world. Then one can 247
find some retirees who pursue a hobby with intense zeal. 258
Whatever one wants to do, the most critical factor is that 270
planning must be done with care prior to the date one sets 282
for retirement. In this way, one can be sure to have a 293
retirement that brings much success. 300

| 1 | 2 | 3 | 4 | 5 | 6 | 7 | 8 | 9 | 10 | 11 | 12

The value of team play and of team effort has been a | 11
topic of great interest to many different people. There | 22
are experts who look at the actions of people in a variety | 34
of research studies in order to find out the impact of a | 45
unified effort on how much the group is able to achieve. | 57
The results are always the same. When a group of people | 68
tries to meet a shared goal, it is quite likely that more | 80
will be gained. This is true in many environments--office, | 92
plant, home, school, or church. It is especially true when | 104
one looks at the success of athletic teams. | 113

Many business firms have now begun quality circles in | 124
their offices and plants. The goal of these circles is to | 136
encourage small groups of workers to meet on a periodic | 147
basis to find out if any of the procedures or steps that | 158
they follow in the jobs they do can be improved. The small | 170
groups give each person in the unit a stake in the way the | 182
unit functions as a whole. A quality circle recognizes the | 194
benefits that can come from a team effort. | 203

The concept of team effort is most evident when it | 213
comes to athletic events. Each time that a study is made | 225
of a championship team in any sport or event, many comments | 237
can be made about the team play and the team spirit that | 248
were observed. This point is often discussed after a big | 260
game by sportswriters and the many fans of a team. A lot | 271
of experts, in fact, would back the notion that team effort | 283
is more important than the talents of any single player or | 295
players on any one team. | 300

| 1 | 2 | 3 | 4 | 5 | 6 | 7 | 8 | 9 | 10 | 11 | 12

Spacing: Double

For over three decades, firms have been trying, with   11
higher and higher levels of success, to harness information   23
technology. The role that top management has played has   34
often not been as useful as it could have been. Managers   46
have helped things happen rather than made them happen.   57
People today must know something about the technology that   69
helps them do their jobs. Telecommunications involves some   81
fairly simple concepts that quickly expand into complex   92
details. The jargon alone is often enough to numb the mind   104
and cause some concern.   109

It makes no sense for managers to try to learn the   119
nuts and bolts of the technology. The field is moving too   131
fast for experts to keep up their knowledge base. What   142
managers need is the same level of basic understanding that   154
a person involved in business has to have about accounting.   167
They should have a sense of the major sections and terms,   178
such as debits and credits. They must be able to interpret   190
a computer plan in the same way that they read a financial   202
statement. That level of knowledge in no way means they   213
are experts, but it enables them to take part in planning   225
and not be scared off because they don't know the topic.   236

When managers deal with technology, they often will be   247
dealing with change because it brings organizational and   259
business issues to the foreground of planning and action.   271
It pushes senior managers to take on a new relationship   282
with what has often been outside their scope. Ten years   293
ago, few executives would have defined an understanding of   305
technology as part of the profile of an effective manager.   317
If they don't do so now, they soon will. Change may be a   329
problem, but it also can bring new growth. Technology can   341
pave the way for new growth for all executives.   350

| 1 | 2 | 3 | 4 | 5 | 6 | 7 | 8 | 9 | 10 | 11 | 12

Pick up any newspaper or turn on any news program on   11
TV, and it seems you will hear yet another story about an   22
oil tanker that has spilled its cargo or a landfill that   34
has reached its limit. As more and more people are paying   46
heed to the environmental concerns, more and more companies   58
are following suit by setting environmental goals.   68

What are the reasons so many firms have a new stance   79
on these issues? First, and foremost, there appear to be   90
more simultaneous threats to our world today than at any   102
other time. Our federal government believes that four out   113
of ten Americans live in places where the air isn't healthy   125
to breathe. Other issues include ozone depletion, acid   137
rain, the fouling of thousands of rivers and lakes by raw   148
sewage and toxic wastes, destruction of rain forests, and   160
the greenhouse effect.   164

A second reason for the growing concern over these   175
issues in corporate America is a response to heightened   186
public awareness of the problem. Nine out of ten people   197
say they would be willing to make a special effort to buy   209
products that show concern for protecting the air, land,   220
and water. Membership in environmental groups is soaring.   232
There are now tens of thousands of conservation groups;   244
each town seems to have two or three doing anything from   255
trying to save a trout stream to questioning the building   267
of a shopping mall.   271

In recent decades over a dozen major environmental   281
laws have been passed. As a result, the overall pollution   293
levels have dropped. New regulations focus on the keeping   305
of records and seem to focus less on the ideal standards   316
that are set up for business firms to follow. While much   328
has been done, strong maintenance is the key to keeping our   340
air, water, and land clean and usable in the future.   350

| 1 | 2 | 3 | 4 | 5 | 6 | 7 | 8 | 9 | 10 | 11 | 12

SUPPLEMENTARY TIMING

Spacing: Double

The perception of time by human beings has grown out
of a natural series of rhythms which are linked to daily,
monthly, and yearly cycles. No matter how much we live by
our wristwatches, our bodies and our lives will always be
somewhat influenced by an internal clock. What is of even
greater interest, though, are the many uses and perceptions
of time based on individuals and their cultures.

Rhythm and tempo are ways we relate to time and are
distinguishing features of a culture. In some cultures,
folks move very slowly; in others, moving quickly is the
norm. Mixing the two types may bring about feelings of
discomfort. People may have trouble relating to each other
because they are not in synchrony. To be synchronized is
to move in union with another person; it is critical for a
strong and lengthy partnership.

In general Americans move at a fast tempo, although
there are regional differences. In meetings, they tend to
be impatient and want to get down to business right away.
They have been taught that it is best to come to the point
quickly and avoid vagueness. Because American business
works in a short time frame, prompt results are often of
more interest than the building of long-term relationships.

Time is also the basic organizing system for all of
life's events. Time is used for establishing priorities.
For example, lead time varies quite a bit from one culture
to the next. When you do business with people of other
cultures, it is crucial to know just how much lead time is
required for each event. For instance, numerous corporate
executives have their time scheduled for months in advance.
Last-minute requests by telephone are often viewed as poor
planning and may be perceived as insulting behavior.

| 1 | 2 | 3 | 4 | 5 | 6 | 7 | 8 | 9 | 10 | 11 | 12

All too often companies place too much importance on
the rational, logical side of the intellect and neglect the
creative, intuitive side. As creative thought occurs in
the mind, it cannot be seen and, therefore, is not easily
measured. Perhaps for this reason, there are only a few
socially accepted roles where it is okay to be creative,
try out new ideas, or seek different methods for reaching
goals. Even when managers claim to want creative ideas
from their employees, the fear of taking risks may squelch
all of these efforts.

As a result, creative people often find themselves on
the outside looking in as new ideas are analyzed over and
over again in an effort to minimize or eliminate the risk.
It may be next to impossible to start a new product which,
in the firm's early days, might have been launched quickly
without excessive controls and approvals. As a response to
this restraint on imagination, thousands of our businesses
are launched every year, many guided by former employees of
large companies who found their creativity and innovative
ideas stifled.

While some creative people leave the corporate world
to find their own niche by starting a small company, many
stay and try to teach their bosses how to better utilize
the talents found right in their own firm. Although some
experts think that creativity comes only from a few special
people placed in top jobs, most believe that creativity
can, and should, be sought from all employees. If given
the right support and enough time, nearly everyone has the
ability to find better systems, strategies, or products.

A part of the challenge of encouraging creativity,
though, is learning to manage creative people effectively,
which is not an easy task. They tend to question policies
rather than accept the way things are always done. Their
high energy levels may result in poor behavior and burnout.
Creative workers tend to be driven by the belief that they
can overcome sizable obstacles and bring about change.

| 1 | 2 | 3 | 4 | 5 | 6 | 7 | 8 | 9 | 10 | 11 | 12

11
23
34
46
57
69
80
91
103
108
119
130
142
154
166
178
190
202
213
216
227
239
250
262
274
285
296
308
319
330
342
353
365
377
389
400

There are a few essential items businesspeople today 11

should know about telecommunications in order to be up to 22

date in their field. Although it may seem confusing at 34

first, it is quite simple once you realize that there are 45

just four main components involved in almost all systems. 57

The first part is called transmission and includes all the 69

links along which the signals are sent and the techniques 80

for coding information. The medium may be cable, microwave 92

radio, satellite, fiber optics, or anything else that can 104

carry the data signal. 109

The next component is the switches. Switches are the 120

specialized equipment at set points of a communications 131

network. At these points the signals from transmission 142

links are processed in order to route them to the terminal 154

or computer, translate them from one message format to the 166

next format, improve the efficiency of transmission, or 177

handle other aspects of the network control. It is in this 189

area that the technology is moving fastest and is the most 201

unstable in terms of products, standards, and vendors. 212

Terminals, devices that access the computer network, 222

are the third area. Most of the time they are personal 234

computers linked to a distant computer for accessing data, 245

processing data, or communicating messages to some other 257

terminals. There are other possibilities, such as word 268

processors, telephones, central mainframe computers, and 279

even some types of workstations. 286

The final part is the network. This is a system of 297

switches and transmission links, as well as a listing of 308

the terminal points that can access them and thus contact 320

each other. The U.S. phone setup is one such network, with 332

the phone number providing the address. The same phone can 344

link itself into other countries' networks. Even though 355

these systems may use different transmission features and 367

conventions, special switches can translate the protocols. 379

In the same way, a single terminal may access many networks 391

which, in turn, can be linked through switches. 400

| 1 | 2 | 3 | 4 | 5 | 6 | 7 | 8 | 9 | 10 | 11 | 12